AGE-PROOF YOUR BODY

Also by Elizabeth Somer

AGE-PROOF YOUR BODY

YOUR COMPLETE GUIDE TO LOOKING AND FEELING YOUNGER

ELIZABETH SOMER, M.A., R.D.

McGraw·Hill

New York   Chicago   San Francisco   Lisbon   London   Madrid   Mexico City
Milan   New Delhi   San Juan   Seoul   Singapore   Sydney   Toronto

Library of Congress Cataloging-in-Publication Data

Somer, Elizabeth.
   Age-proof your body : your complete guide to looking and feeling younger /
Elizabeth Somer.—2nd ed.
     p.   cm.
   Includes bibliographical references and index.
   ISBN 0-07-146264-3 (alk. paper)
   1. Longevity.   2. Aging.   3. Health.   I. Title.

RA776.75 S66   2006
613.2—dc22   2005027986

2 3 4 5 6 7 8 9 0 FGR/FGR 0 9 8 7

ISBN 0-07-146264-3

McGraw-Hill books are available at special quantity discounts to use as premiums and sales promotions, or for use in corporate training programs. For more information, please write to the Director of Special Sales, Professional Publishing, McGraw-Hill, Two Penn Plaza, New York, NY 10121-2298. Or contact your local bookstore.

The nutritional and health information presented in this book is based on an in-depth review of the current scientific literature. It is intended only as an informative resource guide to help you make informed decisions. It is not meant to replace the advice of a physician or to serve as a guide to self-treatment. Always seek competent medical help for any health condition or if there is any question about the appropriateness of a procedure or health recommendation.

This book is printed on acid-free paper.

For my dad, Rolly Somer

I am blessed to have grown up in the current of
my father's passion for life. I may no longer have his
hand to hold, but his vitality continues to shine, illuminating
every day of my life and helping to guide my children
as they grow into their versions of vitality.

Contents

PART 1

Reclaiming Your Vitality

CHAPTER 8   The Antiaging Fitness Program 115

PART 2
Avoiding the Diseases of Aging

CHAPTER 9   Your Defense System Against Aging 139

PART 3
Use Experience to Master Aging

PART 4
Beyond Diet and Exercise

Foreword

The best cooks use the finest ingredients in their recipes; they wouldn't dream of using wilted lettuce in their salads or rancid oil in their dressings. Each one of us is like a chef, blending the ingredients from our daily habits, which contribute to or detract from our recipes for healthy, long lives. We don't often think of our lives as we age as being a result of the ingredients we put into them, but what we eat, how we move, and the way we think contribute importantly to how and when we grow old and to what degree we enjoy living in the meantime.

We live in an age of medical miracles where bone marrow transplants and coronary bypass surgery have become routine procedures. These technological breakthroughs of modern medicine still reflect the old paradigm of "rescue and repair," which emphasizes treating rather than preventing disease. Abundant evidence now indicates that a health-care approach with a goal of promoting health and preventing illness costs less than the disease-care approach with its expensive diagnostic and therapeutic interventions. More importantly, focusing on prevention will help us achieve the ultimate goals: a high-quality life and sustained good health. The best news is that the individual has considerable control in reaching these goals. We can improve our diets. We can become more active, both physically and mentally. We can choose to stop the insult from cigarette smoke and more.

Most people are willing and eager to make changes that will improve their chances of living well; however, there is a bewildering, and often contradictory, array of information available to the general public on ways to achieve optimal health and reduce the risk for age-related declines in health and function. Some of that information is accurate, but much of it is not. Some popular information is even harmful.

Elizabeth Somer has worked to summarize the vast and still-growing scientific literature about ways to age-proof our bodies, covering basic advice (such as to eat more vegetables and exercise more) to the latest research on supplements, hormones, and phytochemicals. Employing her esteemed professional judgment and drawing on the help of many experts, she has separated the facts from the hype and provided the essential take-home messages about what really works, what doesn't, why, and at what cost.

She recognizes that as we age, health is more than the absence of disease. What we ultimately want is to live vital and passionate lives filled with purpose, joy, and fulfillment. The skills, tools, and guidelines for transforming our lives to achieve and maintain health and vitality for a lifetime are in this book. Elizabeth Somer makes it easy to understand that when you age-proof your body, you begin to engage in an ongoing, dynamic process that brings rewards far greater than just longevity. She even shows you how to make it fun!

Here is a fact-based, comprehensive, easy-to-read book on how to empower yourself to die young—as late as possible.

Jeffrey Blumberg, Ph.D., FACN
PROFESSOR IN THE FRIEDMAN SCHOOL OF NUTRITION AND SCIENCE POLICY
TUFTS UNIVERSITY

Acknowledgments

Many friends and colleagues donated their valuable time and thoughts to this book. A special thank-you to Jeanette Williams, who developed the recipes; Deborah Brody, my editor and bike buddy; David Smith, my agent and friend; Victoria Dolby Toews, who found all the research; and especially my children, Lauren (who checked all the resources and updated the references) and Will, just because I'm so blessed to have them in my life.

I also want to thank the researchers who have pioneered the theories and ideas on vitality and aging and who were so gracious in explaining these concepts and their research with me, including George Armelagos, Ph.D.; Holly Atkinson, M.D.; Lydia Bazzano, M.D., Ph.D.; Gladys Block, Ph.D.; Jeffrey Blumberg, Ph.D., F.A.C.N.; Kelly D. Brownell, Ph.D.; Robert N. Butler, M.D.; C. Wayne Callaway, M.D.; Larry Christensen, Ph.D.; Nancy Clark, M.S., R.D.; Leonard Cohen, Ph.D.; William Connor, M.D.; Douglas Darr, Ph.D.; Bess Dawson-Hughes, M.D.; Johanna Dwyer, D.Sc., R.D.; Sharon Edelstein, Sc.M.; Mary Enig, Ph.D.; Harinder S. Garewal, M.D., Ph.D.; Helen Gensler, Ph.D.; Barry Goldin, Ph.D.; Michael Green, Ph.D.; Robert Heaney, M.D.; Ben Hurley, Ph.D.; Robert Jacob, Ph.D.; David Jenkins, M.D.; Robin Kanarek, Ph.D.; Darshan Kelley, Ph.D.; Susan Krebs-Smith, Ph.D., R.D.; Sarah Leibowitz, Ph.D.; David Levitsky, Ph.D.; Susan Mayne, Ph.D.; Paul Mills, Ph.D.; Byron Murray, Ph.D.; Daniel Nixon, M.D.; Pamela Peeke, M.D.; Herbert Pierson, Ph.D.; William Pryor, Ph.D.; Judy Putnam, Ph.D.; George Roth, M.D.; Robert Russell, M.D.; Robert Sack, Ph.D.; Howard D. Sesso, Sc.D., M.P.H.; Adria Sherman, Ph.D.; Gary Stoner, Ph.D.; Varro Tyler, Ph.D., Sc.D.; Thomas Wadden, Ph.D.; Ronald Watson, Ph.D.; Walter Willett, Dr.P.H.; Margo Woods, D.Sc.; Margo Wootan, D.Sc.; and Gary Zammit, Ph.D.

Before You Begin This Book

When I was twenty-one
I had just begun.
When I was fifty-two
I was nearly new.
When I was sixty-three
I was hardly me.
When I was seventy-four
I was not much more.
When I was eighty-five
I was just alive.
But now I am ninety-six, I'm as
clever as clever.
So I think I'll be ninety-six for
ever and ever.

—ADAPTED FROM
THE END BY A. A. MILNE

Most of us are eager to push back the hands of time. In fact, three out of every five of us want to live to be 100, according to a survey by the Alliance for Aging Research. Of those polled, 67 percent believe it's within their control, and nine out of every ten people say they'd adopt a more positive outlook on life, eat more nutritious foods, and exercise regularly to reach this goal.

Their hopes are not far off the mark. The evidence shows that up to 70 percent of cancers result from lifestyle, including what we eat and how we live. One in every two cases of heart disease is preventable, and osteoporosis, a disease of thinning bones, is almost entirely preventable with a change in lifestyle. The list of avoidable age-related diseases is seemingly endless. That's particularly good news, since most of us are more concerned with illness, disability, and loss of independence in our later years than we are with dying. Few people want a longer life if it means years spent in a nursing home or lost to Alzheimer's disease.

But the powerful benefits of a few simple changes in lifestyle go beyond just being a healthy great-grandparent. New research from respected institutions shows that we easily can stretch our life expectancies from the current 76.9 years to as much as 100 years by making some simple changes in what we eat and how we move. We might even push beyond life's ultimate finish line of 120 years by making additional dietary changes. The sooner you take the longevity plunge, the better; however, it's never too late to jump on the antiaging bandwagon and reap the benefits of all that good food and activity have to offer.

Improving on a Good Thing

Effort is the measure of a man.

—WILLIAM JAMES

Improving the odds of living as long and fully as you can imagine is not as monumental a task as you might think. Most of us include at least some healthy foods in our daily diets. We have at least some joy, laughter, and playfulness in our daily routines. We are fortunate to have a few, if not many, nurturing relationships. We even do a bit of exercise every day, even if it's only walking from the parking lot into the grocery store.

All that most people need to do is improve on a good thing. That's what this book is all about. *Age-Proof Your Body* provides a wealth of suggestions on how to tweak a pretty healthy life into a very healthy one to boost your chances for living a lot longer, happier, and better.

What Can You Expect from This Book?

Begin at once to live.

—SENECA

Perhaps you picked up this book because you're noticing the beginnings of aging, such as a stiff joint here or a wrinkle there. Or maybe you like the hand you've been dealt and don't want to lose your edge as you age. Perhaps you are a little farther down the road and have been told by your doctor to make some changes fast. Whatever the longevity recipe you have been handed by inheritance or chosen, you can make use of those ingredients to the fullest, starting today.

In this book you'll gain the tools to begin a quest for well-being and passion that will last a lifetime. If you follow the simple guidelines outlined in *Age-Proof Your Body*, you can expect to:

- Decrease your risk for numerous diseases
- Improve your immunity and resistance to colds, infections, and disease
- Lose weight and reduce your body fat

- Increase muscle strength, flexibility, and balance
- Improve your chances of living a long life without having to rely on others or a nursing home for your daily care
- Experience enhanced sexuality in your second fifty years
- Look younger
- Enjoy life more
- Have more energy for what you want to do and waste less energy on needless worries, tensions, and negative thoughts
- Heal more quickly from injuries and recover more quickly from illnesses
- Increase your aerobic capacity (that is, your endurance)
- Feel more fully alive

Not bad for starters! And it's only the beginning.

Living Vitally

Let each of you discover where your chance for greatness lies. Seize that chance, and let no power on earth deter you.

—FROM THE MOVIE *CHARIOTS OF FIRE*

I reviewed literally thousands of scientific studies while researching this book. All of the antiaging guidelines in this book reflect this thorough review of the current literature. While more pieces of the antiaging puzzle will continue to unfold, we already have in our grasp reliable, sound, and necessary habits that slow aging and prevent age-related diseases.

But the goals of this book extend far beyond just living longer or even living more healthfully. My wish is that all who read this book will incorporate into their vision of their future selves the quality of vitality. I hope that you will strive every day not only to live well but to live passionately—to incorporate into your daily routine some small glimmer of your higher self so that by the time you reach your hundredth birthday, vitality and the joy of life will have settled on you like an elegant cloak. The focus of this book is to provide the tools to fashion a life that will let you live both long and joyfully. Your vitality quest starts today, and everything you need for the journey is in the following pages.

PART 1

Reclaiming Your Vitality

CHAPTER 1

What Is This Thing Called Aging?

I always wanted to be somebody, but I should have been more specific.
—LILY TOMLIN

What does it mean to age? Technically speaking, biological aging, as defined by Dr. Denham Harman from the University of Nebraska College of Medicine, is "the accumulation of changes in the cells and tissues that increase the risk of death." If this is the only biomarker of aging, then from birth on and escalating after age thirty, we all are in the process of dying.

Luckily, that's not the case. When we analyze each component of aging—from loss of cell function to the onset of most degenerative diseases (from heart disease to cancer)—we repeatedly find that it is not age but years of abuse that wear down the body's ability to regenerate itself. Stop the abuse and encourage the repair processes, and all physiological functions should retain much of their youthful vitality.

Even the superficial signs of the passage of time—from wrinkles and stooped posture to a feeble or frail appearance—can vanish when a person's approach to life is vital and enthusiastic. An eighty-year-old who climbs mountains, takes ballet classes, is working on her college degree, or tackles life with a passion not seen in most twenty-year-olds is hardly "old" by anyone's standards, and she radiates the beauty unique to healthy, happy people.

Researchers are finding that the oldest old are much healthier than traditional views of aging would predict. Often they are more vital than people twenty years younger. When the oldest old in the world are compared, from the Okinawans to the Hunzas living in the Himalayas (both peoples typically live past a hundred years), they all exhibit the same qualities. They have stretched their middle years, not prolonged their old years, and they are remarkably healthy and robust. Even in the general population, people with healthful lifestyles live longer and are more likely to live disease free compared with their unhealthy neighbors.

What Are Your Vitality and Longevity Goals?

In your journal or on a piece of paper, answer the following questions:

1. What does aging mean to you?
2. What is your image of the perfect older person?
3. What aspects of aging do you want to avoid?
4. What aspects of aging do you want to nurture and encourage?
5. Reflect on your subtle beliefs about aging. Do you assume people's minds deteriorate with age? Do you expect people to become more debilitated or more serene as they age? Do you expect to become weakened or empowered in later years? What negative and positive images do you have of aging, and where did they come from? What body shape do you assume old people should have? Make a list of your assumptions on the left-hand side of the page, and then argue against these assumptions on the right-hand side.
6. List your most precious memories, and then review your list. What has given your life the most meaning up to this point? How can you add more meaning to your life every day to extend your years and boost your enjoyment of life?

The message is loud and clear. Aging has much more to do with how you live and who you are than with chronology. Having a clear mental picture of who you want to be when you're a hundred years old can help shape your life each day to reach that goal.

How Long Can We Expect to Live?

No life that breathes with human breath has ever truly longed for death.

—ALFRED, LORD TENNYSON, 1830

We've more than tripled the average life expectancy since the 1700s, from 25 years then to 77.6 years today. But that still is a far cry from what scientists estimate is our maximum life span of 120 years.

The Span of a Lifetime

1 LIFE =

120 years

480 seasons

1,440 months

6,240 weeks

43,800 days

1,051,200 hours

63,072,000 minutes

3,784,320,000 seconds

Before we begin our longevity journey, there are a few terms that should be clarified, such as *life span*, *life expectancy*, and *active life expectancy*. These terms might sound as though they mean the same thing, but they are very different. While the second has changed exponentially in the past century, the third has made only modest improvements, and the first hasn't given an inch in the entire history of humankind.

Life span refers to the maximum number of years any human has ever lived. With everything on your side—from the best longevity genes nature has to offer to a perfect lifestyle and a lot of good luck—the longest a person can hope to live is approximately 120 years. (There are no hard facts to back up isolated reports of extreme longevity.) Anything short of this 120-year mark essentially is premature aging.

With the research accumulating on why we age and the advancements in genetic engineering (see Chapter 2), there is the possibility that future generations will tamper with this cutoff point. But for now, 100 to 120 years is the best you can hope for. Reaching this maximum life span eludes most of us.

What Do You Expect Out of Life?

That brings us to the most important issue of longevity: life expectancy. *Life expectancy* is how long a person can expect to live. It is based on a number of factors, most of which are within our control.

Longevity is a modern luxury. Life expectancy for the human race in general has seen dramatic changes in the past hundred years. The human species survived for hundreds of thousands of years—more than 99 percent of our time on earth—with a life expectancy of only about eighteen years. Chinese archaeological finds dating back ten thousand years show that most people died young and violently. In one dig, only three of the 173 total skeletons uncovered (or 1 percent of the population) showed signs of having lived more than fifty years. Early Iron Age and Bronze Age cave dwellers had the same maximum life span as modern humans, about 120 years, but life was so violent for most men and childbirth was so risky for women that most would not reach drinking age. Up until the Roman Empire, only 2 to 3 percent of the population survived past the age of sixty-five. Even by the late 1700s, half the population of the world was under the age of sixteen.

In short, in the old days, the elderly were honored because they were more rare than gold. In those days, most of our current health and aging concerns—from eating well and exercising to getting routine dental checkups and deciding whether to take hormone replacement therapy at menopause—would have been moot.

As recent as the beginning of the twentieth century, life expectancy was still only forty-nine years. Since then, almost thirty years have been added to the average person's life expectancy at birth, primarily because of improved diagnosis, treatment, and prevention of infectious disease, along with lifestyle habits that include better diet, more exercise, and improved work conditions.

In the twentieth century alone, women increased their average life expectancy by 71 percent, while men's life expectancy improved by 66 percent. This steady improvement is expected to continue, although at a slower rate and always with the cutoff point at 120 years.

The good news about life expectancy statistics is that they improve with age. That is, the longer you live, the farther you are ahead of the population average. So while your life expectancy at birth is 74.5 years if you're a man and 79.9 years if you're a women, if you can make it to forty-five in good health and are not a smoker, you have a good chance of living to age eighty to eighty-five. If you live to eighty in good health, your chances of living even longer increase compared with the average person. Longevity is the one race in life where the farther you get, the longer you've got.

In essence, you have time on your side when it comes to life expectancy—if you use that time well. The amazing variation in the signs of aging from one person to the next is evidence that the underlying causes of these changes are modifiable.

One person wrinkles heavily by age forty-five; another appears virtually wrinkle free at seventy. One eighty-year-old is stooped and shuffles; another walks upright and briskly. Many seventy-five-year-olds are world travelers, taking college classes, playing tennis daily, or starting new careers, while how many fifty-year-olds do you know who already complain of stiff joints and low energy?

These vast differences are constant reminders that besides the genes you were given, much of what we consider as "getting older" is a reflection of what we think and how we live. Studies on twins repeatedly show that only about 15 to 20 percent of aging is due to genetics; the other 80 to 85 percent is linked to lifestyle and attitude. The better care you take of yourself today and the more vitality you welcome into your life, the more healthy tomorrows you are likely to have.

Actively Pursuing Life

Which leads us to the most important longevity term, active life expectancy, which is what this book is all about. *Active life expectancy* is the maximum number of healthy, disease-free years a person can expect to have. This is where a person has the most control, since the majority of chronic and crippling diseases that undermine health in the later years can be avoided with a few changes in what you eat, how you live, what you think and believe, with whom you spend your time, and how much you move. The choice is yours.

What Are the Biomarkers of Age?

If a man hasn't discovered something that he will die for,
he isn't fit to live.

—DR. MARTIN LUTHER KING JR.

Wouldn't it be wonderful if there were simple tests you could take at your annual physical that would chart your biological age—that is, how fast your body is aging? That way you could tell if taking the latest antiaging hormone or making a change in your diet was turning back the clock.

Unfortunately, identifying predictable biomarkers—accurate and specific measurements of how fast the body is aging—is easier said than done. As yet scientists have not found a measurable sign of aging that arrives predictably during a limited time span and that is inevitable and irreversible. What makes the hunt even harder is that the aging process begins much earlier than is commonly assumed. At the very core of your trillions of cells, aging already has set in by the time you are twenty or thirty years old. It's just that the signs don't show up on the surface for another thirty to forty years. For example, by the time people are thirty-five years old, they have attained their maximum bone density. From this point on, they are losing bone. How quickly they lose it depends on what they eat and how they exercise. Muscle mass and strength also start to wane in the thirties, while heart disease is percolating as early as the teen years.

Another confounding factor is that individual uniqueness increases as we age; thus, two sixty-year-olds are biologically and psychologically less akin than two eighteen-year-olds. Consequently, the older you get, the more difficult it is to determine how old your body really is.

That doesn't mean no one is trying. Researchers at the National Institute on Aging are exploring reliable biomarkers, from loss of short-term memory to changes in pain sensitivity. In the future, we probably will take a series of longevity tests that produce a score. A score of 95 might mean you would live to age 110, while a score of 60 might mean you have only until age seventy-two, give or take a few years. A low score at an early age could be the incentive to make changes while there's still time.

One rough estimate of aging can be obtained from monitoring athletes over time. Even a fine-tuned athletic body loses about 0.5 percent of performance for every year of life after about age thirty. If this is a true benchmark for decline, then any greater loss of function is not aging but is an indicator of abuse or disuse. If you maintain optimal function through diet, exercise, attitude, and lifestyle so that you lose only 0.5 percent of mental or physical function each year after age thirty, then by age sixty-five you will have lost only 15 percent of your original vigor and you should have a wealth of vitality left by the time you reach 120.

On the other hand, a sedentary life with little attention to how you fuel your body through diet and thoughts can speed the aging process to 2 percent or more each year. By the time you reach age sixty-five, you will have lost up to 70 percent or more of the vigor you had in your youth. The numbers add up and are all in your favor if you choose to play your cards well.

Do Women Live Longer than Men?

Honor women! They entwine and weave heavenly roses in our earthly life.

—JOHANN VON SCHILLER

Until recently (relatively speaking, in terms of human history), more women died during childbirth than did men in battle, making the life expectancy for women even worse than men's. It wasn't until the 1600s that wealthy women could expect to live as long as their husbands (into their twenties). Surviving childbirth for the average woman did not improve until the mid-1800s to early 1900s.

That all changed in the twentieth century. Today men may sit in the Oval Office, may have walked on the moon, and may hold the record for running a marathon, but it is women who will live to talk about it. In the matter of only a few decades, women not only closed the gap but raced ahead of men in life expectancy.

Worldwide, women are winning the longevity race. Compared with men, Greek women enjoy the Mediterranean sun five years longer, Japanese women have six more years to spoil their grandchildren, U.S. women have five and a half more years of retirement, and Russian women have ten more years of smelling the roses and gathering memories. In fact, only the men in Nepal outlive the women there — and only by one year.

Modern women also are hardier than men when it comes to surviving disease. For example, 170 boys are conceived for every 100 girls, but girls have closed the gap by adolescence, primarily because more male fetuses are miscarried and those boys who are born are more likely to die from infections, disease, and accidents. In later years, men are up to seven times more likely than women to die from heart

Average Life Expectancy

YEAR	MEN	WOMEN
1900	48.3 years	51.5 years
1950	66.0	71.7
1990	72.1	79.0
2005	74.5	79.9

attack, stroke, cancer, respiratory diseases, accidents, and AIDS. "Approximately one-third of the difference in life expectancy between men and women is attributed to biological or genetic factors," says Robert N. Butler, M.D., director of the International Longevity Center at Mount Sinai Medical Center in New York. According to Dr. Butler, women have stronger immune systems, possibly as nature's way of ensuring that they survive pregnancy and childbearing.

Why Can't a Man Be More like a Woman (or Vice Versa)?

Women have time on their side for a number of reasons. First, there is the hormone factor. A high ratio of the female hormone estrogen to the male hormone testosterone protects a woman from heart disease and stroke—at least until menopause, when estrogen levels drop and a woman's heart disease risk escalates to that of men's.

Second, the secret might be in the genes. One theory states that the male sex chromosome Y might contain the stumbling block for reduced life span. Some disorders (such as muscular dystrophy) affect primarily men and can be traced to that missing segment of DNA that makes a Y chromosome a Y instead of a female X. Dr. Harman speculates that the female X chromosome is protected from damage during the early stages of development in the womb and that this allows girl babies a better chance at long-term survival.

A third possibility is that men's greater muscle mass and increased metabolic rate undermine longevity by speeding cell death, much in the way the remote control on a television fast-forwards a movie. On the other hand, men's battle with longevity could be traced to their generally feistier, more aggressive and competitive natures or to the fact that they work in higher-risk jobs. Whether it's in their cells, their lifestyles, or their attitude, men in general tend to live faster and harder and die younger than women.

While women live longer than men, they don't always live better. Women, once they get sick, are less likely than men to regain their health, and the extra years are likely to be spent depending on the care of others. Women are more likely to struggle with rheumatoid arthritis, depression, osteoporosis, and other "age-related" diseases, while men who live longer than average also live stronger and more independently.

For example, after retirement, 71 percent of men live independently, while only 54 percent of women can boast the same. By the age of eighty-five, a man has about a fifty-fifty chance of still maintaining his independence; a woman has only a one-in-three chance. The main reasons why older women fare worse than older men are economics and lifestyle. One in every five women over the age of seventy-five is below the poverty line; lack of resources has as much if not more to do with health status and longevity as gender. Women also start out with less muscle and are less likely than men to maintain what muscle they do have. Consequently, their weakened physical condition leads to disability, frailty, osteoporosis, and other debilitating conditions.

Women don't have to take the decree of frailty as gospel, just as men don't have to take this longevity news lying down! "Up to two-thirds of the difference in longevity between men and women can be traced to choices, such as drinking and smoking, diet, and exercise," says Dr. Butler. By making a few healthy changes, a woman can prepare for a robust and independent life in later years, while a man can significantly shrink the longevity gap.

Most men aren't willing to trade in their testosterone for more estrogen, but they would do well to live (and act?) a little more like a woman. For example, they could eat more like a woman. Women, on average, consume more fruits, vegetables, and whole grains, while men consume more red meat, beer, and liquor. Trading in the eight-ounce steak and alcohol for more dark green leafy vegetables, whole-wheat rolls, and fruit salads would help men lower blood fat levels and manage their weight, which in turn lowers the risk for heart disease, hypertension, and diabetes.

Women also are more apt to attend to routine medical tests that increase the chance of early diagnosis and treatment of disease. In addition, they seek medical attention more readily when things go wrong.

Then there's the communication issue. "While men may have their old boy networks and camaraderie in the locker room, they generally aren't willing to go so far as to admit they have emotional issues, let alone share them with friends," says Dr. Butler. Women are much freer in venting grief, worries, and intimate issues with friends and family.

All of these behaviors are associated with improved health, speedy recovery from illness, and longer life. Something as simple as taking a few moments to relax each day or seeking advice can help protect men from a variety of ills, ranging from depression and alcoholism to arrhythmias and cancer.

In short, women can avoid frailty and men can close the longevity gap by taking charge of their health today. "Adding life to your years requires *physical fitness* that includes a healthful diet, regular exercise, and not smoking; *purposeful fitness*, which means developing a purpose beyond yourself; and *social fitness* by developing a network of friends you can turn to during a crisis," recommends Dr. Butler.

Diet and Exercise Maximize Longevity: Promising New Findings

It is much cheaper and more effective to maintain good health than it is to regain it once it is lost.

–KENNETH H. COOPER, M.D., M.P.H.,
CHAIRMAN AND FOUNDER OF THE COOPER AEROBICS CENTER IN DALLAS

Of all life's gifts, none is as important as health. You can have boundless money, fame, possessions, experiences, and opportunities, but all of these pale without health. With health, almost anything is possible. A fit, healthy body and mind provide the stamina and energy to achieve most goals.

No one can avoid getting older, but there's no reason to look or feel old. Change how you eat, think, exercise, and live, and not only will you add years to your life but you will be able to count on those extra years as some of your finest. In fact, the traditional enfeebled and ailing elderly person will someday be a distant and vague memory of an unenlightened era.

However, while more than 70 percent of people believe they can stretch their years, only one in every one hundred people meets even minimum standards for a healthful diet or engages in even modest daily activity. It takes determination to live long and vitally, and it requires a daily commitment to take care of yourself.

Remember, the purpose of antiaging is not to extend life in order to live more years as an "old" person but to delay the onset of the aging process and lengthen the healthy middle years. That means taking charge of your health today. The sooner you grab on to your health and vitality, the longer you can stretch those healthy middle years and the slower you will glide into old age. The good news is that it is never too late to slow the ticking of the aging clock.

Looking Back to the Future

Developing a lifelong plan for vitality means knowing where you are going. Who do you want to be when you're one hundred years young? What do you need to do today to get there?

Grab a pencil and a piece of paper and find a comfortable spot where you won't be disturbed. Imagine that it is your hundredth birthday. You are healthy, fit, happy, and full of life. What do you look like? How do you feel? Who surrounds you? Where are you? How do you spend your time?

Now, as a one-hundred-year-old, take a moment to look back over your life. What did you do all those years to help yourself stay healthy, fit, and vital? What did you eat? How did you exercise? With whom did you spend time? What relationships did you nurture, and which ones did you discontinue? What were your hobbies? At what fulfilling jobs did you work? What challenges did you assume?

Are you creating a life today that will help you reach your vitality and longevity goals? What are you doing that supports these goals? What will you change?

CHAPTER 2

How Does Aging Happen?

Youth, large, lusty, loving—
Youth full of grace, force,
fascination.
Do you know that Old Age
may come after you with
equal grace, force,
fascination?

—WALT WHITMAN

We can't avoid getting old, but we don't have to age. By following the recommendations in this book, you can avoid most of what once were considered inevitable consequences of aging. By taking good care of yourself, you can sidestep some of the "metabolism melt-down" described next and can expect to look, act, and feel at least twenty years younger. Not bad for a start!

Metabolism Meltdown: What Happens to Our Bodies as They Age?

Nothing is more dishonorable than an old man, heavy with years,
who has no other evidence of his having lived long except his age.

—SENECA

Left to its own devices, starting somewhere between the ages of twenty and thirty, the body starts a gradual decline in many major systems, including the immune and muscular systems. The metabolic rate slows, the digestive tract becomes sluggish, and the endocrine system slips. A decrease in glucose tolerance increases the risk of diabetes, and an increase in blood pressure contributes to heart disease. Hair cells stop producing pigment, so most of us develop at least a few gray hairs, sometimes as early as in our thirties. Some people turn totally gray or white, while others lose their hair entirely. Oil glands in the scalp dry out, so the hair might become more brittle or break more easily. The skin wrinkles, although the extent depends in large part on sun exposure, history of smoking, nutrition, and genetics. The skin also loses some of its elasticity, again more as a result of sun exposure than of age. The skin is less moist and might even feel chalky. The upper layers produce fewer cells, so the skin is thinner and prone to bruising. Reduced blood supply to the skin causes paleness, but this is easily remedied by increased exercise.

Sight, sound, and smell also are affected. By their midforties, most people notice they can't read the print on a food label no matter how far away they hold the package. The lens of the eye thickens and becomes less smooth and elastic, while the pupil gets smaller and the muscles that help it widen and narrow are less responsive. Hearing peaked during puberty and has been on the decline ever since. By a person's forties and fifties, hearing loss is noticeable and a person may find it difficult to block out background noise. High-frequency noises are the first to go, especially in men, which might explain why husbands don't hear their wives as well.

The gradual loss of smell affects appetite by diminishing a person's ability to taste. This partially explains why some older people heavily salt or sweeten their foods. (Zinc deficiency also can lower an older person's ability to taste and can be remedied by taking a multiple vitamin and mineral supplement that contains 15 to 20 milligrams of zinc.)

A person's figure changes over the course of decades. Cartilage is one of the few tissues that continues to grow throughout life. Consequently, the ears and nose grow longer, starting around age thirty. Waistlines broaden, while shoulders might narrow. Unless a person continues to exercise, a loss of muscle and a gain in fat weight are inevitable as the decades pass.

Hormone levels change with age, resulting in cessation of menstruation at menopause for a woman and perhaps loss of libido in a man. The drop in estrogen for women can affect skin tone, vaginal lubrication, emotions, mental function and memory, and sex drive. Men's testosterone levels drop by as much as 40 percent between the ages of thirty and eighty. Other hormones, such as growth hormone and DHEA, also drop with age, possibly reducing muscle strength, vigor, and immune function. (See Chapter 5 for more on these hormones.)

Matter over Mind

Consider the following accomplishments:

- At age seventy-five, film producer-director Cecil B. DeMille premiered his seventieth film, *The 10 Commandments*.
- At age seventy-one, Michelangelo was appointed chief architect of one of the world's greatest architectural undertakings—St. Peter's in Rome. He worked on the project for eighteen years, until his death at age eighty-nine.
- At age sixty-nine, America's most famous architect, Frank Lloyd Wright, began what is often considered his best work—the house at Fallingwater.
- After age eighty, Italian composer Giuseppe Verdi wrote two of his greatest operas, including *Falstaff*.
- At age sixty-nine, Mother Teresa won the Nobel Peace Prize.
- Until his death at age eighty-six and despite failing eyesight, Claude Monet, the father of French Impressionist painting, was still painting his famous water lilies.

It is obvious from these and many other examples that talent and intellectual ability can bloom in the later years. Yet no other aspect of aging causes more distress and confusion than the thought of losing mental acuity and, with it, our personalities, talents, and memories. Many people incorrectly assume that mental function deteriorates with age; consequently, serious mental problems such as Alzheimer's disease often progress undetected because they are misdiagnosed as natural memory loss. But senility is not inevitable with age.

Almost all deterioration of mental function comes from disease, not from the aging process. Granted, people lose a few brain cells as they age, but they don't lose brain function. In fact, most brain cells are lost prior to puberty. After that, the rate slows considerably, at least until about age sixty.

Any normal reduction in mental capacity, such as slowed reaction time or trouble with short-term memory, might result from increased blood pressure, reduced blood supply to the brain, alterations in sleep patterns that affect brain activity, stress, or changes in hormones or brain chemicals called neurotransmitters. Not paying attention also might explain why you misplace your keys. Of course, some changes in the brain could result from self-fulfilling prophecies: the more a person complains of memory loss, the more likely he or she will experience more of the same. Many of these alterations in body and mind are modifiable by making a few simple alterations in diet, exercise, and thinking.

Theories of Aging

*People grow old only by discarding their hopes and dreams. Years
may wrinkle the skin, fade vision, or stoop posture, but only loss of
passion wrinkles the spirit!*

—ANONYMOUS

Why does the body change with time and age? In essence, aging is the result of accumulating loss of functioning cells. These effects are most noticeable in muscles and nerves, since their capacity to regenerate is limited.

Numerous theories attempt to explain this gradual decline in cell function, but no one really knows why we age. In centuries past the ravages of old age were attributed to demonic forces. In the machine age it was postulated that aging was a sign that the body's machinery had worn out. Today scientists theorize that aging might result from a number of factors acting alone or together in the body.

The Abuse Theory

The most practical of all the current theories on aging is the Abuse Theory. According to this theory, longevity depends on how well we treat our bodies. An abundance of evidence shows that people live longest when they:

Eat a low-fat, fiber-rich diet
Exercise regularly
Limit alcohol and avoid tobacco and drugs
Maintain a healthy weight
Have a positive attitude toward life
Wear seat belts
Effectively handle stress
Seek medical care when needed
Have ample money, education, support, and self-confidence
Live in middle- to upper-income communities

How Fast Are You Aging?

Here's a quick test of how your lifestyle is affecting your aging process. All the statements that follow pertain to lifestyle habits that you can improve or modify. Of course, family history of disease, your age, the age at death of your ancestors, and luck also are key influences of life expectancy and would modify the final score.

Women, on average, live about five and a half years longer than men. Your average life expectancy is your starting point. Respond to the following statements and add and subtract years as directed to obtain your approximate life potential.

Women: average life expectancy—79.9
Men: average life expectancy—74.5

1. Add two years for every "yes" answer to the following statements:
   a. I am in excellent health.
   b. I maintain a trim weight.
   c. I exercise daily.
   d. I consume a low-fat, high-fiber diet.
   e. I avoid consuming excess calories.
   f. I average eight servings of fruits and vegetables every day.
   g. I maintain a cholesterol level lower than 200mg/dL.
   h. I get at least seven hours of quality sleep each night.

2. Add an additional one year for every "yes" answer to the following statements:
   a. I am in good health (ignore if you already answered "yes" to 1a).
   b. I limit meat intake to three weekly servings (three ounces each).
   c. I take a moderate-dose multiple vitamin and mineral supplement with extra vitamin E.
   d. I am generally happy and satisfied with my life.
   e. I cope with stress and avoid unnecessary stress when possible.
   f. I average six servings of fruits and vegetables every day (ignore if you already answered "yes" to 1f).
   g. I am in a long-term, satisfying relationship.

3. Subtract five years for every "yes" answer to the following statements:
   a. I am overweight.
   b. My blood cholesterol is higher than 200mg/dL.

Continued

c. I eat too much fat and not enough fruits and vegetables.

d. I use tobacco.

e. I don't have an annual physical examination by an M.D.

4. Subtract two years for every "yes" answer to the following statements:
   a. I am in poor health.
   b. My blood pressure is high.
   c. My blood sugar is high.
   d. My blood cholesterol is greater than 200mg/dL or my HDL cholesterol is lower than 60mg/dL.
   e. I drink more than five alcoholic beverages each week.
   f. I am very overweight or obese.

5. Subtract one year for every "yes" answer to the following statements:
   a. I don't use sunscreen.
   b. I don't use seat belts.
   c. I am not in a long-term relationship.
   d. I have no close friends.

Total the numbers to obtain a rough estimate of what your life expectancy is, given your current habits. Keep in mind that you can improve these odds by making changes today in what you eat, how often you exercise, and how you live.

The Wear-and-Tear Theory

Life can kill you—or so say proponents of the Wear-and-Tear Theory of aging, who assert that daily life simply wears out the body's tissues. Consuming too much fat over time raises blood cholesterol levels, which leads to heart disease. Sunbathing makes skin susceptible to wrinkling and cancer. Alcohol consumption wears down the liver and leads to premature disease and death. Almost anyone older than sixty-five has some joint damage from years of walking, lifting, bending, jogging, squatting, or dancing.

Unlike machines produced on an assembly line, however, every human body is different. Some people are more prone to osteoarthritis, possibly because their cartilage is less resilient. Others increase their chances of developing osteoarthritis by being overweight, which places additional stress on the joints. Atherosclerosis, wrinkling, loss of muscle tone, and numerous other wear-and-tear disorders can be greatly modified by diet, exercise, and how you live. In short, genetics and lifestyle are as much to blame as aging for how the body "wears."

Furthermore, the Wear-and-Tear Theory doesn't explain why the body stops repairing itself. Machines can't fix themselves or build new parts, but our bodies have a complex repair system that quickly remedies engine problems every day, usually putting us back in action without a sign of malfunction. What causes the body to stop repairing broken parts? Other theories, discussed next, address this question.

The Cross-Linkage Theory

Repair processes cease when cell communication breaks down, according to the Cross-Linkage Theory of aging. This theory states that cells generate defective cell "messengers" that then tell the cell to produce defective or cross-linked proteins including enzymes. These useless proteins accumulate and eventually reduce cell function, interfere with cell repair, or cause cell death. What causes the defective messengers is unknown, but many researchers suspect that highly reactive compounds called free radicals are to blame.

The Free-Radical Theory

Like David and Goliath, the body may be brought down by infinitesimal oxygen fragments called free radicals found in air pollution, fried foods, tobacco smoke, and normal metabolic processes. A free radical attacks and damages the genetic code and the protective coatings (membranes) of cells. Free radicals also halt energy production by damaging the cells' powerhouse centers (the mitochondria). Some researchers speculate that the rate of mitochondrial damage might determine life span.

After thousands of free-radical attacks on each cell every day, the cells over the course of decades become damaged or abnormal. Due to immune cell damage, the body gradually loses its resistance to colds, infections, and disease. Eventually the cell dies and only a "clinker" remains. In fact, the cell age of tissues is determined by the number of clinkers present.

Luckily, the body's antioxidant system, comprising vitamins, minerals, enzymes, and other compounds, sweeps up and deactivates free radicals. This is why it is essential to stockpile a strong antioxidant defense and minimize any lifestyle habit that generates free radicals.

The body is exposed to free radicals throughout life, yet the damage seems to escalate in the later years. This suggests that the aging human body needs greater amounts of antioxidants to compensate for other lagging systems. (See Chapters 4 and 9 for more information on free radicals and antioxidants.)

The Immune Theory

The main job of the body's immune system is to separate friend from foe, letting normal cells flourish while destroying everything abnormal or damaging, from germs to renegade cancer cells. Sometimes immune processes malfunction as a result of aging and attack body tissues, rather than foreign substances, leading to tissue destruction. Studies on animals support this theory of aging. Animals with vigorous immune systems live approximately 77 percent longer than those with poorly functioning immune systems.

While there's a big difference between humans and mice, the link between immunity and aging might cross species. Poor diet and medication use in later years can interfere with nutrient absorption and compromise immunity. In addition, intestinal absorption and the availability of some immune-enhancing nutrients, such as vitamin B_{12}, decrease as a person ages, thus increasing dietary requirements to maintain health. Several studies report improved immunity when a person follows the guidelines of the Antiaging Diet (see Chapter 7) and consumes a portion-controlled, high-fiber diet, takes a moderate-dose multiple supplement, and exercises in moderation.

The Waste Products Theory

Like your car, your refrigerator, and the earth itself, the body depends on an efficient means of removing waste. Anything that interferes with this system could contribute to aging. When one or more of the body's waste-removal systems malfunctions, by-products accumulate in cells, clogging normal metabolic processes and potentially damaging or killing the cells.

No one knows why the aging body becomes less efficient at handling wastes. However, accumulation of damage caused by free radicals, including the buildup of yellow-brown pigments called lipofuscin, is likely a primary contributor. Low intake of vitamin E results in greater accumulation of lipofuscin, and marginal deficiencies of several nutrients, such as the B vitamins and iron, are associated with accumulation of abnormal by-products of metabolism and reduced mental functioning.

The Ticking Clock Theory

In the 1960s a scientist named Leonard Hayflick noticed an interesting characteristic of cell growth. Cells placed in a flask and fed well continued to thrive by reproducing themselves but only up to a point. Then after a set number of replications, the cells grew old and died. No cell tested lived forever.

This "Hayflick limit" is specific to each type of cell. For example, cells from chickens divide fifteen to thirty-five times, while cells from mice achieve only fourteen to twenty-eight replications. Human cells fare better, at about fifty to sixty generations. Hayflick theorized that some kind of cellular clock counts the generations and triggers cell death. According to the Ticking Clock Theory, life span and aging might be arranged and enforced somewhere within the cell.

That "somewhere" might be at the ends of the DNA strands within each cell. These end segments, called telomeres, are like the handles on a jump rope. They protect the DNA cord from unraveling and allow complete replication of the entire DNA strand during cell division. However, each time the DNA splits during cell replication, one notch on the telomere handle is lost. After a set number of cell divisions, the telomere is used up and the cell can no longer replicate. These dead or damaged cells interfere with neighboring cells, creating a haphazard cascade effect that could result in aging. In essence, the telomere is like a ticking clock that determines life span. If scientists could measure telomere length, it might serve as the most accurate biomarker of aging. In the future there may be ways to directly affect telomere length by tampering with the enzymes responsible for its shortening. According to this theory, stop that internal clock and you can stop the aging process.

In the meantime, even if you can't stop the clock, you can slow it a bit. Several things speed up cell division, which amplifies telomere demise. Sun exposure, infections and injury, radiation exposure, stress, and tobacco use increase cell turnover. On the other hand, restricting calories slows cell turnover and extends life span.

Protecting the DNA from free-radical attacks also might extend the life of the telomere. Preliminary evidence shows that building antioxidant defense systems does, in fact, lengthen the life of some species. Granted, extrapolating results from roundworms to humans is a big leap, but the possibilities are exciting. Extending the life span from three to an unheard-of six weeks in a worm is equivalent to giving the average human life span a boost to 150 to 240 years!

You Can Reverse the Aging Process

To know how to grow old is the master work of wisdom, and one of the most difficult chapters in the great war of living.

—HENRI FRÉDÉRIC AMIEL

Aging doesn't happen overnight. The slow loss of youth begins in your twenties, when you still think you're indestructible. The sooner you jump on the antiaging bandwagon and start supplying your body with all the nutrients it needs for optimal functioning, the more likely you will hold on to that youthful health, sidestep the slow demise of aging, enjoy life to its fullest, and dramatically reduce medical costs later in life. For this reason, it's important to be aware of the subtle first signs of poor health. For example, did you know that mood swings might be caused by a vitamin deficiency rather than a glitch in your personality? That dry skin might be easily remedied with a little more oil in your diet? Or that fatigue might be a sign you need more iron, not more coffee?

Most of us know that what we eat is important to how we feel, and we've made some changes. We've cut fat intake from 42 to 34 percent of total calories and are trying to eat the recommended servings of fruits and vegetables. We've switched from potato chips to baby carrots and from chocolate ice cream to fat-free frozen yogurt, and we put low-fat milk in our caffe lattes. Hey, many of us even know our cholesterol levels!

While all of these changes are commendable, many of us think we're doing better than we really are. According to a survey by the American Dietetic Association, 90 percent of adults think they eat a healthful diet, when in fact only 1 percent

■ *Signs of a Bad Diet*

HAIR AND SCALP

- Dry, thin, lackluster hair
- Hair that splits or breaks or is dry and tangles easily
- Hair loss and/or dandruff
- Premature graying or changes in hair color

NAILS

- Poor growth
- Nails that chip or are weak
- Brittle, fragile nails or nails with ridges

SKIN

- Dull, dry skin
- Sun-damaged skin, sagging skin, easy bruising
- Flaky, itchy, or rough skin

MOUTH, TEETH, AND GUMS

- Cracks at the corners of the mouth, soreness, or burning of the tongue
- Bleeding gums
- Periodontal disease
- Cavities

EYES

- Vision loss caused by cataracts or macular degeneration
- Sensitivity to bright light, burning, itching
- Bloodshot eyes, poor vision

MOOD AND ENERGY

- Tiredness, lethargy
- Mild depression, irritability
- Mood fluctuations

meet the dietary guidelines outlined in the U.S. Department of Agriculture's (USDA's) MyPyramid.

Seeking medical help and having an annual physical exam to monitor blood cholesterol, blood sugar, weight, blood pressure, and other parameters of health status are important. But being healthy is about taking charge of your health every day.

One place to start is your diet. Do you really know how well you're doing diet-wise? You might be surprised at how what you eat might be affecting how you look, feel, and age. Marginal nutrient intakes can have profound yet subtle effects on well-being, vitality, and aging. The symptoms of poor nutrition are vague, so they progress unnoticed or we explain them away as being "all in our heads" or with the observation "I'm just getting older" or "I was born this way." In fact, all it might take is a few simple dietary changes to look and feel good, if not great.

The effects also can be immediate. While heart disease or osteoporosis may require a lifetime of poor eating habits, the sparkle in your eye or a healthy smile is a sign of what you've eaten in the last few months. The warning signs of a bad on page 25 will help you assess your dietary intake and decide what, if anything, needs improvement. Use this information to work with your physician to prevent age-related diseases and to help slow the aging process. Chapter 10 includes information on how to improve your diet to prevent specific conditions.

CHAPTER 3

Exploring Vitality

Sow a thought, reap an act;
Sow an act, reap a habit;
Sow a habit, reap a character;
Sow a character, reap a
destiny.
—ANONYMOUS

We are surrounded by living examples of vitality:

- Tina Turner, who at sixty-seven and despite a rocky life still struts her stuff like a twenty-year-old.
- Lance Armstrong, who has won seven Tour de France races after overcoming testicular cancer and having been given almost no chance of survival.
- Jimmy Carter, who at eighty-one is a tireless humanitarian and recipient of the Nobel Peace Prize.
- Paul Newman, actor and owner of Newman's Own foods, who makes eighty years old look sexy!
- Barbara Boxer, the sixty-five-year-old senator from California, who is bright, fiery, and gorgeous.
- Then there is Gloria Steinem, Paul McCartney, Madonna, Christiane Amanpour, Susan Sarandon, Annette Bening, Robert Redford, Nelson Mandela, Michael Jordan, Sophia Loren, Ed Harris, Bono, Bonnie Raitt, Tom Brokaw, or any of thousands of other people who exude a passion and purpose for living.

Others who have left us, such as Christopher Reeve and Katharine Hepburn, continue to shape our image of what a purposeful life looks like.

These are just a few of our mentors of vitality. Each of us has people much closer to us—in our homes, offices, schools, or neighborhoods or sitting next to us at church—who possess that same passion for living. Most of us ourselves have experienced the joy and aliveness of vitality though perhaps not as often as we'd like.

■ *A Road Map to Vitality: Advice from Vital People*

I interviewed many vital people for this book. Here are a few of their recommendations for getting the most out of life:

- Live in the present, and enjoy it.
- Think positive.
- Don't take your health for granted.
- Be grateful for every single thing life has to offer.
- When you're feeling down in the dumps, do something for someone else; it will help you forget your woes.
- No matter what comes along, know that you can handle it.
- Be good to people; it always pays off.
- Don't take yourself too seriously.
- Accept that no one goes through life scot-free.
- Do what you love and love what you do.
- Keep moving.

Most vital people, in fact, live what they would call ordinary lives, yet they're filled with extraordinary experience.

Vitality is the spark of life itself and is the fuel for a happy life. Choosing to live longer is not the goal—the true goal is to live those extra years vitally.

What Is Vitality?

They want somebody to tell 'em they have a chance at the i-n-g of
life and not the e-d.

—TOM ROBBINS, FROM *JITTERBUG PERFUME*

There is more to longevity than a low cholesterol level and more to vibrant living than an exercise program. Vitality provides the passion that makes getting older worth it.

Vital people exude a spirit, gusto, or joie de vivre (joy of life) so radiant that it forms our first impressions of them. We're attracted to them like moths to a light.

■ *Vital Dreaming*

One way to nurture vitality is to visualize it, or picture it in your mind. Visualizations give you the chance to see life as it could be if vitality and health were in full bloom. There are no right or wrong ways to visualize; just accept and enjoy whatever comes to mind.

Find a comfortable, quiet place where you won't be disturbed, preferably just before you go to bed at night or just after awakening in the morning. Close your eyes, and for a few moments pay attention to your breathing—the drawing in and the going out of your breath. When you feel calm, consider the following questions and try to picture in your mind and even feel in your body the answers:

1. What does vitality mean to you?
2. How does it feel to be energized with vitality? What does it feel like to be emotionally at peace, feeling no anger, fear, or depression? How does it feel to have a heart filled with love, trust, and compassion?
3. What would you look like as a vital person?
4. What would you do in your life to nurture your vitality?
5. What brings you joy? What helps you feel and give love, delight, and wonder?
6. At what moments in your life have you felt vital? Describe how you felt.
7. What people, events, traits, experiences, or other things tie your life together and give it meaning? Look to these as a starting point to vitality.

Now take a long look at yourself in a mirror. What do you see that you like? What resembles the looks and feelings of vitality you just identified in the visualization? What do you see that you want to change? How will you go about bringing your daily life into a focus on health and vitality?

Vital people make us smile. They wake us up. We feel better, happier, and more hopeful just being around them. We describe them as positive, energetic, comfortable with themselves, centered, curious, uplifting, optimistic, or resilient; they describe themselves simply as normal or happy but wonder why other people aren't having as much fun. Vital people appreciate all of life. They enjoy life in general and in almost all of its aspects, while other people glimpse only isolated moments of the same enthusiasm.

Vitality goes even deeper than just taking joy in life. According to the Oxford Dictionary, the word *vitality* means "the principle of life" or "the ability to sustain life." Vitality is life or aliveness expressed to its fullest. The quest for longevity, therefore, is an empty goal unless it encompasses the striving for vitality or life's source.

Where Does Vitality Come From?

Seize the moment of excited curiosity on any subject to solve your doubts; for if you let it pass, the desire may never return, and you may remain in ignorance.

—WILLIAM WIRT

Everyone has the potential for and the right to vitality. Granted, growing up in a household of encouragement, joy, silliness, and vitality certainly boosts the odds of developing it yourself, but many vital people came from less-than-happy childhoods. Still more have suffered serious illness or tragedy yet continued to appreciate life despite the odds.

With no research on the topic thus far, we can only speculate that there might be a genetic predisposition to vitality. Even if some aspects of vitality are inherited, in large measure it is how you nurture your genetic potential that makes all the difference in life. In essence, each of us comes into this life as a canvas bearing only the rough outline of a picture. Life hands us the paints, the brush, and the palette; it's up to us whether we create a Monet or a fiasco.

The Vitality Continuum

Like most aspects of our physical and mental makeup, each of us probably has a unique continuum for vitality that ranges from merely existing to sheer joy—say, on a scale of 1 to 10 where 1 equals existing and 10 equals maximum vitality. Where you are on that continuum depends on the choices you make each day. The ultimate goal is to live at the upper end of the scale most of the time.

Babies are born overflowing with vitality and wonder at life. It takes practice for adults to hold on to or rekindle that natural-born vitality by adding a depth that comes only from experience and maturity. Vital people are exposed to the same world as everyone else; their adversities might be no different from those of their neighbors. The difference is that vital people focus on positive times and try to view

■ *More Advice from Vital People*

- When things seem overwhelming, remind yourself that it's only life.
- Be necessary.
- Practice random acts of kindness (for example, put a dime in someone else's parking meter, cook a hot meal for a housebound senior, hold the door for a stranger, let someone with fewer purchases go ahead of you in line, or buy someone flowers when it isn't his or her birthday).
- Don't fret about the future—fretting is a waste of time.
- Never retire.
- Learn something new every day.
- Don't be afraid to make mistakes; they're only signs that you're stretching your wings and growing a little.
- Be resourceful. If you can't get where you want to go one way, try a different route.
- Do things because you love them, not because you expect fame or fortune.
- Throw out the television and get involved in life.
- Be outrageous.
- Hang out with happy people.

even hard times in a positive light. As a result, uplifting experiences, feelings, thoughts, and beliefs come far more frequently and intensely to them than to other people. We all can push our natural-born right to vitality by taking charge of our life and our physical, emotional, mental, and spiritual well-being.

The Link Between Health, Attitude, and Vitality

When fate hands us a lemon, let's try to make lemonade.

—DALE CARNEGIE

Taking care of the body by eating well and exercising, not smoking, drinking in moderation, and sleeping well clears the way for vitality to shine. But vitality also has an emotional component. It is difficult to feel vital when you're depressed, fatigued, or stressed. People who develop a positive, trusting attitude toward life are

■ *Even More Advice from Vital People*

- Take responsibility for yourself—don't blame anyone else for what happens in your life.
- Be the kind of person you would want to have as a friend.
- Love others because you want to, not because you expect anything from them.
- Take risks.
- Don't let pain get you down. If something hurts, it's going to hurt whether you're lying in bed or climbing a mountain. You might as well enjoy the view!
- Don't bear grudges.
- Be curious about everything.
- You're old when you feel sorry for yourself.
- You may not be perfect, but you're good enough.
- What makes people young or old is how they think.
- Never give up!

less likely to suffer from disease, ranging from cancer and heart disease to migraines and urinary problems. For example, studies from both the University of Wisconsin and the University College in London found that people who focus on positive attitudes and work hard to be happy also benefit by experiencing less heart disease. Researchers at Geneva University Hospital in Switzerland report that vital people also show better mental health throughout life. When vital people are ill, they're more likely to recover and recover quickly. Vitality can even master terminal illness and shine through amidst some of life's biggest challenges. In fact, often it is during a crisis that a person realizes that life is too short and too precious to be spent any other way but vitally.

When faced with a terminal condition, vital people look for meaning, purpose, and humor in their experience, discovering ways to appreciate life even when they're dealt a bad hand. They also are less likely to be dependent on others for their daily care in their later years than people who clutch on to negative, angry, or hopeless thoughts.

The link between vitality and health is a win-win relationship. Embracing vitality boosts energy, helps maintain health, and reduces the risk of disease and premature aging. In turn, a healthier body encourages positive thinking and fuels vitality. Nurturing both works in your favor for health, happiness, and longevity. Conversely, not taking care of your health, eating poorly, not exercising, living a stressful lifestyle, allowing negative thoughts, or surrounding yourself with depressing people dampens or even snuffs out vitality, which leads to more damaging behaviors, disease, and premature death.

Put all the vital people in the world into one room and you wouldn't find a curmudgeon in the batch. Vitality begins and ends with attitude. Vital people are grateful for life. They don't avoid life's problems, but they do minimize the things they can't change and view unpleasant experiences as temporary. Vitality is the opposite of the victim mentality, whereby people blame anyone and anything but themselves for their problems. Vital people instead ask, "How can I change, fix, or improve this situation?"

You can reach that upper end of your vitality continuum by filling your mind and life with vital thoughts and actions, layer upon layer. Listen to your thoughts. Do they reaffirm vitality or bury it?

Thoughts that negate vitality sound like this:

"I can't do this."
"I can't handle this."
"I am likely to fail."
"This is going to be awful."
"This will never work."

Thoughts that nurture and reinforce vitality sound like this:

"I can handle this."
"I'm enjoying this adventure no matter what the outcome."
"I'll learn and grow from this experience."
"I love what I'm doing."
"This is fun!"

Remember, attitude is everything, and attitudes spring from thoughts. You choose your thoughts. If you want to be old, think "can't," "won't," or "shouldn't." The sooner you start, the quicker you'll age.

If you want to live vitally and long, on the other hand, choose to think youthfully and be playful. Focus on all you have to be grateful for and take good care of it. Try new experiences, surround yourself with nurturing relationships, and keep your sense of humor. If you plan to live a long life, be prepared to work on your attitude.

Keep Laughing

"Keep your sense of humor." That is the most common advice given by vital people. "Don't take yourself too seriously" is another.

Vital people are playful. They're not afraid to be silly, spontaneous, or vulnerable. Vital people get a kick out of things and find humor even when life tries to bring them down. This ability to laugh might be one reason why vital people are less prone to illness. Numerous studies, including one from Osaka University in Japan, conclude that laughter helps cure disease, possibly by boosting the body's immune system, which fights off infection and cancer. Laughter is so important that even if you don't feel like it, hang around someone who does. The humor is contagious!

One way to nurture this playfulness is to never act your age. If when you're forty you act your age by slowing down instead of taking up in-line skating, mountain climbing, ballet, the clarinet, or any other hobby (because "people your age don't do those sorts of crazy things"), imagine how feeble, dependent, and inactive you'll be by the time you hit ninety! How can you live to be 120 if you stop living at forty?

Some of the healthiest and oldest people in the world live in Okinawa, where it is common for people to celebrate their hundredth birthday. When asked, these oldest old attribute their longevity to diet and to *yuimaru*, which comes from the Japanese words for *circle* and *connection*. Feeling necessary and sharing gives meaning and fun to everyday living.

Another way to kindle joy is to challenge set patterns. Routine and habit, though comfortable, can dampen an inventive, lighthearted approach to life. Try living from a new angle, even if it's by taking a small step, such as reading the paper at a different time of day or ordering something new at a favorite restaurant. Keep each day fresh and open to joy.

Curiosity vs. Fear

Vital people are curious, open, and willing to learn. They ask questions, want details, and have an insatiable appetite for knowledge. That's what makes a vital person so interesting, someone you want to know. Curiosity and playfulness keep vital people young.

Anxiety, stress, and fear kill curiosity and, thus, vitality. As Dr. Gerald G. Jampolsky says, "Love is the absence of fear." Being curious and willing to try new things requires that a person push past fear, self-doubt, or negative beliefs and take the risk. It means viewing problems, troubles, barriers, and fears as opportunities for growth rather than as reasons to retreat from life. It takes courage to live a long and vital life, but when you think of the alternative, it's worth it!

Have a Purpose

British philosopher Bertrand Russell resigned at age eighty-eight from the Campaign for Nuclear Disarmament to establish a more militant group called the Committee of 100. The year before he died (at age ninety-seven), he stated that his purpose in life was sparked by three passions: "the longing to love, the search for knowledge, and the unbearable pity for the suffering of mankind."

What is your life's purpose? How would you want to answer the question of what good came from your life? Your answer tells a lot about how you should live each day and also gives you insight into the source of your vitality. As the German philosopher Friedrich Nietzsche said, "He who has a why to live can bear with almost any how."

When life loses its meaning, one's desire to live fades. "The highest suicide rates are in white men over the age of 80 who have lost a purpose in life and are absorbed in meaninglessness," says Robert N. Butler, M.D., director of the International Longevity Center at Mount Sinai Medical Center in New York. As we age the search for meaning in life can take on a new depth, being given dimension by our experience, pain, struggle, triumphs, loss, and discovery.

Vitality is closely woven into the meaning and purpose we give to every moment of our lives. It has nothing to do with possessions, fortune, fame, or status but much to do with how open we are to love and happiness. Vital people have a clear sense of what gives their lives meaning. This personal philosophy underlies their daily decisions and actions. Usually the purpose involves giving—that is, being of service to others, helping to make the world a slightly better place, or bringing joy to others' lives.

Sometimes we actively define what gives our lives significance; other times it lands in our laps unexpectedly. My life's purpose was revealed years ago while I participated in a guided imagery in a college class. The teacher had asked us to close our eyes, relax, and let our imaginations carry us. She asked us to imagine we were climbing a mountain. The path was winding, and it took some time to reach the summit, where someone was waiting. The person was to hand us a present, and then we were to walk back down the mountain. After the guided imagery, the class discussed what each one of us had visualized.

Like many of the students in the class, I had been met by a sage, sort of a Gandolf- or Merlin-like character. My sage was sitting at a fire overlooking the surrounding mountain peaks. It was that magic time when daylight meets darkness. I sat down by the fire next to my imaginary sage, who pulled from his robes a simple brown suede pouch tied with twine, much like those little bags that hold marbles. I peeked into the bag to find a fistful of pea-sized crystals that caught the firelight and twinkled. I put the bag into my back pocket, stood up, and started back down the mountain. As I walked, the crystals fell out of the pouch and sprinkled on the ground, covering my trail with jewels.

From that brief journey into my imagination, I realized that my purpose in life was to leave sparkles wherever life took me, knowing that I could always find my way back up the mountain by following the joy I had left behind.

If you plan to live a long life, you'd better know why you're here. Each person's life purpose and source of vitality is as unique as his or her fingerprints. No two people can follow the same path to vitality. You must take time to ask yourself some very important questions, such as these:

- What do I choose as the meaning and purpose of my life?
- What do I want to accomplish during this lifetime?
- What do I want to be remembered for?
- If it were the last day of my life and I was reviewing my time here on earth, what would I want to look back on with pride? What regrets do I want to avoid?
- Why do I want to live a long and healthy life? How will I use those extra years constructively?

Go for It

If you want to live to be 100 or older, you can't just sit around
waiting for it to happen. You have to get up each day and go after it!

—GEORGE BURNS

Developing a vital personality and approach to life isn't achieved overnight; it takes a lifetime of practice to grow into and strengthen your vitality, just as it takes daily exercise to keep your muscles strong. It isn't easy to change, but it is possible, and it's the desire to better ourselves that makes us human and makes life valuable.

First, you must build a healthful life that fulfills basic needs for feeling safe, feeling connected to other people through family and friendships, nurturing love in every act of life, building respect both for yourself and for others, and taking care of your body with healthful habits. According to the psychologist Abraham Maslow, only when these basic needs are fulfilled can a person focus on more profound issues of vitality and spirituality. Sometimes you have to begin gradually, finding small ways to work joy and health into daily experiences, starting with any aspect of your health, from the physical, mental, and emotional to the social or spiritual.

Act As If . . .

If you don't feel vital, start by changing how you think or act. The feelings may catch up. Anything becomes a habit if repeated often enough. Research shows that when people adopt a healthful lifestyle, eat well, exercise regularly, and keep stress at bay, they start feeling better about themselves. They also enjoy life more and have a more positive attitude. A study from the University of Manitoba found that people who exercised also scored higher on happiness scales and lived longer. Vitality is like a snowball rolling downhill. The more you incorporate vital qualities into your life, the more vital and enthusiastic you will feel and the easier it will become to connect with that wellspring of life within you.

Identify one aspect of your life that you want to change. Even if you don't feel that way yet, start by acting as if you already have mastered that change. For example:

- If you are struggling to start an exercise program, tell yourself several times daily that you are an exerciser, then act as if you feel comfortable with your new exercise routine. Rehearse success by visualizing yourself exercising effortlessly and enjoying the experience. To support this attitude, surround yourself with people who are enthusiastic about their exercise, read books that will motivate you to stick with it, and/or put stars on the calendar for every day you successfully meet your exercise goals.
- To feel more energetic, start with something as simple as how you walk. Start walking as if you were self-confident and energetic. Walk with long, powerful

strides, with your head high, your shoulders back, your chin up, and your arms swinging freely at your side. Do it every day until it becomes habit.

- If you want to bring more laughter into your life, surround yourself with people who make you laugh, watch comedy shows on television, rent silly movies, put up a bird feeder in the backyard, get a kitten, volunteer at a day care center, and/or read funny books. Avoid people, activities, thoughts, and behaviors that rob you of humor, and slowly replace them with more positive people and experiences.

Include something every day in your life that excites you and brings you joy (if possible, make it your job, your family, and your friends or community). Stop reading the paper or listening to negative news reports, and start spending the extra time with positive-thinking people and listening to music or motivational tapes. Replace negative thoughts with positive ones, and repeat positive affirmations throughout the day. Slowly, without even noticing it, vitality will come to you.

Just Do It

When it comes to changing attitudes, the basic advice to just do it is about as useful as a crash course in walking on water. However, there is a pearl of wisdom in this advice. Attitudes—from optimism to hopelessness—are learned responses, not cut-in-stone personality traits. Basically, negative thinking is just a bad habit, and habits can be changed. Here are a few tips for adjusting your attitude:

- Start replacing negative thoughts with positive ones. Interpret setbacks as temporary and specific learning experiences. Attribute favorable situations to enduring causes.
- Surround yourself with positive people; attitudes often rub off.
- Don't let one setback contaminate your whole life; keep it contained and in perspective.
- Believe in your ability to stretch your limits. (Studies of college students found that their level of hope more accurately predicted college performance than did SAT scores or high school grades.)
- Improve your diet and exercise regularly, to alleviate depression, hostility, and negative thinking.

- Push the limits of your comfort zone. Research from the University of Chicago shows that peak experiences come from matching challenges to abilities. People are most likely to feel invigorated when their skills are pushed to the limit by a hefty challenge. On the other hand, anxiety is likely when the task is more than their skills can handle, while apathy is a product of never taking risks or stretching boundaries.

The secret is to keep learning, experimenting, adventuring, and challenging yourself. Cultivating a positive approach to life takes time and effort, but it's well worth it. If nothing else, think of the alternative, which is living a dull, drab life!

Ageless, Timeless

Go outside to the fields, enjoy nature and the sunshine, go out and try to recapture happiness in yourself and in God. Think of all the beauty that's still left in and around you and be happy.

—ANNE FRANK

Vitality is the fuel that makes the journey of life fun and possibly longer. It is a process, not an endpoint. Even one-hundred-year-young vital people say they are still learning more about how to appreciate life. Each of us must pass through many of life's doors and experience many failures, successes, losses, and gains before vitality reaches its full expression. We are like roses slowly unfolding. Only age can bring us into full bloom.

CHAPTER 4

Stack the Deck Against Aging

Should you fail to pilot your own ship, don't be surprised at what inappropriate port you find yourself docked.

—TOM ROBBINS,
FROM *JITTERBUG PERFUME*

Staying young depends on a healthful diet, daily exercise, a positive attitude, and a supportive lifestyle, with a hefty dose of heredity thrown in. Basically, nature deals us the cards, but we play our own hand. And we're allowed to stack the deck.

While specific guidelines for each of these facets in the longevity game will be outlined in future chapters, there are a few antiaging cards that are so potent they deserve a chapter all to themselves. Read on!

Antioxidants Against Age

Today, you don't have to worry about growing old, you have to worry about rusting.

—GEORGE BURNS

As was discussed in previous chapters, disease is not a matter of age but is a result of accumulating damage over time. Antioxidants are key players in damage control.

A wealth of evidence shows that the antioxidant nutrients (including vitamins C and E, the carotenoids, selenium, and zinc, as well as thousands of phytochemicals) do the following:

- Play a leading role in the prevention of age-related diseases
- Stimulate the immune system, thus protecting the body from disease and infection that can lead to premature death

- Protect the nervous system and brain from oxidative damage associated with age-related memory loss and nerve function
- Function at the very foundation of the body's biological clock, preventing or at least slowing the damage that underlies aging itself

Free-radical damage to our cells' genetic code escalates as we age. Consequently, anything that reduces free-radical production or counteracts free radicals, including the antioxidants, becomes important to our staying young as we grow older. (See Chapters 2 and 10 for more on free radicals.)

What You Can Expect from Antioxidants

Studies consistently show that diets rich in antioxidants prevent disease and possibly premature aging. Hundreds of studies alone show a protective effect of fruits, vegetables, and their antioxidants in preventing numerous types of cancers, including cancers of the bladder, breast, pancreas, esophagus, lungs, larynx, oral cavity, cervix, stomach, endometrium, colon, and rectum. "Although every study done to date, and probably every future trial, can be critiqued over one issue or another, the accumulating evidence is such that this approach [increasing intake of antioxidants] may turn out to be one of the most important disease prevention strategies," states Harinder S. Garewal, M.D., Ph.D., assistant director of Cancer Prevention and Control, Arizona Cancer Center and Tucson VA Medical Center.

Among the studies showing the benefits of antioxidants are the following:

- A study from Brigham and Women's Hospital in Boston found that women with the highest blood values for antioxidant-rich carotenoids had up to a 35 percent lower risk of developing breast cancer.
- Researchers at the University of Utah found that women with the lowest intakes of vitamin E were more than twice as likely to have rectal cancer than women with the highest intakes. Low intakes of certain forms of vitamin E, such as alpha- and gamma-tocopherol, were associated with more than a threefold greater risk of rectal cancer among women age sixty or older. In addition, women with the lowest intakes of lycopene, an antioxidant-rich carotenoid, were 70 percent more likely to have rectal cancer.
- According to a study from the Unit of Nutritional Epidemiology Surveillance in Paris, women who consumed the most antioxidant-rich flavonoids lowered

their risk for heart disease by 69 percent compared with women who ate few fruits and vegetables containing these phytochemicals.

- Researchers at the Harvard School of Public Health say that men who load their plates with antioxidant-rich fruits and vegetables can lower their risk for stroke by up to 41 percent.
- Antioxidant-rich diets lowered ovarian cancer risk by up to 67 percent, as reported in a study from the Roswell Park Cancer Institute in Buffalo, New York.
- People who consume antioxidant-rich diets might lower their risk by up to 41 percent for developing diabetes down the road, according to a study from the National Public Health Institute in Helsinki.

How Antioxidants Combat the Radicals

On a cellular level, antioxidants are the advocates of vitality because they are uniquely effective in combating the oxygen fragments called free radicals (also called oxidants). Free radicals have an extra electrical charge called an electron. Since electrons usually come in pairs, having an unpaired electron makes free radicals highly unstable. In an effort to neutralize their extra charge, free radicals attack cell membranes, proteins, and even the genetic code within cells, stealing an electrical charge. This reaction neutralizes the free radical but generates a new one, since the attacked membrane or protein is now short one electrical charge.

Left unchecked, this chain reaction of destruction is much like the process of oxidation, which rusts metal or turns butter rancid, but in your body it means cell membranes are weakened, the powerhouse centers of the cell called the mitochondria break down, proteins are scrambled, and the genetic code is altered. The end result is damaged, devitalized, or dead cells. As discussed in Chapter 2, the accumulation of free-radical damage in tissues is a major contributor both to the aging process and the diseases associated with aging.

Unless you're willing to give up breathing, which is a main source of these oxygen fragments, there is no avoiding free radicals. We also ingest them in food, especially fried or fatty foods, and the body generates these renegades as natural by-products of metabolism. Even damaged tissue spews out free radicals, which interferes with the repair and healing of new tissue. In fact, the DNA in each cell of your body alone receives about 100,000 free-radical "hits" every day. If you smoke or breathe cigarette smoke, drink alcohol, eat a high-fat diet, live in an area with air pollution, or are exposed to ultraviolet light from the sun, your hits per day are likely to be much greater.

You can't avoid the free radicals that gradually undermine youth and vitality, but you can combat them with antioxidants. In fact, the body has an elaborate antioxidant defense system consisting of enzymes (such as superoxide dismutase, or SOD, catalases, and glutathione peroxidase), molecules (including numerous phytochemicals, the carotenes, and coenzyme Q10, to name only a few), vitamins (vitamin C and vitamin E), and minerals (selenium, manganese, and zinc) that have the job to block the action of free radicals.

Our antioxidant system might be efficient, but it can be overwhelmed when exposed to excessive amounts of free radicals. Even if 99.9 percent of all free radicals were erased by an active antioxidant system, the remaining free radical "tears" each day to your cells' genetic code, proteins, and membranes would result in millions of wounds over the course of a lifetime. It is this backlog of cellular debris that contributes to the aging process and its associated diseases. Although you cannot entirely prevent this buildup (nor would you want to), you can slow it down by boosting your antioxidant defenses.

Boosting the body's antioxidant system takes effort. Most people don't eat enough fruits, vegetables, and other antioxidant-rich foods when they're young, and the deficit worsens with age as intake drops even further and the body's needs rise to an all-time high—in some cases to levels higher than can be supplied realistically from diet alone. That's why you must stockpile your antioxidant defense system so it is well armed every day.

This means combining diet with supplements. William Pryor, Ph.D., Boyd Professor of Chemistry and Biochemistry and director of the Biodynamics Institute at Louisiana State University, suspects that the level of many antioxidants needed to stimulate immunity and prevent disease can be met only by combining food and supplements. Supplements provide the extra levels of many antioxidant nutrients, but fruits and vegetables are gold mines for the thousands of health-enhancing phytochemicals.

How Do You Know You're Getting Enough Antioxidants?

While you can't peek into your cells to judge the war's outcome, you can get a frontline report by how you feel and look. A well-stocked antioxidant system will help maintain a youthful appearance, healthy body, and clear mind. Numerous studies report that people who consume ample amounts of antioxidants from either food or supplements and maintain high blood levels of these nutrients also are the least likely to develop heart disease, cancer, cataracts, arthritis, and other diseases. They additionally are more likely to be physically strong and active and least likely to require assistance in caring for themselves as they age.

Attempts to boost antioxidant defenses to offset oxidative damage to tissues have been focused on increasing the intake of the antioxidant nutrients, such as vitamins E and C. A study from the University of Colorado Health Sciences University in Denver proposes a potentially more effective approach than antioxidant supplementation. In this study, people were given a supplement containing five widely studied medicinal plants, including green tea extracts, turmeric, and milk thistle. Blood samples were taken before supplementing and after 30 and 120 days and were analyzed for levels of antioxidant enzymes, such as superoxide dismutase (SOD), catalase, and lipid peroxidation markers for oxidative stress, such as TBARS, uric acid, C-reactive protein (CRP), and cholesterol. Within 30 days of supplementing, TBARS had decreased 40 percent. By 120 days, SOD levels had increased 30 percent, and catalase levels had increased by 54 percent, suggestive of enhanced antioxidant enzyme activity, a boost in defenses, and a drop in oxidative stress. Dr. Joe McCord, a researcher on the study and the man who first discovered SOD back in 1969, concludes that modest stimulation of the antioxidant enzymes might be a more effective and potent a method of boosting antioxidant status than just supplementing alone with antioxidant nutrients.

You also can assess your status with a new test. Researchers at the University of Utah have developed an antioxidant laser scanner, a version of which is marketed and sold as the Pharmanex BioPhotonic Scanner, that measures levels of a family of antioxidants, the carotenoids, in skin. The scanner shines a blue laser onto your hand. The amount of carotenoids present changes the light to green, which is analyzed and converted into an "antioxidant score" by the scanner. "The technology is very promising, although there are some unresolved issues, such as does skin pigmentation affect the readings," warns Susan Mayne, Ph.D., associate professor of epidemiology and public health at Yale University and lead researcher on a study investigating the validity of this technology. In addition, the scanner only measures a handful of carotenoids, not the entire gamut of more than twelve thousand antioxidants in fruits, vegetables, and other real food. Don't get swayed into buying the company's supplements. The scanner should be used not as an excuse to take more pills but as a fun way to keep track of whether you're eating enough beta-carotene-rich leafy greens, sweet potatoes, and peaches. Ask your physician about the availability of this scanner in your area, and make sure you're getting enough antioxidants by doing the following:

- Adhere to the Antiaging Diet outlined in Chapter 7.
- Avoid foods that generate free radicals, such as fried foods, processed foods made with oils, and fatty foods in general.
- Take antioxidant supplements.

Choosing an Antioxidant Supplement

There are no "magic bullets" or one-pill approaches when it comes to turning back the hands of time. No nutrient works in a vacuum, so it's no surprise that the antioxidants also work as a team, one facilitating the effects of another. For example, vitamin C is very efficient at recycling vitamin E, thus prolonging and strengthening the antioxidant defense system. In turn, other antioxidants help recycle vitamin C. Although beta-carotene is less potent than vitamin E, it functions at the interior of membranes or lipoprotein compartments more effectively. On the other hand, many of the antioxidant phytochemicals, such as the flavonoids or polyphenols in fruits and vegetables or coenzyme Q10 (see Chapter 5), inhibit the formation of free radicals, thereby increasing concentrations of antioxidant vitamins in tissues. So when considering an antioxidant supplement, choose one that supplies a wide variety of antioxidants, not just a single nutrient. (See Chapter 6 for specific dietary guidelines and supplement dosages to ensure optimal antioxidant intake.)

Phytochemicals

You can't turn back the clock. But you can wind it up again.

—BONNIE PRUDDEN

Phytochemicals are not vitamins or minerals, nor are they fiber, protein, fat, or carbohydrates. While they have no specific nutritional value, phytochemicals are the

Examples of Phenolic Compounds

PHENOLS	COMMON FOODS
Vanillin	Vanilla beans, cloves
Sesamol	Sesame seeds
Caffeic acid, ferulic acid	Oats, soybeans, blueberries, prunes, grapes
Quercetin	Tea, coffee, cereal grains, onions
Epicatechin, epigallocatechin	Tea leaves
Ellagic acid	Grapes, strawberries, raspberries
Curcumin	Turmeric, mustard

nutrients of the future and explain why fruits and vegetables, soybeans, whole grains, nuts, red wine, and green tea help prevent cancer and heart disease.

Phytochemicals are naturally occurring compounds found in real foods, from fruits and vegetables to legumes and nuts. They are lost when foods are processed. *Phyto* is derived from the Greek word for "plant." Every vegetable and fruit contains thousands of these chemicals that protect plants from harmful effects of the environment. They also help human cells stay normal by blocking one or more stages of cancer development, inactivate cancer-causing substances, stimulate the immune system, protect the heart against disease, and help prevent cataracts.

While scientists have long known that vitamins, minerals, and fiber in fruits and vegetables are beneficial, more recent evidence shows that, beyond nutrients, certain phytochemicals in these foods are particularly health enhancing and disease preventing.

Take cancer, which is a multistage disease. One or more phytochemicals that slow or even reverse the process can be found at almost every step along the pathway leading to cancer. For example, several studies on animals show that phenolic compounds in vegetables, soy, and red wine protect against the formation of cancers of the colon, esophagus, lung, liver, breast, and skin. People who eat the most fruits and vegetables, or at least eight servings daily, are about half as likely to have cancer as those who eat the typical three to four servings daily.

Phenolic compounds also are linked to a reduced risk of developing atherosclerosis and heart disease and might explain the lowered incidence of heart disease in the French population, who generally consume a high-saturated fat diet but drink phenolic-rich red wine. Phenolic compounds are more effective than vitamin E at inhibiting oxidation of LDL cholesterol; they also inhibit oxidative enzymes, which reduces atherosclerotic risk.

Following are other examples of how phytochemicals are important to your anti-aging program:

- Lutein and zeaxanthin, two carotenoids found in spinach and other richly colored produce, slow the progression of macular degeneration of the eyes, a leading cause of blindness in older people, according to researchers at Wageningen University in The Netherlands.
- Sulforaphane, an antioxidant-rich phytochemical in broccoli, bolsters the body's natural defense mechanisms. This plant nutrient also boosts the production of detoxifying enzymes that usher harmful substances out of cells before they can cause problems, such as cancer.
- Limonene, a phytochemical in citrus fruits, enhances the activity of enzymes that help dispose of harmful substances before they jeopardize health.
- Phytochemicals called proanthocyanidins, found in cranberries, aid in the prevention of urinary tract infections.
- A mixture of carotenoids, such as lutein, lycopene, and beta-carotene, protect the skin from sun damage caused by ultraviolet light, according to a study from the Heinrich-Heine University in Düsseldorf. The topical use of tea polyphenols, along with certain antioxidant vitamins and sunscreen, might be an effective means of lowering sun-induced skin damage and cancer, according to researchers at Duke University.

The research on phytochemicals is in its infancy, but it appears that some fruits and vegetables have an added phytochemical punch. Carrots and leafy green vegetables are particularly effective in lowering the risk of lung cancer. For lowering the risk of colon cancer, the cruciferous vegetables, such as broccoli and cabbage and possibly carrots, are very effective. For lowering the risk of cancer of the larynx, throat, mouth, or esophagus, fruit seems to be consistently important. But a lower cancer risk is really related more to high intake of a variety of fruits and vegetables than to overconsumption of any one plant.

Does cooking destroy phytochemicals? Yes and no. Some phytochemicals, such as beta-carotene, are lost to a certain extent during cooking. Others, such as lycopene in tomatoes and the indoles in cabbage and broccoli, increase as a result of cooking, either because heat softens undigestible plant tissue, making the compound more accessible for digestion, or because cooking converts inactive compounds into health-enhancing substances. The bottom line is to eat a wide variety of cooked and raw colorful vegetables and fruits to maximize your intake of all phytochemicals.

Green Tea

Replacing coffee with green tea once or twice a day might be good for your health. In studies on animals, green tea reduces risk for numerous cancers, including skin, lung, oral cavity, esophagus, stomach, small intestine, colon, pancreas, and breast cancers. Researchers at Tufts University report that tea is a rich source of polyphenolic flavonoids with potent antioxidant abilities. These compounds help reduce the risk for heart disease and cancer and possibly also benefit bone density, cognition, dental health, and weight loss, as well as help prevent kidney stones.

Lycopene

For those who shamefully admit that the ketchup on a hamburger is the only vegetable they get, there's good news. Eating something tomato-y nearly every day is one way to protect the heart.

Lycopene is one of hundreds of carotenoids in food, beta-carotene being the most famous. Lycopene is a pigment in red fruits and vegetables; tomatoes are the richest source of lycopene, but other good sources include watermelon, papaya, pink grapefruit, and guava. (Strawberries are red, but they get their color from a compound other than lycopene.) Like beta-carotene, lycopene is an antioxidant, which might be one of the reasons why lycopene lowers the risk of heart disease. It also might explain why diets rich in lycopene are associated with lower risks for all sorts of cancers, especially cancers of the prostate, cervix, skin, bladder, breast, lung, and digestive tract. Eating lycopene-rich foods also might help protect skin from sun damage.

No one knows how much lycopene is needed, but studies show that people who include anywhere from seven to ten servings a week of lycopene-rich foods have the lowest risk for heart disease. Blood levels of this heart-healthy compound decrease with age, so the older we are, the more we need. Women with the lowest

Mother Nature's Best Inventions

FOOD	PHYTOCHEMICAL	FUNCTION
Fruit	Ferulic acid, caffeic acid	Decrease cancer-causing nitrosamines. Solubilize carcinogens.
Dark green or orange fruits and vegetables	Carotenoids: lutein, lycopene, alpha- or beta-carotene, canthaxanthin	Antioxidants. Help prevent blindness in seniors by replacing lost pigment in the retina. Lower the rate of cancer of the lung, breast, and other sites. Protect the immune system.
Berries, nuts, grapes	Ellagic acid	Antioxidant. Stops DNA mutations.
Green tea	Flavonoids	Antioxidants
Cruciferous vegetables	Indoles	Help regulate estrogen. Decrease cancer risk.
	Phenethyl isothio-cyanate (PEITC)	Inhibits lung cancer.
	Phenols: flavonoids	Antioxidants
	Sulforaphane	Inhibits cancer growth.
Citrus fruits	Monoterpenes (including limonene)	Inhibit breast cancer.
Tomatoes, green peppers, strawberries	P-Coumaric acid	Inhibits carcinogens.
	Chlorogenic acid	Decreases nitrosamines.
	Lycopene	Protects DNA cell proteins and fats.
Beans	Saponins	Decrease cholesterol.
	Phytosterols	Slow colon cancer growth.
	Phytoestrogens	Help regulate estrogen. Decrease breast cancer.
Garlic, onions	Sulfur compounds	Inhibit cancer. Decrease heart disease.

risk of heart disease in one study averaged about 10 milligrams or more of lycopene a day, the equivalent of about half a cup of tomato sauce daily. The average American gets only 3.6 milligrams, or slightly more than a third of that.

Lycopene is best absorbed and most helpful to the body when it comes from cooked and processed foods. Fresh tomatoes also supply lycopene, each one adding about 4 to 5 milligrams of lycopene to the diet. Studies show that people who include seven or more fresh tomatoes in their weekly diet have up to a 60 percent reduction in cancer. Choose deep red tomatoes, since they have more lycopene than do pale red, yellow, or green tomatoes. Vine-ripened tomatoes have more than those picked green and allowed to ripen later. And those grown outdoors in the summer have more lycopene than those grown in greenhouses. You need a little fat to boost absorption of lycopene, so drizzle olive oil over a salad with tomatoes.

Tomatoes pack a nutritious bang for each bite, but keep in mind that lycopene is only one of twelve thousand phytochemicals in fruits and vegetables that help lower your risk for heart disease and all other age-related diseases and that might even help slow the aging process.

Beans

Navy, black, kidney, or soy—any bean you name is a powerhouse of phytochemicals. Phytosterols in beans might slow or even prevent colon cancer. Phytochemicals in beans, called saponins, prevent cancer cells from multiplying and also might lower blood cholesterol, thus lowering the risk of heart disease. However, the greatest health benefits appear to come from the phytoestrogens in soybeans.

The link between diets rich in phytoestrogens and reduced disease rates is consistent and strong. In cultures where people consume ample amounts of soy-based products, the incidence of heart disease, cancer, osteoporosis, and even menopausal hot flashes is low to nonexistent. When these people migrate to the United States and consume few soy products, their disease rates escalate to that of the local inhabitants.

Phytoestrogens have estrogen-like activity, which explains why these compounds might lower rates of menopausal hot flashes, breast cancer, and heart disease. For example, the incidence of menopausal hot flashes is rare in Japan, where the diet contains up to 200 milligrams per day of soy (compared to 5 milligrams in the United States) and urinary excretion of isoflavones is a hundred to a thousand times that of meat eaters in the West. Since estrogen protects women against heart disease by lowering LDL cholesterol and raising HDL cholesterol, it is not surprising that consuming a diet rich in phytoestrogens also produces similar effects in postmenopausal women. The incidence of breast, colon, endometrial, and ovarian cancers is low in women who consume soy-rich diets, such as vegetarians and people in Asia. Even if these women develop breast cancer, their prognosis and survival time is better than in women who consume small amounts of phytoestrogens.

One of the most controversial issues in nutrition is whether soy decreases or increases the risk of breast cancer. According to researchers at Vanderbilt University in Nashville, soy protects against breast cancer. Overnight urinary samples were taken from 250 women with a history of breast cancer and from a similar number of matched controls. These samples were analyzed for excretion rates of several phytoestrogens, a measure of soy intake. Results showed that urinary excretion of isoflavonoids and lignans, phytochemicals in soy, was 60 percent lower in the breast cancer cases than in cancer-free women. The risk of breast cancer decreased as urinary excretion of these phytochemicals increased; women with the highest excretion rates had a 72 percent lower risk for developing breast cancer than women with the lowest excretion rates. Numerous studies support these findings and suggest that at worst, soy has no effect on breast cancer, while at best it might help lower risk.

Phytoestrogens in soy also might lower the risk for:

- **Thyroid cancer.** Women who include traditional soy-based foods (such as tofu and soy milk) in their diets have a low incidence of thyroid cancer, according to a study from the University of California School of Medicine in San Francisco.
- **Weight problems and diabetes.** Researchers at the USDA and George Washington University in Washington, D.C., report that phytoestrogens in soy might have a beneficial effect on diabetes and obesity in both animals and humans. Numerous studies show that including soy in the diet improves glucose control and insulin resistance. In studies on humans, soy curbs elevated blood sugar and reduces body weight, blood cholesterol, and insulin levels.
- **Bone loss.** The incidence of osteoporosis is low in Asian women compared with their Western counterparts. Japanese women, who eat much more soy, also have lower risks for hip fractures. One study found that a low dose of genistein, one of the phytoestrogens, was equivalent to the medication Premarin in maintaining bone mass in rats.
- **Memory loss.** Adding soy-rich foods to the diet improved memory within ten weeks in a group of men and women at King's College London, while in a

■ The Garlic Lover's Tool Kit: Part 1

For the garlic connoisseur, here are a few tips for selecting top-grade garlic:

- Pick large, plump, and firm bulbs.
- Color is not important between January and May, but from June on, choose the whitest garlic you can find.
- The sheath should be tight and unbroken.
- Avoid soft, spongy, or shriveled garlic.
- Store fresh garlic in a cool, well-ventilated place.
- For long-term storage, place peeled cloves in a jar with olive oil and refrigerate.
- For a few tasty garlic recipes, see Appendix B, "Antiaging Recipes." (Try Fresh Mushroom Soup with Chicken and Thyme, or Moroccan Chicken Stew with Curried Couscous, to name a few.)

study from University Medical Center Utrecht in The Netherlands, postmenopausal women who consumed the most soy-based phytoestrogens had the best memory.

Garlic

Garlic helps prevent and treat numerous conditions, including infections, heart disease, and cancer, and also stimulates the immune system. The wealth of sulfur-containing compounds in garlic have potent antibacterial effects, destroying germs' ability to grow and reproduce, in much the same way that penicillin fights infections. Fresh garlic also is helpful in the treatment of fungal infections, including urethritis, athlete's foot, vaginitis, and *Candida albicans* (yeast infections). Garlic even might help combat viruses, something no synthetic drug is able to do.

Garlic also might help in the prevention of heart disease. Compounds in garlic decrease blood cholesterol levels by as much as 12 percent. Fresh garlic can also raise HDL cholesterol (the "good" cholesterol), and it reduces cholesterol manufacture in the liver as well as the stickiness of blood cell fragments called platelets, which in turn reduces blood clotting and artery clogging. The more garlic that is consumed, the greater the benefit to the heart.

The Garlic Lover's Tool Kit: Part 2

Here are a few suggestions for taming the garlic-breath dragon:

- Eat fresh parsley or watercress with your garlic.
- Mix garlic with other strong flavors, such as fennel, dill, aniseed, or caraway.
- Chew on a coffee bean after a meal.
- Drink lemon juice after a meal.
- Eat lime sherbet for dessert.
- To remove the scent of chopped garlic from your fingers, rub hands with lemon, followed by salt. Rinse and wash with soapy water.

Garlic also might inhibit the development of abnormal cells, slow the progression of established cancer cells (including cancers of the mouth, digestive tract, breast, liver, and skin), and stimulate the immune system. Garlic might do more than fend off disease; it may lengthen your years. Preliminary evidence shows that garlic extends the life span of cells in culture and has some "youth preserving, anti-ageing, and beneficial effects on human [immune cells]," according to researchers at Aarhus University in Denmark.

So how much garlic is enough? According to Jeffrey Blumberg, Ph.D., professor at the Friedman School of Nutrition Science and Policy at Tufts University, "Garlic appears to have a beneficial effect in stimulating immune function and lowering blood cholesterol levels even when consumed in moderate amounts of 1 to 1½ cloves a day." This amount of garlic added to pasta sauces, stews, soups, casseroles, or baked chicken (to name only a few possibilities) adds flavor to your diet and could provide natural health insurance. Whether more is better remains questionable, but it probably wouldn't hurt.

Healthy Fats: Olive Oil, Nuts, and Fish Oils

Although many people still hold to the idea that abstinence from fat is the best way to protect the heart, research overwhelmingly shows that as long as you don't overeat, you can take pleasure in the "good" fats. In fact, if most of the fat in your diet is healthy fat, you don't have to obsess quite so much about following the low-fat diet rules.

While the "bad" fats—that is, saturated fats and the trans fats—increase blood cholesterol levels and your risk for heart disease, monounsaturated fats (in olive oil, nuts, and avocados) and the omega-3 fats (in fish and flax) are healthy fats. These fats lower total cholesterol and the "bad" cholesterol (LDLs) while holding constant or even raising the "good" cholesterol (HDLs), thus lowering the risk of heart disease. In addition, the monounsaturated fats also protect LDLs from damaging free radicals that otherwise make them sticky and more prone to clog arteries. They also reduce blood clots that can lead to heart attack and stroke, and they possibly lower the inflammation in the arteries associated with the risk of heart disease. In fact, following the Mediterranean-style diet (which includes the monounsaturated fat olive oil) can lower risk of heart disease by up to 70 percent!

It's more than just the oil that's good for you. Olive oil also is an excellent source of compounds with strange names like polyphenols and squalenes, which are antioxidants that protect tissues from damage. This might explain why these good fats also show promise in lowering the risk for other health problems, such as hypertension, diabetes, rheumatoid arthritis, angina, and certain forms of cancer, such as breast, colon, and prostate cancers.

Olive oil is linked closely with the heart-healthy Mediterranean-style diet, which conjures images of country tables overflowing with wholesome fruits, vegetables, homemade breads, flavorful cheeses, fresh fish, and nuts, everything doused with olive oil. Interest in this style of eating first drew attention back in the 1950s, when it was discovered that, despite poor medical care and high incidence of smoking, men on the Greek island of Crete had 10 percent the heart disease rate seen in the United States. This was because of their lifestyle and diet. The Mediterranean-style diet gained popularity in the 1990s because of continued evidence that it wasn't total fat but the type of fat that Americans were eating that caused disease. Men in Crete eating the traditional fare consumed relatively high-fat diets, but the fat came from olive oil, not from butter, cheese, meat, and such. This traditional diet was high in minerals, fiber, antioxidants, and healthy fats.

This is *not* what most people in the Mediterranean are eating today, and it's certainly not what is served in many Greek restaurants here in the United States. In fact, much of the Americanized Greek cuisine should be spelled "grease." For example, grape leaves or spinach pie can have more artery-clogging fat than a Big Mac, while a gyro (pita sandwich with lamb and beef) or an order of moussaka has twice as much (760 calories and 20 grams of saturated fat). Closely resembling the Antiaging Diet, the true Mediterranean-style diet includes the following guidelines:

- Use olive oil as the principal fat, replacing other fats and oils.
- Drink wine in moderation (about one to two glasses per day for men and one glass per day for women), typically with meals.
- Choose fruit for dessert; limit sweets with a significant amount of sugar and saturated fat.
- Base the diet on an abundance of food from plant sources, including fruits and vegetables, whole-grain breads and grains, beans, nuts, and seeds.
- Eat minimally processed and seasonally fresh and locally grown foods.
- Total dietary fat should range from less than 25 percent to 35 percent of energy, with saturated fat accounting for no more than 8 percent of total calories.
- Eat low to moderate amounts of cheese and yogurt daily.
- Consume moderate amounts of fish and poultry weekly.
- Limit eggs to no more than four per week.
- Include red meat in the diet only once or twice a month.

Nuts

People who snack on a handful of nuts several times a week have up to a 50 percent lower risk for heart disease. They also might curb their risk for diabetes and lower their blood pressure. The fats in nuts may help improve the body's response to insulin and help maintain healthful blood sugar levels. One study from Purdue University found that when people snacked on nuts, they felt satisfied and were less hungry, so they ate fewer calories later in the day and did not gain weight even though they had snacked on a high-calorie food.

Nuts are good for your heart, lowering cholesterol when consumed along with a heart-healthy diet. Nuts also have been linked to fewer heart attacks. In a Harvard University study, women who ate five or more ounces of nuts a week had a 35 percent lower risk for heart attack than women who rarely or never ate nuts. Even those who ate nuts only once a week had a 25 percent lower risk. The heart-healthy benefits of nuts come from several things. They are high in the monounsaturated fats that lower the risk of heart disease. They have varying amounts of omega-3 fats, also known to be heart-healthy. The vitamin E in nuts might help lower the risk of heart disease, as might arginine (a building block to the artery-protective nitric oxide) and phytochemicals, including flavonoids, phenols, sterols, saponins, and ellagic acid. Finally, nuts are good sources of heart-protecting nutrients, such as folic acid, magnesium, copper, potassium, and fiber.

Fish Oils

For millions of years, our ancestors ate diets rich in omega-3 fatty acids, the fats once found in wild game and now found primarily in seafood. The human body survived and evolved on a rich supply of these fats, concentrating them in tissues, such as the cerebral cortex of the brain, the retina of the eye, the testis, and the heart muscle. Unlike storage fats, such as saturated fats in red meat, omega-3s are structural fats that are important constituents of cell membranes, facilitating cell metabolism and providing the building blocks for hormonelike compounds called eicosanoids. Today researchers are uncovering the diverse roles these fats play in human health, as well as the disorders and diseases that ensue when we don't consume enough omega-3 fatty acids.

The omega-3s are essential for your health.

- Omega-3s protect against certain types of cancer, especially cancers of the breast, colon, and prostate. They suppress the process that converts a normal cell into a cancerous cell, inhibit abnormal cell growth, and enhance abnormal cell death (called apoptosis).
- Omega-3 consumption also is associated with reduced risk for heart disease in high-risk populations. Lower blood concentrations of triglycerides, reduced blood clotting, and improved eicosanoid metabolism with reduced risk of heart disease has been noted in people who regularly consume fish. Eicosanoids are hormonelike compounds in the body that help regulate a wide variety of metabolic processes, including blood vessel function, blood pressure, and water balance. Risk of heart attack decreases by 50 percent when people consume at least 200 milligrams a day of the omega-3 fatty acids in supplements or in foods.
- Docosahexaenoic acid (DHA), a type of omega-3, is essential for growth and development of brain tissue in infants and is critical for the maintenance of normal brain function in adults. Optimal intake of this fat improves learning,

while deficiencies result in mental deficits. Low DHA intake also is associated with increased risk for depression, mood disorders, and even suicide.
■ Preliminary research already shows possible improvements in arthritis, adult-onset diabetes, and inflammation with increased omega-3 intake.

Although an optimal daily dose has not been identified, eating fish at least twice a week appears to be sufficient to obtain the heart-protective effect. Which means Americans should switch from filet mignon to fillet of sole (or salmon, tuna, or mackerel) as their source of meat whenever possible. For vegetarians, a less potent, nonmeat form of omega-3 can be found in flax, walnuts, and soy.

Calorie Cutback

Never eat anything at one sitting that you can't lift.

—MISS PIGGY

There might be a dietary trick to maximize your life span and avoid most of the age-related diseases, but you're not going to like it. If the abundance of research on animals showing that calorie restriction increases life span can be applied to people, then cutting your food intake by about half for the rest of your life is all it would take to make you the healthiest centenarian on the block.

"Calorie restriction is the only manipulation known in mammals to improve both life expectancy and life span," says Dr. George Roth, chief of the Molecular Physiology and Genetics section of the National Institute on Aging in Baltimore. Every mammal the researchers have studied, including mice, rats, hamsters, and monkeys, increases its life span from twofold to fourfold when calorie intake is cut to 60 percent of what's called ad libitum, or 60 percent of what the animals usually eat to feel satisfied and full. Cut the fat at the same time, and the animals live even longer.

The secret is undernutrition, not malnutrition, which means drastically reducing calories while still providing all the vitamins and minerals in optimal amounts for health. Every mouthful must be nutrient-packed. Every mouthful in excess of basic calorie needs increases the risk for disease and aging. The good news is that it's never too late to cut back; even older animals placed on calorie-restrictive diets live longer and age more slowly than their full-fed friends.

The benefits of semifasting far exceed just living longer. The hungry animals also are disease free. Every age-related disorder—from heart disease, diabetes, and cancer to memory loss and dwindling immunity—seems to vanish. Blood levels of the stress hormones and disease-causing free radicals also drop. In fact, people might reduce their cancer risk by half if they simply cut calories. Even the skin and appearance of animals fed calorie-restricted diets appear younger.

No one is sure why drastically cutting calories boosts longevity. Restricting food might decrease free-radical reactions in the body or alter hormone levels. Another theory states that semistarving the body lowers the metabolic rate (the rate of life), consequently slowing the aging process. Calorie restriction also boosts growth hormone levels that otherwise drop as a person ages, which might halt or slow many age-related symptoms.

The big question is whether people are enough like rats to expect the same results. "Calorie restriction has only been studied in animals with short life spans," warns Dr. Blumberg. "It is possible that the lengthened life spans in these starved animals is a survival mechanism that allows them to live a few extra months, long enough to survive the drought or famine and reproduce." There are no published long-term studies on the effects of semifasting on longevity in humans or bigger animals, which live for many decades, not merely several months. However, studies currently in progress on humans show promising results. For example, a study from Washington University in St. Louis found that sticking to a low-calorie diet throughout life slowed the natural decline in heart function associated with aging.

There also is a wealth of indirect evidence showing that humans could successfully trade less food for more life. For example, overweight people die at younger ages than do fit and lean (but not skinny) people. In fact, researchers at the University of Illinois estimate that within the next fifty years, the epidemic of obesity will begin shortening life expectancy rates by at least two, and possibly five, years. In contrast, Seventh-day Adventists, who avoid meat and are leaner than the average American, also live longer. In short, being overweight and unfit is never a benefit to your health, while being lean and fit stacks the deck in favor of a long and healthy life.

To maximize the benefits of calorie restriction while minimizing the deprivation and possible harm, a person's best bet is to achieve a lean and fit weight in the early years and then maintain that weight throughout life. For those beyond their early years, the best bet is to improve fitness (see Chapter 8) and attain a desirable weight by losing pounds gradually and permanently (see Chapter 12).

Move It

Raise your sail one foot and you get ten feet of wind.

—CHINESE PROVERB

If someone said he had a pill that would slow aging, help prevent heart disease and cancer, and make you feel and look younger for the rest of your life—and that it had no side effects other than improved mood and self-image—would you take it? You'd be crazy not to! Well, it may not be a pill, but there is something you can do every day that provides all of these benefits: exercise.

Not only can you slow the aging process, but you can reverse at least some of it with exercise. A weekly routine that includes some weight-bearing exercise (such as walking) with some strength-training exercise (such as lifting weights) helps prevent bone deterioration and even reverses bone loss, reduces the risk of developing heart disease, helps maintain a desirable weight, reduces the risk of losing your independence later in life due to frailty and weakness, might even reduce cancer risk, and is essential to achieving the vitality to enjoy those extra years. In fact, an unfit person at any age can reduce his or her risk of dying prematurely by up to 50 percent by becoming fit, and active people are two decades "younger" than their couch-potato counterparts. (See Chapter 8 for a detailed description of why exercise can turn back the hands of time and how to do it right.)

CHAPTER 5

Antiaging Potions

*Get the facts first. You can
distort them later.*

—MARK TWAIN

With the largest segment of the population approaching middle age, it is not surprising that antiaging potions are hitting the market faster than ever. All of these hormonelike products, from DHEA to melatonin, are backed by scanty research at best; their long-term safety is unknown. Hormones have far-reaching effects on the body, many of which are poorly understood. Like the estrogen derivatives, such as DES, given to pregnant women decades ago that resulted in increased cancer risks in offspring, some of these consequences might not surface for decades. While in many cases the research on the "new" antiaging hormones is promising, anyone who takes these products is playing Russian roulette with his or her long-term health.

Don't Believe Everything You Hear or Read

You can stroke people with words.

—F. SCOTT FITZGERALD

Americans' insatiable appetite for nutrition news has spurred the media to amplify its reporting of the hottest topics, but newsworthy is not always factual. Moreover, there is seldom time for reporters to decipher how one study fits into the wealth of information on that topic. Worse yet, important subtleties in a study's findings often are left on the cutting-room floor. In short, we get a truncated tidbit of nutrition news.

How is someone to decipher truth from tabloid? You should pay attention to how the media report clinical research and how you interpret the stories.

Rule 1: Be wary of overnight breakthroughs. Science is like needlepoint, with each study representing one stitch in the tapestry. A clear perspective and sound dietary recommendations come only when we weigh the preponderance of the evidence.

Rule 2: Count the legs of the subjects in the study and consider any research on quadrupeds with an interested, but skeptical, eye. Studies on animals provide the foundation, but these studies only point us in the direction for more research; they can't necessarily be extrapolated to people. For example, caffeine produces birth defects in mice, but there is no evidence that caffeine or coffee has similar effects in humans.

Even in studies on humans, question whether the population being studied is representative of you. Then select which nutrition changes to make in your life, based on your personal health profile. For example, people who aren't salt sensitive will do little to reduce their risk for hypertension by cutting back on salt, but cutting back on fat intake might reduce a person's risk of more pressing health concerns, such as weight gain, cancer, and heart disease.

Rule 3: Ask some basic questions about the study, such as who conducted it (is it a reliable group of researchers, such as those conducting the Nurses' Health Study from Harvard, who publish ongoing information on women's health?), and where it was published (look for reputable journals, such as the *Journal of the American Medical Association*, the *New England Journal of Medicine*, or the *Annals of Internal Medicine*).

Rule 4: Be wary of any article that thrives on conflict. The media are very good at structuring stories for controversy by finding people to express the most diverse opinions on an issue. Readers would be better served if the reporter discussed the common ground of scientific evidence where researchers agree rather than disagree.

With these rules in mind, here is a brief look at the truth behind some of the latest headlines.

DHEA: The Mother of All Antiaging Tonics

*When you are right, you cannot be too radical; when you are wrong,
you cannot be too conservative.*

—DR. MARTIN LUTHER KING JR.

Since hormones are blamed for everything from moodiness to sterility, it isn't surprising that a hormone should be touted as the cause of the ultimate disorder—aging. And so it goes for DHEA (dehydroepiandrosterone), a steroid hormone produced in the adrenal glands that serves as a building block for the sex hormones, estrogen and testosterone.

DHEA rose to fame in the mid-1980s when researchers at the University of California, San Diego (UCSD) reported that plasma levels of DHEA were linked to all disease-related causes of premature death, from heart disease to cancer. The study showed that low blood levels of DHEA were as important as age in predicting death caused by heart disease. The researchers concluded that low DHEA levels were not a result, but rather appeared to be a cause, of disease and death.

Subsequent research showed that high DHEA levels might increase muscle mass, strength, and immune function, as well as improve mood, energy, libido, mental capacity, memory, and weight loss, while possibly lowering the risk for heart disease, cancer, osteoporosis, diabetes, joint pain, fatigue, high blood pressure, depression, and stress-related diseases.

It also was found that the levels of the hormone drop at a rate of about 3 percent a year; by the time people reach seventy years of age, they have only about 10 to 20 percent of the DHEA they had in their twenties. One study from the University of Bologna in Italy found that older men with high DHEA levels were much more active and vital compared with their same-age colleagues with low DHEA levels.

Why would the body produce so much DHEA early in life and so little later on? Could a DHEA deficit slowly rob people of their youth and health? No one knows the answers to these questions. While DHEA appears to be wasted on the young and dwindling levels in the old go hand in hand with disease, it is a major leap in logic to assume that boosting lagging DHEA levels will turn back the clock any more than growing hair on a bald head will erase wrinkles. Critics warn that most studies have been done on rodents. Besides the obvious differences between man and mouse, rodents also have a short life span, which is a major stumbling block when trying to extrapolate data on longevity to humans.

Despite the controversy, the few studies that have investigated DHEA therapy in people are promising. Studies at UCSD found that DHEA supplements restore the hormone to youthful levels, while raising HDL cholesterol (the "good" cholesterol). While hopes that DHEA might improve immune function have not been proven in recent studies, up to 82 percent of those taking supplements in one study reported they handled stress better, slept more soundly, and rated their general well-being as higher.

The Downside of DHEA

Reaping the potential benefits of DHEA has a price. Opponents warn that DHEA produces unpredictable results, with side effects ranging from acne and facial hair to greater risks for breast and uterine cancer in women and prostate cancer and aggressiveness in men, birth defects in pregnant women, and liver damage. DHEA supplements also might increase the risk for heart disease. No one is even sure how DHEA works in the body.

The biggest risk is that no one knows the long-term consequences of taking DHEA. Granted, DHEA-supplemented subjects in the UCSD study reported no side effects after six months; however, whether it is equally harmless to take DHEA for years—which is what someone might need to do to permanently keep disease and aging at bay—is anyone's guess. Many researchers recommend taking DHEA only with physician supervision and routine checks of steroid and cholesterol levels, glucose tolerance, and, in men, prostate health.

The Food and Drug Administration (FDA) has discouraged the sale of DHEA. Supplements made from wild Mexican yams (claimed to contain the building blocks for DHEA) are available in some health-food stores, but scientists say the body can't convert the compound into DHEA. Supplements might not be the only way to boost DHEA levels. One study found that people who meditated daily maintained higher DHEA levels than nonmeditators.

The bottom line? Until there are conclusive studies on DHEA's effectiveness and long-term safety, the best that can be said is that DHEA may not extend life, but it may help a person age gracefully. The question is whether you're willing to be the guinea pig for an unproven, but promising, antiaging hormone.

Growth Hormone

Take calculated risks. That is quite different from being rash.

—GENERAL GEORGE S. PATTON

As with most antiaging quick fixes, growth hormone started out with a bang but is rapidly fizzling as its effectiveness becomes questionable and the cost and side effects mount.

Growth hormone, also called somatotropin, is released by the pituitary gland in the brain beginning in childhood. The hormone enters the bloodstream in pulses, especially during the early hours of sleep. In the liver, it is converted to other compounds that act as growth messengers throughout the body. In childhood, growth hormone aids in strengthening and lengthening bones and stimulating protein synthesis that results in bigger tissues, muscles, and organs, including the heart, kidneys, and skin.

A wealth of research shows that levels of the hormone gradually drop by about 14 percent for every decade of adult life. By the age of sixty, about four of every ten persons have 20 percent of the growth hormone that they had at puberty. Growth hormone levels in some older people, especially couch potatoes, are so low they can't be measured.

More important is that the physical signs of aging mirror the decline in growth hormone. Dwindling levels of growth hormone are associated with reduced muscle mass and strength, increased body fat, reduced resistance to colds and infections, elevated cholesterol, and increased risk for developing high blood pressure and osteoporosis. Research on older animals and humans shows that those who maintain high growth hormone levels naturally or by injecting the hormone sometimes see improvements in many of these conditions.

Growth hormone is not a panacea, since low levels don't cause aging per se. Rather, this is one pebble in the avalanche of aging. Raising growth hormone levels may restore some age-related symptoms, but it won't affect many other common aging changes.

The Pros and Cons of Growth Hormone

Growth hormone's biggest claim to fame came in 1990 when a study from the Medical College of Wisconsin in Milwaukee reported that injecting this hormone into older men could turn back the clock when it came to body composition, leaving the men packing denser bones, increased muscle, and less fat. In this study, twenty-one men between the ages of sixty-one and eighty-one with low growth hormone levels injected the hormone three times weekly. After six months, the men taking growth hormone showed an almost 9 percent increase in muscle, a 14 percent decrease in fat, and a 1.6 percent increase in bone density, compared with no changes in the control group. Growth hormone also improved skin tone. Even more exciting, the men taking growth hormone reported improvements in well-being, enhanced vitality, and increased mental alertness. It was the first time any drug had so clearly reversed the signs of aging in humans.

In the next few years, however, the tide would turn against growth hormone. A study from the Veterans Affairs Medical Center in Palo Alto, California, investigated the effects of the hormone on eighteen healthy older men, ages sixty-five to eighty-two, who were on a strength-training program while injecting growth hormone daily. The men on growth hormone showed some improvements in muscle and bone, but there were no differences in muscle strength between the hormone-treated group and a control group. Numerous other studies reported similar findings.

In another study, men with initially low growth hormone levels injected the hormone three times a week for six months. While lean body mass increased slightly (4.3 percent) and fat decreased by 13 percent, the men did not show greater strength, endurance, cognitive function, or even mood. Worse still, the men receiving growth hormone were riddled with negative side effects.

The Side Effects and Solutions

The more scientists test growth hormone injections, the more adverse side effects surface. In fact, the side effects are so serious that federal law now states it is illegal to sell growth hormone for antiaging or age-related problems. Long-term use of growth hormone increases a person's risk for insulin resistance and diabeteslike symptoms, water retention possibly triggering heart failure, enlarged bones and increased production of connective tissue possibly resulting in carpal tunnel syndrome and arthritis, and elevated blood pressure. Men are likely to develop tender, enlarged breasts, while women might be at greater risk for breast cancer. The older people are, the more likely they are to experience side effects. One study on animals found that raising growth hormone levels too high actually shortened life expectancy!

Granted, lowering the dose reduces many of these side effects but also might limit the hormone's effectiveness. More importantly, any benefits are lost rapidly when the hormone is discontinued. So to see a lasting effect, a person must take growth hormone for the rest of his or her life. It's anyone's guess what the long-term consequences of that might be. Couple the physical risk with the monetary cost of growth hormone injections (while cheap sources are available in Mexico, estimates in the United States range as high as $30,000 a year) and it is clear that the cost of taking growth hormone might outweigh any minor improvements in strength or skin tone.

There is a safer and more proven alternative: daily exercise significantly boosts growth hormone levels, even in older persons. Other growth hormone stimulators include cutting calories, increasing your intake of vitamin A–rich foods, such as carrots and spinach, and including more arginine-rich foods, such as oatmeal and other whole grains, fish, and cheese in your daily diet. Despite the claims, ginseng does not raise growth hormone levels.

Melatonin

Drink nothing without seeing it; sign nothing without reading it.

—SPANISH PROVERB

Melatonin, a hormone secreted in the evening by the pineal gland in the brain, regulates the body's daily time clock—the ebb and flow of wakefulness and sleepiness. Melatonin levels drop with age, so that by age sixty-five a person has one-third to one-quarter the melatonin levels of a twenty-five-year-old. One can raise melatonin levels by taking a daily supplement.

The theory is that when the daily melatonin cycle deteriorates with aging, other body rhythms are weakened. This gradual loss of function underlies aging and increases a person's susceptibility to age-related diseases. Limited research shows that melatonin supplements might help slow some of the symptoms of aging, but this hormone can't reset the aging clock that underlies these problems, nor can it extend life span.

Melatonin has antioxidant capabilities perhaps more potent than those of other antioxidants, such as vitamin E; consequently, proponents speculate that dwindling melatonin levels expose the body to the free-radical damage that contributes to aging. The brain generates more free radicals than any other organ, so maintaining an active antioxidant system is paramount to maintaining mental acuity as we age. Several studies, including one from the University of Texas Health Science Center, have found melatonin helps protect the central nervous system and that it might help combat the nerve damage that results in dementia.

While no side effects of melatonin supplementation have been identified as yet, the best that can be said is that it helps people get a good night's sleep and glide more easily through jet lag. There is no evidence that it can be counted on as the next antiaging drug. Moreover, melatonin is not regulated by the FDA, so the purity and dosage of any product is not assured. Scientists urge people to be cautious and to consult a physician before self-medicating with such a compound when so little is known about it.

To boost melatonin levels naturally, try following a low-calorie diet, increasing exercise, and consuming more carnitine, which might help stimulate production of melatonin.

Coenzyme Q10: Myth or Miracle Pill?

Avoid the crowd. Do your own thinking independently. Be the chess player, not the chess piece.

—RALPH CHARELL

Every cell in the body depends on a fat-soluble substance called coenzyme Q10 to help convert food and oxygen to energy. Without coenzyme Q10, cells cannot perform their essential functions, and life would cease within minutes. Numerous studies have found that this vital substance also benefits health in many ways, from improving heart function to boosting immunity and possibly aiding in weight management.

Other names for coenzyme Q10 are CoQ10 or ubiquinone, which reflects its ubiquitous distribution throughout the body. Like other coenzymes, CoQ10 assists in metabolic reactions. However, it has a unique ability to aid in the complex process of transforming food and oxygen to ATP (adenosine triphosphate), the base fuel required by the body for everything from running a race to digesting food, making new cells, or even pumping blood through the heart.

Virtually every cell of the human body contains CoQ10; however, the mitochondria, the powerhouses of cells where ATP is produced, contain the most. The heart and liver, because they contain the most mitochondria per cell, have the greatest amount of CoQ10 of any tissue or organ in the body.

CoQ10 levels could be inadequate to meet the body's needs for a number of reasons, including:

- Defects in production
- Impaired synthesis caused by nutritional deficiencies
- Greater cellular need resulting from strenuous exercise or from a disease state, such as cardiovascular disease, diabetes, or Alzheimer's disease
- Interference in CoQ10 levels or function from medications
- Advancing age
- A sedentary lifestyle

In addition to its helper role in the release of energy, CoQ10 might act as an antioxidant, neutralizing free radicals that cause potentially irreversible damage to cells, tissues, and organs. Several studies demonstrate that CoQ10 performs many of the same antioxidant functions as vitamin E and selenium in protecting the blood vessels, heart, brain, and other tissues from free-radical damage.

CoQ10 was discovered in the 1950s. Since then, numerous scientific trials have demonstrated that this natural enzyme fights bacteria, increases antibody numbers, resists viral infections, and produces a greater number of immune system cells. Proponents claim that supplementing with CoQ10 might return an impaired immune system to normal or even optimal levels.

But does it prevent aging? Numerous studies on animals show that by maintaining strong immune and antioxidant systems, increased intake of CoQ10 results in a longer, healthier life. A handful of studies suggest that boosting CoQ10 intake by taking supplements of 30 milligrams to 90 milligrams could have the same effect in people. Since CoQ10 levels decrease with age, maintaining optimal intake of this natural coenzyme throughout life might delay many age-related changes.

CoQ10 should not be viewed as a panacea or a miracle cure. In fact, this substance is an excellent example of how more is not necessarily better. If CoQ10 levels are optimal, ingesting more will not enhance its effects. However, if low CoQ10 levels are contributing to dysfunction, increasing dietary intake could be the "fuel booster" the body needs.

CHAPTER 6

Proaging Foods and Substances: What You Should Avoid to Stay Young

Thou shouldst eat to live; not live to eat.
—CICERO

The antiaging foods are easy to spot. They are the minimally processed, wholesome items that traditionally line the perimeter of your grocery store. You find them in abundance in the produce section, as whole-grain bread in the bakery, and as nonfat milk, soy milk, and yogurt in the dairy case. Other antiaging foods include cooked dried beans and peas, nuts, wheat germ, and dried or canned fruits.

There are a few foods or food ingredients you want to avoid, or at least limit, if you're planning to live vitally. These include saturated fat, meat, and any food that contains trans fats. You also want to steer clear of tobacco smoke.

Saturated Fat

You better live your best and act your best and think your best today, for today is the sure preparation for tomorrow and all the other tomorrows that follow.
—HARRIET MARTINEAU

The best thing you can do dietwise for longevity, besides eat tons of fruits and vegetables, is to cut the saturated fat from your diet. Saturated fats in meat and whole-

Fat Tricks

At a loss on how to cut saturated fat? Here are a few suggestions that maximize taste, while they minimize unnecessary fat and calories:

INSTEAD OF . . .	USE . . .
Whole-milk ricotta cheese	Fat-free ricotta cheese
Cream or whole milk	1 percent low-fat or nonfat milk, evaporated nonfat milk, or nonfat milk mixed with instant nonfat dry milk solids
Sour cream	Fat-free sour cream
Cream cheese	Fat-free cream cheese
Half-and-half	Fat-free half-and-half
Making a roux with flour, whole milk, and butter	Nonfat milk or evaporated nonfat milk thickened with flour or cornstarch
Using the full amount of hard cheese	Low-fat cheese (portions in sauces reduced by ⅓ to ½, sprinkled or grated on top of dishes as a garnish)
Whipped cream	Low-fat or fat-free whipped toppings
Whole eggs	Egg whites, two per whole egg, or egg substitute
Chicken with skin	Chicken breast with skin removed
Preparing 4- to 8-ounce meat servings	2- to 3-ounce servings of extra-lean meat mixed or served with rice or noodles, and vegetables

milk dairy products increase your risk for a host of age-related diseases, from heart disease to cancer.

Most people already know they should cut saturated fat, but many are still consuming far too much. Why? One reason is that misinformation is rampant. Food manufacturers are partially to blame for this confusion. In this carb-phobic nation, a label that reads "carb free," "light," or "low net carbs" gives almost any food the aura of nutritional quality, even if more often than not the food is less nutritious, and possibly even harmful to your health, than the label implies. Fast-food restaurants have capitalized on America's fear of carbs by touting saturated fat–laden disasters as reasonable alternatives to healthful options, while many of these dishes, from salads to deep-fat-fried fish fillet sandwiches, derive up to 56 percent of their calories from fat and teaspoons of saturated fat.

Despite the confusion, the saturated fat issue is the most clearly defined topic in nutrition. We have thousands of studies spanning decades of research repeatedly

Fatty red meats	Ground turkey breast, ground round (7 percent fat by weight)
Frying meat	Baked, roasted, broiled, steamed, or stewed meat, with excess fat drained
Flavoring soup with ham hocks	Lean pork or one to two drops liquid smoke
Fatty stock, stews, and gravies	Stocks, stews, and gravies made from refrigerated meat, with hardened fat skimmed from surface (invest in a defatting cup that pours from the bottom, leaving fat on the top)
Butter for sautéing	Nonstick pans, defatted chicken stock, or nonstick sprays (hint: vegetable and grain dishes should be less than 20 percent fat calories!)
Using the full amount of butter in a recipe	⅓ of the suggested amount; substitute up to half the butter with an equivalent amount of applesauce in quick breads and muffins
Butter on toast	Fruit butter, jam, or thick applesauce
Pound cake	Angel food cake
Ice cream	Sherbet, sorbet, nonfat or low-fat ice cream

showing that diets low in saturated fats help reduce the risk for heart disease, cancer, and possibly a wealth of other age-related diseases. There is no safe amount of saturated fat, and this fat is not needed for any reason by the body, so limiting intake to no more than 10 percent of calories is a good start. The lower the better. However, not all fats are bad. As mentioned in Chapter 4, moderate intake of healthy fats in olive oil, nuts, and fish oils might actually help extend life and maintain health.

What Is Saturated Fat?

The fats that supply calories and texture in foods, that float in your blood, and that accumulate in your thighs and hips are called triglycerides. They can be saturated or unsaturated, and the unsaturated ones can be either monounsaturated or polyunsaturated. All triglycerides supply more than 250 calories per ounce (or 9 calories per gram, equal to the weight of a paper clip or raisin) and can contribute to weight gain when consumed in excess. Only the saturated fats (and trans fats, which are discussed a little later in this chapter) are associated with disease, from heart disease to cancer.

All foods contain mixtures of saturated and unsaturated fats with one fat usually predominating, such as saturated fat in meat, cheese, and other fatty dairy products; monounsaturated fat in avocados, olives, and nuts; and polyunsaturated fats in fish and safflower oil. In general, the harder a fat, the more saturated it is. Beef, butter, and stick margarine are mostly saturated fats. Liquid oils are usually unsaturated fats. Coconut, palm, and palm kernel oils are exceptions to the hardness rule. These liquid vegetable oils are highly saturated fats.

Cholesterol is a no-calorie fat, so it can't be exercised off, sweated out, or burned for energy. It is found only in animal products, including meats, chicken, fish, eggs, organ meats, and dairy products. It can be attacked and damaged by free radicals either during food preparation or within the blood. These damaged cholesterol oxides can set off a chain of events in the body's cells leading to cell death and possibly contributing to premature aging.

Why Is Saturated Fat Bad for You?

Typical American diets are oozing with saturated grease from red meat and fatty dairy products. These fats raise the bad cholesterol (called low-density lipoprotein or LDL cholesterol) and lower the good cholesterol (called high-density lipoprotein or HDL cholesterol). They have been clearly linked to risk of heart disease. Diets high in saturated fat also appear to raise the risk for certain cancers, such as colon and possibly breast cancers, as well as diabetes and a host of other age-related diseases. Cut the saturated fat and blood cholesterol levels and disease rates drop. Researchers at Tufts University found that the combination of high fruit and vegetable and low saturated fat intakes is especially protective against premature aging.

From an evolutionary standpoint, it makes sense that saturated fat would be harmful to our bodies. For tens of thousands of years, our hunter-gatherer ancestors lived on diets consisting entirely of wild game and plants. Along with nuts, seeds, and the occasional avocado or olive, the only consistent source of fat was wild game, which is exceptionally lean, low in saturated fat, and relatively high in heart-healthy omega-3 fats. The domesticated meat we eat today provides just the opposite: it is loaded with saturated fat and devoid of the omega-3s. Humans did not evolve on saturated fats, so today's diets are as alien to our bodies as breathing carbon monoxide. It's no wonder that saturated fats raise disease risk, while the lower people's intakes of these harmful fats, the healthier they are.

Meat and Potatoes

Cultivate only the habits that you are willing should master you.

—ELBERT HUBBARD

With meat linked to everything from heart disease and diabetes to cancer and high blood pressure, some people have taken the plunge and gone vegetarian. Even more have cut out red meat, though they still eat poultry and fish.

Studies from Harvard show that red meat and fried foods are the main sources of saturated fats in the diet and are major contributors to the risk of heart disease. Consuming a typical Western diet high in meat, refined grains, sweets, and French fries raised the risk of heart disease up to 64 percent in one study from the Harvard School of Public Health. Switch from red meat to tofu and heart health improves. Women who eat meat daily have a 50 percent higher risk of developing heart disease compared with vegetarian women, and disease risk for both sexes increases as the duration and frequency of meat consumption increases. Other studies, including one from the American Cancer Society (ACS), have found a strong link between meat consumption and colon cancer risk. In the ACS study, people who consumed the most red meat had up to a 50 percent higher risk for developing cancer compared with people who ate little or no red meat. It's no surprise that people who adopt a vegetarian diet have lower risks of disease, and the earlier they adopt that diet, the better off they are.

In all fairness to meat, it might not be because vegetarians have given up T-bone steak that they have a lower risk of disease; rather, the protective effects of foods in the vegetarian diet are the real boon. Long-term studies on cancer incidence in Seventh-day Adventists, a group with a high percentage of vegetarians and a low cancer rate, found that people who ate lots of fruits, legumes, and vegetables were at much lower risk for certain cancers, probably because they simply didn't have as much room in their diets for other fattier foods. A study from the London School of Hygiene and Tropical Medicine found that lifelong meat eaters had higher rates of breast cancer compared with vegetarians. The researchers concluded that "although it is not possible to exclude the possibility that lifelong meat abstention may play a role, the findings provide evidence that a diet rich in vegetables . . . may be protective against this cancer." Vegetarian diets typically include a variety of anti-cancer foods, including fruits, vegetables, whole grains, nuts, tofu, and soy milk. It could be that the combination of these healthy foods along with no meat is the best way to sidestep some age-related diseases.

Trans Slam

One should be just as careful in choosing one's pleasures
as in avoiding calamities.

—CHINESE PROVERB

For years we've been told to avoid saturated fat–laden butter and instead spread margarine on our toast. Margarine was heart-friendly because it was made from vegetable oil—or so we thought. Now we hear that margarine is as bad as, if not worse than, butter.

Margarine and shortening are liquid vegetable oils made creamy when manufacturers convert some of the unsaturated fats into saturated ones. To do this, hydrogens are added to the strings of carbon atoms that make up the fat molecule—hence the terms *hydrogenation* and *hydrogenated vegetable oils*. Hydrogenation hardens a liquid vegetable oil so it looks, feels, and acts like naturally hard fat, such as butter, beef tallow, and lard. Consequently, the processed oil doesn't ooze out of cookies or corn chips, spreads on an English muffin, and is the current fat of choice for frying everything from chicken to French fries at most fast-food restaurants.

But hydrogenation also leaves a trail of unnatural fats in its wake as it smashes and rearranges the chemical bonds of the molecules, altering the form of up to one-third or more of the remaining unsaturated fats so their natural "c"-shaped "cis" shape is transformed into an abnormal "z"-shaped "trans" shape. It is these trans fatty acids (TFAs) that have caused all the commotion.

"Partially hydrogenated vegetable oils are a real problem," warns Mary Enig, Ph.D., former research associate at the University of Maryland and one of the first

Trans-lating Your Table

How much trans fatty acids are in the foods you eat? Here are some estimates to help you tally your intake:

FOOD	TFAs (GRAMS)
Butter (1 tablespoon)	0.40
Mayonnaise (1 tablespoon)	0.55
Dinner roll (1)	0.85
Diet margarine (1 tablespoon)	0.90
Pound cake (1 ounce)	0.98–2.15
Vanilla wafers (8)	1.00
Liquid margarine (1 tablespoon)	1.21
Sugar cookies (2)	1.33
Chocolate cookies (3)	2.00
Microwave popcorn, with fat (4 cups)	2.00
Cheese Danish (1)	2.24–5.20
Crackers (12)	2.40
Hard stick margarine (1 tablespoon)	2.00–4.60
Vegetable shortening (1 tablespoon)	3.00
Chocolate cake rolls (2)	4.00
Buttermilk biscuit (1)	4.00
Packaged doughnut (1)	5.00–6.00
Apple turnover (1)	6.50
French fries (1 large order)	4.00–7.90

researchers to investigate TFAs in our food. What Dr. Enig began uncovering in the early 1980s has been confirmed by hundreds of subsequent studies: TFAs, in amounts typically consumed by Americans, raise total blood cholesterol and LDL-cholesterol levels in much the same way as saturated fats. Large amounts also might lower HDL-cholesterol levels. These changes upset the ratio of total cholesterol to HDL, increasing heart disease risk by up to 27 percent. Trans fats also increase the risk for heart attack and aggravate inflammation in the arteries, which increases the risk for atherosclerosis and heart disease.

The potential health risks of TFAs wouldn't be an issue if we weren't eating a lot more of them than we think. Until the turn of the twentieth century, the natu-

◾ *Cut the Trans*

To cut back on TFAs:

- Read labels and avoid foods that contain partially hydrogenated vegetable oils. Also avoid foods fried in fast-food restaurants, from doughnuts to French fries, where up to 40 percent of the fats are TFAs.
- If you must use margarine, remember that diet or whipped margarine contains fewer TFAs than tub margarine, and tub margarine contains fewer TFAs than stick margarine. (Look for brands that list water and/or liquid vegetable oil as the first ingredient.)
- Better yet, switch to olive oil and use it sparingly.

rally occurring TFAs in meat and dairy products constituted a small portion of the diet. That changed dramatically when the food industry introduced hydrogenation into commercial food production. "The worst thing that could have happened is that natural fats were pulled out of our diets and replaced with hydrogenated vegetable oils," says Dr. Enig. Now TFAs account for 25 percent or more of the fat in many processed foods. Americans probably average 5 to 10 grams of TFAs daily. Intake is likely to be much higher if a person eats snack foods, fast foods, and highly processed convenience foods.

As TFA intakes increase, health risks escalate. The Nurses' Health Study, conducted by Walter Willett, M.D., Dr.P.H., and colleagues at the Harvard School of Public Health in Boston, compared dietary intakes to disease rates in more than eighty-five thousand women and found that as intakes of TFA-containing foods (including margarine, cookies, biscuits, and cakes) increased, so did women's risk for heart disease. Women with the highest intakes had nearly twice the risk of those who ate few hydrogenated fats. Women who ate four or more teaspoons of margarine a day increased their risk of developing heart disease by 66 percent compared with those who limited margarine to less than one teaspoon a month.

Dr. Willett states that TFAs contribute to more than thirty thousand heart disease deaths in the United States each year, even when intake is moderate. Data from the Nurses' Health Study suggest that the risk might be up to five times higher. The damaging effects of trans fats go far beyond just heart disease. Researchers at the Fred Hutchinson Cancer Research Center in Seattle report that these fats increase prostate cancer risk in men. Other studies suggest that TFAs also elevate the risk for diabetes.

The bottom line? "There is no safe dose for trans fatty acids, so the lower the intake the better," concludes Dr. Willett. These fats perform no necessary functions in the body; essentially, if you never ate another trans fat, you'd be better off. Fortunately, food labels are now required to list trans fats. Your total day's intake for saturated fat and trans fat should not exceed 10 percent of calories. That means if you maintain a desirable weight on 2,000 calories a day, then you can consume no more than 22 grams of these two fats (2,000 × 0.10 = 200 calories ÷ 9 calories per gram = 22 grams).

Smoking

He who puts up with insult invites injury.

—JEWISH PROVERB

Next to eating well, maintaining a desirable weight, and exercising daily, the most important habit a person can adopt is avoiding tobacco. Smokers and people exposed to tobacco smoke age faster and die younger of heart disease and cancer. They are most prone to lung problems, including asthma and chest colds. They suffer from more age-related diseases, look older, and have thinner skin and more wrinkles, possibly because smoking increases the damaging effects of sun exposure, causes the release of an enzyme that breaks down skin elasticity and escalates inflammatory processes associated with aging, and restricts the blood supply to the skin. Smoking also escalates cell turnover, the risk of cell mutations, and the development of cancerous cells because of its damaging effects on the lining of the lungs. Men who smoke have a greater likelihood of erectile dysfunction and high blood pressure, while both men and women smokers are more prone to periodontal disease and tooth loss. As mentioned in Chapter 2, anything that speeds up cell turnover, from sunbathing to smoking, sets the aging clock at high gear. The bottom line: don't smoke and don't expose yourself to other people's smoke. And if you already smoke, quit immediately.

CHAPTER 7

The Antiaging Diet

*Keep yourself alive
by throwing day by day
fresh currents of thought
and emotion into the things
you have come to do
from habit.*

—JOHN LANCASTER SPALDING

**The Eight Dietary Guidelines
for a Long and Healthy Life**

1. Eat at least eight colorful fruits and vegetables each day.
2. Eat legumes (cooked dried beans and peas) at least five times a week.
3. Eat minimally processed foods.
4. Include fish, nuts, and olive oil at least twice a week.
5. Eliminate excess calories by cutting back on sugar, fat, and refined grains.
6. Include three low-fat, calcium-rich foods in the daily diet.
7. Enjoy food.
8. Supplement responsibly.

Feeling energetic and fully alive is a by-product of good health and is fundamental to vitality. What you eat must provide all of the building blocks and fuel to help you attain and maintain that good health. While most people wouldn't dream of putting bad gasoline in their cars, it is common for people to supply their bodies with low-grade fuel and then wonder why their most precious machine is showing wear and tear.

What you choose to eat determines what will happen at the cellular level in your body, where all metabolic processes occur and where life and vitality begin. We have up to one hundred trillion cells in our bodies, each one demanding daily a constant supply of forty-plus nutrients and thousands of phytochemicals in the proper balance in order to function optimally. That's a big responsibility!

You Deserve Better

To accomplish great things, we must dream as well as act.

—ANATOLE FRANCE

What you eat today will determine how you feel in the future. "Aging is not a sudden event," says Robert Russell, M.D., professor of medicine and nutrition at Tufts University. "You don't wake up one morning to find you are old. It's a continuum, so the same nutrition issues related to the elderly, from osteoporosis and cataracts to cancer and heart disease, have their roots in the middle years."

A good example of this is vitamin D, a nutrient essential in calcium metabolism and the prevention of osteoporosis. Your body can manufacture vitamin D when the skin is exposed to sunlight, but it gradually loses this ability with age. "People in their twenties can synthesize only 80 percent of the vitamin D that their bodies made when they were eight years old. By the seventh decade, that production has decreased to about 40 percent," says Dr. Russell. That means dietary sources of vitamin D become increasingly more important to prevent osteoporosis. Vitamin D–fortified milk, orange juice, and soy milk are the only reliable dietary sources of this vitamin, and adults must drink two to four glasses daily to reach their recommended intake. Few people do that.

In fact, most people aren't getting even adequate nutrition, let alone optimal. They are sacrificing long-term health and their chances for vitality. Gladys Block, Ph.D., at the University of California, Berkeley, reviewed the data from three major national nutrition surveys and found that one in every two women—many of whom think they are eating well—consumes inadequate amounts of just about every vitamin and mineral studied, from vitamin A to zinc. On any four consecutive days, 86 percent of women fail to include even one dark green leafy vegetable in their diets and one in every two women avoids fruit, which explains why women's diets are low in beta-carotene, vitamin C, iron, and folic acid—all essential for the prevention of cervical and other cancers, anemia, and possibly heart disease. Most mature women consume about half of the daily recommended 1,200 milligrams of calcium (1,500 milligrams if they are not taking hormone replacement therapy) needed to help offset bone loss associated with osteoporosis. In general, men eat even fewer fruits, vegetables, and whole grains than do women.

The data show ninety-nine out of every one hundred adults need to get much more aggressive about how they fuel their bodies. Keep in mind that not only are you fueling your physical health, mood, and energy level today, but you're setting the stage for your health and vitality tomorrow. The benefits of eating well are astounding! According to a study published in the *Journal of the American Medical Association*, people who follow healthy diets, such as the Antiaging Diet, have up to a 65 percent lower risk for dying prematurely from any disease, including heart disease, diabetes, hypertension, or cancer. Why settle for less out of life when eating well offers so much?

The Antiaging Diet: The Eight Dietary Guidelines

*To live longer and healthier, people must eat a low-fat, low-meat diet
that contains an abundance of fruits and vegetables.*

—ROBERT RUSSELL, M.D.

The Antiaging Diet has three goals:

1. To supply all of the essential nutrients—including vitamins, minerals, phytochemicals, protein, essential fats, and fiber—in optimal amounts to ensure that your body is fueled for life. This eating plan also is low in saturated fat, trans fatty acids, sugar, meat, and other harmful substances.
2. To supply these essential nutrients in a steady balance for optimal energy and emotional, mental, and physical function.
3. To assist the body in removing toxic or disease-causing substances efficiently, before they undermine health and longevity.

The eight guidelines are discussed in detail in the following pages and are put into practice in the week's worth of menus found in Appendix A at the back of this book. Whether you still have children at home or have settled into the empty nest, these guidelines are simple and foolproof. You should notice a marked improvement in your energy level and how you feel mentally and physically within one month of following these guidelines and the exercise guidelines outlined in the Antiaging Fitness Program in Chapter 8.

What the Antiaging Plate Should Look Like

- Eight or more colorful fruits and vegetables each day
- Legumes (cooked dried beans and peas) at least five times a week
- Few processed foods
- Fish, nuts, and olive oil at least twice a week
- Sparse sugar, fat, and refined grains
- Three low-fat, calcium-rich foods in the daily diet

Guideline 1: Eat at Least Eight Colorful Fruits and Vegetables Each Day

Some people wait all their lives for the outside to change their inside.
But it never seems to happen, because change comes from within
us first, then the outside becomes different.

—ELLIOT GOLDWAG, PH.D.

What do the surgeon general, every major nutrition group, and your mother have in common? They all recommend that you eat lots of fruits and vegetables. From luscious strawberries and crunchy carrots to crispy broccoli and juicy oranges, colorful fruits and vegetables are Mother Nature's most nutrient-packed foods.

How many servings of colorful fresh fruits and vegetables did you eat yesterday? If you are like many people, you could double that amount and still barely meet the minimum requirements. To fend off the hands of time, you should consume at least eight servings of fruits and vegetables each day. More is even better. Unfortunately, only one in five Americans eats even five fruits and vegetables each day, more than 40 percent consume three or fewer servings, and 20 percent of adults skip vegetables altogether.

Fresh fruits and vegetables (with the exception of avocados, olives, and coconuts) have no fat, cholesterol, or sodium. They are the most fiber-rich, nutrient-packed

The Ten Commandments of the Antiaging Diet

Thou shalt:

1. Base snacks on colorful fruits and vegetables.
2. Plan an all-plant dinner that includes only vegetables, whole grains, and beans at least three times a week.
3. Limit red meat (even if it's lean) to no more than three servings per week (remember, a serving is three ounces) and include baked or broiled fish, nuts, and olive oil at least twice a week.
4. Consume three glasses of nonfat milk or three cups of nonfat yogurt daily.
5. Choose more whole grains than refined grains.
6. Limit processed or preprepared foods (from canned soups to frozen dinners) to avoid excessive salt intake.
7. Cut back or cut out sweets, including soft drinks, desserts, doughnuts and cinnamon rolls, granola bars, scones, and cookies.
8. Drink lots of water and some green tea and limit alcohol consumption to one 6-ounce glass of wine a day.
9. Cut way back on saturated and trans fats, including added butter or margarine in cooking or food preparation, fatty snack foods, fatty dairy and meat products, and hidden hydrogenated fats in prepared foods.
10. Take a moderate-dose multiple vitamin and mineral supplement with extra calcium, magnesium, and the antioxidant nutrients daily.

foods in the diet, and they are low in calories (a heaping bowlful of greens supplies only 30 calories!). The more color, the higher their antioxidant and phytochemical content. So spinach is better than romaine lettuce, which is better than head or iceberg lettuce. A sweet potato is better than a baked potato, and blueberries are better than an apple. No other food or food group is so closely linked to vitality as colorful fruits and vegetables. If you do nothing else but double your current intake of colorful produce, you'll be well on your way to age-proofing your body!

Your daily need for several vitamins, including vitamin C, folic acid, and beta-carotene (the building block for vitamin A), can be satisfied almost exclusively from fresh fruits and vegetables, especially citrus fruits, dark green leafy vegetables such as spinach and broccoli, and dark orange vegetables such as carrots. Eight servings

What's in a Serving?

Eight servings may sound like a lot, but a serving size is smaller than you think. In general, the USDA specifies one serving as any of the following:

- 1 medium-size piece of fruit or vegetable, such as one orange or one carrot
- ½ cup canned fruit or cooked vegetables
- ¾ cup juice
- 1 cup raw leafy greens

The following also are considered one serving:

FOOD	ONE SERVING
Apple	1 2-inch diameter fruit
Apricots, fresh	4 medium
Artichoke	½ medium
Banana	½ of a 9-inch long fruit
Cherries, fresh	12 large
Figs, dried	2 medium
Grapefruit	½ medium
Raisins	2 tablespoons
Tomato	1 medium
Tomato paste	2 tablespoons
Tomato sauce	3 tablespoons

of fruits and vegetables daily also supplies approximately 27 grams of fiber, well within the daily target goal of 25 to 35 grams!

Studies repeatedly show that people who consume diets loaded with fresh fruits and vegetables are the healthiest, with significantly lower disease rates, more energy, and less risk for memory loss and weight gain compared with people who skip these foods. Many fruits and vegetables supply ample amounts of calcium, iron, magnesium, and many vitamins that prevent age-related crippling diseases. The good news is that it's never too late to enjoy the benefits of these foods; improvements in health risks are noted within weeks of adding more fruits and vegetables to the diet.

▪ *Are You Getting Enough?*

How many fruits and vegetables do you include in your daily diet? If you are like many people, your intake might be short of optimal. Tally your intake on the worksheet that follows to see how close you come to the eight-a-day goal.

Day: _____   Date: _____

MEAL/SNACK	NUMBER OF FRUITS	NUMBER OF VEGETABLES	TOTAL
Breakfast:	_____	_____	_____
Lunch:	_____	_____	_____
Dinner:	_____	_____	_____
Snacks:	_____	_____	_____
Total for the day:	_____	_____	_____
Goal:	3 to 5	5 to 7	8 or more
How many more should you add to reach the recommended goal?	_____	_____	_____

They Taste Good, Too

Fruits and vegetables not only protect your heart, your health, and your waistline—they also taste good. Gone are the days of overcooked spinach and limp asparagus. From lightly grilled eggplant to dribble-down-your-chin watermelon, with their rich assortment of flavors, textures, colors, and aromas, colorful vegetables and fruits contribute as much to the visual and sensual appeal of each meal as to its nutritional quality. Peppers, onions, or garlic add flavor to a main course, from pasta to casseroles. Crunchy pea pods, carrots, or jicama add texture to cooked foods and salads or are tasty appetizers. Luscious kiwi and sweet pears or apples liven up salads. Juicy oranges and strawberries are a low-fat, nutritious sweet treat at the end of a meal. Skip the greasy hash browns and instead slice juicy tomatoes to accompany

How to Make Sure You Get Enough

Making sure you get enough fruits and vegetables takes some planning. Here are the guidelines for meeting the eight-a-day goal:

- Plan ahead. Include at least two fruits or vegetables at every meal and two more for snacks.
- Eat your greens. Include at least two servings daily of a dark green vegetable, such as spinach, romaine lettuce, or chard, to ensure optimal intake of beta-carotene, folic acid, and the phytochemical lutein.
- Grab an orange. Include at least two vitamin C–rich selections, such as citrus fruit, strawberries, or green pepper.
- Nibble on cabbage. Include at least five vegetables each week from the cabbage family, such as Brussels sprouts, kohlrabi, asparagus, cabbage, broccoli, or cauliflower. These vegetables are chock-full of phytochemicals that lower your risk of developing cancer.

your scrambled eggs in the morning. Just say "no" to the trans fat–laden French fries and serve baked sweet potato fries instead. And preparation is a snap: the less you do to colorful fruits and vegetables, the better.

Guideline 2: Eat Legumes (Cooked Dried Beans and Peas) at Least Five Times a Week

It is not enough to do good: one must do it the right way.

—JOHN, VISCOUNT MORLEY, OF BLACKBURN

People who want to live to one-hundred-plus years might do well to switch from meat 'n' gravy to beans 'n' rice. No matter how lean the cut, all meat contains saturated fat, which might explain why high meat consumption is linked to increased risk of disease and shortened life span. Replacing meat with soy products and other legumes, such as cooked dried beans and peas and lentils, increases life expectancy by up to 13 percent. Strive for at least five servings of beans each week. (See Chapter 6 for more information on how meat reduces longevity.)

Fifty+ Ways to Get Your Fruits and Vegetables

BREAKFAST

- Drink a glass of tomato juice, orange juice, grapefruit juice, or another 100 percent fruit juice. (No white grape, apple, or pear concentrate, since these are merely sugar water.)
- Blend a smoothie with soy milk and fresh fruit.
- Stir fresh fruit into plain, low-fat yogurt and sprinkle with granola.
- Top whole-wheat waffles with blueberries and fat-free sour cream.
- Accompany eggs with sliced tomatoes, or make an omelet with steamed broccoli, cauliflower, and sliced carrots.
- Have a slice of Oven-Roasted Vegetable Frittata.*

LUNCH

- Add grated carrots, diced celery or jicama, or green peas to pasta or potato salad.
- Eat at a salad bar and load up on greens rather than fatty toppings.
- Top a baked sweet potato with diced apples, dried cranberries, and nuts.
- Top prepared plain pizza crust with sauce, low-fat cheese, and lots of vegetables, including onions, zucchini slices, artichoke hearts, mushrooms, peppers, tomato slices, and/or asparagus.
- Have a bowl of Chilled Cantaloupe Soup with Coconut and Blueberry Puree.*
- Make a wrap using a whole-wheat tortilla, grilled vegetables, and low-fat cheese.
- Add mandarin orange slices, raspberries, or winter pears to a spinach salad.
- Add leftover vegetables from last night's dinner to soups and salads, or add frozen vegetables to canned soups.
- Pack ½ cup lettuce, slices of tomato, and a slice or two of avocado into your tuna, chicken, or cheese sandwich.
- Pack a ziplock plastic bag with baby carrots, broccoli florets, and other vegetables.
- Mix preshredded coleslaw fixings with apple or pineapple chunks and low-fat coleslaw dressing for a quick salad.
- Have a serving of Mediterranean Salad* along with your sandwich.

DINNER

- Accompany any entrée with at least two vegetables (use frozen when in a hurry).
- Use leftover chicken and lots of vegetables to make a quick stir-fry.

Continued

- Make shish kebobs with more vegetables and less meat (try zucchini, crookneck squash, whole mushrooms, cherry tomatoes, eggplant chunks, baby onions, carrots, or red peppers).
- Top halibut or other fish with salsa made from mango chunks, cilantro, red onion, diced chilies, and lime juice.
- Add broccoli, spinach, or chard to lasagna. Add zucchini, grated carrots, green peppers, or mushrooms to spaghetti sauce.
- Add green peas or other vegetables to rice dishes.
- Toss steamed broccoli or cauliflower florets, green pepper slices, zucchini rounds, and/or pea pods with pasta.
- Serve pasta marinara (the tomato sauce counts as a vegetable) along with a tossed salad and steamed vegetables.
- Serve Oven-Roasted Brussels Sprouts with Apples and Walnuts* with any entrée.
- Puree steamed cauliflower with a little fat-free sour cream, and season with a little horseradish as an alternative to mashed potatoes.

WHEN EATING OUT

- Split an entrée and order extra servings of steamed vegetables.
- Frequent the salad bar and focus on the fresh vegetables and fruits.
- Order à la carte and choose vegetable soups, salads (dressing on the side), baked potatoes, and fresh fruit.
- If vegetables are not listed on the menu, ask which are available.
- Request that a Chinese vegetable stir-fry or chow mein be prepared with little or no oil.
- At a Japanese restaurant, ask for vegetable sushi.
- At an Italian restaurant, order pasta marinara or primavera.
- Order deli sandwiches with extra tomatoes and your pizza with extra helpings of vegetables.
- Order a fresh fruit platter.
- For an appetizer, choose a fresh melon wedge, gazpacho, a fresh fruit medley, or vegetable juice.
- Order tomato juice instead of a Bloody Mary.

DESSERTS

- Pile fresh blueberries on top of low-fat cheesecake or angel food cake.
- Top fat-free frozen yogurt with mango chunks.

- Dip fresh strawberries, sliced kiwi, banana chunks, and orange or grapefruit slices in low-fat chocolate syrup.
- Serve Chilled Blue Moon Dessert.*
- Serve poached pears in a wine sauce.
- Nibble on frozen blueberries or grapes.
- Make a peach cobbler using extra peaches and half the crumble crust.
- Cut up fresh fruit and place on the table after dinner.

SNACKS AND MINIMEALS
- Keep a fresh banana or apple in your desk at work.
- Keep a bowl of fresh fruit on the dining table.
- Keep packages of dried fruit in the glove compartment.
- Use precut vegetables and baby carrots as a crunchy midafternoon snack.
- Steam chopped spinach and mix with fat-free sour cream and seasonings to make a vegetable dip.
- Take a package of snow pea pods to work along with fat-free ranch dressing for dipping.
- Mix ⅔ cup orange juice with ⅓ cup sparkling water, ice, and a dash of lime.
- Dunk apple slices in a little caramel sauce.

*Recipes in Appendix B.

Soy products and beans are easily included in the daily menu.

- Cook dried beans and refrigerate for use in meals throughout the week.
- Toss canned kidney, garbanzo, or black beans into salads, soups, casseroles, and side dishes.
- Add extra beans to chili.
- Use fat-free refried beans in burritos, nachos, and other Mexican dishes.
- Crumble tofu into lasagna, enchiladas, or casseroles.
- Add chunks of tofu to soups, stews, and stir-fries.
- Use soy milk in place of regular milk on cereals, in smoothies, and in baking. Light soy milk has even fewer calories than nonfat milk yet has phytochemicals, calcium, vitamin D, and other nutrients essential to health.

Guideline 3: Eat Minimally Processed Foods

Let him that would move the world, first move himself.

—SOCRATES

Almost all dietary recommendations can be distilled into one rule: eat food in its most natural form. Choose whole grains more often than refined white breads, rice, cereals, or pasta. Choose plain nonfat or low-fat milk and yogurt rather than highly processed ice creams, sugar-laden frozen yogurts, or cheese spreads. Choose corn or corn tortillas instead of corn oil, fresh fruit instead of candy with fruit added, oatmeal instead of a granola bar, and a baked potato instead of French fries or potato chips.

This guideline will help you save money and will improve your health and possibly take the inches off your waistline. Choosing wholesome, minimally processed foods means you shop primarily around the perimeter of the grocery store, focusing on the bakery, produce section, and dairy case.

Guideline 4: Include Fish, Nuts, and Olive Oil at Least Twice a Week

A great secret of success is to go through life as a man who never gets used up.

—ALBERT SCHWEITZER

As mentioned in Chapter 4, fish, nuts, and olive oil are powerful antiaging inclusions in the diet. Each supplies healthy fats that lower disease risk, extend the healthy years, and possibly prolong life. Nuts and olive oil also are rich sources of phytochemicals that protect arteries and tissues from disease.

Fish

Fish is the best dietary source of the omega-3 fats, but some varieties also contain chemical contaminants that come from polluted waters. Some environmental residues, such as PCBs and PBBs, have leached into the water supply and accumulate in some freshwater fish. The toxic metal mercury also accumulates in some fish and is known to cause nerve damage.

To maximize the health benefits while minimizing exposure to chemicals, choose marine fish—with the exception of tuna, shark, mackerel, tilefish, and swordfish—and inshore species, such as bluefish and striped bass. Freshwater fish are the ones most likely to be contaminated with harmful pesticides or metals. However, Gulf Coast oysters, sea bass, halibut, marlin, pike, and white croaker also could contain unhealthy levels of mercury. And finally, choose wild or organic rather than farmed salmon. Your safest bets in order of safety from least likely to most likely to be contaminated are as follows:

Freshwater	Nearshore	Offshore
Yellow perch	Pink salmon	Cod
White perch	Chum salmon	Haddock
Brook trout	Sockeye salmon	Pollack
Rainbow trout		

Nuts

After years of hearing the message that fatty foods should be avoided, it is a breath of fresh air to know that nuts are a healthy inclusion in an antiaging diet! Snacking on nuts also helps a diet not feel like a diet. Of course, you also have to use some common sense. Nuts are high in fat, even if it's heart-healthy fat, so are high in calories, with 160–200 per ounce. Eat them instead of other high-calorie snacks, such as potato chips, and limit your portion to an ounce (1 ounce = 18 cashews, 22 almonds, 36 peanuts, or 15 pecan halves). To add nuts to your diet:

- Eat nuts plain or toss them into salads, cereals, or yogurt.
- Add nuts to meatless stir-fries or to pancake and muffin batters.
- Make homemade trail mix with equal parts nuts and dried fruit.
- Replace pine nuts with other nuts, such as cashews or walnuts, when making pesto sauce.
- Mix cashews into chicken salad.
- Combine nuts with yogurt, apples, and celery to make a quick Waldorf salad.
- Use nuts in cookies and brownies.
- Throw some nuts into your pasta dishes. Toss peanuts into pasta primavera, for example.

- Coat fish or chicken with a nutty flavor before cooking. Mix equal parts seasoned bread crumbs and finely chopped or toasted mixed nuts.
- Top favorite casseroles or soups with finely chopped nuts.
- Add nuts to grain dishes, for example almonds and brown rice.
- Top frozen waffles with a few nuts, berries, and maple syrup.

Olive Oil

The antiaging guidelines recommend limiting total fat to between 20 percent and 35 percent of total calories, with most fats coming from unsaturated fats, such as nuts, fish, and oils. Yes, the fats in fish, nuts, and olive oil are healthy, but that doesn't give you license to binge. Any fat, be it olive oil or butter, supplies about 120 calories and 14 grams of fat for every tablespoon. In the United States, where almost seven in every ten people are already seriously overweight, most Americans cannot afford more calories. These heart-healthy fats need to replace the fats in burgers, fries, cheese, and pizza—they are not to be added to an already fatty diet. These fats won't single-handedly lower the risk of heart disease. You also have to follow the other antiaging guidelines, such as loading the plate with vegetables, whole grains, and legumes.

Like wine, olive oil varies in quality, character, and price. The grade is determined by the International Olive Oil Council and is categorized by taste, color, and the amount of acid (the more acid, the more bitter the taste and the lower the grade). The flavor depends on the olives used (there are more than fifty different varieties), ripeness, climate and soil where grown, and methods used to extract and refine the oil.

- **Extra-virgin olive oil.** This is the most expensive. It is the end result of cold-pressing the olives just once. It has the least amount of acid and is a dark yellow to green oil with a fragrant, full-bodied taste. You will even find that people describe the various flavors as fruity, rustic, peppery, flowery, earthy, and, of course, olivey. Extra-virgin is richest in antioxidants and polyphenols. It's best used straight from the bottle, drizzled over cooked vegetables or salads.
- **Virgin olive oil.** This is slightly higher in acid content and is not as flavorful or as deep in color. It contains some of the antioxidants found in extra-virgin but not as many because they are lost in the filtering process. This oil often has some extra-virgin oil added back to give it flavor.

- **Olive oil.** This has even more acids and is obtained through chemical extraction rather than pressing. It is less flavorful and contains fewer antioxidants.
- **Light olive oil.** This is a tricky one. In most cases, when a food label says "light" it means the food has half the fat or sodium and two-thirds the calories. Not with olive oil. Light only refers to color, not calories. It is sold only in the United States to accommodate our preference for colorless, flavorless oils, such as corn and soy oils. This oil is very refined and contains few of the characteristics of olive oil and almost none of the antioxidants.

Should you only buy extra-virgin olive oil? Not necessarily. Extra-virgin is the most flavorful, but those flavors also break down quickly with heat. Extra-virgin olive oil is best used in salad dressings, as a dip for bread, and drizzled over already cooked foods, where the oil isn't heated. The pure olive oil or virgin olive oil is a more all-purpose oil that can be used for sautéing and in cooking. The light olive oil has no flavor, so it works well even in baking. You might want to aim for three bottles of olive oil in your cupboard: the inexpensive light for baking, the virgin oil for cooking, and the extra-virgin for salads and other delicate dishes where it will add flavor.

Finally, when buying olive oil, don't go just by price. It's really a matter of taste preference. Sample different varieties to find the one that best suits your likes. Also, don't be too concerned with color. The riper the olives used for that particular oil, the paler the color, but color doesn't necessarily imply flavor.

Guideline 5: Eliminate Excess Calories by Cutting Back on Sugar, Fat, and Refined Grains

Subdue your appetites, my dears, and you've conquered human nature.

—CHARLES DICKENS

Cut back or cut out the foods that contribute nothing to your long-term health. These include foods high in sugar, fat, and refined grains. Limiting intake of most alcoholic beverages is also wise. By minimizing these foods in the diet, you save more room for the antiaging foods: fruits, vegetables, whole grains, nonfat milk or soy milk, and legumes. In addition, cutting unwanted calories is the best way to attain and maintain a desirable weight, which is essential to a long and healthy life.

Sweet Indulgences

Americans' sugar consumption has skyrocketed in the past 150 years. Whereas a person in 1840 sprinkled a scant four teaspoons of sweeteners into home-baked jams and desserts, today the average American heaps as much as fifty teaspoons of sugar and artificial sweeteners onto the daily plate.

There is evidence that sugar might speed the aging process. Animals consuming high-sugar diets have significantly shorter life spans than do those given more nutrient-packed diets, despite no differences in body weight or blood sugar levels. Researchers speculate that regularly indulging a sweet tooth might alter body mechanisms, which in turn accelerates aging through free-radical damage.

A national nutrition survey conducted by the USDA found that two of the top three sources of carbohydrates in many adults' diets are not breads and pastas but soft drinks and sugar. Americans consume more than fifty-four gallons of soda per person per year; at up to nine teaspoons of sugar per serving, that equals up to 5,184 teaspoons of sugar annually or more than fourteen teaspoons a day from soft drinks alone.

Soda is directly related to body weight. A study from Harvard University found that people who drink soda pop consume about 200 extra calories a day and a study from the University of Minnesota concluded that people who drink as little as nine ounces of soda a day consume 188 calories more every day than people who don't drink any. Over the course of a year, a person drinking soda every day could gain up to twenty pounds!

One explanation for this is that our bodies handle calories in liquid form differently than they handle calories in food. We don't register those calories, so they don't fill us up—and we overeat as a result. For example, in a study from Purdue University, people were given a snack of jelly beans or a soft drink, both having an equal number of calories. Only the people drinking their calories gained weight. The researchers concluded that the beverage calories were added to other foods and calories in the diet (rather than replacing them), which resulted in overconsumption of calories and weight gain. In addition, soda contains high-fructose corn syrup (HFCS). Experts suspect that HFCS might accelerate weight gain because this sweetener is digested, absorbed, and metabolized differently than regular sugar and is more likely to be packed into fat stores.

The food industry has capitalized on our sweet tooth. At the turn of the twentieth century, sugar was bought directly by the consumer for home use. Today three out of every four teaspoons are added by industry before foods reach the kitchen. While everyone knows they're eating sugar when they munch on a candy bar, fewer people realize that sugar is added to ketchup, dessert wines, cranberry juice, baked beans, spaghetti sauce, canned soups, fruited yogurt, salad dressings, peanut butter, fiber bars, most cereals, flavored oatmeal, and many other processed products. Increased use of products sweetened with white grape, apple, or pear juice concentrate also misleads the consumer, who is unaware that this "juice" is just sugar water. Don't be fooled by the new reduced-sugar cereals, from Froot Loops to Frosted Flakes. They have just as many calories, carbs, fat, and other nutrients as their full-sugar counterparts, according to a study conducted by five universities, including Tufts and Harvard.

Dental caries and periodontal disease have skyrocketed since people began bathing their teeth in a constant supply of sugar. Although a consistent trend has not yet appeared, many researchers suspect that a sugar-laden diet is a culprit in the development and progression of heart disease, depression and mood swings, lethargy, hypoglycemia, diabetes, kidney disease, prostate cancer, gallstones, and ulcers.

When sugar intake increases beyond 9 percent of total calories, people's vitamin and mineral intakes progressively decrease, which compromises their immune systems and might contribute to the development of numerous health problems. Sugary foods added to an otherwise ample diet tip the calorie scale toward weight gain. Animals fed a high-sugar diet, even when fat intake is low, consume more calories and gain more weight compared with those eating more starch and less sugar. In short, excessive sugar intake, with or without a low-fat diet, encourages overeating and obesity. Weight problems, in turn, contribute to the development of cancer, cardiovascular disease, diabetes, and osteoporosis.

How Much Is Safe?

Currently, sugar averages more than 22 percent of our total calories. Although exact recommendations have not been set, it is generally agreed people should cut their intake of added sugar in half. People who consume fewer than 2,000 calories a day must depend on nutrient-dense foods to guarantee adequate vitamin and mineral intakes and should consume even less added sugar.

How can you cut back on a sweet thing? Just follow these few simple rules:

- Avoid sticky, sweet foods, such as processed fruit bars, candy, and caramel, since they are the worst offenders in tooth decay.
- Limit soft drinks to one serving (twelve ounces) or less a week.
- Cut back on doughnuts, pies, cakes, cookies, and ice cream, since these and other sweet foods are doubly harmful because of their high-sugar and high-fat content.
- Read labels. Although manufacturers are not required to list the percentage of sugar calories, you can get an idea of a product's sugar content by reading the ingredients list. A food is too sweet if sugar is one of the first three ingredients or if the list includes several sources of sugar.
- Add more spices. Cinnamon, vanilla, spearmint, and anise provide a sweet taste to foods without adding sugar or calories. Sugar substitutes also can be used in moderation.

All added sugar is essentially calories with no redeemable nutrient qualities. A little sugar in the diet adds enjoyment and variety, especially when it comes from natural sources, such as fruit. Going overboard for sweets, however, will undermine your health.

Fat Attack

Most people know they should cut back on fat, but our average fat intake is still far in excess of optimal. As mentioned in Chapter 6, diets with too much saturated fat and trans fats subtract years from your life, and they steal quality from the remaining years. Such diets are linked to an increased risk of obesity, most degenerative diseases, and premature aging. Eating too much fat in general also is likely to crowd out more vitamin- and mineral-rich foods, thus contributing to nutrient deficiencies. Cutting back on saturated fat and excess calories from too much fat is one of the most important dietary changes a person can make for health and longevity.

Cutting back on saturated and trans fats means reducing or eliminating obvious fats, such as butter, margarine, mayonnaise, gravies, shortenings, cheese, fatty meats, and cream. Use small amounts of olive oil and avocados, and snack on an ounce of nuts instead. It also means cutting back on hidden fats in processed snack foods like potato chips and granola bars, fast foods like hamburgers and French fries, desserts such as cookies and pies, and convenience foods such as high-fat frozen entrées. It means reducing fat in favorite recipes by substituting nonfat milk for cream or whole milk, low-fat cheese for regular cheese, and baking for frying. It means switching from red meat to fish or beans as entrées. Using fat-free items, such as fat-free sour cream, half-and-half, or cream cheese, also helps lower saturated fat intake.

Your saturated fat intake will automatically decrease if you fill your plate with vegetables, legumes, whole grains, nuts, soy milk, and fruit. A rule of thumb is to fill three-quarters of the plate with these foods of plant origin, leaving the remaining space for small amounts of fish and nonfat milk products such as yogurt. (See "What the Antiaging Plate Should Look Like," at the beginning of this chapter.)

Alcohol and Longevity

People who drink too much alcohol, whether it's from beer, hard liquor, or wine, die at a younger age than do teetotalers or people who drink in moderation (less than two drinks each day). In fact, heavy drinking is right behind obesity and smoking as a primary cause of premature death. Women who consume two or more drinks a day increase their risk for breast cancer. Heavy drinkers also are much more likely to suffer from cirrhosis, high blood pressure, mouth and throat cancer, bronchitis and pneumonia, and liver cancer, and they're at high risk of dying from accidents, suicide, and cardiac arrest. People who consume more than four or five alcoholic drinks daily are likely to develop impaired memory and loss of mental ability as well.

On the other hand, people who have an occasional drink live about two years longer on average than do those who abstain, primarily because of a reduced risk for heart disease. When it comes to the heart, red wine is better than beer, which is slightly better than hard liquor.

People who drink a glass or two of red wine daily are much less likely to die from heart disease than people who don't drink or who drink other alcoholic beverages. The benefits might not come solely from the alcohol but instead from other antioxidant compounds in wine.

Red wine contains a wealth of phytochemicals called phenols, ergothionine, and resveratrol that have antioxidant capabilities in protecting the arteries and blood fats from free-radical damage. Phenols are found in most fruits, onions, and tea but are especially high in grapes. Both grape juice and red wine solids (without the alcohol) lower heart disease and cancer risks in animals, so while alcohol might offer additional benefits, such as possibly boosting the antioxidant potency of the phenols, a person can derive at least some benefits from dealcoholized wine or even grape juice.

Alcohol consumption is not a risk-free deal. If you choose to drink, do so in moderation. This means limiting alcohol intake to one drink daily for women, no more than two drinks daily for men, and no more than one drink daily for people over the age of sixty-five, as specified by the National Institute on Alcohol Abuse and Alcoholism. One drink equals six ounces of wine, ten ounces of beer, or one ounce of hard liquor.

Guideline 6: Include Three Low-Fat, Calcium-Rich Foods in the Daily Diet

Never give in! Never, never, never, never, never, never. In nothing great or small, large or petty—never give in except to convictions of honor and good sense.

—WINSTON CHURCHILL

Calcium is the foundation of any plan to prevent osteoporosis, the gradual loss of bone that results in fractures and curvature of the spine. Everyone needs calcium starting at birth, since the greatest bone mass and density (called peak bone mass) are reached by a person's midthirties. Prior to this time, a person is building bone density, which will serve as the bank account for calcium for the rest of his or her life. The more bone a person builds in the early years, the less likely he or she will battle osteoporosis later in life.

Women are at particular risk for osteoporosis because they have smaller bones, hence smaller bank accounts of calcium. Women also are more prone to dieting, which restricts calcium as well as calories. Finally, women are less likely than men to engage in vigorous physical activity, which helps maintain strong bones. As a result, shortly after peak bone mass is reached, the bones begin to lose calcium at a rate of 1 percent a year until menopause. After menopause the loss accelerates, and in the spine it can reach 6 percent per year. High calcium intake (that is, 1,500 milligrams per day), ample intake of vitamins D and K, weight-bearing exercise, and prescription medications, such as hormone replacement therapy and Fosamax, help slow this bone loss.

It is never too late to correct a calcium-poor diet, although the sooner you start, the better. Osteoporosis is a silent disease—the first symptom is often a broken bone. Nothing can mend the damage caused when osteoporosis is allowed to progress unchecked to this advanced stage. In short, calcium provides a protective effect in the development of bone loss and osteoporosis. Hip fracture risk is reduced by as much as 75 percent in people who consume high-calcium diets, whereas people who consume low-calcium diets or who fail to take supplements of calcium and vitamin D are at high risk for severe bone loss as they age.

Aim for at least 1,200 milligrams of calcium daily, 400IU of vitamin D, 350 milligrams of magnesium, and 90 micrograms of vitamin K. You'll need even more vitamin D if you are older than sixty-five. While you can meet these needs by following the guidelines of the Antiaging Diet, you'll probably need to supplement to reach this level of vitamin D, unless you consume four glasses daily of nonfat or low-fat milk or fortified soy milk. (See Chapter 10 for more information on osteoporosis.)

To make sure you get enough calcium:

- Have a spinach salad with raspberries and fat-free vinaigrette (calcium and vitamin K).
- Make salmon patties with canned salmon (vitamin D and calcium).
- Snack on nonfat, plain yogurt with canned peaches (calcium).
- For breakfast, have a bowl of Total cereal topped with nuts and light soy milk (vitamin D, magnesium, and calcium).
- Switch from apple juice to calcium- and vitamin D–fortified juice (calcium and vitamin D).
- Accompany a meal with a glass of light chocolate soy milk (calcium and vitamin D).
- Cook brown rice, oatmeal, and other grains in nonfat milk instead of water (calcium and vitamin D).
- Fill a whole wheat tortilla with low-fat cheese, fresh spinach, black beans, and salsa (magnesium, calcium, and vitamin K).
- Blend onion, garlic, and lots of steamed broccoli, and then combine with low-fat milk, curry powder, salt, and pepper to make a creamed curry soup (calcium, vitamin D, and vitamin K).

■ *Quick, Easy, and Nutritious Little Meals and Snacks*

LITTLE MEALS

- Grilled Salmon with Pesto and Lemon Zest* served with steamed vegetables and a tossed salad
- Barbecued chicken (use bottled sauce) with instant brown rice and Sweet Potato Ramckins with Maple Syrup (sugar free) and Chopped Hazelnuts*
- Baked Halibut with Tomato Salsa and Shaved Parmesan Cheese* with microwaved baked potato, steamed frozen carrots, and spinach salad (use bagged spinach)
- Grilled shrimp and garlic over linguini pasta served with Broiled Asparagus with Sea Salt and Lemon* and a tossed salad

SNACKS

- Fresh strawberries, nonfat yogurt, and pecan bits
- A tortilla filled with black beans, low-fat cheese, tomato, salsa, and lettuce or fresh cilantro
- A smoothie made with soy milk, orange juice concentrate, a banana, and wheat germ
- A slice of toasted whole-wheat bread topped with peanut butter, fat-free cottage cheese, and canned pineapple

Recipes in Appendix B.

Guideline 7: Enjoy Food

*Take pleasure out of life. . . . As much as you can. Nobody ever died
from pleasure.*

–SOL HUROK

Eating is one of life's most pleasurable experiences. Food should taste, look, and smell delicious. It also brings us together with loved ones, is a form of celebration and joy, and accompanies every important tradition and holiday. An extra advantage, according to the National Cancer Institute, is that people who create interesting menus based on a wide variety of wholesome foods are much less likely to die prematurely than those who eat the same few foods day in and day out. Pleasure, health, and vitality are inseparable.

What's in a Serving?

Take a look at people's portions, and you'll find that one person's snack could be another person's meal. The moderate servings on which the Antiaging Diet is based are in stark contrast to what many people are eating. Here are a few guidelines to keep your portions in line with a fork rather than a forklift:

ONE SERVING OF . . .	IS THE SIZE OF . . .
Milk Products	
8-ounce glass of milk or container of yogurt	Two wine glassfuls
1 ounce of cheese	A large marble or pair of dice
Whole Grains	
½ cup brown rice, noodles, or cooked cereal	A tennis ball
1 slice of bread or ½ small bagel, English muffin, or hamburger bun	A CD case
1 pancake	A compact disc
Meat	
3 ounces of meat, chicken, or fish	The palm of your hand, a deck of cards, or a cassette tape
Vegetables and Fruit	
1 cup raw	A baseball
½ cup cooked	Your fist
1 small fruit or vegetable	An apple, a carrot
Fats and Sugars	
1 teaspoon butter or margarine	A postage stamp the thickness of your finger
2 tablespoons salad dressing or peanut butter	A standard ice cube or a Ping-Pong ball
2 tablespoons pancake syrup	A shot glassful

One way to add vitality to your meals is to use spices and herbs, much as a painter uses paint, to color and texture the masterpiece. Enriching meals with enticing flavors helps satisfy on small portions, so you are less likely to overeat and gain weight. Try new or different spices with new foods. Stop depending on salt as your main flavor, and sprinkle basil, thyme, cilantro, curry powder, or other herbs instead. Many spices both flavor a meal and contain phytochemicals that help stop the aging clock. For example, adding a handful of herbs could give your salad quite a boost of antioxidants, according to a study from the University of Urbino in Italy. Aromatic herbs and spices, such as lemon balm and marjoram, increased the antioxidant content of a salad by up to 200 percent. Fresh marjoram added to a salad corresponded to an intake of 200 milligrams of the antioxidant-rich phenolic compounds in one study. Cumin and ginger also pack a high antioxidant punch. Olive oils and wine or apple vinegars provide the highest increase in antioxidants for salad dressings.

Garlic is a perfect example of how vitality, longevity, and taste are combined in a flavoring. Garlic helps lower heart disease and cancer risk and stimulates the immune system. Try some of the following suggestions to maximize the benefits from garlic while enhancing the flavor of meals:

- Chop or mince garlic cloves into Italian sauces, vegetable dips, meat loaf, marinades, soups, stir-fries, homemade salad dressings, and stews.
- Cook green beans, spinach, zucchini, or other vegetables with garlic in a drizzle of olive oil.
- When cooking pasta, add two to three cloves to the cooking water to impart subtle flavor.
- For fat-free garlic bread, first spray vegetable oil on whole bulbs of garlic with the skin on and wrap the bulbs in tin foil. Bake for forty-five minutes at 300°F or until soft. Spread the softened baked garlic cloves on French bread.
- Embed several garlic cloves in meat or poultry before roasting.

Guideline 8: Supplement Responsibly

The way to win a war is to make certain it never starts.

—GENERAL OMAR N. BRADLEY

In the not-so-distant past, the general consensus was that a person should eat a "balanced diet" to obtain all the vitamins and minerals in the right amounts. The reality is that few people actually meet even minimum standards of a good diet, let alone the optimal standards needed to prevent chronic disease and premature aging.

For example, most women average four servings of fresh fruits and vegetables daily (men do even worse, at only three servings), yet the minimum standard is five servings, the Antiaging Diet recommends at least eight, and the latest dietary guidelines from the federal government recommend as many as thirteen servings a day. You also should consume at least six servings daily of whole-grain breads or cereals, but, if you are like most Americans, you average less than one serving a day.

Even if people made perfect choices every day, there still is reason to take a supplement. While the antioxidants, such as vitamins C and E, might be potent antiaging nutrients, the amount needed to fend off the ravages of time is far greater than is realistically possible from diet alone. The Alliance for Aging Research recommends that adults consume the following amounts daily:

- 250 to 1,000 milligrams of vitamin C
- 100 to 400IU of vitamin E

While the Antiaging Diet meets the lower levels for vitamin C, a person must consume one cup of safflower oil or twenty-one cups of spinach daily to consume even 124IU of vitamin E! Not likely. In addition, as we age, requirements for other nutrients, such as vitamin D and vitamin B_{12}, increase to levels unrealistic from just diet. For people who cannot always follow the Antiaging Diet to the letter or for those who want to ensure optimal nutrition, there is reason to supplement— wisely and moderately. In fact, many nutrition experts agree that the supplement-diet controversy is no longer an either-or issue. You need to eat really well *and* supplement responsibly.

Can Supplements Help Prevent Aging?

Research repeatedly shows that those who supplement fare better than those who don't. For example:

- A study from the University of Heidelberg in Germany found that adults who supplemented with calcium and vitamin D were able to reverse bone loss, thus lowering their risk for osteoporosis, while nonsupplementers continued to lose bone throughout the study.
- Researchers at the University Medical Center Nijmegen in The Netherlands report that high doses of B vitamins lowered homocysteine levels, a risk factor

for heart disease and dementia, by 31 percent compared with only 3 percent in the placebo group.

- People who supplement with vitamin C at doses of 700 milligrams or more daily might reduce their risk for developing heart disease by up to 25 percent, according to a study from the National Public Health Institute in Helsinki and Harvard School of Public Health in Boston.
- Researchers at the MRC Neuropsychiatric Research Laboratory in Surrey, England, state that the research on folic acid and depression is substantial and warrants taking 800 micrograms along with 1 milligram of vitamin B_{12} to enhance conventional treatment of depression.
- A study from the USDA Human Nutrition Research Center on Aging at Tufts University found that daily supplements of 200IU of vitamin E lowered the risk for developing respiratory infections in seniors.
- People who take combined supplements of vitamins C and E might have a lower risk for developing Alzheimer's disease, according to a study from Johns Hopkins University.

The Three-Step Approach to Supplementation

Choosing a good supplement program is as easy as 1, 2, 3.

1. Select a broad-range multiple vitamin and mineral supplement. Look for one that contains vitamin D, vitamin K, all of the B vitamins (vitamins B_1, B_2, B_6, and B_{12}, as well as niacin, folic acid, pantothenic acid, and biotin), and the trace minerals (chromium, copper, iron, manganese, selenium, and zinc).

   - Steer clear of "extra" ingredients, such as lipoic acid, enzymes, or inositol; these extras add only cost, not value, to a product since they either are worthless or are supplied in amounts too low to be of use.
   - Save money by avoiding time-released vitamins, chelated or colloidal minerals, or most "natural" supplements, since they promise more than they deliver.
   - Some nutrients in a multiple can be ignored, such as potassium, choline, or phosphorus, since the diet either already supplies optimal levels of

these compounds or they are supplied in supplements in amounts too low to be useful.

- Read the column headed "Daily Value" on the label. Look for a multiple that provides approximately 100 to 300 percent of the Daily Value for all nutrients provided. What you want is a balanced supplement, not one that supplies 2 percent of one nutrient, 50 percent of another, and 600 percent of a third nutrient.

2. Supplement your multiple with extra calcium and magnesium. Size dictates that one-tablet-a-day multiples never supply enough of these minerals. (The pill would need to be the size of a Ping-Pong ball to have enough!) If on a daily basis you don't drink at least three glasses of nonfat milk or fortified orange juice or soy milk and consume several servings of dark green leafy vegetables, wheat germ, soybeans, and other magnesium-rich foods, look for a calcium-magnesium supplement that provides approximately two parts calcium for every one part magnesium (for example, 500 milligrams of calcium and 250 milligrams of magnesium). If your multiple (or your fortified cereal) does not contain vitamin D, make sure the calcium-magnesium tablet also contains 400IU of this vitamin if you are younger than fifty and 600IU if you are older.

3. Consider taking extra antioxidants. If the multiple does not contain extra amounts of vitamin C, vitamin E, and the carotenoids, consider taking an antioxidant supplement that supplies 250 to 1,000 milligrams of vitamin C, 100 to 400IU of vitamin E, and no more than 10 milligrams of beta-carotene. (Smokers should consult their physicians before supplementing with beta-carotene in doses greater than this.)

Can Supplements Be Toxic?

Some experts caution against vitamin toxicities. But are vitamin toxicities really a threat to most people? Not really. In most cases, raising the red flag of toxicity is making much ado about nothing. In fact, many more people suffer toxicities and side effects from over-the-counter and prescription medications than they do from supplements.

The Best Supplement

Designing a good supplement program is easier than you might think. You might have to mix and match one to three products, but in the end your total supplement intake should resemble the following:

NUTRIENT	THE BEST FORM	THE OPTIMAL DOSE
Beta-carotene	Mixture of carotenoids	10mg
Vitamin E	Alpha-tocopherol succinate	100IU–400IU
Vitamin D		400IU–800IU*
Vitamin K		65mcg–90mcg
Vitamin B$_1$		2mg–5mg
Vitamin B$_2$		2mg–5mg
Niacin		20mg–25mg
Vitamin B$_6$		5mg–10mg
Vitamin B$_{12}$		3mcg–15mcg*
Folic acid		400mcg–800mcg
Vitamin C		100mg
Boron		2mg–3mg
Calcium	Calcium carbonate or citrate	1,000mg–1,500mg*
Chromium	Chromium-rich yeast, chromium nicotinate, chromium picolinate	200mcg

Vitamin A is most famous for its overdose effects, and older people are most susceptible to vitamin A overdose. As people age, their livers become less able to clear excessive amounts of this vitamin. Even moderate intake in the later years can raise liver enzymes, an indicator of liver damage. Ironically, up to 40 percent of all vitamin A overdoses are from food, not supplements. Most people know better than to take too much vitamin A, so reported cases of supplemental overdoses are few. Of course, no one is recommending that anyone take huge doses of vitamin A, and you can get all you need of this important nutrient by eating lots of beta-carotene-rich fruits and vegetables (beta-carotene is converted to vitamin A in the body).

Vitamin D also can be toxic when consumed in huge amounts (that is, more than 2,000IU a day) over long periods of time. However, vitamin D deficiency is

NUTRIENT	THE BEST FORM	THE OPTIMAL DOSE
Copper		3mg
Fluoride (needed only if drinking water is not fluoridated)		4mg
Iodine		150mcg
Iron	Ferrous fumarate	18mg (premenopausal women) 10mg (men and post-menopausal women)
Magnesium	Magnesium oxide, magnesium citrate, magnesium citrate-malate	350mg–500mg
Manganese		5mg
Molybdenum		250mcg
Selenium	Selenomethionine, selenocysteine	200mcg
Zinc	Zinc gluconate, zinc picolinate	20mg–30mg

*Amount needed increases as a person ages.

much more common than overdose. Excessive doses of other nutrients, such as vitamin B_6 (in amounts greater than 500 milligrams a day) or selenium (in amounts greater than 400 micrograms a day) also can be toxic.

Granted, there are concerns about vitamin and mineral toxicities, especially in high-risk populations, such as children, people with liver disease, and pregnant women. But decades of research show that the vast majority of people who supplement do so responsibly. They choose a balanced multiple and sometimes supplement it with extra vitamin C, vitamin E, or calcium. Supplementers also tend to eat better and take better care of their health. They are less prone to disease and premature aging and maintain stronger immune systems than nonsupplementers. Now that's much ado about something!

■ *Other Antiaging Supplements to Consider*

SUPPLEMENT	TYPE	DOSE	POTENTIAL FUNCTION
Fish oils	Docosahexaenoic acid (DHA)	500mg	Lowers heart disease, bone loss,
	Eicosapentaenoic acid (EPA)	500mg	memory loss; improves mood
	Phosphatidylserine (PS)	100mg	Might improve memory
Glucosamine		1,500mg	Aids in arthritis
Chondroitin		1,200mg	Aids in arthritis
Ginkgo biloba	Standardized to 24 percent flavone glycosides and 6 percent terpene lactones	120mg	Might improve memory

The Empty-Nest Kitchen

We must not stay as we are, doing always what was done last time,
or we shall stick in the mud.

—GEORGE BERNARD SHAW

An empty nest brings with it many adjustments. Life previously might have revolved around routines of work and raising children. Probably nowhere was the routine more ingrained than at the dining table, where for years it was your job to make sure the kids ate at least one good meal every day. Many parents find that after the children move out or when a spouse dies, their incentive or interest in cooking dwindles to little or none at all. They may eat the same foods over and over, skip meals, or eat at the kitchen counter rather than prepare a sit-down meal for one.

"People in their 50s and 60s are at a crux. Their physiological reserves begin to dwindle and they will age more rapidly if they don't take care of themselves," says Jeffrey Blumberg, Ph.D., professor at the Friedman School of Nutrition Science and Policy at Tufts University. "On the other hand, with the children gone, people have more personal time. If they approach good nutrition with the attitude that it can be fun, they can take advantage of an opportunity to do something good for themselves and their long-term health." In fact, the kitchen might be just the place to foster rediscovery, self-renewal, health, and even romance.

Resurrecting the joy of eating after the kids leave home requires an adventure-some spirit. You must abandon well-worn recipes. Try new fruits and vegetables, such as sliced jicama or radicchio in, a salad. Toss sun-dried tomatoes in pasta. Experiment with different combinations: add exotic fruits, such as mangos or papaya, to chicken dishes. Explore the different flavors of international cuisine. Try forming a dining club with friends, sampling each other's newest creations. Even discovering new places to shop for groceries can open up alternatives. You may find that variety alone is enough to wake up a sleeping palate.

Taking Nutrition for Granted

While scaling down in the kitchen can add adventure and zest to your life, without a little planning some people may fall short nutrition-wise at a time when nutrition is more important than ever.

"People at this age are most likely to meet their nutritional needs and maintain a desirable weight if they stop planning traditional meals around meat, which is a main source of fat in the diet. Instead, they should ask themselves, 'What vegetables and whole grains will I have today?'" recommends Margo Woods, D.Sc., assistant professor of medicine at Tufts University School of Medicine. "Eating well is as simple as preparing a big pot of soup made with lots of vegetables and a little bit of meat. Then, buy a variety of vegetables for accompanying salads and you have several light meals throughout the week." Dr. Woods also recommends that you place sliced fresh fruit on the table every night. "A few bites of fruit after a meal often curb the desire for something sweet. It also gives you something to do that is good for you while your partner is still eating."

Nutritious meals can be easy and quick to prepare if you have stocked your kitchen with nutrient-packed "convenience" foods, such as the following:

- **In a can.** Low-fat soups, tomatoes, tomato sauce, chicken broth, chickpeas, black beans, and tuna packed in water.
- **In a box.** Nonfat milk powder, cold and hot cereals, dried fruit, and instant brown rice.
- **In a bag.** An assortment of pastas and salad greens.
- **In bulk.** Whole-grain flour, bulgur wheat, barley, and other grains.

- **Whole-grain breads.** Tortillas, pita bread, and packaged low-fat pizza crusts.
- **Oil-free, low-sodium condiments.** Mustard, soy sauce, vinegar including balsamic vinegar, salsa, lemon juice, fruit spreads, salad dressings, sun-dried tomatoes, and minced garlic or ginger.
- **In the dairy case.** Fresh nonfat or 1 percent low-fat milk and yogurt, light or regular soy milk, and cheeses such as Parmesan, part-skim mozzarella and ricotta, or Gorgonzola.
- **In the produce section.** An assortment of fresh and frozen vegetables, including sweet potatoes, asparagus, cauliflower, chard, fresh herbs, broccoli, onions, garlic, baby carrots, lettuce (anything but iceberg!), and fresh fruit, such as mangos, lemons, oranges, apples, kiwi, berries, and papaya.
- **In the freezer.** Frozen low-fat entrées (purchased or made at home), chicken breasts, fish fillets, frozen plain vegetables, berries, and whole-wheat waffles.

Planned Overs

One way to minimize the time you spend preparing food is to cook for more than one meal. Rather than thinking of the extra portions as leftovers, consider them "planned overs," or planned ingredients for another meal. Wrap, label, date, and store extra foods quickly. Freeze any portions that will not be eaten within three days.

These foods recycle especially well:

- Pancakes, French toast, muffins, and waffles
- Sandwich fillings (such as tuna, chicken, and pureed beans)
- Steamed vegetables, which can be used in omelets, soups, stews, marinated vegetable salads, or burritos or for cold snacks
- Onions and garlic (chop the whole onion and several cloves of garlic, and then store them individually in sealed plastic bags)
- Soups, to which you can add pasta, kidney beans, or more vegetables to change the character
- Sauces (tomato or creamed sauces are particularly good, since you can spice the sauce as needed after thawing)
- Chicken breasts, which can be used as sandwich fillings or tortilla stuffers, added to pasta or rice dishes, or used in a stir-fry
- Fish, which can be used in fish tacos or pita sandwiches

- Pasta dishes, which actually taste better when reheated—simply add extra sauce to moisten
- Rice or beans, which can be added to casseroles, marinated vegetables, or soups
- Baked potatoes, which can be mashed or pureed with milk to make a "cream" soup base

Seize the Moment

The empty-nest kitchen offers a golden opportunity to break free from cooking ruts and explore new tastes, textures, and aromas. This is also a wonderful chance to nurture yourself, your health, your vitality, and your relationships.

CHAPTER 8

The Antiaging Fitness Program

> *There is no substitute for*
> *learning to live in our bodies.*
> *All the tests and all the*
> *machines in the world will fail*
> *if we do not first become*
> *good animals.*
> —GEORGE SHEEHAN, M.D.

Are you out of breath after walking up a flight of stairs? Is carrying the groceries from the car more tiring than it used to be? Has your back ever gone out from just leaning over to pick up something from the floor? Does crossing the street to make a green light feel like running the hundred-yard dash? Are you stiff in the morning? Tired in the evening? Does an afternoon of gardening leave your muscles sore for days?

If you answered "yes" to any of the preceding questions, welcome to the out-of-shape club! You're not alone. Six out of every ten Americans do not exercise regularly. Only 15 percent of adults come close to Dr. Sheehan's goal of being "good animals" by exercising at least three times a week for twenty minutes or more each time. Worse yet, by age seventy-five, a third of all men and half of all women don't exercise at all. Inactivity contributes to two million deaths each year, including deaths related to diabetes, osteoporosis, stroke, heart disease, and arthritis, as well as several cancers, such as colon and breast cancers.

Sitting on your duff won't do you in when you're ten, fifteen, or even twenty years old. But your muscles will take a nosedive in your thirties. People lose approximately 1 to 2 percent of muscle mass every year after this point, which equates to a five- to ten-pound loss of muscle every decade. The loss doesn't become noticeable until your forties, when you find that pushing a door open takes two hands instead of one or you unconsciously take the elevator to avoid even a two-story climb up the stairs. And that's just the beginning.

As the body ages, it loses muscle and accumulates fat. Fat tissue is like a storage box in your body. Because it is relatively inactive, the more fat you have, the fewer calories you need to maintain a constant body weight. Muscle, on the other hand, is like your car's engine, burning calories when moving and even at rest. Consequently, the fat-for-muscle trade-off results in a lower metabolic rate (called basal metabolic rate, or BMR). It takes fewer calories to keep you going—eat like a thirty-year-old when you are fifty and you'll gain weight.

Letting muscle slip away is the first step in the aging process. The gradual loss of fitness also contributes to bone loss and osteoporosis. The increase in body fat is directly linked to increased blood cholesterol and glucose, elevated blood pressure, increased insulin resistance, and loss of bone density, which place a person at increased risk for most age-related degenerative diseases, from heart disease and diabetes to hypertension and cancer. Excess body fat even has been linked to higher risks for developing dementia down the road.

Where Metabolism Meets Movement

Metabolism is the sum total of all energy-requiring processes in your body. The more you move, the more calories you burn and the higher your metabolic rate. Metabolism is primarily a combination of BMR and physical activity. BMR is the calories needed to maintain basic body functions, such as blinking your eyes, sending electrical messages along the nerves, kidney and liver function, and heartbeat.

BMR accounts for about 60 percent of your total daily energy needs. It can account for up to 75 percent of your energy needs if you do strength training. That's because a physically fit body has a higher percentage of muscle to fat tissue compared with an unfit one. Muscle is the body's calorie-burning furnace, so it is called metabolically active. Fat is metabolically inactive and uses fewer calories. As a person exercises and increases muscle mass, the metabolic rate goes up, more calories are burned during and after exercise, and weight is lost.

The changes don't happen overnight. Body fat increases slowly from 18 to 36 percent in men and from 20 to 44 percent in women between the ages of twenty and sixty-five years. Between the ages of thirty and eighty, breathing capacity gradually declines up to 60 percent, nerve conduction drops 15 percent, and maximum oxygen uptake declines by 70 percent. The changes are so gradual that most people lament their age as the cause, rather than putting the blame squarely where it belongs: inactivity.

As your body becomes less and less fit over time, it takes more effort to do even simple daily tasks; consequently, you do less and less. If you live long enough, you'll reach a point where you can't get up out of a chair without help or even pick up the groceries, let alone your grandchild.

Hold On to Your Youth

"Know thyself" means this, that you get acquainted with what you know, and what you can do.

—MENANDER OF ATHENS

There's good news. Almost all of the weakness, frailty, and loss of function associated with aging is preventable and even treatable! All you must do is keep moving. The fountain of youth is within you. It's the sweat on your brow after a good workout. It also can be found at the water fountain at the local gym, the water bottle strapped to your bicycle, and the tall glass of iced green tea that refreshes after a brisk walk.

Even better news is that you don't have to rearrange your life or spend hours a day working out. For example, in seniors, even modest exercise slowed the rate of aging- and disease-related weight loss, according to a study from the Yale University School of Medicine. All it takes to rewrite the script for aging at almost any age is a few minutes of brisk walking and a few strengthening exercises to escape the perils of inactivity and aging. Better yet, you'll see results within one month of starting the Antiaging Fitness Program in this book.

Studies repeatedly show that weight gain and the risk of dying prematurely from any cause decreases as people increase their participation in vigorous activity. For example, women who exercise daily reduce their abdominal fat, thus potentially lowering their risk for heart disease, diabetes, and the metabolic syndrome, according to a study from Kansas State University. Healthy centenarians exercise more and have more muscle and higher metabolic rates than do seventy-five-year-olds who don't exercise. In short, to avoid the grim reaper, not only should you run away, but you should swim, cycle, row, jump, skate, hike, ski, tap-dance, and walk.

Better than Any Pill

Almost all aspects of aging can be avoided or slowed simply by moving every day. The single most important habit you can acquire to maintain optimal function throughout life is to stay physically active. Here is a partial list of what to expect as a result of being physically active:

- Decreased risk of developing or dying from heart disease
- Prevention or delay of high blood pressure
- Decreased blood pressure in people with hypertension
- Lowered risk of developing non-insulin dependent diabetes
- Maintenance of youthful muscle strength
- Improved range of motion of joints
- Improved joint structure and function
- Control of joint swelling and pain associated with arthritis
- Increased general mobility
- Attainment of peak bone mass
- Slowing of the accelerated bone loss associated with aging, thus reducing the risk of developing osteoporosis
- Reduced likelihood of gaining excess body fat and greater ease losing excess body fat
- Improved lean body mass (muscle, organs, and other fat-free tissue)
- Improved digestive function and reduced risk of constipation
- Improved lung and respiratory function
- Encouragement of other healthful habits
- Improved sleep patterns
- Increased ease in performing daily tasks
- More energy and less chance of suffering fatigue
- Reduced depression, anxiety, and stress
- Improved mood
- Improved psychological well-being
- Improved self-esteem
- Maintenance of physical functioning and independent living
- Reduced risk for falls
- Maintenance of youthful metabolic rate
- Improved recovery from illness
- Improved and more youthful appearance

The Aging Muscle

If you don't run your own life, somebody else will.

—JOHN ATKINSON

The research consistently points to disuse, not age, as the underlying cause of frailty and disease. The older a person is, the more critical this rule of disuse becomes. Weak muscles are more prone to injury and stiffness. The loss of muscle strength in older men and women is a major contributor to disability, osteoporosis, insulin insensitivity and diabetes, and lessened ability to transport oxygen to the tissues (called aerobic capacity or VO_2 max). Unfit older people also are less efficient at burning fat for fuel, which when combined with the lowered metabolic rate results in weight gain and difficulty losing weight.

Anyone, no matter what age, who begins exercising shows increases in strength and metabolic rates. Middle-aged and older persons benefit the most. While twenty-year-olds improve their oxygen capacity by about 29 percent after starting an exercise program, people ages sixty to seventy show up to a 38 percent improvement in oxygen capacity. In just twelve weeks of starting a strength-training program, men between the ages of sixty and seventy-two showed up to a 227 percent improvement in muscle strength. In a study of ninety-six-year-olds, strength improved up to 200 percent. Moderate daily exercise also boosts resistance to both colds and cancer more in older than in younger people.

Compared with an inactive older person, a seventy-year-old who exercises daily has lower blood pressure, lower blood cholesterol, higher HDL (good) cholesterol, and as much as a 40 percent lower risk of developing heart disease. Physically active men and women have lower body weight and body fat and improved insulin sensitivity, thus lowering their risk of high blood pressure and diabetes. They are less likely to experience colon cancer, stroke, or even back injuries. They have stronger bones and are at lower risk of developing osteoporosis. And they are up to 25 percent less likely to injure themselves or fall compared with unfit older people. Even practicing unconventional physical activities, such as tai chi (an ancient Chinese martial art that combines meditation with rhythmic movements), can reduce the chance of falls and injury by almost 50 percent.

Exercise and Vitality

Though our outer nature is wasting away, our inner nature is being renewed every day.

—2 CORINTHIANS 4:16

Watch the faces of people out for a brisk autumn walk, or feel the enthusiasm of the runners lined up for a 10K race. Listen to the conversations of middle-aged or older people at your local gym. You will hear and see the signs of vitality: enthusiasm for life, positive thoughts, and plans for the future. Fitness is the breeding ground for vitality.

The research bears this out. Physically fit people are happier, more satisfied with their lives, and less prone to depression, anxiety, and stress. Exercise becomes their play and brings out the childlike quality inherent in vitality. People who are physically active also think more clearly, concentrate better, remember more, and react quicker than sedentary folks. In short, their physically fit bodies allow them the freedom to do what they want in life.

Staying fit also means living longer. Women who continue to exercise in their second fifty years are as fit as or even fitter than sedentary women who are twenty to thirty years younger. This may explain why they also live longer. Men who take up exercise in the middle years lower their risk of dying prematurely by up to 30 percent. In fact, the more calories a person expends in exercise each week, the longer he or she is likely to live disease free.

Inactivity or Smoking: Name Your Poison

Avoiding exercise is the riskiest vice you can choose. Almost two million deaths globally every year are attributed to physical inactivity. The combination of poor diet and lack of exercise accounts for four hundred thousand deaths alone in the United States. Those staggering figures place lethargy in the same high-risk behavior category as smoking, obesity, hypertension, and driving drunk.

Ironically, those who stick with an exercise program for at least six months report that if only they'd known how good they would feel, they would have started exercising earlier! The secret to a long and healthy life filled with vitality is as simple as getting off the couch and moving—every day for the rest of your life.

Exercise: The Natural High

That still, as death approaches nearer,
the joys of life are sweeter, dearer:
and had I but an hour to live,
that little hour to bliss I'd give.

—ANACREON

A daily workout releases brain chemicals, including epinephrine and norepineph-rine, that boost alertness. It also raises serotonin levels, which boost mood. At the same time, exercise de-stresses the body by lowering blood levels of the "stress hor-mones," including cortisol, that prepare the body for "fight or flight." Over time, the body learns to react less intensely to stress, thus providing a built-in coping mechanism. In addition, the rise in body temperature resulting from a vigorous workout has a tranquilizing effect on the body, not unlike that experienced when soaking in a hot bath. Finally, the hour at the gym or pounding the streets might provide a much-needed time-out from a hectic day. The hidden benefit to this is that when we prevent an overreaction to stress, we also curb cravings for sweets, thus helping to maintain a trim figure. Research from the University of California, San Francisco, found that animals—and probably people—turn to sweets when under stress and that those very foods help curb the stress response and calm us down. Preventing the stress reaction is the only way to curb that tendency to overeat, and exercise is the habit of choice.

The notorious "runner's high" has been attributed to an exercise-induced release of endorphins, the body's natural morphinelike chemicals that help boost pain tol-erance and generate feelings of euphoria and satisfaction. However, the research on endorphins and exercise remains equivocal. Exercise increases blood levels of endorphins up to tenfold, but the key is whether or not brain levels of endorphins are increased.

Endorphins or no endorphins, one thing seems clear: exercise is a great antide-pressant. There is evidence that exercise relieves depression better than psy-chotherapeutic medications, counseling, or a combination of the two. In a study of 357 adults at Stanford University in Palo Alto, California, researchers compared the effects of no exercise and various intensities of exercise on psychological out-comes. After twelve months, the exercisers reported significantly reduced stress, anxiety, and depression compared with their sedentary counterparts, regardless of

The Four Fitness Guidelines for a Long and Healthy Life

Move every day for at least forty-five minutes:

1. Engage in some form of aerobic activity, such as walking, swimming, or jogging, at least four hours a week.
2. Do some form of strength training, such as lifting weights or doing calisthenics (for example, sit-ups), at least twice a week.
3. Warm up and cool down with flexibility and balancing exercises.
4. Always make it fun!

whether they experienced any changes in fitness or body weight. Neither the level of intensity nor even the type of exercise (aerobic activities, such as walking, running, or swimming, or anaerobic sports, such as bodybuilding) seem to matter; all forms of exercise alleviate depression and improve mood.

People want to categorize this effect by saying it's biochemical or psychological, but in reality it's most likely a synergistic effect of these and, as yet, unidentified factors. Whatever the cause, one thing is sure: the best mood-elevating effects come from starting and sticking with a daily exercise program.

The Antiaging Fitness Program

Everyone is an athlete. The only difference is that some of us are in training, and some are not.

—GEORGE SHEEHAN, M.D.

You must be physically active if your goal is a long and healthy life. But you must do it right, which is as simple as 1, 2, 3. That means combining the following:

1. Aerobic activity (such as walking, swimming, or jogging)
2. Strength training (such as lifting weights) or calisthenics (such as sit-ups)
3. Warm-up, cooldown, and flexibility exercises

Aerobic activity strengthens your cardiovascular system and helps burn fat. Strength training increases muscle and metabolism. Flexibility activities keep your joints and muscles elastic, while balance activities keep your brain-muscle systems coordinated. This combined program will slow or halt the changes in body composition associated with aging, aid in weight management, help normalize blood sugar and blood pressure, increase muscle, stimulate the immune system, and even possibly stimulate growth hormone release, which in turn might help build more muscle and denser bones while helping burn fat. The sooner you start the better, but it's never too late for damage control or even reversal.

Get Started

Whether you are one of the almost 90 percent who are inactive or are an avid exerciser, you should be aware of a few important considerations before making a change in your activity level.

First, you need to know where you are before you can decide where you're going. Everyone over the age of forty should obtain medical clearance from a physician before beginning any exercise program. That includes completing a monitored fitness test to determine where you need to focus your exercise goals. If you're like most people, you'll probably find that you need to work on several goals, such as increasing your cardiovascular fitness level and upper-body strength. Or maybe balance and flexibility will prove high priorities. You also need to determine at what level you should start a fitness program and whether there are any undetected health risks that should be taken into account, such as high cholesterol or blood pressure. After a thorough physical evaluation, you and your physician can lay out a plan.

The Plan

You probably wouldn't host a party or go Christmas shopping without having a plan. But many people jump into exercise, join a fitness club, or purchase exercise equipment without first sitting down and thinking it through. Planning will dramatically increase the odds that you will stick with your exercise routine. Even if it's something as simple as riding your bike to work, you need to decide how you'll

■ *Your Activity Quotient*

The first step in a lifetime exercise program is to determine where you are now—physically, that is. To calculate your fitness score, determine your rating for each of the following categories. Next, multiply the numbers to obtain a score (fitness score = activity rating × frequency rating × intensity rating × time rating). Retake this self-assessment six months after starting your exercise program and compare to see how far you've come.

RATING	TYPE OF ACTIVITY YOU ROUTINELY ENGAGE IN
3	A mixture of aerobic, strength training, and flexibility. The day also is filled with activity, such as climbing stairs, vacuuming, walking rather than driving, and using nonelectrical appliances (for example, a hand-held can opener).
2	Either aerobic or strength training/flexibility but not both. The day is somewhat active with house or yard work, walking, and climbing stairs.
1	Recreational sports, such as kite flying, bowling, light gardening, archery, canoeing, fishing, volleyball, table tennis, or baseball. The rest of the day is moderately inactive (for example, using elevators and escalators instead of stairs or driving whenever possible instead of walking).

RATING	FREQUENCY OF PLANNED PHYSICAL EXERCISE
5	More than five times a week
4	Four to five times a week
3	Three times a week
2	Two times or less a week

RATING	INTENSITY OF PLANNED PHYSICAL EXERCISE
5	Very heavy, with sustained heavy breathing and perspiration, as in jogging, aerobic dancing, skipping rope, or cycling
4	Heavy, with intermittent heavy breathing and perspiration, as in a vigorous game of tennis or racquetball

3	Moderately heavy, as in continuous bicycling, swimming, calisthenics, shoveling snow, or heavy yard work.
2	Moderate, as in brisk walking, golf (carrying bag and walking), leisurely bicycling (5.5 mph), rowing, scuba diving, skating, hiking, or horseback riding
1	Light, as in fishing, slow walking, croquet, shuffleboard, horseshoes, billiards, badminton, routine housecleaning, pulling weeds, or planting flowers

RATING	TIME SPENT DAILY
4	More than forty-five minutes
3	Thirty-one to forty-five minutes
2	Twenty to thirty minutes
1	Less than twenty minutes

PERSONAL FITNESS SCORE

SCORE	ESTIMATED FITNESS LEVEL
144–300	This very active lifestyle sustains a very high level of physical fitness.
54–143	This active lifestyle sustains an above-average level of fitness. You'll experience even more benefits if you boost your score to at least 180!
40–53	This moderately active lifestyle sustains an average level of fitness. You'll see improvements in health and longevity if you increase daily exercise to reach a score of at least 54.
24–39	This borderline active lifestyle sustains a marginal level of fitness. Long-term health and longevity are at risk unless you increase physical activity with physician approval and raise your score to at least 40.
Less than 24	This sedentary lifestyle will contribute to disease risk and shortened life expectancy down the road. Start exercising with physician approval to boost your score to at least 40.

carry your briefcase or lunch, how you'll keep mud and grease off your work clothes, and even what route you'll take. You'll also need to repair the bicycle and have an alternate fitness plan for rainy days. Also, you must identify all the reasons you have for not exercising and then devise realistic ways to overcome those barriers.

Establish a Routine

Exercise will be a priority only if you make it one. Establish a routine by setting aside a time or place every day for exercise. Write it on your daily calendar and don't let anything get in the way. Plan ahead. Bring exercise clothes when traveling. At home, put on your exercise clothes when you get up in the morning or when you arrive home after work; keep them on until you've exercised.

Set Goals

The biggest mistake most people make when starting an exercise program is that they try to do too much too soon. The resulting soreness, injury, and discouragement undermine even the best intentions. Devise an exercise program that is well within your capability, knowing that early success will encourage long-term commitment. If you know you can walk twenty minutes at a brisk pace, walk only fifteen minutes at a time the first week. That way you won't feel too sore and will be encouraged to stick with your program.

The adage "no pain, no gain" is outdated. Exercise doesn't have to hurt to be good for you. Brisk walking (at a pace that allows you to cover two miles in less than thirty minutes) is one of the best activities for strengthening the cardiovascular system and burning excess body fat. Fitness gains are greatest in those people who go from being sedentary to doing something; the gains are less dramatic for those who move up a notch from fitness to superfitness.

On the other hand, rousing an out-of-shape body off the couch and into the gym won't feel as good as, say, polishing off a bag of Hershey's Kisses—at least, not at first. You must move enough to see benefits (that means you must sweat) but not so much that soreness or fatigue undermine your motivation. As Dr. Sheehan said, "You must listen to your body. [Exercise] through annoyance but not through pain."

You also must answer the question "How fit do I want to be?" It's important that you realistically plan activity so it will fit into your life. For some people, that means getting up a half-hour earlier in the morning to walk. For others, it may mean creating four ten-minute breaks throughout the day to stretch, lift weights, or ride a stationary bike.

You don't need huge amounts of time to exercise. There are 336 half-hours in a week—all you need is five to six of those set aside for aerobic activity such as walking and another two for strength training. If even that sounds monumental, try breaking your activity sessions into several miniexercise sessions throughout the day. The research shows you can derive the same benefits from two to three mini-workouts as long as the total day's time is still at least forty-five minutes.

In addition, you can increase activity throughout the day by using the stairs instead of the escalator or elevator. Park your car at the end of the lot and walk to the store. Better yet, ride your bicycle to the store. Don't let anything interfere with your plan. Remember, failing to plan is planning to fail.

One Step at a Time

Develop a progressive exercise program. To see results without feeling miserable, gradually increase the duration, intensity, or frequency of your exercise session—but not all at once. A rule of thumb is to increase time or intensity by 10 percent each week. If you're currently walking two miles a day, increase the distance to 2.2 miles the next week, and do it in the same amount of time. Also, add activities to the program as you advance. Your ultimate goal is to accumulate thirty to forty-five minutes or more every day of moderate-intensity physical activity.

Make It Fun

Physical activity should bring out the kid in you. It should be your playtime during the day, during which you laugh, enjoy the company of friends, love what your body can do, and "lighten up." Doing something physical should be pleasurable, active, freeing, and rewarding. Eventually, exercise can become something you'd do even if it had no benefits other than the joy of doing it.

Rather than calling it exercise, call your daily activity romping. As Dr. Sheehan noted, "Fitness has to be fun. If it is not play, there will be no fitness. Play, you see, is the process. Fitness is merely the product." That may mean romping with friends if you are a social animal or choosing a solitary sport if you need some quiet time away from the tensions of work. It may mean alternating three or more activities throughout the week to keep your romping fresh and new or playing sports with the kids. You'll stick with exercise only if it's fun. So ask yourself what you like to do and what is convenient to do, and then use your imagination to keep moving interesting.

Cardiovascular Fitness: Your Target Heart Rate

I'm sixty-five and I guess that puts me in with the geriatrics, but if there were fifteen months in every year, I'd only be forty-eight.

—JAMES THURBER

The first component of the Antiaging Fitness Program is to strengthen your cardiovascular system by strengthening the heart and increasing blood and oxygen flow to the tissues. Aerobic exercise achieves this and burns more calories than any other type of activity. It is the best way to burn excess body fat. It also helps relieve stress by tempering the stress hormones and possibly raising brain chemicals called endorphins.

Aerobically fit people are healthier than anyone else, with a lower risk of developing heart disease, hypertension, and diabetes, as well as of being overweight. The more aerobically fit you are, the greater are your chances of living a disease-free, healthy life. Aerobic fitness goes hand in hand with vitality. It's as simple as that.

How do you know if your activity is aerobic and if you're doing enough to reap the benefits? Aerobic activities use large muscle groups, such as the legs and arms, in a rhythmic and continuous motion. Checking heart rate is the most convenient way to monitor your cardiovascular or aerobic fitness and intensity, since it directly reflects how hard you are working. Your goal is to exercise within your target heart rate, or THR, which is 60 to 90 percent of your maximum heart rate (MHR).

It is also important to do a spot check while exercising. How do you feel when you are working at 40 percent of your MHR, at 60 percent, and at 80 percent? How hard are you breathing? Are you comfortable or gasping for air? Are you perspir-

■ *How to Calculate Your Target Heart Rate*

To identify your MHR, subtract your age from 220. To identify your THR range, multiply your MHR by 0.60 and again by 0.90. For example, a forty-five-year-old man's THR would be:

220 − 45 = 175 (MHR)
175 (MHR) × .60 = 105 beats per minute for 60 percent of MHR
175 (MHR) × .90 = 157.5 beats per minute for 90 percent of MHR

This man's target heart rate is between 105 and 157.5 beats per minute. To take your pulse and monitor your heart rate during exercise, lightly place your two middle fingers on your throat, just to the side of center (carotid pulse). (See illustration below.) Don't press too hard, since this will slow the pulse. You also can use your wrist, placing two fingers on the thumb side (radial pulse). Count the beats starting with the number zero on the first beat. Count for ten seconds and then multiply that number by six, or count for ten seconds and add a zero to the end of that figure to determine the total heart beats per minute. It is important to count the pulse immediately after stopping exercise, since the pulse rate slows quickly once exercise is stopped.

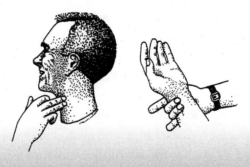

ing? Is your heart pounding wildly or just rhythmically pumping? These spot checks help you learn the signals of how hard you're working out. Eventually, this awareness will be an accurate way to measure exercise intensity.

A general rule of thumb is to exercise at a level that allows you to talk and sweat at the same time. If you can't talk, you are exercising too hard and should slow down, even if you are within your THR. If you are within your THR and can sing or whistle while exercising, you are not working hard enough and should increase your exertion to the higher end of the THR scale.

▪ *Guidelines for a Cardiovascular Workout*

To maximize the benefits from your workout, follow these guidelines:

1. Warm up for five to ten minutes before beginning the activity.
2. Be sure the movements are continual and rhythmic, using the major muscle groups, such as the arms and legs.
3. Periodically monitor your heart rate and perceived exertion level during the activity.
4. Do not exceed your THR.
5. Make the workout fun, playful, and enjoyable.
6. Work up to at least forty-five minutes of continuous motion.
7. Cool down for five to ten minutes after the activity, including some stretching and flexibility exercises in your cooldown.

Strength Training

I am more myself than ever before.

—MAY SARTON

While aerobic activity will soothe the heart, strength training will put a spring in your step. In fact, strength training may be the most important antiaging activity there is. The loss of muscle that accompanies aging slows metabolism, leads to weight gain, and weakens the body, contributing to everything from obesity, osteoporosis, and heart disease to loss of function, coordination, and the ability to perform everyday tasks. Even highly trained runners will start to suffer from weakened muscles, nagging injuries, and weight gain as they age unless they combine their aerobic workouts with at least two strength-training sessions each week.

Strength training is one of the most important components of any weight-management plan. It preserves or restores muscle tissue and is the only effective way to increase muscle mass as a person ages. The increased muscle boosts calorie burning up to about 7.5 percent for up to fifteen hours after the workout. During any weight-loss effort, you will lose more lean tissue and will end up weaker from dieting unless you combine aerobic activity with strength training. Strong muscles also allow you to perform ordinary tasks with less effort, so you can accomplish more and have energy left over!

Why Warm Up?

Warm-up exercises are very important to overall fitness and prevention of injuries. The benefits include:

- Improved oxygen delivery to the muscles
- Improved oxygen release in the muscle tissues
- Stimulation of energy systems within the cell, which improves muscle function during exercise
- Enhanced transfer of nerve messages to the muscles
- Increased blood flow to muscles
- Reduced injuries to muscles, tendons, ligaments, and other connective tissue
- Improved responsiveness of the heart and blood vessels to sudden or strenuous exercise
- Increased range of motion in joints
- Reduced muscular tension and soreness
- Improved coordination
- Enhanced sense of well-being

The ABCs of Strength Training

Improving your muscular strength does not mean bulking up like a bodybuilder. It does mean developing stronger muscles that prevent needless injury as you age. Proper strength training does not require that you join a gym to use their high-tech equipment. It can be as simple as doing well-designed calisthenics at home and, if you want, adding hand and ankle weights as you progress. Of course, you also can purchase free weights or machines to use at home or join the gym. It's up to you.

Here are the most important rules:

- Include exercises that strengthen major muscle groups, such as the muscles at the back of the thigh (hamstrings), the front thigh muscles (quadriceps), the lower-back muscles (erector spinatus), the abdominals, the chest muscles (pectorals), the upper-back muscles, the biceps and triceps in the upper arms, and the muscles in the shoulders and neck.
- Include warm-up and cooldown exercises before and after strength training.

- Work each muscle group to near fatigue, which usually takes two to three sets with ten to twelve repetitions each. Choose weights that are heavy enough that you can't do any more than twelve repetitions at a time. All it may take in the beginning is lifting the weight equivalent of a jug of milk or a hardbound dictionary. When the last few lifts are too easy, it's time to switch to slightly heavier weights or add another set.

- Take it slow. If you start with eight repetitions of fifteen pounds, you might increase to twelve repetitions at the same weight, then increase to two sets of eight repetitions at the same weight, and so forth. The biggest mistake people make is to add too much weight or too many repetitions too quickly, setting themselves up for injury and discouragement.

- Breathe! Inhale before you lift a weight, and exhale as you lift it. Don't hold your breath.

- Take at least one day off between sessions to allow muscles to heal and to maximize strength gains, or alternate upper-body and lower-body workouts every other day. You should notice improvements in strength and energy within six weeks of starting a strength-training program.

Meet with a trained exercise physiologist or fitness expert to devise a strength program for your fitness level. Numerous books also are available. Several are listed in the resource section at the end of this book.

Balance and Flexibility

In the past few years I have made a thrilling discovery . . . that until one is over sixty, one can never really learn the secret of living.

—ELLEN GLASGOW

As people age, they become more susceptible to falls, injuries, stiff joints, and muscle spasms or pains—not because of their age but because they haven't kept their bodies limber and coordinated. After a person's midthirties, subtle changes in muscle and connecting tissues cause joints, ligaments, tendons, and other tissues to become increasingly stiffer and less functional—that is, more prone to injury. The jumping and playfulness that maintained balance is replaced with sitting and more sedentary activities, so the use-it-or-lose-it takes over, and we become increasingly less coordinated and more apt to fall. But older people can stay as limber and balanced as the young, if they are willing to spend a few minutes daily improving their range of motion.

Flexibility is the ability of the joints to move through their natural range of motion. Flexibility and balance exercises can be part of the five to ten minutes of your warm-up and cooldown sessions. Stretch slowly, don't bounce, and never stretch to the point of pain. Practice balancing activities, such as standing on one foot or doing stretching on an exercise ball. Also, don't forget to breathe while stretching or doing any exercise. Of course, vitality and a youthful appearance go hand in hand with good posture. Stretching can help you stand like an exclamation point, not a comma, which might take a bit of effort if you're not used to it, but you'll feel younger and more vital as a result.

Any previous injury to the joints or muscles may require extra precautions. If you are recovering from any injury, consult your physician or physical therapist in designing a safe and effective stretching program.

How do you know if you've sufficiently warmed up? The body temperature rises with good warm-up exercises. You've sufficiently warmed up when you break into a mild sweat.

How to Stick with It

He who postpones the hour of living rightly is like the rustic who
waits for the river to run out before he crosses.

—HORACE

You sign up at the local gym and start lifting weights or taking aerobics classes four times a week. By the third week, you're down to weekly sessions. By the second month, the gym bag is sitting at the back of the closet.

The promise of longevity isn't enough to induce most people to bounce out of bed at 5 A.M. for a jog or a workout at the gym. Some immediate reward must reinforce taking time out of the day to sweat, or you're likely to end up back on the couch. It may take up to six weeks for your body to get used to exercising daily without feeling some degree of fatigue. How do you give exercise a positive spin so you stick with it beyond the initial slump—or even beyond the customary one to six months, after which many people burn out? You need to redefine yourself and establish a system of rewards to stay motivated.

Define Yourself as an Exerciser

Throw out the old vision of yourself as inactive and start visualizing yourself as an exerciser. Look for excuses to exercise rather than reasons why you can't. Hang out with other people who exercise in their free time, or join a gym. Nurture your interests in exercise by reading books and magazines, renting exercise or fitness tapes, taking a tennis class, talking about exercise with other enthusiasts, or attending a motivational lecture. The shift in attitude happens gradually, but it slowly will transform how you view yourself and exercise, which in turn will motivate you to stick with it.

Develop a Motivation Plan

What motivates you to exercise? Is it a feeling of accomplishment? If so, place stars on a calendar for every day you are physically active, record each day's accomplishments in an exercise log, or place a dollar in a jar for every day you exercise and then use the money to buy something you've always wanted. Reward yourself whenever you reach a fitness goal: purchase clothes in your new smaller size, join a health club, or take a fitness-oriented vacation.

Do you crave more time with friends? Then use exercise as a way to enjoy their company. Write a contract with a fellow worker to walk for thirty minutes before work every day. At lunch, walk with friends and grab a light snack afterward at your desk. Do you and your spouse need more time together? Use exercise as an opportunity to discuss your day and share positive time. Research shows that one in every two people who stick with an exercise program do so because of family and social support.

Look for benefits and rewards beyond a drop in pounds or stars on a calendar. Do you notice improvements in your endurance level, your mental focus, or your

Your Workout Journal

The rules for moving are simple: the more consistently you exercise, the better you'll feel. Make a month's worth of copies of the page, or use the sheet as a guidepost and develop your own journal to record your daily activity. Your goal is to move for at least forty-five minutes every day, with four to five sessions of aerobic activity and at least two strength-training sessions per week. Review your journal each week, and summarize the benefits you experienced. By the end of the month, you will prove to yourself how important exercise is to your physical, emotional, and mental well-being!

Dates: _____

Long-Term Fitness Goal: _____

This Week's Goal: _____

DATE/DAY	ACTIVITY ST/AER.	TIME	INTENSITY*	HOW FELT AFTERWARD	OTHER BENEFITS**
_____	_____	_____	_____	_____	_____
_____	_____	_____	_____	_____	_____
_____	_____	_____	_____	_____	_____
_____	_____	_____	_____	_____	_____
_____	_____	_____	_____	_____	_____
_____	_____	_____	_____	_____	_____
_____	_____	_____	_____	_____	_____

ST = strength training
AER. = aerobic

Intensity: 1 = mild, 2 = moderate (broke a sweat), 3 = high

**Did you notice benefits in sleep patterns, energy level, general well-being, ability to concentrate or think, tolerance, stress level, relationships, mood, and so on?*

personal relationships, stress level, or mood? Pay attention to how different life is when you feel good. Maybe the difference is something as simple as not getting angry at the guy who cut you off on the freeway or having the staying power to solve a problem at work. Write down the benefits as you notice them, and tally the results each week.

The Bottom Line

Whenever you are asked if you can do a job, tell 'em, "Certainly I can!" Then get busy and find out how to do it.

—THEODORE ROOSEVELT

The most important message of this chapter is to *move*—for at least forty-five minutes every day for the rest of your life. If thoughts of target heart rates and stationary bicycles turn you off, forget those guidelines, at least at first. Just start by doing something every day. That will eventually lead to a little more until you will have walked away from recreational couch sitting and started on the road to lifelong fitness. Make physical activity a priority, and you'll change the way you grow old.

PART 2

Avoiding the Diseases of Aging

CHAPTER 9

Your Defense System Against Aging

> Do not go gentle into that good night. . . . Rage, rage against the dying of the light.
> —DYLAN THOMAS

While aging is intensely personal, it also is something we all share. That common bond comes with a few inevitables. All women experience menopause, where they cease ovulating and menstruating. Men don't experience anything quite so definite (unless a "male menopause" is verified); however, they share with women many age-related changes. The skin loses some of its youthful elasticity, and hair color changes. Vision worsens, and hearing fails. Joints wear out, giving us varying amounts of pain and disability. Just about every other age-related condition, from heart disease and cancer to sleep problems and osteoporosis, is more a matter of lifestyle than time.

It is not years alone that result in old age but how we choose to live them. The first step in preventing age-related illness is to stockpile your body's natural defense systems, such as the immune system and the antioxidant system.

Immune Power

> Despise no new accident in your body, but ask opinion of it.
>
> —FRANCIS BACON

Everything in the environment—from the air you breathe to the people you meet—constantly exposes you to bacteria, viruses, and other "germs" that cause infection or disease. In the past a person was considered a victim of these factors. Researchers now believe the body is more often than not an accomplice, not a victim, to disease.

Your Family Health History: Blueprint for Change

Any disease that runs in your family puts you at risk. The genes your parents passed to you are like links in a health chain; some links are strong and protect you, while others are weak and can break. Knowing your family health history helps you clarify your health chain, identify the weak links, and develop a personalized plan to prevent breaks.

Use the chart that follows to help identify diseases and health conditions that run in your family. Complete the chart, starting with grandparents. Fill in names, current age or age at death, and any diseases. Discuss the chart with your physician, and give a copy to your children.

Your Family's Health History Chart

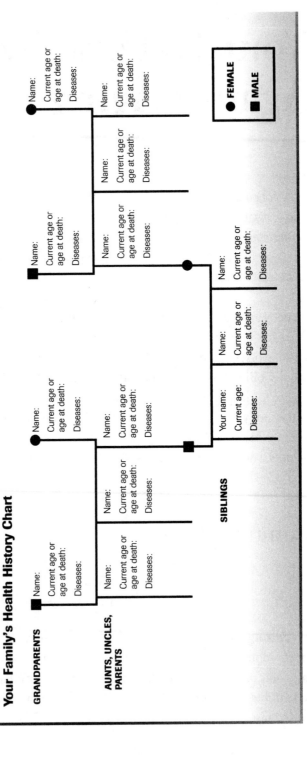

GRANDPARENTS

Name:
Current age or age at death:
Diseases:

AUNTS, UNCLES, PARENTS

Name:
Current age or age at death:
Diseases:

Name:
Current age or age at death:
Diseases:

Name:
Current age or age at death:
Diseases:

Name:
Current age or age at death:
Diseases:

Name:
Current age or age at death:
Diseases:

Name:
Current age or age at death:
Diseases:

Name:
Current age or age at death:
Diseases:

Name:
Current age or age at death:
Diseases:

SIBLINGS

Your name:
Current age:
Diseases:

Name:
Current age or age at death:
Diseases:

Name:
Current age or age at death:
Diseases:

● FEMALE

■ MALE

The condition of the immune system, one of the body's fundamental defense systems against foreign invaders and renegade cell growth such as cancer, is a critical factor in whether a person succumbs to infection, disease, and possibly even premature aging. (Keep in mind that the maximum life span of humans is currently set at 120 years; anything less than this is premature aging!)

A healthy immune system correctly recognizes a foreign substance, multiplies, calls for reinforcements, destroys the enemy, calls off the troops, and creates "memory" cells that file data on subversive invaders. A weakened immune system fails to recognize an invader or mounts a weak attack. The results can be chronic or repeated infections, more serious illnesses such as cancer, and an increased likelihood of dying before your time.

Immunity and Aging

Until recently, dwindling immune function was considered a natural consequence of aging. Upper respiratory infections, cancer, shingles, tuberculosis, and other immune-related disorders occur more frequently as people age, and older persons with suppressed immunity are the most likely to fall ill, develop complications from surgery, and even die earlier than their healthy counterparts. The link between suppressed immunity and advancing years was so strong that for some time researchers thought it was the drop in a person's immune system that caused aging.

Today we know that it is not age but the damage caused by years of eating poorly, inactivity, medication use, and/or illness that destroys the older body's ability to fight disease. The sooner you stop the damage, the less likely you are to become a victim to diseases later in life.

Vitality and Immune Function

People who are optimists have stronger immune systems and are less likely to succumb to disease than pessimists. If a person is stricken with disease, his or her tenacity in fighting the disease can marshall the body's defenses in ways modern medicine cannot equal. Granted, optimism and vitality can't ensure a disease-free life, but embracing these qualities increases the likelihood of health and makes any road you travel a lot more fun!

Boosting Immunity with Food and Supplements

"Unfortunately, you can't just look in the mirror to judge the immune system. A person can look healthy and feel good, but that is not an accurate indicator of a well- functioning immune system," says Adria Sherman, Ph.D., professor of nutritional sciences at Rutgers University. Dr. Sherman recommends good nutrition to help ensure the immune system remains intact and functions optimally. Research shows that seniors who eat well and supplement responsibly can stimulate immune activity, prevent many of the diseases once thought to be age related, and recover more quickly than someone whose immune system is weakened by inadequate nutritional supplies. For example, beta-carotene-rich produce, including carrots, sweet potatoes, apricots, and mangos, could be a fountain of youth, at least when it comes to immunity in the later years. Studies show that immune activity increases when beta-carotene intake is increased, even in people who prior to the study had low immune responses. In fact, beta-carotene-rich diets might bring immune function in seniors up to that of younger people, while seniors consuming beta-carotene-poor diets show continued low immune activity.

Studies from the USDA Human Nutrition Research Center on Aging at Tufts University and the International University of the Sciences in Switzerland show that supplementing seniors with single nutrients, such as vitamin B_6 or vitamin E, or with broad-range multiple vitamins and minerals boosts immune function. One study from the Memorial University of Newfoundland found that seniors who took multiple vitamin and mineral supplements for one year maintained or enhanced their bodies' natural defenses against disease, while the seniors who took placebos showed a decline in immune function.

All it takes is a moderate-dose multiple vitamin and mineral supplement to see significant improvement in disease resistance. Exceptions to this rule of moderation are vitamins E and C. Taking doses greater than can realistically be obtained from the diet—or approximately 100 to 400IU for vitamin E and 250 to 500 milligrams for vitamin C—might help adults keep their immune systems in peak performance.

Other nutrients, such as vitamin B_6, zinc, folic acid, vitamin B_{12}, and the phytochemicals, also are essential for proper immune function in the later years, yet often they are not consumed in optimal amounts, as evidenced by the following:

- In a study from Oregon State University in Corvallis, women who supplemented their diets with as little as 1 milligram of vitamin B_6 showed enhanced immune function.

- A study from Maimonides Medical Center in Brooklyn found that vitamin B_{12}-deficient elderly were less responsive to vaccines and, thus, were more susceptible to pneumococcus infections that could result in illness or death.
- Folic acid absorption often is reduced as a person ages, and poor dietary intake only worsens the deficiency, undermining immunity. In addition, folic acid is easily damaged by many medications, including antacids, diuretics used for high blood pressure, and anti-inflammatory medications.
- Researchers at Duke University in Durham, North Carolina, report that zinc contributes to immune function, along with protecting against ultraviolet (UV) radiation and enhancing wound healing. Other minerals, including iron, copper, magnesium, and selenium, also might aid in maintaining the immune system. Dr. Sherman adds, "Balance is the key with the minerals. These nutrients interact and it is their unified effect on immunity that is important." Dr. Sherman emphasizes that this balance is best found in nutritious foods, not supplements. The minerals also are examples of how some is good, but more is not necessarily better. For example, although moderate doses of zinc (15 to 30 milligrams a day) are beneficial, doses of 150 milligrams actually suppress immune function and might increase a person's risk for infection and disease.

A healthy immune system depends on more than just vitamins and minerals. Heart-healthy fats, such as the omega-3 fats in fish and the monounsaturated fats in nuts and olive oil, as well as soy, such as tofu and soy milk, also appear to boost immunity. Preliminary research also suggests that the phytochemicals in fruits and vegetables might help protect the immune system. In contrast, just as saturated fat clogs arteries and increases cancer risk, these fats also might suppress the immune response, increasing susceptibility to colds, infections, and disease.

The Antioxidant Defense System

Your man ages because he lets his body rust.

—TOM ROBBINS, FROM *JITTERBUG PERFUME*

Antioxidants—including the phytochemicals, vitamin E, and vitamin C—are key players in immunity, preventing the accumulation of free-radical damage to the immune system, much like oiling a cast-iron pan prevents it from rusting. "The

■ Snacks That Boost Your Immune System

- Red bell pepper slices and hummus dip
- Leftover chicken and vegetables wrapped in large, crisp spinach leaves and dipped in bottled hoisin sauce
- A bowl of kiwi halves and orange sections
- Bottled carrot juice or a glass of fresh-squeezed orange juice
- A serving of coleslaw made with low-fat dressing
- Vietnamese Black Bean Salad*
- Baked tortilla chips and homemade guacamole (avocado, diced tomato, chili peppers)
- A handful of almonds and dried plums
- Frozen blueberries
- Thai Ginger Cabbage Salad*
- Mango slices drizzled with lemon juice
- Lightly steamed vegetables (broccoli, asparagus, green beans, cauliflower, carrots, and so on) with low-fat ranch dressing or bean dip
- Apple slices and peanut butter
- Fresh Bowls of Berries with Sour Cream and Yogurt*
- Large tomato cut into quarters and topped with tuna salad made with fat-free mayonnaise

*Recipes in Appendix B.

gradual accumulation of free-radical damage results in many of the age-related changes we've grown accustomed to, from suppressed immune function to vision loss," states Dr. Blumberg, Ph.D., professor at the Friedman School of Nutrition Science and Policy at Tufts University in Boston.

The antioxidants protect the membranes of immune-related cells, thus strengthening the immune response, increasing resistance to infection, and reducing the risk for developing immune-related diseases such as cancer. Heaping the plate with antioxidant-rich broccoli, spinach, asparagus, dried plums, berries, mangos, oranges, and other colorful produce is one line of defense. Vitamins E and C in foods are very effective at stimulating immune function and the body's resistance to colds, infections, and disease. Additionally, ample intake of beta-carotene-rich

The Five Guidelines for Managing Medications

Here is a checklist to ensure your medications are used safely and only when needed:

1. Before you leave the doctor's office, ask the doctor about any possible side effects for any prescribed medications. If you are concerned about any medication being prescribed, say so and discuss your concerns. Ask about alternatives, such as counseling instead of tranquilizers or ice packs instead of anti-inflammatory medications.
2. Always ask your pharmacist these questions:
   - What is the name of the medication?
   - What is the medication for?
   - When is the best time to take it?
   - Are there any side effects? If so, what are they?
   - Are there any possible interactions with nutrients or other drugs?
3. Take only medications prescribed for you. Don't take anyone else's medications, and don't share your own.
4. If you take more than one prescription medication, especially if prescribed by more than one physician, take all the medications to a pharmacist to check interactions, dosages, and compatibility.
5. Take all expired medications to the local pharmacy for disposal.

foods, such as carrots, apricots, and broccoli, maintains the skin and mucous linings in the nose and lungs, which are the body's first line of defense against invasion.

Even marginal deficiencies of one or more of the antioxidant nutrients can compromise the body's defense system. Since typical American diets are low in the antioxidants, many people are at nutritional risk and don't even know it. In addition, diet alone might not be enough. "Recent evidence shows that a person must consume at least 400IU of vitamin E daily to experience immune-enhancing effects. You must resort to odd eating habits and be the size of a small whale to get that much vitamin E from food," says William Pryor, Ph.D., Boyd Professor of Chemistry and Biochemistry and director of the Biodynamics Institute at Louisiana State University. Consequently, some researchers recommend supplements.

However, other researchers disagree. "With a proper diet, a person can get all the nutrients needed for optimal immune function," says Robert Jacob, Ph.D., at the Western Human Nutrition Research Center, USDA Agricultural Research Service in San Francisco. According to Dr. Jacob, it takes approximately 200 milligrams of vitamin C (the amount obtained from one cup of orange juice and two-thirds of a cup of strawberries) to keep the immune system running smoothly. However, many people do not eat even recommended levels of 60 milligrams of vitamin C each day. The key is to combine responsible supplementation with a fruit- and vegetable-rich diet to maximize intake of both antioxidant nutrients and phytochemicals.

The Total Picture

Never give up and never give in.

—HUBERT H. HUMPHREY

"Whether the attacking organism or the immune system prevails depends on many factors, including a person's nutritional status, general health, stress level, and sleep patterns, as well as the force of the onslaught," says Darshan Kelley, Ph.D., research chemist at the Western Human Nutrition Research Center in San Francisco. Consequently, the dietary guidelines outlined in the Antiaging Diet can't guarantee protection from all infections and diseases, but, until the last piece in the diet-immunity puzzle is found, they will greatly improve your odds of winning the war.

Medications on the Menu

Always carry a flagon of whisky in case of snakebite and furthermore, always carry a small snake.

—W. C. FIELDS

Half of all Americans take at least one prescription medication. Five in every six seniors take a medication, and half of the elderly take three or more prescriptions, according to the Centers for Disease Control and Prevention. Few are aware of the impact many medications have on nutritional status.

Drug-Nutrient Interactions

DRUG	NUTRIENTS AFFECTED	WHAT TO DO/CONSEQUENCES
Acetaminophen	Liver damage caused by this pain reliever might be reduced by beta-carotene.	Consume several daily servings of beta-carotene-rich carrots, apricots, and spinach.
Alcohol	Replaces nutritious food. Increases requirements for B vitamins. Increases need for antioxidants. Inhibits absorption of vitamin C, B vitamins, calcium, and fat-soluble vitamins. Alters metabolism of vitamins D, B_1, B_6, and folic acid. Depletes tissues of vitamins A and E and selenium.	Limit alcohol intake to fewer than five drinks per week. Consume a nutrient-rich diet and take a moderate-dose multiple vitamin daily.
Antacids	Reduce absorption of vitamins A and B_{12}, iron, and folic acid. All-calcium antacids may upset magnesium balance.	Take antacids between meals and not with supplements. Take extra magnesium.
Antiarthritic medications (d-penicillamine)	Reduce absorption of iron, zinc, and vitamin B_6.	Increase intake of legumes, whole grains, bananas, and wheat germ.
Antibiotics	Alter production and absorption of biotin and vitamins C and K.	Consume several dark green leafy vegetables and citrus fruits daily.
Tetracycline	Reduces absorption of calcium in milk products. Reduces tissue levels of vitamins A and C.	Drink milk at opposite time of day from when taking the antibiotic. Consume five or more servings of fruits and vegetables daily.

Continued

DRUG	NUTRIENTS AFFECTED	WHAT TO DO/CONSEQUENCES
Arthritis medications (penicillamine)	Reduce absorption of zinc, iron, and other minerals. Increase requirements for vitamin B_6.	Take medication between meals. Consult a physician about drug-nutrient interactions.
Aspirin	Irritates digestive tract, leading to internal bleeding, and consequently reduces iron stores. Large doses can reduce absorption of folic acid and vitamins C and B_{12}.	Take aspirin in the morning and supplements at night. Have a physician monitor status.
Caffeine	Tannins in coffee and tea reduce iron absorption.	Take extra vitamin C. Drink coffee or tea between meals rather than with food.
Cholesterol-lowering medications (cholestyramine and colestipol)	Reduce absorption of folic acid; iron; vitamins A, D, E, B_{12}, and K; and beta-carotene.	Increase intake of chicken, leafy vegetables, and nonfat milk, and/or take a supplement that contains these nutrients.
High blood pressure medications	May increase urinary excretion of potassium, calcium, or magnesium.	Consume potassium-rich fruits and vegetables; magnesium-rich green leafy vegetables, soybeans, and wheat germ; and calcium-rich milk. Or take a moderate-dose supplement.
Laxatives	Increase excretion of calcium, potassium, and vitamin D.	Deficiencies can result with long-term use. Consult a physician about these effects and the need for supplements.
Mineral oil	Increases excretion of vitamins A, D, E, and K.	Consult a physician about long-term effects of taking this laxative.
Phenobarbital	Reduces absorption of folic acid and vitamins B_{12} and D.	Increase intake of nonfat milk, dark green leafy vegetables, and lean meat.

DRUG	NUTRIENTS AFFECTED	WHAT TO DO/CONSEQUENCES
Prozac	May reduce cravings for carbohydrates.	Some people experience a temporary loss of appetite and weight. Eat small meals and snacks throughout the day to sustain energy.
Sulfasalazine	Reduces absorption of folic acid.	Increase intake of dark green leafy vegetables, orange juice, and wheat germ.
Tobacco	Increases requirements for or lowers tissue levels of beta-carotene; folic acid; vitamins A, E, C, B_6, and B_{12}; and other nutrients.	Don't smoke or inhale others' smoke.

Medications can affect nutritional status in four ways:

1. They increase or decrease appetite, which reduces vitamin and mineral intake or results in overconsumption of nutrient-poor foods. Some medications also produce side effects that influence appetite, such as nausea, heartburn, or an altered sense of taste.
2. They interfere with the absorption of nutrients, resulting in marginal vitamin and mineral deficiencies even when dietary intake is adequate.
3. They alter how the body uses or transports a nutrient or might entirely block the body's use of a vitamin or mineral.
4. They increase vitamin and mineral excretion, so nutrients are drained from the body faster than they are replaced.

The best defense against drug-nutrient interactions is to consume a nutrient-packed diet rich in fruits, vegetables, whole grains, nuts, soy, olive oil, extra-lean meat, legumes, and nonfat milk products. In addition, always read the medication label and consult your physician and pharmacist to learn everything you can about the medications you are asked to take.

CHAPTER 10

How to Prevent the Diseases of Aging

Our body is a machine for living. It is organized for that, it is its nature. Let life go on in it unhindered and let it defend itself, it will do more than if you paralyze it by encumbering it with remedies.

—LEO TOLSTOY,
FROM *WAR AND PEACE*

Old is what you get if you're lucky. Disease is what you get if you're not. Eating well, exercising regularly, managing stress, avoiding tobacco, maintaining a desirable weight, limiting alcohol, and adhering to other positive lifestyle habits can have profound effects on lowering your risk of developing disease in the second fifty years. In fact, a recent study found that seniors who followed healthy diets, drank alcohol in moderation, exercised daily, and did not smoke (in other words, followed the Antiaging Diet and Fitness Program in this book) lowered their risk for dying from any cause by 65 percent!

Unfortunately, many diseases just happen despite the best habits. Even then, a healthful lifestyle can help minimize the effects of a disease, shorten its duration, lessen the symptoms, improve the odds for recovery, and help give you the vitality and energy needed to fight for your health.

This chapter provides an overview of the latest research on how diet can reduce the risk of most age-related diseases, from arthritis and cancer to aging skin and osteoporosis. In all cases, the foundation for prevention is the Antiaging Diet and Fitness Program. Modify these guidelines based on the dietary recommendations for each disorder.

The Big Four

Work and struggle and never accept an evil that you can change.

—ANDRÉ GIDE

Most people would extend their lives if they avoided the four main diseases: heart disease, hypertension, diabetes, and cancer. For example,

- More than 105 million Americans have blood cholesterol levels higher than 200mg/dL, placing them at risk for heart disease. Of those, approximately 42 million have levels greater than 240mg/dL.
- More than 71 million Americans already have cardiovascular disease—that's one in every three persons.
- More than 50 million Americans have high blood pressure.
- More than 2,500 Americans die each day—or at least one person every 35 seconds—from heart disease.
- Almost 21 million people, or 7 percent of the U.S. population, have diabetes, and the numbers increase every day.
- Almost 1.4 million new cases of cancer will be diagnosed in the United States this year, or about 1,500 every day.

The statistics on the Big Four are staggering, especially when you consider that two out of every three people whose lives are affected by one or more of these diseases could have prevented the pain, suffering, and loss of life merely by making a few simple changes in their diet and exercise.

A Common Bond

These diseases have a lot in common. If you have either hypertension or diabetes, your risk of heart disease doubles; if you have both conditions, the risk is fourfold. In fact, heart disease is the leading cause of diabetes-related deaths. Combine either diabetes or hypertension with smoking and your risk for heart disease goes up eight-fold. Smoking also elevates your risk for hypertension and cancer.

Inactivity and excess body fat, especially if it's around the waist, dramatically increase a person's risk for developing all of the Big Four. Inactivity leads to weight gain, elevated blood fats, and reduced blood sugar regulation, setting up a condition called the metabolic syndrome, which will be discussed later in this chapter. For example, compared with lean people, overweight people have the following:

- A 7.37 times greater risk for developing diabetes
- A 6.38 times greater risk for high blood pressure
- A 1.88 times greater risk for elevated blood cholesterol

Exercising daily, avoiding tobacco smoke, consuming a healthful diet, and coping effectively with stress result in lower body weight, reduced blood cholesterol levels, elevated HDL (good) cholesterol levels, improved glucose tolerance, normalization of blood pressure, and possibly a lowered risk of developing cancer. Heart disease, diabetes, hypertension, and cancer are linked to free-radical damage to the tissues, while increased intake of the antioxidant nutrients minimizes the damage and possibly lowers disease risk.

Most of these diseases are preventable. The vast majority of cancers caused by cigarette smoking or alcohol—especially cancers of the lungs, bladder, esophagus, and stomach—could be prevented by making healthier choices. Up to 95 percent of many cancers can be effectively treated if diagnosis is made in the early stages of the disease. Most diabetics and people with hypertension could be free from their disease just by losing excess body weight. Heart disease is preventable, curable, and even reversible in one out of every two cases by making better food, exercise, and lifestyle choices.

Heart Disease and Hypertension

A man is only as old as his arteries.

—SIR WILLIAM OSLER

Heart disease remains the number-one killer disease in this country, despite a drop in death rates in the past few decades. The best news is that heart disease is preventable and treatable in most cases and gives most people fair warning—elevated blood cholesterol levels and low HDL cholesterol levels. Keeping total cholesterol at or below 200mcg/dL and the ratio of total cholesterol to HDL cholesterol at or below 4.5:1; maintaining normal blood pressure, homocysteine levels, and C-reactive protein levels; and preventing or managing diabetes can lower your risk dramatically.

▪ *Red Flags for the Metabolic Syndrome*

Pudgy stomach:	Women—more than 31-inch waist
	Men—more than 37- to 40-inch waist
Blood triglycerides:	150mg/dL or higher
Total cholesterol:	Above 200mg/dL
HDL cholesterol:	Women—under 50mg/dL
	Men—under 40mg/dL
Blood pressure:	Systolic—greater than 120mmHg
	Diastolic—greater than 80mmHg
Blood sugar:	Fasting is 110mg/dL or higher (100 to 125 is "prediabetes")
C-reactive protein:	Above 3mg/L
Homocysteine:	Above 7mmol/L

The development of heart disease and its underlying cause, atherosclerosis (narrowing of the arteries caused by cholesterol accumulation), is often part of a more complex condition, the metabolic syndrome, that includes an increased risk for high blood pressure, glucose intolerance and diabetes, excess body fat, and high blood fat levels (such as cholesterol and triglycerides). Increased weight elevates blood pressure and cholesterol and places increased stress on the heart and blood vessels. While virtually everyone has some degree of cholesterol accumulation in the arteries by the second decade of life, the condition progresses to disease states for about half the population.

The Good and Bad Fats

The three most important habits you can adopt to prevent, treat, and even reverse heart disease is to maintain a desirable weight, exercise daily, and not smoke. After those three factors, cutting back or cutting out saturated and trans fats is critical to reducing heart disease risk. Reducing dietary saturated and trans fats lowers blood cholesterol levels, slows the progression of atherosclerosis, and decreases your risk for heart attack. Cutting back on saturated fat also helps lower levels of C-reactive protein, a risk factor for inflammation of the arteries and atherosclerosis. Even modest changes in the diet can lower blood cholesterol as much as 10 percent, with a subsequent reduction in heart disease risk of 20 percent.

The oil in fish, nuts, avocados, and olive oil are exceptions to the fat–heart disease connection. These healthy foods—when combined with a low-fat, high-fiber, calorie-controlled diet—decrease blood fat levels and help lower blood pressure, which in turn lowers the risk for atherosclerosis and heart disease. As little as four ounces of salmon or one and a half ounces of nuts can benefit the heart if consumed on a regular basis.

Fiber for Your Heart and Arteries

The second most important dietary change a person can make is to increase fibrous foods in the diet. The soluble fibers in oats, cooked dried beans and peas, and fruit lower blood cholesterol and low-density lipoprotein cholesterol (LDLs), the "bad" cholesterol linked to heart-disease risk. Both soluble fibers in oats, beans, and fruit and the insoluble fibers in whole grains and vegetables help decrease the production and increase the excretion of cholesterol and help reduce blood pressure, all of which lower a person's risk for heart disease.

Fiber-rich whole foods offer more protection against heart disease than processed foods. In a study from the Harvard School of Public Health, men who consumed the most whole grains had an 18 percent reduction in heart disease risk, while a high intake of bran lowered risk by 30 percent. The researchers concluded that the bran component of whole grains could be a key factor in the relationship between grains and heart disease. Researchers at Wageningen University in The Netherlands found that boosting fiber intake by as little as an additional 11.5 grams is enough to lower both systolic and diastolic blood pressures. The benefits are greatest in people over the age of forty and in people with high blood pressure, but lesser benefits also are noted in younger people and in people with normal blood pressure. While fiber-rich whole grains lower the risk for stroke, women who chow down on too many refined carbohydrates might increase their stroke risk, according to a study from the Harvard School of Public Health.

The Bottom Line on Salt

The National Institutes of Health warns that everyone should reduce his or her intake of salt to prevent hypertension, and the latest U.S. dietary guidelines recommend limiting salt to no more than 6 grams (slightly more than a teaspoon) per day. Further reduction to 4.5 grams or less is best for people who are "salt sensitive" and develop high blood pressure when they consume excessive amounts of salt. Salt (sodium chloride) is 40 percent sodium, so this recommendation is the equivalent of 2.4 grams (2,400 milligrams) of sodium.

To prevent or treat hypertension, include several servings a day of calcium-rich foods and lots of potassium-rich fruits and vegetables. Numerous studies show that it is the combined effect of too much salt and too little calcium and potassium that might predispose a person to hypertension (along with excess body fat!). You should consume the equivalent of three to four glasses of nonfat or low-fat milk, yogurt, or fortified soy milk each day and at least eight servings of fruits and vegetables to get enough of these two minerals.

Vitamins, Minerals, and Your Heart

Even the most carefully designed diet can fall short of optimal when daily calorie intake is below 2,000 or when disease or medication use increases nutrient needs above normal requirements. In addition, some nutrients, such as vitamin E, are needed in amounts far greater than are realistic from diet alone. Consequently, a moderate-dose multiple vitamin and mineral plus an extra dose of vitamin E should be considered.

Several B vitamins are important in the prevention of heart disease or hypertension. Nicotinic acid (a form of niacin) lowers both total cholesterol and LDL cholesterol while raising high-density lipoprotein cholesterol (HDLs), the beneficial form of blood cholesterol. Pharmacological doses (doses greater than are typically consumed from foods) of niacin in conjunction with cholesterol-lowering medications are effective in the management of heart disease. Niacin therapy can cause adverse side effects, however, and should be monitored by a physician.

Optimal intake of vitamins B_6 and B_{12} as well as folic acid also are associated with a reduced risk for heart disease. These B vitamins are essential in controlling a compound called homocysteine. Levels of this compound rise when the diet is low in these vitamins, increasing a person's risk of heart disease even if other factors, such as blood cholesterol, remain low. "It appears that the amount people need are greater than current recommendations," states Robert Russell, M.D., professor of medicine and nutrition at Tufts University. The Antiaging Diet plus a supplement that supplies at least 400 micrograms of folic acid, 3 micrograms of vitamin B_{12}, and 2 milligrams of vitamin B_6 will help keep homocysteine levels in the normal range.

Adequate intake of the antioxidant nutrients and phytochemicals might lower the "bad" blood cholesterol levels while elevating the "good" HDL cholesterol. The phytoestrogens in soy milk and tofu, the flavonoids in fruits, lycopene in tomatoes, and vitamins C and E all show promise in lowering cholesterol, possibly reducing inflammation associated with atherosclerosis, and reducing heart disease risk.

Magnesium relaxes artery walls and the heart muscle. A deficiency of this mineral results in hypertension, irregular heartbeat, chest pain associated with reduced blood and oxygen to the heart, atherosclerosis, and damage to the heart. Supplementing with magnesium might return the heartbeat and blood pressure to normal and reduce the chances of experiencing a heart attack. In addition, the doses of many heart and blood pressure medications often can be reduced when magnesium intake is optimal. Some hypertension medications increase urinary loss of magnesium and increase the risk for marginal deficiency of this essential mineral.

The guidelines for a healthy heart are simple:

- Maintain a desirable weight. This is *the* most important step a person can take to lower risk. Even a modest weight loss of ten to twenty pounds can reduce blood pressure, cholesterol levels, and heart disease risk, while improving glucose tolerance and other indicators of the metabolic syndrome.
- Consume no more than 30 percent of total calories as fat (that is, choose nonfat dairy products and lean meats, and use little or no fat in food preparation) with most of that fat coming from fish and monounsaturated fats in olive or canola oils and nuts.
- Limit saturated and trans fats to no more than 10 percent of total calories (the lower the better).
- Limit salt by choosing unprocessed foods, avoiding fast foods, and using herbs instead of salt when cooking or preparing foods at home.
- Limit cholesterol to no more than 300 milligrams a day (one egg contains 220 milligrams of cholesterol; whole milk contains 34 milligrams of cholesterol per cup; one ounce of cheddar cheese contains 28 milligrams).
- Include 25 to 45 grams of fiber in the daily diet by choosing a wide range of fiber-rich whole-grain products, cooked dried beans and peas, and fresh fruits and vegetables. Make sure that three out of every four foods you eat are plant derived, including vegetables, fruit, whole grains, and legumes.
- Exercise every day for at least thirty minutes at a moderate-intensity pace (you are breathing heavily and/or sweating).

Diabetes Under Control

Don't fight forces, use them.

—RICHARD BUCKMINSTER FULLER

Diabetes is a disease characterized by the body's inability to produce or properly use insulin, the hormone that regulates blood-sugar levels. One form of diabetes, insulin-dependent (or type 1) diabetes, is an autoimmune disease that usually develops in children and young adults; it can be controlled through diet, exercise, and daily insulin injections.

Up to 95 percent of diabetics have the other form, non-insulin-dependent (or type 2) diabetes (sometimes called adult-onset diabetes), which results from the body's inability to make enough or efficiently use insulin. This form of diabetes is almost always caused by inactivity, poor eating habits, and excess body weight. Maintain or regain a desirable body weight, and blood sugar levels almost always normalize.

Why Do People Develop Type 2 Diabetes?

The body uses a simple sugar called glucose for energy. Glucose is obtained from carbohydrates in the diet, including starches and sugars. That energy is obtained when we eat and digest food. Glucose enters the bloodstream from the digestive tract, and the rising blood glucose levels signal the pancreas to release a hormone called insulin, which helps transport the rising blood glucose into the cells of the muscles, brain, liver, and other organs. This process provides fuel for the tissues and returns blood glucose levels to normal.

In overweight people, the body's cells are insensitive to insulin, so blood glucose levels remain high. The pancreas tries to overcompensate by secreting more insulin, and the result is a condition called insulin resistance or hyperinsulinemia (high insulin levels in the blood). Left unchecked, this condition can progress to diabetes, in which both insulin and glucose levels remain high. In diabetics, elevated insulin levels also promote the conversion of glucose into fat. Insulin resistance is part of a larger health problem known as the metabolic syndrome, which is associated with above-the-belt fat accumulation, high blood fats, diabetes, hypertension, and an elevated risk for developing heart disease as well as possibly some forms of cancer.

Low-carb diets state that carbohydrates make us fat and cause diabetes, but these fad diets have put the cart before the horse. In reality, eating too many calories from any combination of foods causes excess body weight, which in turn causes hyperinsulinemia and diabetes. Lose the weight, by eating right and exercising, and insulin and blood sugar levels normalize in the vast majority of people. In people who exercise, less insulin is needed to move more glucose into the cells, so less of the hormone is secreted by the pancreas in response to food intake. Consequently, more incoming glucose is burned in the muscles for energy and less is stored as fat. Exercise also protects against insulin resistance by improving the body's ability to mobilize fat from storage for fuel, which prevents fat accumulation. The leaner cells also respond more quickly and efficiently to insulin, so less of the hormone is needed to transport glucose out of the blood. Consequently, daily exercise reduces diabetes risk even in the absence of weight loss.

To prevent type 2 diabetes, do the following:

- Attain and maintain a desirable weight by following the Antiaging Diet and Fitness Program.
- Emphasize fiber-rich foods in the diet, especially cooked dried beans and peas, oats, nuts, and vegetables. These foods help normalize blood sugar levels.
- Keep refined sugar, fat, alcohol, and unnecessary calories in check. In particular, cut back or cut out high-fat fast food and soft drinks. Studies, such as those from the University of Minnesota and Harvard University, repeatedly find that people who eat at fast-food restaurants as few as three times a week or who drink soda gain an extra ten pounds and have twice the risk of developing insulin resistance, a warning sign of diabetes.
- Eat quality carbs. The American Diabetes Association states that low-carb diets are not recommended for diabetics, since whole grains are an important source of energy, nutrients, and fiber. Carbohydrate intake should range from 45 to 65 percent of total calories and should not fall below 130 grams a day. However, monitoring the amount and type of carbohydrate, by using diabetic exchanges or carbohydrate counting, remains a key strategy in achieving blood sugar control.
- Take a moderate-dose multiple vitamin and mineral that contains 200 micrograms of chromium, 400IU of vitamin D, the antioxidants including vitamins E and C, and the B vitamins. Make sure you consume ample amounts of magnesium-rich foods, such as bananas, dark green leafy vegetables, nuts, and wheat germ, or take a magnesium supplement.

Cancer Cures

If I'd known I was going to live so long, I'd have taken better care of myself.

—EUBIE BLAKE

Today fewer people older than fifty are dying from heart disease, but more are dying from cancer. By far the greatest contributor to cancer is smoking, with women being five to six times more likely to die from tobacco-related cancers than their grandmothers who didn't smoke. In fact, if lung cancer is excluded from the statistics, the cancer death toll has dropped in this country since the 1930s. Unfortunately, however, breast cancer is on the rise and is twice as common today as it was in women a hundred years ago.

The good news is that you can decrease your risk. One in every two people with cancer could avoid an untimely death and suffering if they had made a few changes in their lifestyles, state researchers at the Harvard Center for Cancer Prevention in Boston, who recommend the following guidelines:

- **Don't smoke.** Tobacco is the major cause of preventable death, accounting for 5 million deaths each year. Smoking also costs a person more than thirteen years of life.
- **Exercise.** More than six out of every ten Americans do not exercise regularly. Inactivity contributes to 2 million deaths each year, including deaths related to diabetes, osteoporosis, stroke, heart disease, and several cancers (such as colon and breast cancers).
- **Stay lean.** Overweight or obesity contributes to 2.5 million deaths each year. Currently, almost seven out of every ten Americans are overweight, and 30 percent are obese. Excessive body fat is linked to an increased risk for colorectal, breast, endometrial, renal, and esophageal cancers. It also might raise risks for prostate, liver, gallbladder, pancreas, stomach, ovary, and cervical cancers.
- **Eat well.** People who consume lots of fruits, vegetables, folic acid–rich foods, selenium-rich foods, and fiber—and who consume little or no saturated or trans fat and red meat—have the lowest risk for cancer.
- **Drink in moderation.** Excessive alcohol consumption is associated with more than 1.8 million deaths each year, including deaths from liver, oral,

esophageal, breast, and colorectal cancers. Women should limit intake to no more than one drink a day, men to two drinks or less per day.

- **Use sunscreen.** Sun exposure increases the risk for basal cell carcinoma, squamous cell carcinoma, and malignant melanoma. The incidence of skin cancer is rising faster than any other cancer.
- **Practice safe sex.** Unsafe sex is responsible for 2.9 million deaths each year, primarily because of HIV transmission but also because of the transmission of cancer-causing viruses that contribute to cervical, vulvar, penile, and anal cancers.
- **Get tested.** Regular screenings for cervical and colorectal cancers reduce cancer death rates through early detection and treatment.

Hormones, Fat, and Cancer

The causes of cancer have evaded researchers for years. One link, at least with breast cancer, seems clear-cut: women in cultures with a low breast cancer incidence, such as Japan, also have significantly lower levels of a group of female hormones called estrogens. Women in the United States, where breast cancer risk is high, have up to a 75 percent higher level of estrogen than do women in Japan.

The lower hormone levels might have more to do with diet than with genetics. Studies show that when Japanese women migrate to the United States and adopt a Western lifestyle, their risks and their children's risks of developing breast cancer rise to match those of American women. One possible explanation is that breast cancer rates soar as Japanese women abandon their low-fat diets in favor of high-fat American cuisine. Other studies report similar findings. In fact, one study found that women's risk for breast cancer increases as much as 30 percent for every 10 percent increase in fat calories. The fat issue also is firmly documented in studies on animals. Animals fed high-fat diets get cancer, while those fed leaner fare don't. Research is contradictory, however, when the fat-cancer link is studied in people living in the same country. Without consistent findings, the effect of dietary fat on cancer remains controversial.

"Regarding breast cancer, there is a huge amount of data showing that the large amounts of fat in the U.S. diet are doing something and it's not good," warns Leonard Cohen, Ph.D., section head of nutrition and endocrinology at the American Health Foundation in Valhalla, New York. According to Dr. Cohen, dietary fat is a promoter, not an initiator, of the cancer process and probably exerts its effects by altering expression of the genetic code within cells, affecting regulatory processes in cell membranes, and upsetting estrogen balance. The effects of fat on estrogen also make it reasonable to assume that a high-fat diet of hamburgers and French fries during puberty, when these hormones kick in to initiate breast development, could set the stage for cancer later in life. Dietary fat also shows harmful effects when it comes to other cancers, such as colon and rectal cancers.

Another theory highlights the type, not the amount, of fat in the diet. "Just like people have different personalities, different fats also have different effects on cancer risk and shouldn't be lumped together as all bad," says Dr. Cohen. For example, polyunsaturated fats in safflower and other vegetable oils raise levels of hormonelike compounds called prostaglandins, which in turn promote some types of cancers, such as prostate and breast cancers. Saturated fats in meat also escalate risk for several types of cancer including colon cancer, while olive or canola oil, nuts, and the oils in fish might suppress cancer growth.

"There is more evidence that monounsaturated oils [such as olive and canola oils] lower cancer risk, than there is evidence that total fat intake raises risk," says Walter Willett, M.D., Dr.P.H. at the Harvard School of Public Health. One study found that omega-3 fats in conjunction with a healthy diet lowered the risk for developing breast, colorectal, and prostate cancers by up to 70 percent. Unfortunately, no one knows exactly how much olive oil or fish oil is best, but most agree that cutting back on total fat—with more coming from olive or canola oil and fish and less coming from meat, dairy, and other vegetable oils—is a safe and potentially healthful start.

Another advantage of switching to a low-fat diet is that this eating style might help a person maintain a desirable body weight. Obesity is related to several cancers, from colon to breast cancer. You don't have to be obese to develop cancer. Even moderately overweight people are at elevated risk, with the risk rising as body weight increases. Even the chances of surviving cancer are worse if a person is overweight. Studies on animals consistently show that cutting back on calories lowers cancer rates. People who store more fat above the belt compared with those who carry their extra weight in the hips and thighs also are more likely to have higher estrogen levels and higher risks of developing cancer. This link between belly fat, disease, and estrogens might explain why cutting calories and increasing exercise, two ways to reduce fat weight, also lower estrogen levels and disease risk.

Fruits and Vegetables

Follow the Antiaging Diet guidelines by boosting your intake of fruits and vegetables, and you might reduce the risk for cancer by 25 percent or more. Fruits and vegetables are packed with cancer-fighting nutrients, including fiber, folic acid, and the antioxidant nutrients. Diets rich in produce are linked to lower estrogen levels and breast cancer risk in women and to lower risk for numerous cancers, from lung cancer to colon cancer, in men and women. Studies show up to a 76 percent lower risk for certain cancers, such as ovarian cancer, when people consume produce-rich diets.

They also are Mother Nature's best source of phytochemicals. Researchers at Cornell University explain that it is the wealth of phytochemicals in fruits and vegetables that give them their health-enhancing capabilities. For example, the vitamin C in apples accounts for only 0.4 percent of the total antioxidants, the other 99.6 percent coming primarily from phytochemicals, such as phenolics and flavonoids. Examples of how phytochemicals lower cancer risk include the following:

- The phytochemicals in cranberries, such as the flavonol glycosides, anthocyanins, proanthocyanidins (tannins), and organic and phenolic acids, lower cancer risk.
- Women who consume the most fiber or lignans reduce their cancer risk by 57 percent, while risk is reduced by 67 percent with high carotenoid intake, by 58 percent with high intake of stigmasterol (a phytosterol), and by 53 percent with high vegetable intake.
- A study from the University of Arizona Cancer Center in Tucson found that women who consumed the most fruits and vegetables rich in carotenoids, such as lutein or zeaxanthin and beta-cryptoxanthin, had a lower risk for cervical cancer.
- Phytochemicals in pomegranates and grapes might help protect against skin damage associated with the million cases each year of skin cancer diagnosed in the United States, according to a report from the University of Arizona.
- Researchers at the University of Illinois at Urbana-Champaign report that fresh and processed tomatoes and their phytochemicals reduce the risk for prostate cancer.

Are You Getting Enough Lycopene?

You need approximately 10 milligrams a day of lycopene.

LYCOPENE	MILLIGRAMS/3-OUNCE SERVING
Tomato paste	42.2
Spaghetti sauce	21.9
Chili sauce	19.5
Tomato ketchup	15.9
Tomato juice	9.5
Pink grapefruit	4.0
Raw tomato	3.0

Soy Good

Fat is not the only link to low estrogen levels in Japanese women. These women also consume thirty to fifty times more soy foods—which contain an arsenal of anti-cancer compounds called phytoestrogens, with genistein and daidzein appearing to be the most potent—than do women in the United States.

The protective effects of phytoestrogens have been substantiated in studies on animals. Only 60 percent of newborn female rats exposed to chemicals known to cause breast cancer actually develop cancer when their diets are supplemented with phytoestrogens, while 100 percent of unsupplemented rats develop cancer. Soy products also are an excellent source of fiber, which might lower estrogen and cancer risk in its own right. One study from the American Health Foundation in New York reported that estrogen levels dropped significantly within two months when people increased their fiber intake from 15 to 30 grams a day.

How do phytoestrogens work? According to Johanna Dwyer, D.Sc., R.D., professor of medicine and community health at Tufts University School of Medicine, phytoestrogens might bind to receptor sites on breast cells that otherwise bind to estrogen, which reduces the cell-altering effects of the hormone. While suspicions that soy might increase cancer risk in some people have not been substantiated by the research, it is probably best to err on the side of caution and consume only modest amounts of soy foods if you have a personal history of breast or prostate cancer and avoid supplements containing soy or isoflavones. Otherwise, while the optimal daily or weekly dose of soy products has not been established, two or more servings weekly would provide a low-fat, high-fiber alternative to meat and should

Soy Solutions

In a quandary over how to add soy to your diet? Here are a few tasty suggestions:

- Add tofu to enchiladas, pasta primavera, lasagna, and stir-fries.
- Blend silken tofu to make a creamy base for soups, dips, salad dressings, and sauces.
- Crumble tofu into salads (it picks up the flavor of the dressing).
- Use fortified soy milk in preparing packaged pudding mixes, on cereal, in cream sauces, or as a coffee creamer.
- Replace hamburgers with textured vegetable patties (made from soybeans) from the frozen food section.
- Snack on roasted soy nuts.
- Serve edamame (green soybeans) as a side dish or mix into rice dishes.

benefit overall health as well as possibly aid in cancer prevention. For women at low risk for breast cancer and men in general, no upper limit for soy has been established.

How to Prevent Cancer

We don't have firm answers yet about what factors—dietary or otherwise—affect cancer risk. What we do know is that cancer is a multistage process, so a person's best bet is to block that process with a host of healthful foods at as many steps along the way as possible. To do this:

1. Limit your intake of potential initiators or promoters of cancer by cutting back on red meat, processed meat, saturated fat, snack chips, French fries and other fried vegetables, and alcohol. Prepare meats by baking, broiling, or poaching rather than by frying or charbroiling.
2. Base your diet on foods that contain cancer-fighting compounds, such as fiber-rich fruits, vegetables, herbs and spices, and whole grains. Make sure some vegetables come from the cabbage family, such as broccoli, asparagus, Brussels sprouts, and cauliflower. These vegetables are rich in phytochemicals, called indoles, that reduce cancer risk.

3. Consume a diet rich in calcium and vitamin D (nonfat milk and fortified soy milk or orange juice are the most reliable sources). These nutrients combined with a low-fat diet lower colon cancer risk by up to 25 percent.

4. Consume moderate amounts of monounsaturated fats from nuts and olive or canola oil as a substitute for other fats. Choose wild fish instead of farmed fish, which is higher in cancer-causing contaminants.

5. Include several servings weekly of soy foods, such as tofu, soy milk, and/or soybeans.

6. Don't smoke or expose yourself to other people's smoke.

7. Exercise daily and for life. As little as a two-mile walk each day throughout life can cut your risk in half for developing several types of cancer. The minimum is thirty minutes of at least moderate activity five or more days a week. Vigorous activity for forty-five minutes or more will further reduce cancer risk. Children need at least sixty minutes of vigorous activity daily.

8. Maintain a desirable weight throughout life.

9. Take a supplement that includes additional antioxidant nutrients, including vitamins C and E.

10. Drink tea, green or black, decaffeinated or regular. Phytochemicals in tea help lower cancer risk. The same does not hold true for herbal teas.

Dr. Dwyer is right when she says, "There isn't a magic or miracle food that will cure or prevent cancer." However, there might be many health-enhancing compounds in a variety of wholesome foods that could do the trick.

Arthritis: Staying Limber

Let me tell you the secret that has led me to my goal.
My strength lies solely in my tenacity.

—LOUIS PASTEUR

You can wrap your wrists in copper bracelets, drink vinegar and honey, chug Dr. Smedley's miracle potion, take shark cartilage capsules, or inject snake venom, but don't expect any of these quick-fix remedies to cure arthritis.

No one knows exactly the cause of, let alone how to cure, arthritis in the seventy million Americans who currently suffer from the disease. What we do know is that arthritis is probably as old as the human race, with the bones of Java man and mummies from ancient Egypt showing signs of joint damage.

Arthritis is an umbrella term for hundreds of conditions that cause pain and discomfort in the joints and the surrounding tissues. The most common forms of arthritis are osteoarthritis and rheumatoid arthritis. Osteoarthritis develops after a lifetime of use and abuse to the joints, which roughens and wears away the cartilage (the material that cushions the surface of the joints). As a result, the joint—especially the weight-bearing joints in the back, hips, knees, and the bones in the hands and wrists—becomes stiff and painful. With rheumatoid arthritis, the joints are inflamed and swollen, rather than worn, with stiffness and pain. Compared with osteoarthritis, rheumatoid arthritis usually affects the whole body and can range from mild discomfort to severe crippling.

Osteoarthritis (from now on called arthritis) is easily confused with aging, since its incidence increases as people get older. One in eight people under the age of fifty have arthritis, while 25 percent of people older than fifty and one in every two people age sixty-five or older have one or more stiff joints. Arthritis is often more a matter of time and use than age. You have some control as to whether you develop arthritis, how serious the condition is, and at what rate it progresses. Since developing a reliable, effective cure remains elusive, your best bet is to prevent the disease in the first place.

Feed Youthful Joints

Abusing the joints contributes to the development and progression of arthritis, so it makes sense that excess body weight—or more specifically, fat weight—is directly linked to arthritis. Even a modest weight gain of twenty-five pounds equates to constantly carrying a backpack of that weight; over time the extra burden damages cartilage. A study from the Centers for Disease Control and Prevention found that men and women who are overweight are 30 percent more likely than lean adults to develop arthritis, regardless of age. Shedding weight also can help relieve symptoms in people already afflicted with arthritis. In contrast to body fat, extra muscle strengthens the bones and joints and maintains good posture, and both help prevent arthritis. Strength training is essential to the prevention of the disease.

To maintain a desirable weight, focus on the fruits, vegetables, cooked dried beans and peas, nonfat milk, and whole grains in the Antiaging Diet. People who develop arthritis often consume too few of these foods and miss many essential

■ *Rheumatoid Arthritis*

Although no evidence exists that rheumatoid arthritis is caused by diet or that diet can cure the disease, several studies show a reduction in symptoms from a few dietary changes.

- Eat primarily vegetarian. Numerous studies show that switching to a vegetarian diet reduces pain, morning stiffness, the number of joints affected, and the number of swollen joints in people with rheumatoid arthritis.
- Include fish in the weekly menu. Fats in fish oils called omega-3 fatty acids reduce levels of hormonelike compounds in the body called prostaglandins and leukotrienes that aggravate the inflammation associated with rheumatoid arthritis. Eating fish or taking fish oil capsules might reduce morning stiffness and joint tenderness in some arthritis sufferers. The effects appear to be dose related, with greater improvements at higher doses. (Don't supplement with more than 1 gram of omega-3s without consulting your physician, since these fats act as a blood thinner at high doses.)
- Take a moderate-dose multiple vitamin and mineral. Numerous studies report that people with rheumatoid arthritis consume insufficient amounts and have low blood levels of several nutrients, including vitamin E, beta-carotene, folic acid, vitamin B_{12}, selenium, zinc, iron, vitamin B, and niacin. These deficiencies undermine general health and aggravate arthritis.
- Consume three to four servings daily of nonfat milk or fortified soy milk to ensure optimal intake of calcium and vitamin D.

nutrients. Whether this contributes to the development of the disease is not clear, but why take the chance?

Consuming too little calcium, selenium, and zinc from foods such as nonfat milk, cooked dried beans and peas, and fresh vegetables contributes to skeletal damage in humans. Preliminary research shows that some nutrients, such as vitamins E, B_2, and C, inhibit the development of arthritis, while vitamins E, B_1, B_6, and B_{12} improve joint function in some animals. Bioflavonoids in oranges and other citrus fruits and vitamin D in milk also might help prevent the disease. Since the only reliable dietary source of vitamin D is milk and fortified soy milk or orange juice, anyone who doesn't drink at least two glasses daily should consider taking a moderate-dose supplement.

Several supplements show promise in treating the symptoms of arthritis, including glucosamine, chondroitin, collagen hydrolysate, avocado soybean unsaponifiables (ASU), and the omega-3 fats in fish oils. Since there appear to be no harmful side effects, anyone suffering from arthritis might want to discuss their use with a physician. No recommended dosages have been set, but common intakes are as follows:

- 1,500 milligrams of glucosamine
- 1,200 milligrams of chondroitin
- 7 to 10 grams of collagen hydrolysate
- 300 milligrams of ASU
- 1 gram of omega-3s (500 milligrams of DHA and 500 milligrams of EPA)

Move It

Consider the following two scenarios:

Cathy started feeling some stiffness in her joints at age sixty-five. When her joints hurt, she moved less. She spent more time sitting, while her muscles became weaker and her joints became stiffer. After several years, she was in constant pain and seldom left her easy chair.

Joan is eighty years old and has had arthritis for years, but she doesn't let it slow her down. She walks or swims daily, in spite of the discomfort. By staying active, she has maintained strong muscles, maximum joint flexibility, a positive attitude, and an active life.

While the two women have the same disease, its effects on their lives, vitality, and longevity are very different, for two simple reasons: attitude and exercise. Cathy's "give up" attitude hastened the progression of arthritis. Joan's "never give up" optimism motivated her to keep moving when she learned she had arthritis. As a result, her disease has progressed slowly, allowing her to live a full and active life. Exercise is vital for both the prevention and the treatment of arthritis. Runners who pound the pavement actually have a lower rate of arthritis and less overall disability than their couch-potato friends. To reduce your risk of developing arthritis later in life, start moving today.

Times have changed when it comes to exercise for the treatment of arthritis. When our parents developed arthritis, they were told to take it easy. Today the recommendation is to *move*. Exercise is essential to keep the disease under control once it has developed. Staying physically active stretches the joints, helps move fluids and chemicals through the surrounding tissues, and reduces stiffness. Exercise also keeps the bones, muscles, and tendons strong around the joint. One study found that walking, stretching, and strength training in patients with arthritis in the knees lowered their pain by 27 percent and improved their movement by 30 percent.

If you have joint pain or stiffness, first consult a physician to confirm that arthritis is really the problem, since some joint problems other than osteoarthritis are better treated with physical therapy, not exercise. If arthritis is the cause, discuss with your physician the exercise options, including walking, swimming, water walking, water aerobics, or other nonjarring exercise. Remember to always warm up prior to exercise.

Eyesight Survival Skills

*If eyes were made for seeing, then beauty is its own
excuse for being.*

—RALPH WALDO EMERSON

Life is filled with unforgettable sights, pictures we hold in our mind's eye that give meaning and joy to our daily lives. Not so long ago, loss of sight was considered an inevitable consequence of aging. That belief is changing as evidence shows that vision is as much a matter of lifestyle as age, which means that many of the 1.4 million cataract procedures performed each year in the United States might be needless if people made a few changes in what they ate and how they supplemented.

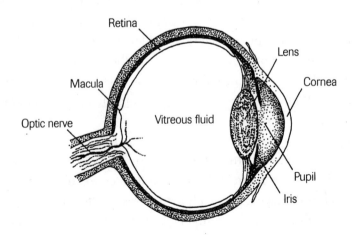

Age-related eye diseases that once led to blindness, such as cataracts and macular degeneration, might be prevented if you make a few simple changes in what you eat today.

Cataracts and Antioxidants

For good vision, the eye lens must collect and focus light on the retina, and to do so, it must remain clear. With age, many people suffer clouding, or opacification, of the lens, a condition called cataracts and one of the leading causes of blindness.

Cataracts are an excellent example of how lifestyle is the problem in disorders once thought to be the natural consequence of aging. People who eat healthy diets have less than half the risk for developing cataracts compared with people who eat typical American diets, high in fat and low in fruits and vegetables.

Research shows that long-term exposure to free radicals, not just aging, is one of the underlying causes of cataracts. Repeated exposure to sunlight and/or tobacco smoke generates oxygen fragments or free radicals that attack and damage proteins within the lens. Damaged proteins clump together and, over a lifetime, cause clouding and cataracts. The greater the exposure to ultraviolet light, the higher the incidence; people who work outdoors or who live close to the equator or at high elevations are at highest risk.

The development of cataracts indicates that the body's protective antioxidant system isn't keeping pace with the damaging onslaught of free radicals. Consuming ample amounts and maintaining high tissue levels of the antioxidant nutrients, such as vitamin C, vitamin E, and the carotenoids, and counteracting sun damage to the lens might delay development of cataracts and help prevent vision loss.

Studies show that people with cataracts have low tissue and blood levels of antioxidants, while people who consume ample amounts of antioxidant-rich foods or supplements and maintain optimal tissue levels of these nutrients reduce their risk by up to 70 percent. Researchers at Harvard Medical School report that of the more than seventeen thousand men they studied, those who took supplements reduced their risks of developing cataracts by more than 25 percent.

When researchers at the University of Wisconsin Medical School investigated the development of nuclear sclerosis (cloudiness and discoloration in the lens of the eye characteristic of precataracts) in 1,919 people and compared that incidence with dietary habits during the preceding ten years, they found that the people who supplemented with vitamins A, C, E, B_1, and B_2 as well as niacin and who also consumed lots of vegetables rich in folic acid, beta-carotene, fiber, and the phyto-chemicals lutein and zeaxanthin cut their risk for developing cataracts by half com-pared with people who did not supplement. These dietary habits also might protect the eyes from other age-related disorders, such as macular degeneration.

What Is Macular Degeneration?

The number-one cause of vision loss is age-related macular degeneration, or ARMD. The term refers to an area of the eye called the macula, the light-sensitive portion of the retina that is responsible for central vision. When the macula is work-ing well, a person can read fine print, drive a car, work on hobbies, thread a nee-dle, or recognize a face. Damage to the macula, however, causes gradual vision loss, creating a blur or blind spot in the center of vision. In the early stages of ARMD, the person may see shapes but can't see well enough to read. Then objects become blurry, and finally they disappear.

Not everyone in the early stages will progress, but there is no way to know who will and who won't develop ARMD. While surgical procedures and clot-busting medications are useful treatment in a small number of cases, by far the best strat-egy is to prevent the damage in the first place.

Antioxidants, Fat, and ARMD

Long-term exposure to air and light generates free radicals that damage the mac-ula. Fortifying the eye with the antioxidants vitamin C, vitamin E, selenium, beta-carotene, lutein, and zinc should help protect against the development of ARMD. People with high levels of antioxidants are at low risk of developing ARMD.

Vitamin C is the antioxidant found in oranges, strawberries, and other fruits and vegetables. The eye naturally stockpiles vitamin C to levels twenty times and higher than those found in the blood. Interestingly, vitamin C levels in the eyes of noc-turnal animals are very low in comparison. Donita Garland, Ph.D., at the National Eye Institute in Bethesda, Maryland, theorizes that the high concentration of vita-min C in our eyes might be an adaptation that protects against solar radiation.

A host of other antioxidant-rich phytochemicals in fruits and vegetables have been identified as sight savers. The potential benefits of phytochemicals were dis-covered after studies showed that people with ARMD consumed significantly fewer fruits and vegetables than did those who maintained healthy eyesight. In contrast, people who consume diets rich in fruits and vegetables, particularly tomatoes and dark green leafy vegetables like spinach, maintain higher blood levels of phyto-chemicals (such as lycopene, lutein, and zeaxanthin). One study found that when people consume 30 milligrams of lutein daily, serum lutein levels rise tenfold within twenty days. Macular pigment densities also increase. As a result, people are less likely to develop ARMD and, if they do, the disease is less likely to progress to advanced stages.

Dietary fat also might play a role in the development of ARMD. Saturated fats in meat and fatty dairy products might increase risk, while the healthy fats, such as fish oils, appear to lower risk. For example, researchers at the University of Wisconsin at Madison surveyed more than two thousand people age forty-five or older and found that those who ate the most saturated fat and cholesterol had an 80 percent greater risk of developing ARMD compared with those who ate little fat. At this time, it's not clear whether consuming a diet high in saturated fat contributes to vision loss or whether filling up on vegetables and whole grains instead of fat protects the eyes.

The Visionary Diet

The secret to preventing age-related vision loss is to start the prevention program immediately and to continue throughout life.

- Consume daily at least eight servings of fresh fruits and vegetables (including two servings of dark green leafy vegetables rich in lutein and two servings of vitamin C–rich citrus fruits).
- Take a moderate-dose multiple vitamin and mineral supplement (see Chapter 7 for guidelines on choosing a supplement).
- Take an antioxidant supplement that contains 250 to 1,000 milligrams of vitamin C and 100 to 400IU of vitamin E. A mix of carotenoids including beta-carotene, lutein, and zeaxanthin also might be useful.
- Limit or avoid saturated fat by reducing intake of meat and fatty dairy products, and focus any fat intake primarily on healthy fats, such as olive or canola oil, nuts, and fish.
- Wear protective sunglasses year-round that filter out 100 percent of the sun's ultraviolet rays.

Radiant Smile, Beautiful Teeth

This bread of life dropped in thy mouth doth cry: Eat, eat me, soul,
and thou shalt never die.

—EDWARD TAYLOR

Until recently, gum disease (called periodontal disease and characterized by swollen and tender gums, bad breath, and a bad taste in the mouth) was considered an inevitable consequence of aging. While infections of the gums and loss of calcium from the jawbone still contribute to dental problems in the second fifty years, the vast majority of gum disease could be prevented. In fact, with proper care and good diet, dentures could become obsolete.

The first step in caring for your teeth is proper daily and yearly care. That includes brushing at least twice daily with a quality toothbrush (most dentists recommend replacing your brush every three months), flossing once a day, and getting a professional cleaning twice yearly. Fluoride helps neutralize acid formation and strengthens the enamel, making it more resistant to decay. Consult your dentist about the possible need for fluoride supplements or rinse if your water isn't fluoridated.

Hormonal changes occurring during menopause can trigger a condition called menopausal gingivostomatitis, characterized by dry or bleeding gums, a burning mouth, abnormal taste sensations, and/or a sensitivity to hot or cold foods. Hormone replacement therapy (HRT) alleviates this condition. If you suffer from these menopausal symptoms and are not on HRT, try a saliva substitute for dry mouth, which can be purchased from most local pharmacies, or drink plenty of water and chew sugarless gum to keep the mouth moist and stimulate saliva. Also, floss and brush gently, using a soft-bristle brush, and use toothpaste especially formulated for sensitive teeth. Consult your dentist if the sensitivity persists or worsens.

Sweet Tooth

Virtually all Americans have some decayed teeth by the time they reach adulthood, not because their teeth wear out but because they eat too many sweets. In cultures where refined sugar is nonexistent, cavities are an oddity, even in the oldest old.

While children are warned to limit their sugar intake to avoid cavities, little attention is paid to the sugar consumed by adults. Yet studies show that seniors consume more sugar-containing foods than do younger adults. (See Chapter 7 for more information on sugar.)

The bacteria that normally live in the mouth break down sugar to form acid, which wears away tooth enamel. Sugar also fuels the growth of plaque, the colonies of bacteria that cause periodontal disease. The cure is easy. Follow the guidelines outlined in the Antiaging Diet, and do the following:

- Cut back on sweets, from desserts and candy to honey and soda.
- Eat sweets only with meals.
- Avoid sticky sweets, such as dried fruits, toffee, and caramelized desserts.
- Keep the exposure short (that is, don't suck on candies or cough drops or sip soft drinks throughout the day).

Since Americans consume more than twice as much sugar as is generally recommended for health, or up to 25 percent of their daily calories, a general rule is to cut your current sugar intake by half. Moderate amounts of nonnutritive sweeteners, such as aspartame or Splenda, don't fuel acid-forming bacteria so are a safe way to sweeten your day.

Snacking also can be a problem, since even natural sugars from fruit, yogurt, or grains can stimulate oral bacteria. Rather than not snack, combine some anticavity foods, such as a small amount of cheese or a few peanuts, which help neutralize acids, with the more problematic foods that tend to stick to teeth, such as crackers and raisins. Chewing on sugarless gum after a meal produces saliva, which helps neutralize tooth-decaying acids. Brushing after every meal and snack is the best option.

Feed a Healthy Smile from the Dairy Case and Produce Department

The number-one rule for maintaining a healthy smile is to replace sugar calories with more nonfat milk, fortified soy milk, fruit, and vegetables. Milk and fortified soy milk supply calcium, vitamin D, magnesium, and phosphorus, which are needed to build and maintain strong teeth and the jawbone (also called the alveolar bone). Fruits and vegetables supply antioxidants, such as vitamin C and beta-carotene, which reduce the risk for gum disease and oral cancer.

Dental problems might be a signal for osteoporosis later in life. One study of postmenopausal women found those who needed dentures before age forty also were at highest risk for the depleted bone density in the spine, wrist, and hip indicative of a high risk for osteoporosis later in life. Consuming three to four calcium-rich foods each day—including nonfat milk, yogurt, calcium-fortified soy milk, or canned salmon with the bones—helps remineralize tooth enamel, buffer acids that otherwise would contribute to tooth decay, and maintain strong bones throughout the body, from the jaw to the hip.

A diet rich in fruits and vegetables cuts the risk for oral cancer by two-thirds. Numerous studies support this link between a high intake of antioxidant-rich foods and the prevention of oral cancers. Antioxidants also reduce the risk by up to 71 percent of developing oral leukoplakia, a precancerous condition characterized by white patches in the mouth. Consuming lots of fruits and vegetables, while cutting back on or eliminating alcohol, fatty meats, and tobacco, could reduce oral cancer rates by more than 80 percent!

Maintaining a radiant smile is within your grasp. The health of your mouth, teeth, and gums depends a great deal on what you eat and whether you take a few moments each day for proper dental care.

Battling the Blues

Drag your thoughts away from your troubles—by the ears,
by the heels, or any other way, so you manage it:
it's the healthiest thing a body can do.

—MARK TWAIN

Depression is caused by a multitude of factors ranging from the physical, dietary, or lifestyle induced to the psychological. While serious depression requires medical attention, in many cases how you feel is a result of what you're eating and how you're living.

If you have ever used food to soothe a bad mood or found yourself craving sweets when your energy is low, join the club. Many people at one time or another have turned to food to feel better. An occasional indulgence is harmless and comforting. However, some people unknowingly choose foods that make them feel worse and that set up a vicious cycle of depression and overeating.

Sweet Delusions

People crave carbohydrate-rich foods when they feel down in the dumps. These foods have a profound effect on the body chemicals that regulate how a person feels and acts.

Carbohydrates raise brain levels of a nerve chemical called serotonin, which regulates both mood and appetite. When serotonin levels are low, people feel blue and crave carbohydrates. Within an hour or so of eating a carbohydrate-rich snack (such as crackers and fruit, candy or a granola bar, a bagel, or a handful of popcorn), serotonin levels rise and the person feels better. The catch is that some carbs are a quick fix that can leave you feeling worse in the long run, while others help you rise above the blues.

The two biggest offenders in the food-mood link are sugar and caffeine. These quick pick-me-ups actually can bring you down. Research conducted by Larry Christensen, Ph.D., chair of the Department of Psychology at the University of South Alabama, shows that depression often vanishes when sugar or caffeine is removed from the diet. "For the person who is sensitive to sugar or caffeine, simply removing these substances from the diet may be all it takes to reduce or even eliminate depression," says Dr. Christensen. "The person suffering from depression who turns to sugary foods may relieve the depression and feel better for a short while, but the depression returns." The person then often reaches for another sugar fix, which sets up a spiral that can last for months, years, and even decades, where food choices fuel the depression. In contrast to the temporary sugar high, eliminating sugar and/or caffeine ("Seldom are people sensitive to both," says Dr. Christensen) from the diet and replacing it with pasta, bread, or other complex carbohydrates might be a permanent solution to depression for some people.

How sugar affects mood is poorly understood. One theory is that concentrated sugars in the diet affect blood sugar levels, sending them from too high to too low. This leaves a person feeling depressed and lethargic. A second theory states that the taste of sugar on the tongue releases morphinelike chemicals in the brain called endorphins, which produce an immediate, but temporary, pleasurable feeling followed by withdrawal-like symptoms of fatigue, mood swings, and cravings for more sweets. Finally, the more sugar you eat, the more likely your diet will be low in vitality-giving vitamins and minerals.

The majority of evidence shows that moderate intake of sugar substitutes is safe. A study from Kansas State University reported that women showed no changes in mood (including tension, depression, anger, fatigue, and confusion) one hour after drinking either water or aspartame-sweetened beverages.

Is Your Diet Affecting Your Mood?

Rate how often you practice the following dietary habits. Then total your score for a quick check on how your diet might be contributing to your mood.

	ALWAYS 3	OFTEN 2	SELDOM 1	NEVER 0
1. Do you eat four or more meals and snacks throughout the day, including breakfast?	____	____	____	____
2. Do you limit sugar intake?	____	____	____	____
3. Do you limit caffeinated beverages to three 5-ounce servings or less each day?	____	____	____	____
4. Do you consume at least 2,000 calories each day of fresh fruits and vegetables, whole grains, low-fat milk or fortified soy products, nuts, and extra-lean meats or legumes?*	____	____	____	____
5. Do you take a moderate-dose multiple vitamin and mineral supplement on days when you do not eat "perfectly"?	____	____	____	____
6. Do you drink at least six to eight glasses of water each day (8 ounces each)?	____	____	____	____
7. Do you avoid tobacco and limit alcohol intake to five drinks or fewer each week?	____	____	____	____

Vitamins, Minerals, Herbs, and Depression

Many people with depression are deficient in vitamins B_2, B_6, and B_{12} and folic acid. Supplementing the diet often improves their moods. In addition, when your diet is low in vitamin B_6, or if you take medications, such as birth control pills, that upset vitamin B_6 levels, your nerve cells are unable to manufacture adequate amounts of serotonin and other nerve chemicals. The result might be insomnia, depression, irritability, and nervousness. In fact, vitamin B_6 deficiency is reported

8. Do you get at least seven hours of restful sleep each night?   ____ ____ ____ ____

9. Do you practice some form of relaxation daily?   ____ ____ ____ ____

10. Do you exercise regularly?   ____ ____ ____ ____

Totals

More than 23. Your diet and lifestyle support a good mood. If you still suffer from depression, consult your doctor.

15–23. Your diet and lifestyle might be contributing to depression, irritability, or mood swings. Select two changes from the preceding list that you will make to improve your diet.

Less than 15. Your diet and lifestyle are major contributors to your doldrums. Select four or more changes, based on the preceding list, to get yourself back on track. After you have successfully implemented the dietary and/or lifestyle changes, expect at least three weeks before your mood improves.

It is very difficult to consume optimal amounts of all vitamins and minerals on a daily intake of fewer than 2,000 calories. For example, a well-balanced diet supplies approximately 6 milligrams of iron per 1,000 calories. Women (of childbearing age) must consume at least 2,500 to 3,000 calories daily to meet their iron needs of 15 to 18 milligrams. Postmenopausal women not taking HRT need the calcium equivalent of at least four eight-ounce glasses of milk each day; most consume two glasses or less.

in as many as 79 percent of people with depression compared with only 29 percent of other people. Marginal dietary intakes of vitamin C, calcium, iron, magnesium, selenium, and zinc also might contribute to depression, irritability, or mood swings.

The research on herbs and mood is sketchy. However, Saint-John's-wort shows promise in boosting mood. An optimal dose has not been identified, but this herb appears relatively safe and free from side effects at doses of 300 to 900 milligrams a day. Always discuss taking any herb with your physician, especially if you are already taking a mood-elevating medication.

Blues Free

If you frequently skip meals or turn to sweets, colas, or coffee for a quick pick-me-up, then making a few changes in your diet could be all it takes to feel better. The Antiaging Diet outlined in Chapter 7 will supply all the vitamins and minerals in the right proportion and spaced evenly throughout the day to fuel your spirits. In addition, the following six dietary rules are the guideposts for a better mood.

Rule 1. Every meal should contain some whole grains or starchy vegetables. Breakfast can include French toast, waffles, pancakes, cereal, toast, or an English muffin. Lunch and dinner can include pasta or rice dishes, bagels and cheese, or vegetable soup and a sandwich. Snacks should include fruits, crackers, bread, or starchy vegetables, such as sweet potatoes or corn, along with yogurt or slices of lean meat. Plan a carbohydrate-rich snack, such as whole-grain crackers and peanut butter, an onion bagel with low-fat cheese, or baked tortilla chips and low-fat bean dip, to curb midafternoon snack attacks.

Rule 2. Cut back on sugar-filled desserts, cereals, candy, beverages, and snack foods, such as granola bars. Replace these foods with nutrient-packed foods, such as fresh fruit, crunchy vegetables, whole-grain bagels, or low-fat yogurt. Include a dessert only at the end of a meal and never as a snack eaten alone.

Rule 3. Cut back on or eliminate coffee and other caffeinated beverages, foods, and medications. That includes tea, chocolate, cocoa, colas, and certain medications. It may take three weeks or more after you have eliminated sugar and caffeine from your diet before you notice an improvement in mood.

Rule 4. Increase dietary intake of vitamin B_6 by including several servings daily of chicken breast, legumes, fish, bananas, avocados, and dark green leafy vegetables. Whole grains are preferable to refined, enriched grains, since more than 70 percent of the vitamin is lost during processing. Consume at least two folic acid–rich foods daily by scrambling an egg substitute with spinach for breakfast, complementing a sandwich at lunch with a plate of raw broccoli spears and low-fat dip, drinking a glass of orange juice, mixing steamed collard greens into mashed potatoes, or using romaine lettuce for salads.

Twelve High-Powered Snacks to Fuel Your Mood

1. Spread fat-free cream cheese on whole-wheat crackers and top with mango chutney. Serve with a glass of light vanilla soy milk.
2. Top a slice of toasted pumpkin or zucchini bread with low-fat cheese and a slice of tart apple. Serve with orange juice.
3. Serve Marinated Four-Bean Salad* with warm whole-wheat bread and a glass of nonfat milk.
4. Toast a half bagel and top with smoked salmon, red onion rings, lettuce, and tomato. Serve with pineapple juice.
5. Top canned mandarin orange sections with crystallized ginger. Serve over orange-flavored, low-fat yogurt.
6. Make a smoothie by blending a banana, orange juice concentrate, toasted wheat germ, and canned apricots. Serve with three graham crackers.
7. Serve Creamy Oatmeal with Blueberries* with a glass of fortified soy milk.
8. Top a bowl of whole-grain cereal with light soy milk, dried plums, and almonds.
9. Microwave a sweet potato and top with crystallized ginger and pecan bits.
10. Thai Ginger Cabbage Salad* served with half a turkey sandwich on whole-wheat bread.
11. Cube leftover roasted sweet potatoes and top with crumbled blue cheese and toasted pecans. Serve with a glass of sparkling water flavored with lemon.
12. A slice of pizza made from commercial pizza crust topped with bottled pizza sauce, low-fat cheese, and lots of vegetables (red pepper slices, mushrooms, onions, garlic, zucchini slices, broccoli florets, and so on). Serve with sparkling water.

*Recipes in Appendix B.

Rule 5. Review your eating habits over the past few months. Have you made dramatic changes in your normal eating patterns? Are you dieting, frequently skipping breakfast, indulging a snack attack in the evening, or limiting your daily food intake to fewer than three snacks and meals? Any of these habits will alter brain chemistry and might contribute to mood swings.

Rule 6. Make changes gradually. Select two or three small changes, and practice these until they are comfortable. This assures long-term success in sticking with your plan and will allow your brain chemistry time to adjust to the new eating style.

What you eat is only part of the blues battle. Regular exercise, effective coping skills, a strong social support system, and limiting or avoiding alcohol and cigarettes that compound an emotional problem also are important considerations. Depression can be a symptom of other problems as well, so always consult a physician if emotional problems persist or interfere with your quality of life and health.

Fatigue Busters

Be master of your petty annoyances and conserve your energies for
the big worthwhile things. It isn't the mountain ahead that wears you
out, it's the grain of sand in your shoe.

—ROBERT SERVICE

Fatigue is one of the most common complaints voiced by both men and women, and it's the most likely to undermine vitality. But before you blame your lack of oomph on your busy schedule or the fact that you're getting older, think again. The answer to waning energy could be as simple as your diet.

The Calorie Crisis

Any eating habit that interferes with a steady supply of carbohydrates to the body—from erratically skipping meals to following a low-carb diet—will undermine your energy level. Blood sugar levels begin to drop within four hours of eating, so frequent, small meals and snacks, rather than two or three big meals, are your best bet for maintaining a constant energy supply and avoiding fatigue. Complex carbohydrates in whole grains and starchy vegetables—from breads, rice, and pasta to lima beans and yams—are the fuels of choice, since they are digested gradually, maintain an even blood sugar level, and provide a constant fuel supply for the body and the brain.

Dieting is a common cause of fatigue. "Cutting calories at breakfast and lunch to lose weight is likely to leave most people in an energy drain that interferes with the daily routine, exercise, or even enjoying life," says Nancy Clark, M.S., R.D.,

Fatigue Fighters

Too busy to rest and too tired to fix a big meal? Energizing snacks can be quick and easy. For example, try some of the following:

- Whole-wheat fig bars, a glass of nonfat milk, and fresh berries
- A raisin bagel topped with fat-free cream cheese and served with baby carrots
- Vietnamese Black Bean Salad* and a glass of pineapple juice
- A bran muffin spread with apple butter and served with a glass of nonfat milk
- An ounce of nuts and a sliced mango
- Whole-wheat pita bread stuffed with hummus and red pepper slices
- Fat-free cottage cheese topped with canned pineapple chunks
- A slice of Fruit Pizza* with a glass of light soy milk
- A slice of toasted whole-wheat bread topped with peanut butter and canned fruit
- Pear, cantaloupe, strawberry, and banana slices dipped in vanilla-flavored nonfat yogurt

*Recipes in Appendix B.

author of *Nancy Clark's Sports Nutrition Guidebook*. For example, one in four Americans skips breakfast; half of us eat this important meal only sporadically. That means many people force their bodies to run on "fumes" during the morning hours. It's no surprise that research shows breakfast skippers are more prone to fatigue, moodiness, poor concentration, and food cravings later in the day compared with people who took five minutes to eat a nutritious breakfast.

Rather than drastically cutting calories to maintain a desirable weight, people should increase exercise, which burns calories, boosts energy levels, and decreases fatigue-related moods, such as depression and despondency.

Breakfast Basics

Skipping breakfast is a big mistake. Eight or more hours have passed since your last meal. Demanding that your body shift into full gear without stopping to refuel is like expecting a car to run on an empty tank. You may feel fine at first, but people who skip breakfast struggle more with fatigue later in the day than do those who take time in the morning to eat. People often skip breakfast in an attempt to cut calories, but research shows that breakfast skippers are more likely to overeat later in the day.

The breakfast rules are simple: avoid sugar, limit caffeine, and choose foods with a mix of protein and starch to maintain blood sugar and energy levels throughout the morning. Examples include egg substitutes, whole-wheat toast, and juice; a whole-grain bagel or English muffin with low-fat cheese and fruit; or a bowl of oatmeal with low-fat milk and a banana. Or try nontraditional foods, such as leftover pizza, toast and soup, or a sandwich. Other five-minute meals include the following:

- A toasted frozen whole-wheat waffle topped with fat-free sour cream and fresh blueberries
- A whole-wheat tortilla filled with cottage cheese and fresh fruit, warmed in the microwave
- A low-fat bran muffin with applesauce and yogurt
- A bowl of low-fat whole-grain cereal with low-fat milk and fresh fruit

Midday Energy Boosters

What and how much you eat at lunch can make or break your energy level for the rest of the day. First, keep it light (a light meal of 500 calories or less will fuel your energy without leaving you drowsy). A tossed salad and crackers might sound nutritious but can leave you short on energy and hungry again too soon. Add some kidney beans or grilled chicken to the salad, go light on the high-fat dressing, and complement it with a glass of nonfat milk and a slice of whole-wheat bread.

Second, keep lunch low in fat. Fatty meals will prime you for a nap rather than a get-things-done afternoon.

Third, combine protein- and carbohydrate-rich foods. An all-carb meal, such as pasta with marinara sauce, raises brain levels of a chemical called serotonin, which leaves you feeling relaxed and drowsy. In contrast, a turkey sandwich and a bowl of minestrone or a bean-cheese burrito with rice and spicy carrots (the protein-carb combination) raises brain levels of another chemical, called norepinephrine, which increases alertness and mental clarity.

In-Between-Meal Boosters

Your body's high performance requires frequent stops for fuel and nutrients, which means eating a small meal or snack every three to four hours. Here are the rules for energy-boosting snacks:

Rule 1. Keep it simple. A nutritious snack must be convenient; that is, it must be readily available and take little time to prepare.

Rule 2. Include at least one fruit, vegetable, or whole grain at every snack, plus one or more of the following:

- Nuts and seeds
- Fortified soy milk or nonfat milk products, such as yogurt or milk
- Cooked dried beans and peas

Rule 3. While cookies, candy, colas, and other sugary treats are quick fixes for dwindling energy levels, they may produce a short-acting response. According to Robin Kanarek, Ph.D., professor of psychology at Tufts University, "Sugar leads to a release of insulin, which results in an increase in sugar uptake and use by the cells. It is possible that once the sugar is used, feelings of fatigue will follow."

Instead, snack on whole-grain bagels, fat-free crackers and cheese, fresh fruit and cottage cheese, crunchy vegetables, or low-fat tortilla chips and bean dip. "Our research shows that a snack in the late afternoon improves performance, especially on tasks that require sustained attention and alertness," says Dr. Kanarek.

One cup of coffee can kick-start your day, but more than three cups and you're likely to spiral into needing more coffee to fend off fatigue from caffeine withdrawal, yet you'll sleep poorly and wake up tired the next morning.

Rule 4. Plan ahead. Pack your purse, briefcase, glove compartment, desk drawer, and office refrigerator with fresh fruit, bagged baby carrots, pita bread, dried fruit, boxed juice, and yogurt. Eat a nutritious snack at the first signs of hunger; a starving body is likely to grab anything to curb the hunger pangs—and usually that means candy from the vending machine!

Fluid Fuels

Water is the most available and inexpensive way to boost your energy, but we often don't drink enough of it. Over the course of days or weeks you can become mildly dehydrated, with a common symptom being fatigue.

Drink six to eight glasses of water, fruit juice, and other beverages every day. Since thirst is a poor indicator of fluid needs, a general rule is to drink twice as much water as is needed to quench thirst. That means about one glass of water every other hour during the day. Also, sip on a glass of water while preparing meals to help replenish fluids and curtail nibbling. Exercisers need even more water and should drink at least a glass of it prior to, during, and following all training and sports events, as well as regularly throughout the day.

Other Fatigue Fighters

If your energy level is in perpetual low gear, your problem could be lack of iron. While only 8 percent of premenopausal women are anemic, as many as 80 percent of active and up to 39 percent of sedentary women are iron deficient, a preanemic condition that results in fatigue and other energy-related problems. For these women, a moderate-dose iron supplement (18 milligrams) and iron-rich foods will boost lagging iron stores. Seldom do men or postmenopausal women need to supplement with iron.

Exercise also is essential in the battle against fatigue. Physically active people have more energy to accomplish routine tasks and ample energy left to enjoy life. The energy-boosting effects of exercise become increasingly important as a person ages. (See Chapter 8 for more information on exercise and energy.)

Learn to recognize the mental or physical symptoms of fatigue and what time of day they usually occur—that is, are you a lark or an owl? Keep a journal to identify when you are most energized, tired, or in the best and worst moods. What precedes your periods of high and low energy, including sleep, stress, diet, and exercise patterns? (Remember, fatigue can be a symptom of something more serious, so always consult a physician if it persists.) Then develop a plan that works with your natural energy cycles and combats the blahs.

Listening Well

It takes two to speak the truth—one to speak, and another to hear.

—HENRY DAVID THOREAU

Without hearing, we'd miss the sound of our loved ones' voices, the splash of water over rocks, the rustle of wind through the trees, the emotions stirred when listening to music, the warning signal of a fire alarm, and the millions of other noises that enrich and protect our lives. Loss of hearing robs some of our interaction with the world and others, which can bring loneliness and speed the aging process.

Hearing is the most likely of the five senses to be lost with age. Approximately one in three people age sixty-five or older and half of those age eighty-five or older report hearing loss ranging from mild to severe. Presbycusis (derived from two Latin words meaning "old" and "hearing") is a gradual, progressive loss of high-frequency hearing. As people age, they are still likely to hear the deep tones of a man's voice but will struggle with the higher-pitched voice tones of children and women.

Noise abuse is the most likely cause of presbycusis, with exposure to 85 decibels or higher being enough to damage the ear. (For example, a firecracker at ten feet is 160 decibels, a stereo headset at volume number 6 is 115 decibels, and a car horn is 100 decibels.) The noise level at a rock concert can permanently damage the ear in less than half an hour! The damage becomes worse as a person ages. Medications, such as antibiotics and diuretics, also can affect hearing.

Besides the obvious—avoid loud noises and wear protective hearing devices when loud noises are unavoidable—there are a few nutrients that might be useful.

Vitamins and Minerals

A deficiency of vitamin D is associated with progressive cochlear deafness. (The cochlea is the spiral-shaped bone in the ear canal that converts sound waves into electrical impulses to be sent to the brain.) Poor intake of vitamin D might produce calcium loss from the bones, including this fragile bone within the ear, which would affect the cochlea's ability to conduct impulses. Whether deafness caused by changes in the cochlea is responsive to vitamin D supplementation is not clear.

Optimal intake of vitamin D, fluoride, magnesium, and calcium also shows promise in reducing the symptoms of hearing disorders, such as tinnitus (ringing in the ears). Until more is known about these nutrients and hearing, it is safe and potentially helpful to consume 200 to 400IU of vitamin D and at least 1,000 milligrams of calcium, either from fortified milk, soy milk, orange juice, or cereal or from supplements, throughout life; drink fluoridated water; and consume magnesium-rich foods, such as whole grains, nuts, legumes, and tofu.

Low intake of vitamin B_{12} and zinc might contribute to the development and progression of tinnitus and hearing loss. Increasing intakes of zinc-rich foods, such as turkey, lima beans, wheat germ, and yogurt, or taking a moderate-dose supplement might be effective in preventing hearing loss or in restoring hearing.

Vitamin C also might help with noise-induced hearing loss, according to a study from the University of Buffalo. Guinea pigs were raised on normal, supplemented, or deficient levels of vitamin C and then were exposed to loud noise for six hours. Animals that received the highest levels of vitamin C developed significantly less hearing loss compared with the animals on normal or deficient diets. These results show that dietary factors might influence individual susceptibility to hearing loss and that high vitamin C intake might help prevent damage to hearing.

Sleepless Nights?

For fast-acting relief, try slowing down.

—LILY TOMLIN

Do you enjoy about eight hours of uninterrupted sleep each night?
Do you awaken easily and feel refreshed without the aid of an alarm clock?
Does it take you at least ten minutes to settle down before you fall asleep?
Do you feel awake and alert all day long?

If you answered "no" to any of these questions, you might not be getting enough sleep.

Busy lifestyles have reduced the average night's sleep by 20 percent. While most adults used to sleep at least nine hours a night and need at least eight hours, most average closer to seven; seniors do even worse and average five to seven hours a night.

This chronic sleep debt impairs memory, logical reasoning, decision making, and the immune system. It also undermines vitality and your sense of humor. Most people would be more productive, healthier, happier, and more vital if they slept more.

While sleep deprivation is sometimes self-imposed, in many more cases it is caused by some form of insomnia. Up to 95 percent of adults experience some form of insomnia during their lives; one in three battles insomnia on a regular basis. Many people assume that insomnia refers only to chronic sleeplessness, but they are wrong. Insomnia is any sleep problem, from occasional difficulties falling asleep or waking in the middle of the night to awakening too early or sleeping too lightly. Insomnia is a complex issue with numerous causes; however, sometimes the answer to sleep problems starts at the diningroom table, not in the bedroom. The most likely dietary culprits that undermine sleep include caffeine, alcohol, spicy or gas-forming foods, and some additives, such as MSG.

Caffeine, Alcohol, and Snooze Control

"People eat chocolate or drink coffee during the day and then wonder why they can't sleep at night," says Robert Sack, Ph.D., professor of psychiatry and director of adult sleep disorder medicine at the Oregon Health & Science University in Portland. "Even small amounts of caffeine can affect sleep architecture, especially in caffeine-sensitive people." If you are a coffee drinker troubled by sleep problems, try eliminating caffeine for at least two weeks and see if your sleep habits improve.

A nightcap might make you sleepy, but actually it will undermine a restful night. Alcohol and other depressant drugs suppress a phase of sleeping called REM (rapid eye movement), during which most of your dreaming occurs. Less REM is associated with more night awakenings and restless sleep. One glass of wine with dinner probably won't hurt, but don't drink alcohol within two hours of bedtime, and never mix alcohol with sleeping pills!

Snacking by the Light of the Moon

"If you don't consume enough calories throughout the day, you're likely to wake more frequently during the night because you're hungry," warns Gary Zammit, Ph.D., director of the Sleep Disorders Institute in New York City and author of the book *Good Nights*. If dieting is causing your sleep problems, increase your calorie intake throughout the day and include some protein-rich foods at the evening meal to help fend off hunger at midnight.

Midnight snacking also can signal underlying medical conditions. For example, if you are eating in the middle of the night in an effort to relieve digestive discomfort, you might have an undiagnosed ulcer that should be checked by your physician. Hypoglycemia, although relatively rare, might be causing your nighttime eating.

Evening Meals

Spicy or gas-forming foods can cause nagging heartburn, indigestion, or gas that disrupt sleep. Eating too fast (too much air is swallowed when you gulp food) also can cause abdominal discomfort, which interferes with sound sleep. Avoid spicy foods at dinner, limit your intake of gas-forming foods to the morning hours, and thoroughly chew food to avoid gulping air.

"Big dinners, especially high-calorie meals, make you temporarily drowsy, but they can cause stomach discomfort and prolong digestive action, which keeps you awake," cautions Dr. Zammit. Dinner should be low in fat, light in calories, and consumed at least two hours before bedtime.

An evening snack might be the best alternative to sleeping pills. A carbohydrate-rich snack triggers the release of a brain chemical called serotonin that aids sleep. Serotonin-enhancing snacks include low-fat popcorn, half of a toasted English muffin topped with jam, or graham crackers and honey. The traditional glass of warm milk, a protein-rich beverage, probably doesn't affect serotonin levels, but the warm liquid soothes, relaxes, and fills you up, which might help you fall asleep.

MSG: Sleep Robber or Innocent Bystander?

People have been concerned about MSG (monosodium glutamate) since the 1970s, when research found that this additive used to enhance flavors in processed foods might cause brain damage and other serious side effects in animals. While these serious consequences have not been reported in humans, some people are sensitive to MSG. The most common symptom in people is numbness in the back of the neck that can radiate down the arms and back. Other people report insomnia and vivid dreams, mild to severe headaches, tightness in the chest, pressure around the cheeks or jaw, or mild mood changes.

A safe dose of MSG has not been established and probably varies from person to person. Generally, the higher the dose, the more people develop symptoms. "The average American consumes between one-third and one-half gram of MSG each day," says Margo Wootan, D.Sc., a senior scientist at the Center for Science in the Public Interest. "But it is easy to consume two grams in one meal at a Chinese restaurant." Fortunately, most foods don't contain this much MSG.

If you suspect you might react to MSG, check with a physician who specializes in allergies or test yourself by eliminating all MSG-containing foods for at least two weeks. (This will take a bit of sleuthing, since MSG comes in a variety of names and in many foods, so it is difficult to avoid all the sources.) If symptoms disappear, then slowly add one food at a time to your diet and monitor your sleep patterns. In addition, frequent only restaurants that promise to serve MSG-free food.

What About Melatonin?

Melatonin has been touted as the latest cure for the one in every three Americans who suffers from mild to severe insomnia. The hormone is naturally manufactured at night in the pineal gland of the brain. Melatonin's job is to tell the body that it is rest time by synchronizing its internal biological clock.

While the gland pumps out melatonin throughout life, it secretes less and less as people age, which might partially explain why sleep problems increase as people get older. Research shows that melatonin supplements, in doses as low as 1 milligram, reduced the time it took to fall asleep from twenty-five to six minutes.

Not everyone is convinced that this hormone-in-a-pill is safe or effective long term. Researchers at Oregon Health & Science University in Portland caution that taking melatonin orally alters the sleep cycle and reduces the amount of deep sleep a person gets, at least in young people. Moreover, the brain naturally secretes melatonin in a wave pattern that causes melatonin levels to rise early in the night, peak around 2 to 4 A.M., and then gradually taper off by dawn. In contrast, melatonin supplements boost blood levels like a flash flood, leaving the user high and dry at 2 A.M. Researchers at Tel Aviv University in Israel might have a solution to this problem. In their studies, time-released melatonin supplements improved sleep quality even in seniors.

◾ *Tricks of the Sleep Set*

A day filled with good eating, exercise, little stress, and healthy habits leads to a good night's sleep. You also can maximize your sleep quotient by following these seven rules:

1. Go to bed and get up at the same times each day.
2. Don't take naps.
3. Establish an evening ritual that relaxes your body and signals your brain that it's time to sleep. At the same time each night, take a warm bath, read or listen to music, sip a cup of hot herbal tea, or have a light all-carb snack.
4. Use the bedroom for sleeping only, not for working or reading in bed or for watching TV.
5. Get out of bed and the bedroom when you can't sleep.
6. Dim the lights in the evening, and keep the bedroom dark at night.
7. Don't depend on sleeping pills.

The biggest concern is not with the pure melatonin used in well-controlled research studies, since this high-quality melatonin is assured of purity and safety, but rather with the unregulated products on the market. The long-term effects of ingesting commercial melatonin are unknown, especially with regard to women, as the hormone's effect on the female reproductive system is unexplored territory.

Your Wake-Up Call

Sleepless nights can be caused by stress, emotional problems, hormone changes during the premenstrual period, menopause, medical conditions, smoking, a busy lifestyle, or a snoring bed partner. Often solving these troubles or tensions eliminates sleep problems.

A major difference between good sleepers and poor sleepers is not what they do at bedtime but what they did all day. Good sleepers exercise and use every opportunity to move. Physical activity helps a person cope with daily stress and tires the body so it is ready to sleep at night. Older people who battle sleep problems report they fall asleep faster and sleep longer after starting a daily exercise program. (Beware of exercising too hard or too fast, however, since strenuous exercise stresses the body and might disrupt sleep.) Sleeping pills are a temporary fix, while a few simple dietary and lifestyle changes could do wonders for your snooze control.

No More Kidney Stones

But I would not be so all alone. Everybody must get stoned.

—BOB DYLAN

Kidney stones come in all shapes and sizes. The small ones usually pass with the urine, but 20 percent of stones are large enough to require medical attention and surgery. Stones also are composed of different substances, including uric acid, oxalate, struvite, and cystine, but by far the most common—accounting for up to 85 percent of all kidney stones—are calcium oxalate stones. Nine times out of ten, it's a man passing the stone.

The evidence shows that kidney stones are a product of lifestyle. Millions of research dollars are spent investigating treatments, but surprisingly little effort has focused on prevention. Consequently, dietary guidelines to avoid kidney stones are rudimentary. In all cases, the treatment of any kidney disease, including kidney stones, should be designed and monitored by a physician and dietitian and include dietary, medication or medical, and lifestyle components.

How Not to Get Stoned

Many age-related diseases come down to being overweight. Numerous studies, including one from Harvard Medical School, show that overweight people excrete more calcium, oxalate, and uric acid and are at much higher risk for developing kidney stones than are lean people. In addition, diets that contain too much meat and salty foods and not enough fruits, vegetables, legumes, calcium, and water are associated with the highest risk for kidney stone formation. Since the turn of the twentieth century, Americans have become increasingly fatter and have doubled their intake of animal protein compared with vegetable protein from a ratio of 1:1 to 2:1, and, not coincidentally, the incidence of kidney stones also has increased.

How to Avoid a Kidney Stone

- Base your diet on fresh fruits and vegetables, whole grains, and cooked dried beans and peas.
- Consume at least three servings a day of calcium-rich foods, such as nonfat milk or yogurt or fortified soy milk or orange juice.
- Drink at least eight 8-ounce glasses of water a day, even more if you exercise or work in hot climates. Also drink green tea and/or fruit juices.
- Include several servings of magnesium-rich foods in your daily diet, such as bananas, beet greens, cashews, nonfat milk, and wheat germ.
- Limit daily intake of meat and fatty or salty foods, and use little or no fat and salt in cooking.
- Ask your physician about reducing oxalates in the diet.

- **Meat.** Some studies show that vegetarians have a lower incidence of kidney stones than do meat eaters. However, you probably don't need to give up meat; just curtail consumption to three ounces daily, fill the plate with lots of fresh vegetables and other foods of plant origin, and you will substantially cut your risk. In addition, eating more beans and less meat will automatically reduce fat intake, which also lowers kidney stone risk.
- **Fluids.** Drink lots of fluids, enough to produce at least two liters of urine each day. The rationale is that stones are less likely to crystalize in diluted, as compared with concentrated, urine.

  While drinking at least eight glasses of water is the foundation of an anti-stone-forming diet, there might be additional protection in including other beverages in the daily menu. Antioxidants in green tea might explain why people who drink this beverage also have lower risk for kidney stones. Researchers at the Harvard School of Public Health compared the intake of twenty-one different beverages and the incidence of kidney stones in more than forty-five thousand men ages forty to seventy-five. They found that drinking fruit juices daily reduced kidney stone formation by up to 37 percent. Cranberry, black currant, and prune juices might be especially useful in the prevention of kidney stones. However, coffee increases urinary excretion of calcium; whether this predisposes a person to kidney stones is unknown.
- **Calcium.** In the past, people were warned to limit their intake of calcium and oxalate-containing foods based on the false assumption that by not

consuming the main constituents of a kidney stone, they would avoid its formation. Research has proven just the opposite. Both men and women who consume high-calcium diets have up to a 31 percent lower risk of developing kidney stones compared with people who consume less calcium. Calcium supplements, especially when taken with a meal, also are not associated with an increased risk.

Research is sketchy when it comes to limiting oxalate-containing foods. The largest contributor to oxalate levels is not from the diet but from the body's manufacture of this compound. Limiting intake might or might not have a significant impact on stone formation. In addition, a low-oxalate diet is complex and difficult to follow, requiring elimination of an unpredictable assortment of foods, from spinach and rhubarb to nuts and chocolate. Since low intake of calcium increases intestinal absorption of oxalates, it is likely that too little calcium, rather than too much oxalate, is the dietary risk factor for kidney stone formation. Until the controversy is resolved, anyone at risk for kidney stone formation should discuss with a physician the usefulness of switching to a low-oxalate diet.

- **Vitamin C.** A handful of studies report that large doses of vitamin C might encourage the formation of oxalate-containing kidney stones in people prone to stone formation. Other studies show that up to 8 grams of vitamin C consumed daily has no effect on kidney stone risk, even in adults prone to stone formation. Not that anyone is recommending this dosage, but it does show that the link between vitamin C and kidney stones remains controversial.

- **Vitamin B$_6$.** A vitamin B$_6$ deficiency might increase the risk for developing oxalate-containing kidney stones. Supplementation with the vitamin reduces the amount of oxalate in the urine and reduces a person's risk for developing kidney stones or kidney damage.

- **Magnesium.** Magnesium inhibits the formation of crystals in the urine, possibly by improving the ratio of magnesium to calcium in the urine. The magnesium content of the urine of those who form stones and those who don't is similar; however, stone formers excrete greater amounts of calcium, making their urinary ratio of calcium to magnesium very high. Increased intake of magnesium alters the ratio of calcium to magnesium in the urine to resemble that of stone nonformers and reduces the formation of kidney stones.

Osteoporosis: The Silent Thief

*The leadership instinct you were born with is the backbone. You
develop the funny bone and the wishbone that go with it.*

—ELAINE AGATHER

Osteoporosis is a silent condition that slowly robs the body of its strongest and most
durable tissues, the bones, much like ocean waves erode the shoreline. Neither the
patient nor the physician may notice the damage until a bone fractures, showing
the disease is in its final stage. The lifelong depletion of bone minerals also
increases the likelihood of disability from a hip fracture, the loss of mobility and
independence, stooped posture from collapsing vertebrae, pain, anxiety, and sometimes death.

More than one and a half million bone fractures are caused by osteoporosis each
year, and more than twenty-five million Americans, 80 percent of them women,
live with the daily fear that a simple movement, such as sneezing or stepping off a
curb, will result in a serious bone break.

Dispelling the Myths

Bones are the body's bank account for calcium, containing 99 percent of all the
calcium in the body. Every minute of our lives, our bones are releasing calcium
into and absorbing it from the blood in order to maintain a constant blood concentration of calcium.

Up until a person's midthirties, more calcium is absorbed and deposited into
bone than is removed. The more calcium is consumed in the first third of life, the
larger the calcium bank account and the less likely a person will develop osteoporosis later in life. After about age thirty-five, bones slowly lose calcium faster than
they absorb it. Consuming ample amounts of calcium after age thirty-five can delay
calcium loss and diminish the seriousness of fragile bones later in life. Most people consume too little calcium; consequently, the bones become increasingly
porous and brittle, and the result is osteoporosis.

Brittle bones are largely the result of lifestyle choices, not aging. Robert Heaney,
M.D., a calcium expert at Creighton University in Omaha, Nebraska, estimates
that women can reduce their risk for bone fractures by up to 60 percent if they consume diets rich in calcium and vitamin D.

Milk Bones

Low-fat milk products, especially milk and yogurt, contain more calcium than any other food regularly consumed in the diet. Fortified soy milk and orange juice are other reliable sources. Women need the calcium-containing equivalent of at least three glasses of milk daily. However, milk is not without controversy.

One belief is that the protein in milk interferes with calcium metabolism. "This statement is partially true and mostly wrong," says Dr. Heaney. A high-protein diet does increase urinary excretion of calcium. "Sulfur-containing amino acids in all dietary protein act much like acid rain on limestone in flushing some calcium out of the body," says Dr. Heaney. However, these amino acids are found in all protein foods, from milk and meat to beans and grains.

According to Dr. Heaney, it is the ratio of calcium to protein that is important. A cup of milk supplies 300 milligrams of calcium for only 8 grams of protein (a ratio of 37:1), while a three-and-a-half-ounce hamburger supplies 5 milligrams of calcium for 32 grams of protein (a negative ratio of 1:6.4). A cup of black beans contains twice the protein but only one-sixth the calcium of milk, for a calcium-to-protein ratio of 1:3.

"Protein's effect on calcium metabolism is primarily theoretical; no one has shown that the amounts typically consumed in this country cause bone loss," reports Bess Dawson-Hughes, M.D., chief of the Calcium and Bone Metabolism Laboratory at the USDA Human Nutrition Research Center on Aging at Tufts University. In fact, recent evidence suggests that moderate protein intake aids in building strong bones resistant to osteoporosis.

Researchers at the University of Illinois surveyed women's attitudes about, and intakes of, calcium. They found that calcium intake averaged only 591 milligrams per day, and only 25 percent of women met the recommended levels of 1,000 to 1,200 milligrams. Postmenopausal women might need up to 1,500 milligrams daily. "Women's calcium needs are greater than we previously thought and might be as much as four to five times higher than they are getting from their diets," says Dr. Heaney, who adds "While the effect is most strongly associated with calcium, milk is the best dietary source of this mineral, and the weight of the evidence comes down on the side of including [two to three servings of] milk in the diet." You can take several calcium pills each day instead of drinking milk, but this goes against all dietary recommendations. "There is no evidence that calcium supplements are superior to milk [in preventing osteoporosis] and food always should be a person's first choice when it comes to obtaining optimal nutrition," advises Dr. Dawson-Hughes.

Milk contains other factors that enhance calcium absorption and help prevent osteoporosis. The most important of these is vitamin D, a deficiency of which results in poor calcium absorption and rapid bone loss. Dr. Dawson-Hughes's research shows that increasing vitamin D intake, even without extra calcium, can help reduce bone fractures and slow the progression of osteoporosis. Aging reduces vitamin D absorption by up to 40 percent. Several studies show that adding 1,200 milligrams of calcium and 800IU of vitamin D to the diets of older women reduces the number of hip fractures by 23 percent or more. Vitamin D–fortified milk, soy milk, and orange juice are the only reliable sources of this vitamin, so your diet could be inadequate if you avoid milk and instead snack on yogurt or cheese.

Many nutrients are important in maintaining overall health and preventing osteoporosis, including boron, copper, magnesium, zinc, manganese, vitamin A, vitamin K, and some B vitamins. These nutrients are found in milk and other foods but would be lacking if a person supplemented only with calcium.

However, for both the young and old who cannot meet the three daily servings goal for low-fat milk and other calcium-rich foods, supplements are a must. "It's prudent to take a 1,000 milligram supplement of calcium, since most women average only 500 milligrams of calcium from their diets," says Dr. Heaney. In addition, avoid colloidal minerals or the "natural source" calcium pills, such as oyster shell and bone meal, since they might contain toxic metals, such as lead.

Beyond Milk

Preventing osteoporosis involves more than just consuming enough calcium and other vitamins and minerals. Researchers at the USDA Human Nutrition Research Center on Aging at Tufts University say the diet-bone issue is more about total diet and less about individual nutrients. Dietary patterns were assessed in a group of 907 people between the ages of sixty-nine and ninety-three. Six dietary patterns were identified with relatively greater proportions of intake from (1) meat, dairy, and bread, (2) meat and sweet baked goods, (3) sweet baked goods, (4) alcohol, (5) candy, and (6) fruit, vegetables, and cereal. Results showed that people in the last group had the greatest bone density, while people in the candy group had the lowest bone density. The researchers conclude that dietary patterns are associated with osteoporosis risk. High intakes of fruits and vegetables protect against bone loss, while a diet high in junk foods promote bone loss.

Lowering your intake of salt to improve blood pressure also could help protect your bones. Researchers at the University of Western Australia in Perth found that

Getting Your Milk Without Drinking It

Can't bring yourself to down three glasses of milk each day? Try these tricks for sneaking calcium-rich nonfat milk into your diet:

- Use canned nonfat evaporated milk instead of heavy cream in creamed sauces.
- Use nonfat milk instead of water when preparing packaged hot chocolate mixes.
- Drink a caffe latte made with nonfat milk instead of regular coffee.
- Switch from regular orange juice to calcium- and vitamin D–fortified orange juice.
- Use nonfat milk or dry nonfat milk powder instead of water when preparing canned creamed soups or tomato soup.
- Use nonfat milk or fortified soy milk instead of water when preparing baked goods, such as cookies, muffins, breads, waffles, or pancakes.
- When making mashed potatoes, add extra dry nonfat milk powder to the nonfat milk and cut back on the butter or margarine.
- Make a morning smoothie with fortified soy milk, concentrated orange juice, and fresh fruit, such as a banana or a peach.
- Make a sweet whipped topping by mixing one-half cup dry nonfat milk powder in one-third cup water and chill. Whip until the milk stands in soft peaks, and then add one tablespoon lemon juice and whip. Add three tablespoons powdered sugar and whip until blended. Refrigerate until ready to use.
- Add dry nonfat milk powder to meat loaf, muffins, meatballs, or other menu items.
- Have a calcium chocolate chew supplement for dessert.
- Layer fruit, nonfat plain yogurt, and granola in a parfait glass, and top with a dollop of fat-free whipped topping.

cutting sodium (salt) intake in half was as effective as increasing daily calcium intake to 891 milligrams in slowing bone loss and preventing osteoporosis.

Soy also shows promise in helping maintain strong bones throughout life. Isoflavones in soy reduce bone loss and might aid in the prevention of osteoporosis. Soy also might reduce calcium loss in urine, resulting in improved calcium retention. According to researchers at the University of North Carolina, Chapel Hill, optimal intake of the key phytoestrogens in soy—genistein and daidzein—has a modest positive effect on improving bone mass. The tricky word here is *optimal*. In Asian cultures where women consume 40 milligrams of phytoestrogens daily (compared with Western intakes of 0 to 3 milligrams) and excrete one thousand times the levels of phytoestrogens in their urine, bone fracture rates are a fraction of what they are in the United States and other Western cultures.

Alcohol abuse and smoking escalate bone loss, so drink in moderation, if at all, and don't smoke. Compounds in coffee increase urinary loss of calcium, but the research has not confirmed a direct link between this beverage and osteoporosis. Until the controversy is settled by well-designed studies, it is best to drink coffee in moderation and with milk.

Exercise also is essential to maintaining strong muscles. Researchers at the University of Cincinnati Medical Center in Ohio report that people can exercise or consume more calcium, but they're not likely to maximize bone density unless they do both. A careful review of seventeen trials of physical activity that also reported calcium intake showed that the benefits of exercise on bone density were apparent only when calcium intake was high. Both weight-bearing exercise, such as walking or jogging, and strength training are essential to maintaining strong bones for life. If you already have osteoporosis, work with your physician to develop a safe activity program.

Bone loss escalates rapidly after menopause, when the protective effects of estrogen on maintaining bone mass are lost. Hormone replacement therapy (HRT) significantly slows the rate of bone loss after menopause and reduces a woman's risk of developing osteoporosis. In addition, many new drugs for the treatment of osteoporosis are now available, including Fosamax, which slows mineral loss and might build new bone and prevent fractures.

Skin and Hair: Turning Back the Hands of Time

For age is opportunity no less
Than youth itself, though in another dress.
And as the evening twilight fades away
The sky is filled with stars, invisible by day.

—HENRY WADSWORTH LONGFELLOW

A person's skin is an outer reflection of his or her inner health. Those who are healthy and vital also are radiant—with clear, moist, glowing skin. The skin is a sensitive timeline for aging. Youthful skin is soft, moist, and smooth, while wrinkles and sagging gradually develop over time as the skin's elastin and collagen fibers deteriorate. The process begins around age thirty and progresses throughout life. Heredity and gravity influence how and when the skin ages, but by far its greatest enemy is sun exposure.

Because the cells of the skin have a short life span, signs of poor nutrition show up quickly in this tissue.

Healthy Skin from Within

Radiant, youthful skin requires a steady supply of all nutrients, including protein, calories, fat, vitamins, minerals, and water. Maintaining an optimal blood supply is critical to delivery of oxygen and nutrients to the skin and the hair and for removing waste products from these tissues. Red blood cells and the blood supply depend on ample amounts of protein, iron, folic acid and other B vitamins, copper, vitamin C, selenium, and vitamin E. An iron deficiency alone can leave the skin looking pale and drawn.

Some nutrients directly affect the health of the skin and hair. An essential fat in vegetable oils called linoleic acid helps maintain smooth, moist skin. Very low-fat diets often are low in this fat and cause dry, scaly skin. Adding a little safflower oil, a handful of nuts or seeds, or a tablespoon of wheat germ to the daily diet can reverse the condition within a few weeks.

Vitamin C helps build collagen, the "glue" that holds the body's cells together. Poor intake of this vitamin results in bruising, loss of skin elasticity, poor healing of cuts and scrapes, and dry skin. A glass of orange juice or a bowl of strawberries daily provides enough vitamin C to ensure adequate collagen formation, although more might be better if you want to protect the skin from sun damage.

Antioxidants Against Skin Aging

With free radicals accused of being the dark force behind aging, it's no surprise that antioxidant nutrients have hit the market with a vengeance. Major cosmetics companies are spiking their face creams with everything from vitamin C to green tea extract.

The antioxidant nutrients help neutralize free radicals generated in the skin from sun exposure before they can irreversibly damage the skin. Basically, antioxidants prevent free radicals from destroying the fats that form a protective moisture bar-

Healthy Hair

As with skin, the health of your hair is a reflection of internal health. Shiny, flexible, vibrant hair signals an optimally nourished body, while dry, dull, or lifeless hair is a gauge for nutritional deficiencies.

Granted, nutrition cannot work miracles. It can't reverse graying or balding caused by heredity. And while hair loss caused by a nutrient deficiency is reversed when the nutrient is added to the diet, consuming extra nutrients in hopes of regaining lost color, hair, or length is likely to end in disappointment. The following is a summary of how deficiencies and toxicities of certain nutrients can affect hair.

SYMPTOMS	COULD RESULT FROM
Hair loss or baldness	Deficiency of vitamin A, biotin, iron, zinc, protein, or molybdenum
Dandruff	Vitamin A deficiency
Dry or dull hair	Vitamin A overdose or a deficiency of vitamin C, linoleic acid, or protein
Hair lacks luster	Deficiency of vitamin B_6 or B_{12} or folic acid
Premature graying or loss of color	Deficiency of pantothenic acid or copper
Itchy scalp	Vitamin A overdose
Poor hair growth	Vitamin D overdose
Hair splits, breaks, and tangles easily	Vitamin C deficiency

rier in the skin and prevent the dryness, loss of elasticity, and wrinkles caused by sun damage. Free radicals also are suspected of attacking the skin's collagen, which keeps the skin firm and supple. If antioxidants can prevent the breakdown of this spongy material, then a person could expect to see fewer deep wrinkles over time. Antioxidants also might act as a weak sunscreen, comparable to an SPF 3.

Unfortunately, the body's antioxidant supply is often caught short when bombarded repeatedly by large doses of ultraviolet (UV) light. "Concentrations of the antioxidants, such as vitamin E, are reduced following exposure to UV radiation, which implies that these nutrients protect the skin," states Helen Gensler, Ph.D., associate professor in the Department of Radiology/Oncology at the University of Arizona Cancer Center. For example, as much as 70 percent of the vitamin C in skin is destroyed after a single UV exposure. Stockpiling the antioxidant nutrients theoretically should reduce skin damage caused by environmental pollutants and sunlight.

Interesting Facts About Hair and Skin

- The use of hair dyes is linked to an increased risk for developing non-Hodgkin's lymphoma and leukemia.

- Hair analysis is useful for determining long-term exposure to toxic metals, such as lead, but is unreliable for assessing nutritional status.

- Although they are touted as hair tonics, there is no credible evidence that inositol, PABA, or vitamin E prevents hair loss or restores color to hair.

- Herbs such as jojoba oil, nettle, and royal jelly do not prevent hair loss.

- Does using sunscreens that block ultraviolet light increase a person's risk for vitamin D deficiency? Apparently not. Blood vitamin D levels remained within the normal range and risk for osteoporosis does not appear to be affected in people who used sunscreen lotion.

- If you get a sunburn despite using sunscreen, try pouring cold tea over your aching skin. Tannins in tea help take the sting out of a sunburn, and researchers at the University of Arizona report these compounds also help curb the sun's cancer-causing effects.

- Rubbing aloe gel on sunlight-exposed skin helps prevent ultraviolet light damage associated with immune suppression and disease.

Preliminary research supports this assumption. A study from Cornell University showed that chronic exposure to sunlight lowered blood levels of beta-carotene. The researchers concluded that repeated sun exposure might increase daily requirements for this antioxidant. Other studies showed that diets enriched with antioxidant nutrients, including selenium, beta-carotene, vitamin E, and vitamin C, inhibit the formation of UV-induced tumors.

These findings suggest that UV damage to the epidermis affects deeper layers of the skin and even blood and other tissues. Antioxidants obtained from the diet probably are stored in the deeper subcutaneous layer of the skin, leaving the corium and outer epidermis only partially protected. That's where applying antioxidants directly to the skin can complement dietary intake.

Studies show that topical application of vitamin C, vitamin A, vitamin E, or a mixture of antioxidant nutrients in the presence of UV light might reduce skin cancer risk, premature aging, and liver spots. Because UV-induced skin damage continues for hours or days after sun exposure, application of vitamin C after sun exposure also might help repair long-term damage. In one study, delaying application of vitamin E for up to eight hours after UV exposure still offered protection.

Douglas Darr, Ph.D., former director of Technology Development at the North Carolina Biotechnology Center, has conducted several studies showing the effectiveness of vitamin C in preventing sun damage to the skin. In one study, the forearms of volunteers were treated with a 10 percent vitamin C solution or placebos and then exposed to UV light. The sites treated with vitamin C showed significantly less sun damage compared with that experienced by the untreated group. Rub vitamin C on your skin, and you might notice improvement in wrinkles within twelve weeks, according to a study from the University of California, San Diego.

"Antioxidants are not a panacea because not all UV damage to the skin can be attributed to [free radicals]; however, antioxidants plus sunscreens might be much better together than either one alone," recommends Dr. Darr. Dosage is important here. Many commercial creams contain 3 percent vitamin C or less, while the research shows at least a 10 percent mixture is needed.

Water-soluble vitamin C is not the only antioxidant that promises relief from premature aging. Selenium, lycopene and other carotenoids, and antioxidants in green tea all show potential for protecting the skin from premature aging. For example:

- Selenium and vitamin E applied directly to the skin might be the best protection against sunburn, according to a study from the University of Connecticut Health Center in Farmington.
- A mixture of carotenoids, such as lutein, lycopene, and beta-carotene, protect the skin from sun damage caused by UV light, according to a study from the Heinrich-Heine University in Düsseldorf.

Antioxidants might not turn back the hands of time and reverse the damage already done by too much sunbathing, but combined with a daily sunscreen lotion, they might help slow the future ticking of that clock.

Feeding Your Skin

The dietary guidelines for healthy, youthful skin are simple.

1. Consume daily at least 2,000 calories of fresh fruits and vegetables, whole-grain breads and cereals, cooked dried beans and peas, soy foods such as tofu,

The Nutrition and Healthy Skin Connection

All nutrients are related to healthy skin. Here are a few examples why:

NUTRIENT	THE SKIN CONNECTION	SOURCES
Protein	Maintains underlying muscles and skin structure, elasticity, and resiliency; maintains hormones that regulate skin moisture; regulates skin pigments.	Milk, meat, fish, chicken, legumes, soy milk
Fat	Essential fatty acid maintains skin moisture. Deficiency results in scaly, dry skin. Fish oils lower skin cancer risk.	Safflower oil, nuts, seeds, whole grains; seafood, including salmon
Water	Maintains skin moisture; helps maintain normal oil secretion.	Water, green tea
Vitamin B_2	Deficiency causes blisters and cracks at corner of mouth, oily and flaky skin.	Milk, dark green vegetables
Niacin	Deficiency causes dermatitis.	Chicken breast, peanut butter, green peas
Vitamin B_6	Deficiency causes itching, dry skin, and anemia.	Bananas, lean meat, fish, chicken breast
Folic acid	Deficiency causes anemia and pale skin.	Dark green vegetables, orange juice
Vitamin B_{12}	Deficiency causes anemia and pale skin.	Milk, lean meat, fish, chicken
Pantothenic acid	Deficiency causes dry, flaky skin.	Milk, chicken breast, peanut butter, vegetables, rice
Vitamin C	Maintains oil-producing glands, collagen, and skin elasticity and resiliency; is an antioxidant against premature aging and skin cancer.	Citrus fruits, vegetables
Vitamin A (beta-carotene)	Maintains outer layer of skin; protects against skin cancer and premature aging.	Dark green or orange vegetables

Continued

NUTRIENT	THE SKIN CONNECTION	SOURCES
Vitamin E	Antioxidant against premature aging and skin cancer.	Safflower oil, nuts, wheat germ
Copper	Prevents anemia.	Oysters, avocados, fish, soy
Iron	Prevents anemia.	Dark green vegetables, lean red meat, legumes, dried apricots
Selenium	Antioxidant against skin cancer.	Organ meats, seafood, whole grains
Zinc	Maintains collagen and elastin; might prevent stretch marks; helps heal cuts. Deficiency causes dry, rough skin.	Oysters, turkey, wheat germ

two to three servings of nonfat milk or fortified soy milk, and no more than four to five ounces of fish, chicken, or very lean meat.

2. Include several servings daily of antioxidant-rich foods, such as citrus fruits for vitamin C, dark green leafy vegetables for beta-carotene, and wheat germ and nuts for vitamin E.

3. Cut back on fat. A high-fat diet increases risk of skin cancer, while cutting back on fat reduces risk. Exceptions to this rule are the omega-3 fats, which lower skin cancer risk, and linoleic acid–rich safflower oil, which helps prevent dry, flaky skin.

4. Drink six to eight glasses of fluids, especially water and green tea, daily to maintain the skin's moisture.

5. Avoid repeated bouts of weight loss and regain, since weight cycling can result in premature sagging, stretch marks, and wrinkling.

6. Take a moderate-dose multiple vitamin and mineral that contains extra amounts of the antioxidant vitamins.

7. Try mixing vitamin E with your sunscreen. (The natural form of vitamin E, called alpha-tocopherol, is best but should be refrigerated.) Vitamin E oils and creams are already available on the market. Many cosmetics, skin creams, and even sunscreen lotions also contain vitamin C.

CHAPTER 11

Thinking Clearly, Remembering When

For as I like a young man in whom there is something of the old, so I like an old man in whom there is something of the young; and he who follows this maxim, in body will possibly be an old man, but he will never be an old man in mind.

—CICERO

Aging is on everyone's mind after we pass the forty-year milestone. Wisdom may flower in the later years, but brainpower sometimes dims in the middle years. Rather than blame the loss of swift thinking on your genes or your age, take a look at your diet. What you eat and how you live affects how well you think, remember, and react.

From the billions of nerve cells and the chemicals (called neurotransmitters) that relay information between these cells to the circulatory system that carries oxygen to the brain, the entire system depends on a constant supply of nutrients to function properly throughout your life.

As the years pass, your mental function is affected long before you notice physical problems. Consequently, vague yet profound changes, such as cloudy thinking, mental fatigue, or impaired memory, can progress undetected because you otherwise feel fine.

Smart Foods

The test of a first-rate intelligence is the ability to hold two opposed ideas in the mind at the same time, and still retain the ability to function.

—F. SCOTT FITZGERALD, FROM *THE CRACK-UP*

Most people recognize that what they eat will affect their physical health. Yet the link between brain function and food, while not visible, is more immediate. What you eat (or don't eat) for breakfast, or even whether you snack during the day, can affect how clearly you think or how well you can recall information by midafternoon.

Take, for example, skipping meals. Big mistake, especially if one of those meals is breakfast. Breakfast restocks dwindling glucose stores, the brain's sole source of fuel. Keeping glucose levels in the optimal range enhances learning, memory, and thinking. Breakfast should be light and comprise complex carbohydrates and a little protein, such as a bowl of shredded wheat, nonfat milk, and a handful of blueberries; oatmeal topped with toasted wheat germ and light soy milk and served with a glass of pineapple juice; or a whole-wheat English muffin with peanut butter, a banana, and a glass of calcium- and vitamin D–fortified orange juice.

Simply as providing your brain with a constant supply of high-quality fuel by spreading food intake into four to six minimeals and snacks evenly distributed throughout the day might be all it takes to think more clearly. Keep these minimeals light. Avoid high-fat or heavy meals containing more than 1,000 calories, which divert the blood supply to the digestive tract and away from the brain, leaving you feeling sluggish and sleepy.

Eat to Think

It's not only when but what you eat that could undermine thinking. While the typical American diet high in fat and sugar alters brain chemistry and reduces spatial learning performance and memory, the eight servings of fruits and vegetables in the Antiaging Diet can help avoid the ravages of time. These foods are loaded with the antioxidants—vitamin C, vitamin E, beta-carotene, and the thousands of phytochemicals—that help prevent premature aging of the brain and nervous system. Excellent antioxidant sources include any fruit or vegetable that is richly colored, such as green or red bell peppers, berries, mangos, orange or grapefruit juice, carrots, sweet potatoes, spinach, apricots, wheat germ, chard, kale, and broccoli.

Iron is essential to quick and clear thinking. Iron helps transport oxygen to and within the brain's cells and works closely with the nerve chemicals that regulate all mental processes. Low intake of this trace mineral results in shortened attention span, lowered IQ, lack of motivation, inability to concentrate, poor educational achievement, and reduced work performance. Premenopausal women should include at least four, and postmenopausal women should include two to three, iron-rich foods in their daily diet, including extra-lean meat, cooked dried beans and peas, oysters, dried apricots, dark green leafy vegetables, and lima beans. Also, cook in cast-iron pots and drink orange juice, not milk, with high-iron meals to improve absorption of this mineral.

B vitamins are essential in the development of the nervous system. They help maintain the insulating sheath around nerve cells that speeds nerve communication, convert energy to a usable form for the brain, and regulate the chemicals that allow brain cells to communicate. Consequently, a deficiency of any one of the several B vitamins, including vitamins B_1, B_2, B_6, and B_{12}, or folic acid, can impair thinking, concentration, memory, reaction time, and mental clarity.

Low blood levels of B vitamins increase the risk for memory loss as a person ages, according to a study from Justus Liebig University of Giessen in Germany. Blood levels of homocysteine, vitamin B_6, vitamin B_{12}, and folate and intake of coffee, tea, and alcohol were assessed in a group of 252 seniors. Results showed that blood homocysteine levels, a marker for heart disease and memory loss, were higher in seniors than in younger populations, especially in women. The higher homocysteine levels in seniors were closely linked to low blood levels of the B vitamins. Other studies support the need for optimal vitamin B intake. For example, researchers at the University of New Mexico School of Medicine report that seniors who consume a diet rich in niacin, folic acid, and vitamins B_1, B_2, B_6, and C score higher on tests measuring memory and thinking ability than do people who eat poorly. Good sources of B vitamins in the Antiaging Diet include nonfat milk and yogurt, wheat germ, bananas, seafood, and green peas.

All forty-plus essential nutrients are important in maintaining a healthy mind. For example:

- Learning and memory slow in the presence of even a mild zinc deficiency. Low zinc intake is common in people, especially women, as they age. Include in the daily diet several zinc-rich foods, such as wheat germ, yogurt, almonds, cooked dried beans and peas, and dark green leafy vegetables.
- Choline is a vitamin-like component of acetylcholine, a nerve chemical that facilitates memory. Choline-rich foods include whole-wheat bread, peanut butter, cauliflower, egg yolks, liver, and leaf lettuce.
- Even coffee can help. Caffeine in coffee and a related compound called theobromine in tea directly stimulate the nervous system and can sharpen your reaction time and improve concentration, alertness, and short-term memory. But more than about three 5-ounce cups of coffee can give you the "coffee jitters" and muddle your concentration and thinking.

The Antioxidants and Memory

The brain consumes more oxygen than any other body tissue, which exposes it to a huge daily dose of oxygen fragments called free radicals. Free radicals are troublemakers, attacking, damaging, and destroying every brain cell in sight. The wear and tear after decades of free-radical attacks is thought to contribute to the gradual loss of memory and thinking associated with aging, even Alzheimer's disease.

That's where the antioxidants once more come in. People most prone to develop age-related memory loss also have the highest levels of free radicals, suggesting that this oxidative stress contributes to the disease. In contrast, people who consume the most antioxidants have lower levels of free radicals and are most likely to retain their faculties as they age. For example, a study from Erasmus University Medical School in The Netherlands found that thinking ability remained high throughout life when people consumed the most beta-carotene-rich foods, such as sweet potatoes, carrots, and apricots. To keep your antioxidant defenses strong, consume daily at least eight, preferably more, servings of colorful, fresh produce.

Soy and Your Mind

Preliminary evidence suggests that adding soy to the menu could help save your memory. It is unclear how soy improves memory, but researchers speculate that the phytoestrogens in soy are protectors of brain tissue or that other compounds in soy might help lower homocysteine levels, which reduces inflammation and circulatory problems associated with impaired memory. What is clear is that memory appears to improve in postmenopausal women when they add soy phytoestrogens to their diets. In a study from the University of California, San Diego, women who consumed soy on a regular basis performed better on mental and memory tests compared with their baseline tests and with the placebo group. You can boost soy intake simply by adding a serving or two of tofu to your weekly menu or by switching from milk to soy milk on occasion.

Healthy Fats, Sharp Minds

Just as some dietary fats lower heart disease while others raise your risk, the type of fat you include in the diet could make or break your thinking later in life. Researchers at the University of Bari in Italy investigated the impact diet has on memory and cognition throughout life. They found that diets high in monounsaturated fats found in nuts, olives, avocados, and canola or olive oils were protective against cognitive decline. Fish and whole-grain cereals also lowered risk for memory loss. Large amounts of aluminum-containing additives or aluminum from drinking water elevated risk, as did deficiencies of vitamins B_6 and B_{12}, folic acid, and the antioxidants vitamins C and E.

Phosphatidylserine (PS) is a type of fat that acts like a revolving door for brain cells, allowing nutrients easy access to the cell and providing a quick escape for toxic cellular debris. PS helps nerve cells conduct nerve impulses, thus enhancing communication within the brain. The body also uses PS to make acetylcholine, the memory-enhancing nerve chemical. Although additional research is necessary, preliminary evidence is promising for the use of PS in preventing or treating mild memory loss. To supplement with this compound, the typical starting daily dose is 300 milligrams, with a maintenance dose of 100 milligrams after that.

The Dumbing Effect of Diet

If your head is wax, don't walk in the sun.

—BENJAMIN FRANKLIN

Cutting calories might boost brainpower or make you dumber, depending on how you cut. Paring down your calorie intake, while still eating a nutrient-packed diet, and doing it for life is the only dietary habit known to increase life span. Paring calories also prevents age-related mental and memory decline.

In contrast, jump on any quick-fix diet bandwagon, and you might come out dumber as a result. Michael Green, Ph.D., senior research psychologist, and colleagues at the Institute of Food Research in the United Kingdom have studied the dumbing effect of diet for several years. In one study, fifty-five women between the ages of eighteen and forty—some of whom were currently on a diet while others were not—were seated in front of computer terminals where a continuous stream of single numbers was displayed. The women were asked to press a response button whenever they detected a sequence of three odd or three even numbers. A total of forty such groupings were presented in random fashion over the course of five minutes.

"The women who were currently dieting to lose weight displayed poorer reaction speeds, immediate memory, and ability to sustain attention," concludes Dr. Green. They processed information slowly, took longer to react, and had more trouble remembering sequences compared with their nondieting counterparts.

Common sense tells us that any drastic reduction in calories will cut off the brain's main fuel supply—carbohydrates. Starved nerves, in turn, relay messages halfheartedly, which means that thinking and emotions suffer. Restricting carbohydrates and calories also upsets the production of nerve chemicals, such as serotonin, that regulate both appetite and mood. Dieting also wreaks havoc with other appetite-control chemicals, such as neuropeptide Y (NPY), galanin, and the endorphins. This disruption can undermine the best weight-loss intentions while also potentially affecting mood and mental state, according to research conducted by Sarah Leibowitz, Ph.D., professor of neurobiology at Rockefeller University in New York.

While glucose levels dwindle, blood levels of fat fragments called free fatty acids are on the rise during restrictive dieting, which is a clear indicator of stress. The stress of dieting, in turn, would contribute to the heightened emotions, increased distractibility, and clouded thinking. "The degree of impairment . . . is similar to that found with other types of extreme preoccupying worry," says Dr. Green.

Finally, cut back too far on calories, and you also jeopardize nutrient intake. In fact, it's virtually impossible to guarantee optimal vitamin and mineral intake on less than 2,000 calories. The dumbing effect is limited only to quick-fix diets. In contrast, "Weight loss in a slow, steady fashion (about two pounds a week) will lead to a more permanent weight reduction and also will be less likely to lead to feelings of frustration and anxiety," concludes Dr. Green.

Is There a Dietary Cure for Alzheimer's Disease?

The heart does not grow old, but it is said to dwell among the ruins.

—VOLTAIRE

Alzheimer's disease seems like the most sinister of all the incurable diseases. This degenerative brain disorder first kills a person's identity by slowly erasing all memories, names, dates, places, and personality. Only after the simplest tasks, such as chewing or swallowing, are lost in the fog of confusion does the disease take the body. The process is excruciatingly slow, unfolding over the course of six to twenty years.

Age is a contributor to Alzheimer's but not a decree. In some cases, age works in a person's favor. While nearly 50 percent of people over the age of eighty-five have Alzheimer's, the numbers drop in people in their nineties. In fact, as few as 25 percent of people over the age of ninety-three have symptoms of this debilitating disease. This suggests that the oldest old are in better shape mentally than their children. Whatever helps these people reach a ripe and active old age also enables them to avoid or delay the diseases that commonly are linked to aging.

A Weak Link with Diet

It is likely that environmental factors contribute to the disease, especially if it occurs later in life. Early studies reported an increased accumulation of aluminum in the brain of Alzheimer's patients, which led to speculation that the use of aluminum cookware, antacids, or even deodorant could trigger the disease. However, subsequent studies have found little to link aluminum with the onset of Alzheimer's.

Poor nutrition is probably related to Alzheimer's disease, but it is unclear whether it is a cause or an effect. Early damage to brain cells located in the region of appetite control might explain changes in food intake. A poor diet resulting in low vitamin and mineral intake might encourage a predisposition to the disease. Once the disease has reached advanced stages, the patient loses interest in or the ability to choose or consume nutritious foods, which only speeds the loss of memory and function.

Consuming enough of certain nutrients, such as the B vitamins, might at least slow the progression of Alzheimer's. The B vitamins, especially B_{12}, are essential for the synthesis and release of acetylcholine, the neurotransmitter involved in memory. Poor intake and low blood levels of vitamin B_{12}, folic acid, and vitamin B_6 could be linked with Alzheimer's disease. Scores on cognitive-function tests are lowest in Alzheimer's patients with the lowest vitamin B_{12} blood levels. In addition, older persons with low vitamin B_{12} levels are at highest risk of developing the disease. It is unknown whether the vitamin deficiency causes or results from deterioration of brain tissue. One of the functions of vitamin B_{12} is to maintain healthy nerve tissue, which might explain how a deficiency of the vitamin contributes to the progression of Alzheimer's disease. Poor intake of any or all of these B vitamins results in elevated levels of a nerve toxin called homocysteine, which impairs memory and mental alertness.

In fact, elevated levels of homocysteine are a red flag for Alzheimer's disease, according to a study from Boston University School of Medicine. Homocysteine levels were measured in 1,092 men and women without dementia with an average age of seventy-six. These measurements were compared with 111 cases of dementia (including 83 diagnosed with Alzheimer's disease) on follow-up eight years later. Results showed that as homocysteine levels increased, the risk for dementia increased. Those subjects with the highest levels of homocysteine at baseline had an 80 percent increased risk for developing Alzheimer's disease. A plasma homocysteine level greater than 14umol/L nearly doubled the risk for Alzheimer's disease. The good news is that you can easily lower homocysteine levels by ensuring your diet is rich in vitamin B_{12}, vitamin B_6, and folic acid. For example, people with the highest folate status score significantly higher on memory than people with low folate status. You can't take these nutrients for granted. Up to one in every four seniors is low in these B vitamins, according to a review of the literature by researchers at USDA Human Nutrition Research Center on Aging at Tufts University.

Choline, a vitamin B–like compound, and its dietary source lecithin have shown varying effectiveness in the treatment of memory loss and Alzheimer's disease. A neurotransmitter called acetylcholine contains choline, suggesting that memory might be enhanced with oral intake of choline. Supplementing with choline or lecithin (containing 90 percent phosphatidylcholine) sometimes has improved brain function in patients with memory loss. Unfortunately, both choline and lecithin have been ineffective in other cases; they raised blood levels of choline but had no affect on acetylcholine levels or brain function. If choline and lecithin are effective in the treatment of memory loss, they are probably useful only in the beginning or mild stages and are then useful only in prolonging the onset of more advanced stages of the disease. According to researchers at Duquesne University in Pittsburgh, caffeine and choline administered together might be more effective for enhancing memory than either one alone.

Fish oils also show promise in slowing age-related memory loss. A diet high in fish oils might slow the progression of Alzheimer's disease, state researchers at the University of California, Los Angeles. In fact, even one serving of fish each week could lower Alzheimer's risk by up to 60 percent.

Finally, the antioxidants might help prevent, or at least slow, the progression of Alzheimer's. People who consume antioxidant-rich diets have a lower risk of developing Alzheimer's disease. At Erasmus Medical Center in The Netherlands, dementia incidence and dietary intakes were monitored during six years in a group of 5,395 people who were fifty-five or older and dementia free at the start of the study. Results showed that high intakes of vitamins C and E lowered the risk for developing Alzheimer's by 18 percent. High intakes of beta-carotene and flavonoids also showed protective effects. Numerous studies found that vitamin E supplements helped prevent and slow the progression of Alzheimer's and might lower the risk for developing Alzheimer's disease by up to 70 percent.

More than Diet

The old man keeps all his mental powers so long as he gives up neither using them nor adding to them.

—CICERO

Hormones, medications, lack of sleep, and disease can undermine mental clarity. Lagging estrogen levels in menopausal women can cloud thinking, while women on hormone replacement therapy (HRT) or people who manage their high blood pressure report improvements in mental function. HRT also reduces a woman's risk for developing Alzheimer's disease. Many commonly prescribed drugs, including antihypertensives and antidepressants, can slow memory. If you're taking any medication and notice changes in your mental abilities, ask your pharmacist or physician if there could be a connection. Anything that disturbs sleep, from arthritis pain and prostate problems to worry or caffeine, can undermine mental function.

A couple of herbs also might help lagging memory. Ginkgo biloba and ginseng improve memory and reaction time, according to a study from the University of Northumbria in the United Kingdom. People received 360 milligrams of ginkgo, 400 milligrams of ginseng, 960 milligrams of a combined ginkgo and ginseng supplement, or placebos and were tested for cognitive ability one, two and a half, four, and six hours after supplementation. All three treatments improved memory, while ginseng also made improvements in the speed of performing memory tasks and in the accuracy of attention.

Avoid exposure to mercury, lead, and other toxic metals that damage brain and nervous tissue and are associated with subtle neurological and psychological disorders, including learning disabilities, reduced attention span, poor reasoning and concentration skills, and reduced IQ.

Work a Muscle, Improve a Mind

People who stay physically active maintain the highest level of cognitive function. When tested, their brain waves are remarkably youthful in patterning. The more years a person exercises, the greater the benefits in cognitive ability. Exercise increases blood flow, oxygen, and nutrients to the brain. It helps maintain low levels of stress hormones while increasing levels of nerve chemicals such as norepinephrine. Exercise also increases the demand on the nervous system to maintain coordination and reaction times during exercise. Any of these responses could explain why physically active people have faster reaction times and retain more information than do sedentary people.

Vitally Thinking

Prepare yourself for the great world, as the athletes used to do for their exercises; oil your mind and your manners, to give them the necessary suppleness and flexibility; strength alone will not do, as young people are too apt to think.

—LORD CHESTERFIELD

Vitality often is the fuel that keeps a person thinking clearly. Those who read, travel, or expose themselves to new experiences at every age keep their minds active. They also live longer and are less likely to develop Alzheimer's disease. Our capacity to remember quantities of information declines somewhat as we age, which has more to do with disuse than with age. The average older person can remember only six items from a memory test compared with a younger person's eight items; the same older person after undergoing a memory training course can remember thirty items, while the younger person's recall jumps to forty. Age might make a difference but not half as much as keeping the brain active and alert. The problem may not be that the mind fails as we age but that we fail to keep our minds engaged.

PART 3

Use Experience to Master Aging

Middle-Age Spread

> *Use, do not abuse; neither*
> *abstinence nor excess ever*
> *renders man happy.*
> —VOLTAIRE

The typical American gains twenty pounds between the ages of twenty-five and fifty-five. Every extra pound of fat beyond ten costs a person one month of life and affects the quality of life. More than three hundred thousand deaths each year in the United States are attributable to obesity, which is quickly catching up to smoking as the leading cause of death. Within the next fifty years, the epidemic of obesity will begin shortening life expectancy rates by at least two and possibly five years, according to researchers at the University of Illinois.

The percentage of overweight people has jumped from one in four to almost seven out of every ten people since the 1970s, according to the Centers for Disease Control and Prevention. More than sixty million Americans are obese, with a body mass index (BMI) of 30 or greater. The rates coincide with a similar increase in hours of television viewing and miles logged in automobiles, a drop in hours of physical activity, and burgeoning portions of restaurant and home-cooked meals. The obesity issue is an issue having to do with lifestyle, not genetics.

Is Weight Gain Inevitable?

> *Success rests in having the courage and endurance and, above all,*
> *the will to become the person you are, however peculiar that may be.*
> *Then you will be able to say, "I have found my hero and he is me."*
> —GEORGE SHEEHAN, M.D.

- You ran track in high school. Now you are out of breath just darting across the street before the signal changes.

- You remember when you could sit cross-legged on the floor for hours. Now you can barely get down on the floor, and if you do, it takes a forklift to get you back up.
- You used to do backbends, cartwheels, and handstands. Now you're too stiff to touch your toes.
- You once fit into size 6 pants. Now finding a pair of size 12s that look good on you is like searching for a needle in a haystack. Buying pants with elastic waistbands is beginning to sound realistic.

Most people gain weight as they age. They also get flabby, choose sightseeing instead of backpacking for a vacation, and spend their free time in front of the television instead of on a bicycle. Until recently, there were few avid exercisers in this age group, and no fit group to compare with the average pudgy, sedentary, middle-aged man or woman. As more people in their thirties, forties, fifties, and beyond adopt active lifestyles, the results are amazing. So don't make excuses about how you're just getting old. Endurance, flexibility, and strength needn't fade, and you don't have to gain weight as you age.

"Much of what we have thought was the inevitable result of aging is actually caused by inactivity," says Lawrence Golding, Ph.D., professor of exercise physiology at the University of Nevada, Las Vegas, and the primary researcher in a study that has followed exercisers for years. In your thirties and forties, as your career or family demands more of your time, you spend less of your life jogging or taking a spin class and more of your free time resting. You trade muscle for fat, metabolism slows, and weight creeps up. You become weaker and stiffer and less flexible, so you do less, which leads to further weight gain and loss of muscle. Middle-age spread is just the beginning of a continuum that will eventually put you in a wheelchair or walker if you don't stop trading muscle for fat.

It is much more about disuse than aging that causes muscles to gradually break down and waistlines expand. The good news is you speed metabolism, maintain flexibility and strength, and curb, if not halt, weight gain by rebuilding lost muscle mass with exercise. Aerobic activity will burn the fat and weight training will build muscle. "Starting at age forty in women and at sixty in men, we lose six to eight percent of our muscle per decade," says Dr. Ben Hurley, from the University of Maryland. "However, after only two months of strength training, women recover a decade of loss and men recover two decades." Research on people who walk for two to three miles each day and eat calorie-controlled, low-fat diets indicates they do not gain the pounds their nonexercising peers gain between the ages of forty-five and fifty. It's never too late to turn back the hands of time—but the sooner you start, the better.

What's a Desirable Weight?

The term *obesity* refers to a body weight that is 20 percent above a person's desirable weight. If someone's desirable weight is approximately 140 pounds, then that person is obese when the scale tips at 168 and the added 28 pounds are fat, not muscle.

Another measurement is the body mass index, or BMI, which calculates body fat by dividing body weight in kilograms by height squared. The American Health Foundation states that optimizing the cardiovascular risk profile corresponds to a BMI of 22.6 or less for men and 21.1 or less for women. A BMI greater than 27 is a warning for postmenopausal breast cancer, while the highest prevalence of diabetes occurs when the BMI is greater than 28. The lowest mortality and morbidity rates occur with BMIs between 19 and 25, which should be attained by twenty-one-years-old and maintained throughout life. As a reference point, for a 5'10" man to have a BMI of between 19 and 25, his body weight must be 128 to 169 pounds. For a 5'5" woman to reach a BMI of 19 to 25, her body must be 114 to 150 pounds.

Prevention is the best medicine when it comes to health and weight. The American Health Foundation's Expert Panel on Healthy Weight states, "The healthiest weight is one that is attained by the age of 21 years old and maintained throughout life." If you are gaining a few pounds every year and those extra pounds are fat, not muscle, you should start and stick with a daily exercise routine and a calorie-controlled diet. If you are already above your weight goal but are not yet at risk for weight-related diseases, the Expert Panel recommends losing between ten and sixteen pounds.

Are You an Apple or a Pear?

*Make the best use of what is in your power, and take the rest
as it happens.*

—EPICTETUS

It's not only how much body fat you have but where it's stored that influences how healthy you are and how long you will live. The good news is that a few extra pounds in the hips and thighs might dent your vanity, but they won't hurt your health. On the other hand, a spare tire or beer belly, even in an otherwise slender person, could signal health problems.

Apple-shaped people carry most of their weight in the chest and abdomen (called an android pattern), while pear-shaped people store fat below the belt and remain relatively slender in their upper bodies (called a gynoid pattern). A man with a waist greater than thirty-seven inches and a woman with a waist of thirty-one inches or greater are likely to be Apples.

Apples are more likely to be men or postmenopausal women. They also are more likely to develop heart disease, diabetes, high blood pressure, gallbladder disease, and possibly cancer; their diseases progress faster and more seriously—and they are more apt to die prematurely from disease than are Pears, even when the two have similar body weights and body fat percentages. In addition, blood cholesterol and triglyceride levels are high in Apples, while HDL (good) cholesterol is low. The health risks apply to both slim and plump Apples.

The type of abdominal fat associated with health risks is called visceral fat, the firm fat that surrounds the internal organs. Subcutaneous fat that lies close to the skin is not the culprit. So a firm, big belly is more indicative of health problems, whereas one or two inches of pinchable fat around the middle might force you to loosen your belt but probably won't hurt your health.

Fat above the waist is more likely to be stocked with saturated fats, so it's firmer than fat below the waist. This fat also is more metabolically active. Extra upper-body fat is associated with a condition called the metabolic syndrome, which includes increased blood levels of fats called free fatty acids, poor regulation of blood sugar and fat, and an increased risk for diabetes and heart disease. Upper-body fat increases both estrogen and testosterone levels, which elevate the risk for developing cancer.

Dieting and Body Shape

Whether body shape changes when you lose weight depends on if you're an Apple or a Pear. Thomas Wadden, Ph.D., professor of psychology at the University of Pennsylvania School of Medicine, monitored body measurements in overweight women who lost weight. Apple-shaped women lost more of their weight in the chest and abdomen; consequently, their body shapes noticeably changed as they lost weight. Women with big hips and thighs (Pears) lost as much if not more weight but lost weight in both the upper and lower body, maintaining essentially the same shape as they slimmed down. "They come into a weight-management program as large Pears and leave as small Pears," says Dr. Wadden.

Losing weight lowers what is called the waist-to-hip ratio (WHR), the proportion of fat above the waist compared with the fat at hip and thigh level (an Apple has a high WHR, while a Pear has a low WHR). Apples derive greater benefits from weight loss, because they lose more weight from the upper body; even a 10 percent reduction in weight significantly improves the Apple's health status. "In short, a person can get rid of the Apple shape, but a Pear will always be a Pear," states Dr. Wadden, who adds, "The only way a pear-shaped person can change body shape is to weight train and build the upper body so the lower body looks smaller."

How you lose the weight might be as important as where you lose it, since preliminary research shows that women who go on and off fad diets have greater fat distribution above the waist and less fat accumulation in the thighs, placing them at greater risk for heart disease and the metabolic syndrome compared with non-weight cyclers. Learning to love your body the way it is might be a more healthful alternative to repeated dieting for Pears.

Stressed-Out Apples

Pears tend to live healthful lives, while Apples are more likely to be smokers, be stressed and sedentary, drink alcohol, or consume high-fat diets. The link with stress is particularly interesting, since this might be a contributing factor in weight gain.

The stress hormone—cortisol—encourages the body to accumulate fat, especially around the middle, where it does the most harm, increasing the risk for heart disease, diabetes, high blood pressure, and other ills. The issue here is chronic, not temporary, stress. A single bout of stress—say you swerve to avoid a collision on the highway—causes cortisol levels to rise instantly and then return to normal. Cortisol is meant for these occasional stresses and is meant only as an "in case of emergency" hormone. Chronic stress is an unnatural state for the body that jams cortisol levels into high gear.

One function of cortisol is to help the body replenish calories after a stressful experience, such as running away from an attacker, and to store those calories in the abdomen for future use. Cortisol triggers both a hike in levels of insulin (a hormone that further increases appetite and fat storage) and a drop in levels of serotonin (the nerve chemical that, when low, increases depression, irritability, and cravings for sweets). Cortisol is useful for the occasional worry, but chronic stress bathes the body in a flood of cortisol that leads to an around-the-clock, insatiable appetite, typically for sweets and fatty foods. You pack on the pounds, and typically that extra weight is stored in your midsection, turning a Pear into an Apple. People who cut back on their fat intakes, stop watching television and start including exercise in their daily routines, and stop smoking are the ones most likely to lower their stress hormones, maintain a healthy weight, lower their WHR, and improve the length and quality of their lives.

How to Lose Weight and Keep It Off

Eighty percent of success is showing up.

—WOODY ALLEN

The only sound, time-proven skills for permanent weight management are:

- Burn more calories than you take in by exercising daily and cutting back on excess calories from refined grains, sugar, and fat.
- Make changes gradually to allow for a one- to two-pound weight loss each week.
- Establish an eating and exercise program you can live with for life.

While you cut calories, you don't want to sacrifice health by cutting vitamins, minerals, fiber, essential fats, and phytochemicals. You must make every bite count! The Antiaging Diet can be tailored to your weight-management needs. But even this excellent eating plan can't guarantee optimal intake of all nutrients when calories drop too low. Consider taking a moderate-dose, well-balanced vitamin and mineral supplement if you're consuming fewer than 2,000 calories a day.

Weight in Motion

Daily exercise is the number-one predictor of whether a person will succeed at lifelong weight management. Working out revs up your metabolism, builds muscle that burns calories, and keeps the weight off. Diet alone won't work and, in fact, might shrink muscles and slow metabolic rate. Diet without exercise means that up to half of the weight lost will be in lean muscle tissue, not fat weight. Metabolic rate slows, which means calories must be cut even more or you gain back the weight. Combining cardiovascular exercise that burns fat, such as walking or jogging, with strength training that builds muscle and revs up the metabolic rate is the only way to maintain muscle and lose fat as you get older. Plan on exercising almost daily for the rest of your life.

Permanent weight loss, like vitality, takes practice. You want an eating and exercise plan you can live with for life and that will allow a gradual weight loss of no more than two pounds a week. Make changes gradually as you adopt the Antiaging Diet and Fitness Program, and consume no fewer than 1,500 calories if you are a short or relatively inactive woman. Add 500 calories if you are a tall and/or active woman, and add up to 1,000 calories if you are an active man. You should increase exercise, not cut calories further, if you can't lose weight on this low-calorie plan.

It All Comes Back to Calories

Calories from fat, alcohol, and possibly sugar are more likely to end up as body fat than are similar amounts of carbs or protein. In addition to being twice as calorie-dense as other foods, dietary fat is more readily converted to body fat.

Sugar also could be to blame for expanding waistlines. High-fructose corn syrup is the sugar of choice in many processed foods, especially soft drinks, yet is linked to increased weight gain and insulin resistance, according to a review by researchers at the University of California, Davis. Fructose, compared to glucose, is preferentially metabolized to fat in the liver and might be a risk factor for weight gain. It also induces insulin resistance, impairs glucose tolerance, and elevates blood insulin levels.

Starting Out

Before you begin a diet, review what really needs changing and where you should start. You want to lose the right kind of weight—fat weight—and you want to lose it for good without sacrificing your health. Here are the three predieting steps to take before starting a weight-management plan:

Step One. Throw out the scale and check your body-fat percentage—that is, how much of your total body weight is fat weight. Body-fat percentages can be calculated by trained professionals using a variety of techniques, including calipers and underwater weighing. Women should aim for a range somewhere between 20 and 30 percent. Men should aim for a range between 12 and 20 percent. Or use the ballpark measure of "overfatness"—the waist-to-hip measurement, which requires nothing more than a tape measure and third-grade arithmetic skills. Divide the waist measurement by the hip measurement; if the ratio is greater than 0.80 or, in women, if the total waist measurement is greater than thirty-one inches, you probably need to lose some fat weight.

Step Two. What are you eating? Any "no" answers to the following questions is a starting place for making dietary changes.

1. Do you consume daily at least five servings of colorful fruits and vegetables?
2. Of these five servings, is at least one a dark green vegetable and one a citrus fruit?
3. Do you consume daily at least three servings of whole-grain breads, pasta, cereals, and other grains?
4. Do you consume daily at least three servings of nonfat or low-fat milk or other low-fat calcium-rich foods, such as fortified orange juice or soy milk?
5. Do you consume daily at least three servings of iron-rich extra-lean meat, chicken breast, fish, or legumes?
6. Do you typically bake, steam, or broil rather than fry, sauté, or use sauces or gravies? When you use sauces, are they tomato based rather than cream based?

When you eat those calories also is important. Large, infrequent meals might set up a scenario in which the body stores more calories as fat as a safeguard against what it perceives as a famine. Dividing the same amount of calories into five or more little meals and snacks encourages the body to burn the food for immediate energy rather than store it in the hips and thighs. Space your meals similarly to those in the seven-day meal plan in Appendix A, starting with breakfast, so that no more than four hours go by between a light meal or snack. Your ultimate goal is not just a certain figure or a number on the bathroom scale—it is a lifelong commitment to be the best and healthiest you.

7. Do you eat at fast-food restaurants less than once a week?
8. Do you avoid or strictly limit butter, margarine, and foods that contain trans fats? When you add fats to your foods, is it olive or canola oil, nuts, or avocados?
9. Do you read food labels and choose only foods that contain 3 grams of fat or less for every 100 calories?
10. Do you strictly limit high-sugar or high-fat snack items to no more than one or two per week?
11. Do you limit (to no more than one drink a day) or avoid alcohol?
12. Do you take a moderate-dose multiple vitamin and mineral supplement?

Step Three. The following questions might help you identify whether managing your emotions, thoughts, and stress should be at the forefront of your weight-loss plan. This time, any "yes" answer is a red flag.

1. Do you eat with a frenzy when under stress?
2. Do you constantly think about food and/or dieting?
3. Do you eat when you're bored, tired, lonely, depressed, anxious, scared, or excited?
4. Do you eat to relax, as a reward or treat, or to calm down?
5. Does extra body weight give you a sense of self-protection?
6. Do you try to ignore hunger but then feel deprived?
7. Are you driven by a desire to be fit or thin, and do you believe that thinness is synonymous with success, beauty, or personal power?
8. Do you overeat in secret or when you are alone?
9. Do you feel that physical hunger is more an enemy than a friend?
10. Do you eat unconsciously—that is, in front of the TV, while reading a book or magazine, or when preparing dinner?

Knowing Where You're Going

Goals are your road map to weight management. Without them you won't know where you are going or even if you got there. For a goal to be useful, it must be specific, realistic, and flexible. Instead of a vague goal to "exercise more" or "reduce fat intake," write specific goals that include what, when, where, and how, such as "I will jog for thirty minutes during my lunch hour, five days a week, for the next six months" or "To reduce my fat intake, I will spread a little jam instead of butter on my toast in the morning."

■ *Stick with It*

In addition to exercising daily and adhering to a healthy, calorie-controlled diet, people who are most likely to successfully lose weight and maintain the weight loss also keep a daily food journal to monitor their eating habits. They also learn from their slipups and return quickly to balanced eating and exercise patterns. As Kelly D. Brownell, Ph.D., professor of psychology at Yale University, says, "If you are changing any aspect of your life, expect setbacks and be prepared to recover. A smart person minimizes mistakes. A smarter person knows how to recover." Following are a few suggestions to help you steer your course to success.

MANAGE EATING AND THE ENVIRONMENT

- Sit at a designated place, such as the dining room table, to eat.
- Eat without reading, watching TV, driving, or doing other activities. Chew slowly and pay attention to flavors and textures.
- Make food less visible, convenient, and available. For example, store food out of sight, ask someone to clean up the leftovers, remove serving dishes from the table, or don't bring tempting foods into the house.
- Plan another activity—such as riding a stationary bike, taking a bath, putting polish on your nails, writing a letter, or walking with a friend—during times of the day when you're prone to eat.
- Avoid or eliminate cues that signal you to eat inappropriately. If a doughnut shop on the way to work is too tempting, then take a different route to work.
- On returning home from work, go for a walk rather than opening the refrigerator.
- Take nutritious foods to work or play so you won't be tempted by the vending machine, fast-food restaurant, or cookie counter.

Realistic goals take into account where you are today and what you are likely to accomplish with reasonable effort. Unrealistic goals are a setup for failure, so avoid perfectionist goals that use words such as *always*, *never*, or *every day*.

For a goal to be realistic, it should be broken down into ministeps. For example, a long-term goal to lose twenty pounds can be broken down into short-term goals to lose one to two pounds a week for the next ten to twenty weeks. Ministeps also include walking an additional three miles a day to burn 250 calories, replacing negative thoughts with supportive ones, and substituting baby carrots for potato chips for your midafternoon snack.

MANAGE THOUGHTS, EMOTIONS, ATTITUDES, AND BELIEFS

- Avoid using food as a reward, a treat, or therapy.
- Listen to your body, and eat only when you are physically hungry.
- List your beliefs about yourself and food. Replace negative beliefs (such as "Everyone must like me" or "I should be good at everything") that interfere with weight management with positive ones (such as "Everyone doesn't have to like me" or "It's all right to make mistakes"). Replace negative thoughts (such as "I can't do this" or "I deserve a treat") with positive ones (such as "I am in charge of my weight and health" or "I've worked hard and made progress in my weight management—I won't stop now!").
- Most people have one or more problem foods that are hard to refuse. Plan ahead when, where, and how much of a "trigger" food you will eat and how you will stop eating.
- Focus on what you can have rather than what you can't have.
- Use thought stopping. Visualize a stop sign in your mind whenever you catch yourself thinking a negative thought about your weight-management efforts.

STAY MOTIVATED

- Reward yourself frequently with nonfood rewards. Place tally marks on a calendar, tokens in a jar, or money in a piggy bank each time you accomplish a ministep.
- Give yourself credit for daily successes.
- Visualize yourself ahead of time successfully handling food issues and social situations involving food.
- Recognize that changing habits will require an initial investment of time.
- Focus on gradual lifestyle changes rather than on dieting or weight loss.

Stay flexible. Modify your ministeps if you find they are too easy or too difficult. Goals should be challenging, not overwhelming.

Snack Rules in the Antiaging Diet

Unplanned nibbling can make or break your weight-management efforts and health. The secret is not to add more snacks to your usual diet but to divide your current food intake into five or six little meals, while continuing to emphasize fiber

My Road Map to Success

Make photocopies of the following worksheet and fill it in each week. Use the checklist to monitor your success. First summarize your ministeps in the left-hand column. Then give yourself credit by placing a tally mark under the appropriate day each time you accomplish a ministep. There can be more than one tally mark per day.

Date/week: _____

Long-term goal: _____

This week's short-term goal: _____

Each day's ministeps (include details such as when, where, how often, with whom)

1. _____

2. _____

3. _____

	MON.	TUES.	WED.	THURS.	FRI.	SAT.	SUN.
Ministep 1: ____							
Ministep 2: ____							
Ministep 3: ____							

and nutrients and to deemphasize fat, sugar, and salt. Have the oatmeal with raisins and orange juice for breakfast, but save the glass of milk and banana for a mid-morning snack. Have a sandwich, raw vegetables, and tomato juice for lunch, but save the dessert of yogurt and fruit for a midafternoon snack. Dine on spaghetti, salad, and steamed vegetables in the evening, and then have a slice of French bread and a cup of nonfat cocoa for a late-night snack. Looking good and feeling great might be as simple as leaving the house each day with your gym bag in one hand and a brown-bag snack and little meal in the other.

In essence, the Antiaging Diet and Fitness Program are also your ticket to weight management. Just adjust the calories in the diet and boost activity to lose weight.

Menopause: A Change for the Better

We do not count a [wo]man's years, until [she] has nothing else to count.
—RALPH WALDO EMERSON

By the year 2015, almost one in every two women in the United States will be in or past menopause. Between 1990 and 2020, the number of menopausal women will double. At no other time in the history of this country have we had so many people facing the same health issues. With that many women experiencing a major life transition, even the change (as menopause is sometimes called) is undergoing a transformation.

As recently as the late 1800s, many women did not outlive their ovaries, so menopause was a moot point. Today menopause, the cessation of ovulation, is only a halfway mark through life for many women. While our grandmothers weathered the experience in silence, women today have brought menopause into boardrooms and offices and onto magazine and book covers and have made it the topic of nationwide television talk shows. Many of the symptoms that women once suffered in silence are now preventable, or at least can be lessened, by a few simple changes in diet and activity.

Just Another Milestone

Keep constantly in mind in how many things you yourself have witnessed changes already. The universe is change, life is understanding.
—MARCUS AURELIUS

The term *menopause* literally means the cessation of menstruation. To be considered menopausal, a woman must be menstruation free for twelve months. By the time she is officially diagnosed as menopausal, the experience is over. Of course, a woman knows long before this that something is different. Her memory or concentration might fail her at all the wrong times, causing her to doubt her competence or sanity. She might break out in drenching sweats during the day (called hot flashes or hot flushes) or at night (called night sweats). Her moods might fluctuate and intensify, while energy levels can fall to an all-time low.

When the diagnosis of menopause is unclear or when a woman enters menopause early, a test to measure follicle-stimulating hormone (FSH) helps. This hormone is manufactured by the pituitary gland in the brain. Levels of FSH increase as estrogen levels drop. Therefore, the higher the FSH level, the more likely the woman is in menopause. The problem with this test is that FSH levels fluctuate as estrogen levels rise and fall, from month to month and even from day to day, over the course of several years when a woman is premenopausal, a period called perimenopause. One test might not be an accurate assessment of a woman's condition, and a physician might need to run more than one FSH test to obtain reliable information.

The menopausal experience is as varied as the personalities of the women who pass this milestone. The average age at menopause is fifty-one, but eight out of a hundred women go through the change before they hit forty, and fertility has been documented in women pushing sixty. Often a woman goes through menopause at about the same time as her mother did, suggesting a strong genetic link. What is certain is that since the average life expectancy for women is eighty years old, tens of millions of women can expect to spend up to 40 percent of their lives after menopause.

Most of the symptoms can be traced to the hormonal roller coaster a woman rides during menopause. A woman's ovaries are the manufacturing center for the female hormone estrogen. As the ovaries begin to shut down, estrogen levels surge, fluctuate, and eventually decline. Anything that levels the surges in estrogen will help curb the symptoms of menopause. While hormone replacement therapy (HRT) is by far the most effective method of balancing estrogen swells, a few studies suggest that for some women this might not be an option. The good news is that diet and exercise is a natural way to help handle many of the discomforts and health risks associated with the menopausal and postmenopausal years.

The Soy Connection

Change not the mass but change the fabric of your own soul and
your own visions, and you change all.

—VACHEL LINDSAY

The hot flash is the hallmark of menopause for many women. A hot flash is the sudden rise in body temperature accompanied sometimes by intense perspiration, a flushing of the skin, and waves of heat that can range from mild to tormenting. The hot flash is the external sign of internal swells in estrogen levels.

Estrogen-like compounds, called phytoestrogens, found in soy help offset the drop in a woman's natural estrogen. While not exactly like estrogen, phytoestrogens act much like the female hormone, binding to the body's estrogen receptors and supplementing the effects of estrogen when levels are low. Whether phytoestrogens actually curb menopausal hot flashes remains controversial, but some women swear soy works and some studies show a possible effect, while other studies conclude soy is no better than placebos. Switching from hamburgers to soy burgers, milk to soy milk, and pork to tofu does reduce a woman's risk for heart disease and possibly lowers her risk for breast cancer, weight gain, and dementia.

This link between food and flush was first suspected when researchers noted the dramatic difference in the incidence of hot flashes across cultures. Only 14 to 18 percent of women living in China and Japan ever experience a hot flash, while up to 80 percent of women in the United States and Europe can describe their last hot flash in detail. Women in Japan and China also add soy to their diets daily and excrete up to a thousand times more phytoestrogens in their urine. One study found that hot flashes decreased up to 44 percent when women added soy to their diets. However, other studies found soy and/or its phytoestrogens to have no effect on hot flashes, vaginal dryness, or other symptoms of menopause.

What should you do? Preliminary evidence suggests that as little as two glasses of soy milk or two ounces of tofu daily might be all a woman needs to lower her risk of heart disease. Whether soy foods also curb those pesky hot flashes is unclear, but it won't hurt to try adding soy to your diet for a few months and see if this dietary change helps cool you down. Always choose soy foods over soy supplements.

■ *The Hot Flash: A Lifestyle Approach*

Except for possibly including soy foods in the daily diet, there is no surefire way to eliminate hot flashes, but there are a few tricks that might ease the symptoms.

- Avoid coffee, chocolate, alcohol, and spicy foods, all of which alter blood flow and can increase the symptoms of hot flashes.
- Eat small meals and snacks regularly throughout the day. Large meals increase body temperature and might aggravate a hot flash.
- Place a glass of ice water by the bed at night to drink at the first sign of an approaching night sweat. Try opening the bedroom window to keep the cool air flowing, use 100 percent cotton sheets, and turn on a small fan by the bed.
- Be careful of what herbal teas you drink. Some herbs, such as dong quai, cause blood vessel dilation and could aggravate a hot flash.
- Some women report that vitamins E and C or the herb black cohosh help improve symptoms of hot flashes; however, this evidence is sketchy.
- Dress in layers so you can add or subtract clothes as your body's temperature fluctuates.

Food and Mood

Time cools, time clarifies; no mood can be maintained quite
unaltered through the course of hours.

—THOMAS MANN

As the female hormones fluctuate during menopause, so does brain chemistry, including a powerful nerve chemical called serotonin. Peri- and postmenopausal women who struggle with mild depression might have lower serotonin levels than do other women. When serotonin levels are low, a woman is more likely to crave sweets and feel grumpy, while a rise in serotonin turns off the cravings and restores a more agreeable mood. An all-carb snack raises brain levels of serotonin and helps boost mood. Including a carbohydrate-rich snack, such as a cinnamon bagel with jam or a bowl of fat-free popcorn, could be all it takes to boost serotonin levels and mood.

■ *Mood-Boosting and Energizing Snacks and Meals*

■ Mix fresh or frozen blueberries, nonfat plain yogurt, and a dollop of apricot jam together in a bowl. Serve with a whole-wheat bagel topped with peanut butter.

■ Mix fresh herbs, such as basil, with fat-free ricotta cheese. Spread on whole-wheat crackers, top with a slice of red pepper or cherry tomato, and serve with fresh fruit.

■ Serve a Flaxseed Blueberry Muffin* with orange sections.

■ Dip whole-wheat pita wedges in hummus. Serve with yellow bell pepper slices.

■ Sprinkle a six-inch whole-wheat tortilla with grated low-fat cheese, drained black beans, chopped cilantro, and salsa. Top with a second tortilla and heat on a griddle, flipping to toast both sides. Serve with orange juice.

■ Serve a bowl of Chilled Cantaloupe Soup with Coconut and Blueberry Puree* with whole-grain crackers.

■ Serve baked tortilla chips, bean dip, and orange slices.

■ Make individual pizzas using whole-wheat English muffins, commercial pizza sauce, low-fat cheese, and leftover vegetables. Bake at 350°F until cheese melts.

■ Top a bowl of whole-grain cereal with vanilla soy milk and serve with sliced mangos.

■ Snack on an ounce of nuts, a sliced apple, and a tub of nonfat yogurt.

■ Snack on two whole-wheat fig-filled cookies, a glass of nonfat milk, and melon slices.

■ Serve a Mediterranean Salad* with half a whole-wheat bagel.

*Recipes in Appendix B.

Salt Cravings

*Your lordship, though not clean past your youth, hath yet some
smack of age in you, some relish of the saltiness of time.*

—WILLIAM SHAKESPEARE, FROM *THE MERRY WIVES OF WINDSOR*

Women approaching and during menopause often report changes in taste and food preferences that reflect fluctuating estrogen levels. However, cravings for salty snack foods—because they almost always are also high in fat and calories—can interfere with a woman's attempts to maintain a desirable weight and can increase the risk for developing high blood pressure.

In some cases, the craving for salt is a biological drive to maintain health. Some pregnant women who restrict salt intake have more complications in the final months of their pregnancies than do those who satisfied their cravings for pickles and other salty foods. In menopause, fluctuating estrogen levels result in water retention, and the increased desire for salt might be the body's attempt to maintain the normal concentration of sodium in the expanded body fluids.

Cravings also can be a learned response, especially in the case of salt. The more you eat, the more you want, with the taste for salt gradually becoming more habit than need. Animals fed low-salt diets in infancy are less likely to overconsume salt later in life, while adult animals accustomed to salty diets crave the taste when salt is restricted. Going cold turkey probably will upset taste buds, just as eliminating sugar too quickly from the diet can lead to sugar cravings. So gradually wean yourself off excessive salt.

Finally, salt cravings sometimes are a desire for tasty or crunchy foods. Try snacking on crunchy baby carrots dunked in flavored fat-free dips or oven-baked tortilla chips dipped in salsa (or the Mediterranean Salad in Appendix B). Try adding more spice to typical foods, such as adding a canned chili pepper or gourmet mustard to your sandwich.

Bone Up on Calcium

One is not born a woman, one becomes one.

—SIMONE DE BEAUVOIR

Women during and after menopause face an escalating risk for osteoporosis. Women who consumed ample calcium throughout life enter menopause with strong bones and are at low risk of developing osteoporosis. Unfortunately, however, most women don't get enough calcium. In fact, one of every two postmenopausal women consumes less than half the recommended calcium allotment of 1,200 to 1,500 milligrams needed to prevent age-related bone loss and osteoporosis. (See Chapter 10 for more about osteoporosis.)

Failing to consume enough calcium after menopause could have consequences beyond just bone loss. Low calcium intake increases the risk for colon cancer and possibly high blood pressure and weight gain. In addition, lead is a toxic metal that

What Does a Vegetarian Heart-Protection Diet Look Like?

Breakfast. Hot oat-bran cereal with soy milk, strawberries, sugar, and bran; and oat-bran bread with margarine or jam.

Snack. Almonds, soy milk, and fresh fruit.

Lunch. Spicy black-bean soup; sandwich made with soy deli slices, oat-bran bread, margarine, lettuce, tomato, and cucumber; and baby carrots.

Snack. Almonds and fresh fruit.

Dinner. Tofu baked with eggplant, onions, and sweet peppers; and cooked pearled barley with steamed vegetables.

Snack. Fresh fruit and soy milk.

accumulates gradually in the bones throughout life and is released as minerals dissolve out of the bones after menopause. This places a woman at increased risk for high lead levels in the blood, a condition associated with nerve damage, anemia, muscle wastage, and mental impairment. Consuming ample amounts of calcium during the early years inhibits lead absorption, and during and after menopause, optimal calcium and magnesium intake might help curb the release of lead from these tissues.

Protect Your Heart

Confront disease at its onset.

—PERSIUS (AD 34–62)

The risk for heart disease escalates quickly as estrogen levels drop, catapulting heart disease to the number-one cause of death after menopause. Heart disease risk can be significantly reduced with HRT and/or diet and exercise. Adopting a low-saturated-fat, low-trans-fat, high-fiber diet based on a wide variety of fresh fruits and vegetables, whole-grain breads and cereals, legumes including soybeans, and nonfat dairy products can keep blood fat levels and heart disease risk low.

In fact, following a vegetarian version of the Antiaging Diet in this book could be as effective at lowering blood cholesterol levels as the typical low-fat diet combined with statin drugs, according to researchers at the University of Toronto. In this study, people with elevated blood cholesterol levels who consumed vegetarian diets rich in whole grains, legumes, soy, fruits, nuts, and vegetables had an average decrease in cholesterol of 28.6 percent, which was about the same drop as seen in a second group who took statin medications. The vegetarian and statin groups also experienced similar reductions in C-reactive protein, a blood marker of inflammation associated with heart disease.

This is certainly not the first study to show that diet works, but it does confirm that diet can be just as effective as medication in treating this country's number-one killer disease—and without the side effects and costs that come from taking any medication! Adopting a few simple healthful Antiaging Diet habits—such as switching from beef to soy, increasing fruits and vegetables, and adding nuts and whole grains to the diet—not only is as effective in lowering heart disease risk but also is the sane way to manage your waistline, mood, and overall health.

The Dietary Nuts and Bolts for Menopause

When she stopped conforming to the conventional picture of
femininity she finally began to enjoy being a woman.

—BETTY FRIEDAN

A woman who goes through the change at fifty could theoretically have another seventy years of healthful living if she is aiming to reach her maximum life span of 120! The Antiaging Diet is the foundation for looking and feeling your best for that majority of life after menopause. Low in saturated and trans fats, salt, and sugar, it is high in fiber, phytochemicals, and the nutrients that help protect against mood swings, cancer, heart disease, and menopausal symptoms. The only adjustment menopausal women might consider is to add one to two servings of soy to the diet daily. Avoid or limit charcoal-cooked meats, processed meats, and smoked meats, all of which increase cancer risk.

Women before, during, and following menopause should supplement responsibly. Approximately half of middle-aged women do not consume even two-thirds of the recommended amounts for many vitamins, including the B vitamins and vitamins C and D, as well as many minerals. Marginal dietary intake of these nutrients is linked to many mental, emotional, and physical problems, including memory loss, mood swings, depression, irritability, osteoporosis, and more. Taking a moderate-dose multiple vitamin and mineral supplement that contains extra vitamin E, plus a second supplement of calcium and magnesium, provides nutritional insurance on those days when a woman doesn't eat well enough. (See guideline 8 of the Antiaging Diet in Chapter 7 for information on how to choose the best supplement for you.)

What's Exercise Got to Do with It?

I had been my whole life a bell, and never knew it until at that moment I was lifted and struck.

—ANNIE DILLARD, FROM *PILGRIM AT TINKER CREEK*

Women in their second fifty years not only can slow the aging process, they might even reverse it with exercise. A weekly routine that combines some weight-bearing exercise, such as walking or aerobic dance, with some strength-training exercise, such as lifting weights, helps prevent bone deterioration and even reverses bone loss in postmenopausal women. Exercise reduces the risk of developing heart disease, lowers the risk of losing your independence later in life due to frailty and weakness, and might even reduce cancer risk. In fact, an unfit woman at any age can reduce her risk of dying prematurely by up to 50 percent by becoming fit. Active women are two decades younger than sedentary couch potatoes. Best yet, exercise is one healthy habit that might reduce or even eliminate hot flashes during menopause, possibly because exercise helps normalize nerve chemicals that, in turn, regulate body temperature.

Exercise also keeps you trim. Being menopausal doesn't mean one has to gain weight. According to studies from the University of California, Berkeley, and the University of Washington, regular physical activity, particularly moderate-intensity exercises such as brisk walking, prevents much of the weight gain associated with aging. If you haven't started already, now is the time to begin a daily exercise routine, based on the guidelines of the Antiaging Fitness Program in Chapter 8.

■ *Menopause: Signs, Symptoms, and Solutions*

Mood Swings, Depression, Irritability, and Anxiety

Diet. Consume several small meals and snacks throughout the day. Include one or more servings of complex carbohydrate at each meal or snack. Avoid sugar, alcohol, and caffeine.

Supplements. Consider a multiple vitamin and mineral if daily intake is lower than 2,000 calories. Also, take a magnesium supplement if daily intake of dark green leafy vegetables, whole grains, legumes, wheat germ, and other magnesium-rich foods is low.

Exercise. Include regular aerobic exercise, such as walking, jogging, aerobic dance, or bicycling.

Habits. Reserve at least twenty minutes a day for relaxing, such as taking a hot bath, meditating, or doing deep breathing exercises. Avoid tobacco. Replace negative thoughts with more nurturing ones. Avoid taking on too many tasks and responsibilities.

Fatigue

Diet. Eat breakfast and divide daily food intake into five to six small meals and snacks throughout the day. Avoid caffeine, sugar, and alcohol.

Supplements. Take a moderate-dose multiple vitamin and mineral with iron if you are perimenopausal and without iron if you are postmenopausal.

Exercise. Exercise daily, including either aerobic exercise, such as walking, or anaerobic exercise, such as weight lifting.

Habits. Get at least seven to eight hours of sleep nightly. Take afternoon naps if possible. Set priorities, and avoid wasting emotional or physical energy on needless activities.

Other. HRT is sometimes helpful. Discuss this option with your physician.

Sleep Problems

Diet. Avoid caffeine, alcohol, and sugar, especially after noon. Eat a light snack of carbohydrate-rich foods, such as fat-free popcorn or a whole-wheat English muffin with honey, an hour before bedtime. Avoid large evening meals or spicy foods at dinner.

Exercise. Exercise daily, including some aerobic and some anaerobic activity, preferably in the morning or afternoon rather than at night.

Habits. Avoid tobacco. Take time to relax before bedtime. Develop a routine before bed that conditions the body for sleep.

Other. Herbs, such as catnip, chamomile, and valerian, might help improve sleep.

Mental Function, Memory, and Concentration

Diet. Consume a low-saturated-fat, high-fiber diet rich in fruits, vegetables, whole grains, and nonfat dairy foods. Drink caffeinated beverages in moderation. Avoid sugar and alcohol.

Supplements. Take a moderate-dose multiple vitamin and mineral. Consider supplements of omega-3s (500 milligrams of docosahexaenoic acid [DHA] and 500 milligrams of eicosapentaenoic acid [EPA]), ginkgo biloba (120 milligrams standardized with 24 percent flavone glycosides and 6 percent terpene lactones), and/or phosphatidylserine (100 milligrams/day).

Exercise. Include at least thirty minutes a day of aerobic exercise, such as brisk walking, jogging, bicycling, or aerobic dance.

Habits. Avoid tobacco. Sleep seven to eight hours nightly. Organize and use lists. Relax.

Other. HRT improves menopause-related memory loss and concentration problems.

Disease Prevention

Diet. Follow a diet that is low in saturated and trans fats and high in fiber. Limit sugar, refined grains, cholesterol, and salt. Drink alcohol in moderation. Consume the calcium equivalent of three glasses of nonfat milk a day.

Supplements. Take a moderate-dose multiple vitamin and mineral. Consider taking extra amounts of calcium, magnesium, vitamin C, and vitamin E.

Exercise. Engage in weight-bearing aerobic activity for at least thirty minutes, five times a week.

Habits. Avoid tobacco. Relax and avoid excessive stress. Have an annual medical checkup.

Looking Forward to the Change

One must never lose time in vainly regretting the past nor in
complaining about the changes which cause us discomfort, for
change is the very essence of life.

—ANATOLE FRANCE

The old myths about menopause causing hysteria and melancholy or signaling the end of life are quickly fading as healthy, active, and vital women approach menopause and revel in the self-confidence and personal fulfillment that can come with maturity.

Many menopausal and postmenopausal women are more emotionally stable, sure of their life's direction, and clear about their priorities than women in their twenties and thirties. They are more at peace with and sure of themselves and happier with their lives than their younger counterparts, especially if they have nurtured their physical and emotional health. That's something to look forward to!

CHAPTER 14

Can Diet Improve Your Love Life?

So, lively brisk old fellow,
Don't let age get you down.
White hairs or not you can still
be a lover.

—GOETHE

The greatest impediment to sexuality in the later years is illness, not ability. People who have an active sex life in their later years are the ones who are free from disease, are physically active, and enjoy life. These people report greater frequency of sexual activity and greater satisfaction compared with inactive people of the same age. If sexual ability wanes, is there anything you can do to stir the fires?

Looking for Mr. Good Potion

The horn, the horn, the lusty horn is not a thing to laugh to scorn.

—WILLIAM SHAKESPEARE, FROM *AS YOU LIKE IT*

For centuries, people have turned to food to enhance fertility and sexual prowess. Eating and loving are so closely entwined that we often speak of "eating our hearts out," "feasting our eyes," or having "lusty appetites." We call our lovers "spicy," "a dish," "a hot tomato," or "good enough to eat." The line separating sexual desire and physical hunger is a thin one.

"The age-old belief that a food or substance does what it looks like is called the Doctrine of Signatures," says Varro Tyler, Ph.D., Sc.D., past dean and Distinguished Professor Emeritus at Purdue University and author of *The Honest Herbal*. According to this belief, the universe reveals the use or virtues of a food by its shape and appearance.

Ginseng is a perfect example. Ginseng's notoriety comes from its shape: this root has leglike appendages and resembles the human body. "Occasionally a ginseng

Lusty Tidbits

- Have you used the term *horny* to describe an especially active sexual state? It is likely this term comes from Asian countries where there was a widespread belief that ground-up horns of various animals, such as rhinoceros and reindeer, could be powerful aphrodisiacs (probably because of their phallic shape). Some people went so far as to recommend unicorn horn; however, finding a supplier must have been difficult.

- The ancient Greeks spread barley around the temple of Demeter to assure fertility. The custom was passed down to subsequent generations and today is perpetuated by the throwing of rice at the bride and groom during weddings. It's a nice custom but a poor fertility pill.

- Spicy foods raise the heart rate and cause a person to break out in a sweat, a physical condition similar to sexual excitement, which is why curry, chutney, pepper, chilies, and cayenne pepper have at one time or another been linked to sexual prowess. Foods and spices linked to love usually are rare or exotic; that is, their very strangeness suggests the existence of secret powers. This is probably why the less-than-glamorous potato (and even white bread) were considered aphrodisiacs when they were introduced into England. Within a few decades, these foods usually sink to the level of delicious but prosaic edibles.

- Researchers at the University of Wisconsin–Madison report that the combined effect of increasing vitamin D and calcium intake (to 400IU and 1,000 milligrams, respectively) might improve fertility rates in men.

- Both too much and too little selenium also might interfere with fertility, while consuming several selenium-rich foods, such as seafood, whole grains, and extra-lean meats, enhances conception.

- Men who smoke jeopardize their reproductive capability—that is, unless they also snack on vitamin C-rich foods, such as strawberries, orange juice, and broccoli. But don't get carried away. Downing megadoses of vitamin C won't turn your couch potato into a Casanova. Since both smoking and exposure to other people's smoke can decrease fertilization rates, you're better off not smoking and avoiding passive smoke whenever possible.

root will sprout an extra appendage that resembles the sexual organ," says Dr. Tyler. "That ginseng root is considered very precious and may sell for hundreds or even thousands of dollars in some countries."

"There is an enormous amount of research on the chemistry of ginseng and its effects on smaller animals," continues Dr. Tyler. "But there is very little research on humans and without additional scientific studies we have no proof whether there is anything more to ginseng than just imagination." Even if ginseng is mildly effective, you can't be guaranteed that the ginseng you buy at the local health food store will work, since there is no quality control of herbs in the United States.

From Lusty Prunes to Rabbit Pie

Sex and beauty are inseparable, like life and consciousness. And the intelligence which goes with sex and beauty, and rises out of sex and beauty, is intuition.

—D. H. LAWRENCE

A food doesn't necessarily have to look, taste, or even smell good to arouse lust. For example, people have dined on dried salamander and fat of camel's hump in preparation for a night of passion. During Elizabethan times, prunes were considered such a powerful aphrodisiac that they were served in brothels.

"If an animal is known for being fertile, such as rabbits, then their sexual organs and even their meat is believed to improve sexual potency," says George Armelagos, Ph.D., professor of anthropology at Emory University in Atlanta and author of *Consuming Passions: The Anthropology of Eating.* "Ancient mythology also has contributed to the aura of aphrodisiacs," he adds. Aphrodite, the goddess of beauty and love, whose name forms the root of the word *aphrodisiac,* was said to have risen from sea foam where Uranus's genitals had fallen in battle—hence the link between sexuality and oysters, clams, lobsters, fish eggs, eels, sea slugs, and almost anything else that comes from the ocean.

Modern-Day Sex Potions

Women complain about sex more often than men. Their gripes fall into two major categories: (1) Not enough. (2) Too much.

—ANN LANDERS, FROM *TRUTH IS STRANGER*

Proponents of dietary aphrodisiacs may mix a little scientific jargon into the promotion of a food or food ingredient, but the same beliefs, myths, and magic are at play. For example, nutrient cocktails rich in vitamin C are billed as "quick-fix climax enhancers." The active ingredients in many of these potions include caffeine or niacin, which appear to be potent only because they give you a temporary flushing of the skin.

There also is the belief that any food that contains hormonelike substances must trigger passions. For example, pheromones are hormonelike compounds naturally produced by many animals to attract members of the opposite sex. These chemicals also are found in minute amounts in anchovies and in some plants, such as parsley, celery, carrots, and young parsnips. Truffles, edible underground fungi that look like a homely version of the testes and have been promoted as a potent aphrodisiac for centuries, actually contain the male pig hormone androstenol. Unfortunately, these hormones have little or no effect on humans when eaten as food.

There is no scientific proof for any of these "remedies." The FDA reports that no product sold over the counter as an aphrodisiac (from ginseng and licorice to vitamins, chocolate, and choline) is effective. "It is very difficult to separate the effect of aphrodisiacs on the mind and their effect on the body," warns Dr. Tyler. "If people believe something is going to work, then it probably will." But was the passion caused by the food, your expectations, or just chance?

Candy Is Dandy, but Liquor Is Quicker

Though I look old, yet I am strong and lusty; for in my youth I never did apply hot and rebellious liquors in my blood.

—WILLIAM SHAKESPEARE, FROM *AS YOU LIKE IT*

Liquor ranks among the most universal love potions of all time. Alcohol acts indirectly as a pseudo-aphrodisiac by its depressant effect on higher brain centers, thus suppressing any fear or guilt about improper behavior and allowing the imbiber to "loosen up." Ironically, more than a couple of drinks does not improve performance, since as a depressant drug, alcohol slows arousal, making for a clumsy and incompetent lover. Researchers at the Harvard School of Public Health report that sexual function in men drops sharply for each decade after age fifty, primarily in men who drink alcohol, watch television as their free-time activity, and don't exercise. As Shakespeare so succinctly wrote in *Macbeth*, "It [alcohol] provides the desire, but it takes away the performance." The good news is that men who are fit and spend more time exercising than sitting on their duffs are the most likely to maintain a normal, healthy, and youthful sex life.

Amorous Edibles: Foods That Really Work

When I'm good, I'm very good, but when I'm bad I'm better.

—MAE WEST

When it comes to sexuality in the second fifty years, the real issue is not the aging process but health. Nutritional deficiencies, from lack of vitamin A to insufficient zinc, can sap your mental and physical energy, while the nutrient-packed, low-fat eating plan outlined in the Antiaging Diet can put a spring in your step and a twinkle in your eye, as well as fuel your wildest desires. When it comes to wooing, even subtle nutritional problems can undermine desire, performance, and fertility. There is strong evidence that reversing the effects of poor nutrition will improve energy, mood, and even conception rates.

Researchers at the University of Utah School of Medicine report that blood testosterone levels plunged by 50 percent in a group of men after they drank high-fat milkshakes. Testosterone levels remained constant in the same men when they downed low-fat shakes. A. Wayne Meikle, M.D., professor of endocrinology and metabolism and the head researcher for the study, concludes, "A high-fat diet over time might curb a man's interest in sex." Fatty diets also clog arteries, and arterial blockages are a common cause of impotence.

Packing excess body weight also leads to performance problems in men. Numerous studies show that unfit and fat men are much more likely to battle erectile dysfunction compared with men who stay fit and lean in their second fifty years, while adopting an active lifestyle improves sexual performance in at least one out of every three overweight men. At the Center for Obesity Management at the Second University of Naples, 110 obese men (average age 43.5 years) with erectile dysfunction were assigned to a control group or an intervention group that included an intensive weight-loss and exercise program. Results showed that after two years, men in the intervention group had lost an average of thirty-three pounds (or 15 percent of their initial weight), cut 300 calories from their daily intake, and increased their exercise to 195 minutes a week. The control group had lost some but nowhere near as much weight as the intervention group. Almost three out of every ten men in the diet-and-exercise group also had erectile function restored, while only 5 percent of the men in the control group reported similar benefits. Women with metabolic syndrome, who typically are overweight, also are likely to be unsatisfied with their love lives. In short, too little or too many calories, dietary fat, or body fat might interfere with a person's love life.

Oyster Ambrosia

Be good, sweet maid,
And let who will be naughty.
If you grow better every day,
How good you'll be at forty.

—WILLIAM HAZLITT

The belief that oysters increase fertility might have some scientific basis. Oysters are the richest dietary source of zinc: one oyster supplies most people's daily requirement for the mineral. Several studies have shown that even short-term poor intake of this trace mineral reduces fertility, including reduced semen volume, levels of blood testosterone (the male sex hormone), and zinc concentrations in semen, and impaired ovulation and fertilization in women.

While consuming 15 to 25 milligrams of zinc each day will help sustain a person's normal sexual function, consuming larger doses will not produce superhuman fertility. It takes more than oysters—or any other food, for that matter—to effectively treat serious sexual dysfunctions or infertility.

Candlelight, Soft Music, and a Smidgen of Nutrition

The most fun I've ever had without laughing.

—WOODY ALLEN, FROM THE MOVIE *ANNIE HALL*, DESCRIBING SEX

Romance has a lot more to do with "chemistry," lingering glances, and subtle body language than it does with aphrodisiacs and zinc. The delicious complexities that attract you to someone are as much, if not more, likely to include qualities such as

■ *Galvanize Your Reproductive System*

A person should consume approximately 15 milligrams of zinc each day. Here are a few ways to increase your zinc intake:

FOOD	AMOUNT	ZINC (MILLIGRAMS)
Oysters, raw	6 medium	76.70
Amaranth grain	1 cup	6.20
Wheat germ	½ cup	6.15
Ground beef, extra-lean	3 ounces	4.44
Baked beans, vegetarian	1 cup	3.55
Cashews	½ cup	3.09
Lentils, cooked	1 cup	2.50
Chicken, dark meat	3 ounces	2.38
Bean burrito	1	2.37
Rice, wild, cooked	1 cup	2.20
Clams, canned	½ cup	2.18
Yogurt, low-fat	1 cup	2.02
Tofu, firm	½ cup	1.98
Spinach, cooked	1 cup	1.37
Avocado, Florida	1	1.28
Oatmeal, cooked	1 cup	1.15
Chicken, light meat	3 ounces	1.05
Milk, nonfat	1 cup	0.92
Cheese	1 ounce	0.70–1.10

humor, intelligence, vulnerability, and integrity than sexual prowess alone. Good old common sense, combined with presentation when it comes to food, will go a lot further than the most potent "love potion" in boosting energy and health. All you need is the nutrient-packed, low-fat Antiaging Diet, which supplies all the vitamins and minerals in optimal amounts; a moderate-dose multiple vitamin and mineral supplement; and to stay fit and maintain a desirable weight.

Lusty Lifestyles

People who are physically active engage in sexual activity more often and enjoy it more than do couch potatoes. Additionally, daily relaxation (chronic stress inter-

Little Sexy Meals

Here are just a few ideas that are simple, elegant (or slightly risqué), and guaranteed to perk up your love life:

- Dim the lights and share a salad of watermelon and dark chocolate on the floor in front of a fire.
- Have a backyard picnic of lemon pasta with steamed asparagus spears, sparkling apple cider, and caviar.
- Steam New Zealand greenlip mussels in wine and herbs, serve with chunks of sourdough French bread, and let the juice dribble down your chin.
- Feed each other Fresh Bowls of Berries with Sour Cream and Yogurt*—while blindfolded.
- Peel grapes and feed them one by one to your lover.
- Pack a picnic lunch that includes juicy fruits, such as mangos, papaya, oranges, and honeydew melon. Eat the fruit with your fingers.
- Rent a copy of the movie *Tom Jones* and take notes during the "eating scene," then plan your own food orgy.
- Bring fresh strawberries and champagne to a drive-in movie.
- Serve your lover breakfast in bed, including fresh-squeezed orange juice and French toast topped with fresh raspberries.
- Eat plums, a bowl of custard, or a banana with your eyes closed, savoring the taste, texture, and smell.
- Eat mashed potatoes, pudding, spaghetti, or Baked Eggplant with Vegetable Ragu Sauce* with your fingers.

Recipes in Appendix B.

feres with sexual desire), avoidance of tobacco, limiting alcohol and caffeine, and restricting medications to only those prescribed by a physician will go much further in boosting your desire, energy, and interest than rhino horn, ginseng, or fish eggs. The rest is up to you. According to Dr. Armelagos, "The most important sexual organ and the best aphrodisiac in the world is the imagination."

PART 4

Beyond Diet and Exercise

Mind over Aging

> *I don't know about you, but
> the way I figure, I can't change
> the world, but I can change
> the channel.*
> —GEORGE BURNS

The true light of vitality comes from within. There's a lot more to life, health, and longevity than just your reflection in the mirror. It is the shape of a person's inner life that shines through the body and keeps it fired with youth.

Attitude: The Science of Happiness

> *Optimism: An inclination to put the most favorable construction
> upon actions and happenings . . . to anticipate the
> best possible outcome.*
>
> —WEBSTER'S THIRD NEW INTERNATIONAL DICTIONARY

As discussed in Chapter 3, all of the qualities of vitality start with an optimistic and positive approach to life. Optimism is like a self-fulfilling prophecy. People who believe they have control over their health and lives take charge of their health, make changes in diet and exercise that will promote health, and experience fewer diseases and disabilities, take fewer medications, recover more quickly from illnesses, and have a lower incidence of depression. Pessimists who believe that their bodies automatically deteriorate with age are less likely to practice healthful behaviors, and their health suffers as a result. In one study, fewer than half of pessimists questioned were willing to make even simple changes in their diets even when they were told the changes would benefit their health.

Our thoughts literally help shape our bodies. The field of psychoneuroimmunology, which studies the connection between the brain and nervous system and the immune system, has found that the central nervous system communicates with the immune and endocrine systems through a network of neurotransmitters, hormones, and chemicals. The power of the mind to heal or hurt appears unlimited. Worrying, brooding or ruminating, feeling depressed or hopeless, or harboring pessimistic thoughts affect the heart rate, suppress the immune system, change skin temperature, and alter blood and brain chemistry. This toxic effect on the body leaves a person vulnerable to disease, abnormal cell growth, and organ damage.

On the other hand, positive attitudes, high hopes, humor, being carefree and lighthearted, and experiencing harmony, laughter, and peace of mind help healthy people stay that way. Vital people are more likely to educate and take care of themselves, and their attitudes also stimulate the immune system and allow the body to keep itself healthy.

While agelessness springs from inner attitudes, there is something that underlies even this inner realm: the will to be vital. A person must first want to strive for vitality. From that determination blooms the drive to get there. As Leo Buscaglia says, "The only thing that stands between us and a happy life is the belief that we deserve it, that it is possible, and that the tools to achieve it exist."

Stress: Sorting Out the Good from the Bad

It is many times more important to know the patient who has the disease, than what kind of disease the patient has.

—SIR WILLIAM OSLER

Most people are born healthy. It is the stress, often self-imposed, of lifelong imbalances in perceptions, behaviors, and attitudes that tips the scale, allowing a person to slide gradually from health and vitality toward disease and despair. Many disorders once thought to be inevitable consequences of aging are now recognized as stress-inflicted and preventable. How you perceive and interpret stressful events, not the events themselves, determines the quality and longevity of your life.

What Is Stress?

To be alive is to be stressed. Stress is the body's response to any demand. The adaptive tools within the body were designed by nature millions of years ago as a protection against any danger, and this fight-or-flight response to any stressor rallies a wealth of physical, emotional, and mental resources to protect you from harm.

The fight-or-flight response is beneficial when it accompanies a real danger for which you need increased alertness, blood flow to the brain and muscles, improved vision and hearing, and other split-second responses that help ensure safety. The response also is beneficial when the stress is a positive one that incites us to stretch our limits, reach for our goals, and explore life. Positive stress actually encourages vitality. However, when stress results in worry, anger, and tension, then our fight-or-flight response might harm health, shorten life span, and undermine enjoyment of life even in someone who is otherwise vital.

Stress and Your Health

High-level or chronic stress accelerates the body's natural aging process and contributes to the development of several disorders, including the major degenerative diseases. The early symptoms are as benign as the following:

- Frequent colds and sore throats
- Restless sleep or insomnia
- Sudden emotional outbursts, hostility, or mood swings
- Headaches or backaches
- Heart palpitations
- Fatigue
- Skin problems
- Stomach and digestive tract upset
- Frequent use of alcohol or pills to help relax or sleep

Left unchecked, stress progresses and undermines vitality and long-term health.

Studies by Ancel Keys dating back to the early 1960s showed that stress raises blood cholesterol levels, increasing a person's risk for developing heart disease. Since then, hundreds of studies have confirmed the detrimental effects of stress on physical and emotional health. One example is a study from the University of Arizona that found that people who overreact to stress are much more likely to suffer heart attacks than those who let stress roll off their backs. In contrast, a study from Duke University Medical Center in Durham, North Carolina, reports that practicing effective stress-management habits lowers heart disease risk.

People who perceive a loss of control over their lives or are overcome by stress are more likely to suffer poor health, elevated blood cholesterol levels, hypertension, heart palpitations, sudden cardiac deaths, bleeding ulcers, colds and infections, asthma, kidney disorders, allergies, joint inflammation associated with arthritis, and possibly cancer. People who suppress their emotions in response to stress are more likely to die from heart disease. Stress also unleashes an army of free radicals, which further damage the body and contribute to disease.

"The effects of stress on aging may be greater than we think," warns Robert Russell, M.D., professor of medicine and nutrition at Tufts University in Boston. For example, up until recently, women usually outlived their spouses. As women have entered the workforce, the burden of juggling family and career has added heavy stress to their lives. Not surprisingly, life expectancy increases in women have slowed down as disease risk rates have begun to increase, not unlike the escalating rates of lung cancer that occurred after women began to smoke.

Future studies might find that many of the diet-related links with disease are more a matter of stress. For example, recent studies show that the stress hormones stimulate fat receptors in the abdomen, funneling extra calories from the diet into fat storage. "Chronic stress jams the stress hormone cortisol into high gear, which increases cravings for sweets and fatty foods, and encourages those excess calories to be stored in the belly where it is readily available to fuel the stress response," explains Pamela Peeke, M.D., assistant clinical professor of medicine at the University of Maryland School of Medicine and author of *Body for Life for Women*. As a result, anyone who overeats during stress also is prone to gaining more fat around the middle, a type of weight gain associated with elevated risks for heart disease, diabetes, hypertension, and cancer.

It's Up to You

Stress in itself doesn't cause disease; it is how we react to stress that determines illness or health. The secret to stress is to welcome it, work with it, and use it to reach your goals. As stress expert Dr. Robert Eliot recommends, "Don't sweat the small stuff, and remember everything is small stuff."

Change may be stressful, but it also is part of a vital life. The people who live their lives to the fullest are those who take the most calculated risks and thrive on positive stress while minimizing harmful stress. Exercise may be the way to make peace with your body, and prayer and meditation are ways to find peace with your soul, but reducing harmful stress is the way to make peace with your life.

How Not to Sweat the Small Stuff

Here is a partial list of ways to sidestep stress and enjoy life more:

- Volunteer at a service that helps other people.
- Get eight hours of restful sleep each night. Take a twenty-minute catnap midafternoon.
- Have a pet. Pet owners live longer and are less prone to disease than people who live alone.
- Develop a hobby.
- Adopt time-management and organizational skills to more efficiently use time and energy.
- Spend twenty minutes each day relaxing; for example, take a stroll outside, do some gardening, throw a Frisbee for the dog, practice a relaxation technique, read a novel, or play a game.
- Meditate daily.
- Cut back on caffeine, alcohol, and tobacco; they only aggravate the stress response.
- Exercise more.
- Let go of "all-or-nothing" thinking. No one is perfect, not even geniuses such as Mozart or Einstein.
- Choose a physician with a positive attitude, one who will talk to you, answer your questions, and respond with sympathy.
- If stress continues to be a problem, join a support group or get counseling.
- Be happily married. People who are happily married are healthier and less stressed than single people or people in bad marriages.

Laugh and Lighten Up

A merry heart doeth good like a medicine.

—PROVERBS 17:22

Anyone seeking to live long and vitally must embrace humor with a passion. Humor diffuses tension and conflicts, boosts morale, enhances relationships, relieves stress, and puts life in perspective. Laughter stimulates the immune system, boosting our resistance to infections and disease.

Laughter also is one of the best stress-management skills. It's almost impossible to be tense or even angry and laugh at the same time. Laughter is like internal jogging. It raises the heart rate, improves circulation and breathing, aids in the transport of oxygen to the brain and muscles, relaxes the muscles, and helps soothe headaches or back problems. Laughter also disrupts negative thoughts and lessens anxiety as well as discomfort. Finally, a good laugh stimulates the release in the brain of endorphins, chemicals that produce a calming, euphoric feeling. Pain and inflammation are reduced and you feel relieved, more peaceful, and more alive. The more you laugh, the happier and healthier you are, and the longer you're likely to live.

The Power of Prayer and Meditation

There is now scientific evidence that belief in prayer is good for you.
First there was exercise and eating right, and now belief.

—HERBERT BENSON, M.D.

Embracing strong spiritual beliefs, with or without belonging to an organized religion or going to church, is consistently associated with better health. People who regularly pray or meditate, who report they feel close to a higher power and feel connected or in harmony with the universe, who define themselves as spiritual, or who practice yoga are happier and healthier than those with little or no spiritual component to their lives. They also are less stressed, suffer less from pain and depression, have better moods, and enjoy higher self-esteem. Patients who pray or meditate need less medication and are less prone to complications than are other patients.

The link between prayer, meditation, and health goes beyond the operating table and mirrors the words of Dr. Albert Schweitzer, who said, "Each patient carries his own doctor inside him." People who develop an active spiritual life have lower blood pressure and half the risk of dying from heart disease, are less likely to suffer from depression or commit suicide, and tend to be in better physical health than those who infrequently pray or go to church. They are less likely to develop colorectal cancer, and even if they do develop cancer, the quality of their lives is better during their illnesses than that of other people.

People with strong spiritual beliefs don't avoid tragedy or suffering, but they are generally better prepared to handle the pain of, and bounce back from, adversity than are others. Prayer and meditation are most effective when combined with, not used as a replacement for, traditional therapies.

A Closer Look at Meditation

Meditation is the simple act of sitting still for twenty minutes or more each day with eyes closed, while focusing attention on either breathing or on a word or phrase called a mantra (a mantra can be a sound, such as "Om," or a gentle "Be still"), which the person repeats. When the mind wanders from this mantra, the meditator simply returns the attention to the mantra or breath. How can something so simple as doing nothing be so good for you?

Meditation aids healing because of its powerful calming effect on the body, which neutralizes the disabling effects of stress. It slows the heart rate, drops blood pressure, increases the flow of blood to the brain, and balances brain wave patterns. Meditation reduces a person's risk for developing arthritis, asthma, chronic pain, diabetes, digestive tract problems, hot flashes during menopause, infertility, and headaches. It also stimulates the immune system and improves memory and mental function.

By quieting the mind for a few minutes each day, one becomes aware of internal thoughts, memories, attitudes, and beliefs that distort perceptions and undermine chances for vitality. Doubts, worries, regrets, desires, and other negative chatter that plague daily life are more easily replaced with positive thoughts when the mind is stilled each day. The result is that the emotional energy wasted on nonproductive thoughts is freed for more positive pursuits.

Forgiveness and Gratitude

> *To offer forgiveness is the only way for one to have it, for in*
> *forgiveness, giving and receiving are the same.*
>
> —JAMES A. KNIGHT, M.D.

Forgiveness and gratefulness are more than just good for the soul—they also are great for the body. People who hold on to anger, disapproval, grudges, thoughts of revenge, and disappointments pay a high price in their physical health, emotional energy, and loss of vitality. They are at much greater risk of developing chronic diseases, such as heart disease. A study from the University of California, Davis, found that people who were grateful for all they had suffered less from harmful emotions, and this grateful optimism helped restore the inner balance that encourages health.

■ *Hold On and Let Go*

How can you bring more gratitude into your life?

■ Make a list of everything you have to be thankful for. Don't leave anything off, no matter how small. Value even the minor things.

■ Focus your thoughts throughout the day on the little things that make life wonderful. This is an example of how more comes from more; the more you emphasize all you have to be grateful for, the more you will find in life to appreciate.

■ Find a way to sympathize with the person who "did you wrong." Think of times you needed to be forgiven in your life. What do you have in common with your offender?

■ Write down how that person wronged you, but also list the unexpected good that came from the other person's actions.

■ Try the following visualization as a way to let go of anger:

1. Close your eyes and visualize the person at whom you are angry.
2. Fill yourself with love, and then send that love and forgiveness to the other person.
3. Ask that person to also forgive you for anything you might have said or done that may have caused pain.
4. See yourself letting go of the person with love and forgiveness.
5. Keep your eyes closed for a few moments to experience the feelings of love, lightness, and freedom.

A Suitcase Full of Vitality

The farther one travels along the journey of life, the more joy and the more pain one experiences. However, for all that is given up even more is gained.

—M. SCOTT PECK

The secret to a joyful journey in life is how you choose to pack your suitcase for the trip. The suitcase will hold only so much, so choose wisely the attitudes, beliefs, ideas, thoughts, and responses you want to bring. Keep in mind that how you choose to think about your life will determine how far down the road you get and, more importantly, to what extent you enjoy the trip.

CHAPTER 16

The World Around You

When an old person dies, it is
like a small library burning.
—ALEX HALEY

If there really is a River of Immortality in Eden, no one swims in it alone. A long and vital life always is intricately intertwined with the lives of others. The importance of developing and maintaining strong, supportive relationships with family, friends, coworkers, and community cannot be overemphasized when it comes to longevity and vitality. We all need to give and receive love—that is what gives life meaning and purpose.

Unless people nurture these relationships when they are in their early and middle years, they are likely to spend the future alone, which can undermine any chances of living longer and healthier. As people age, many tend to loosen the connections they once had with their environments. They make and receive fewer phone calls, write and receive fewer letters, make and pursue fewer friendships, are involved less in other people's lives, participate in fewer meetings and social activities, and use their cars less. They touch and hug and are touched and hugged less, and they take fewer and fewer risks.

Sometimes the gradual isolation is caused by the insidious loss of hearing that can cause a person to slowly step back from social involvement. Physical infirmity, the loss of a loved one, disease, or some other crisis can start the gradual decline in social connections. Whatever the cause, isolation and the stress of loneliness lead to mental and physical decline and an increased vulnerability to disease and premature death.

We humans are social animals, and much of our vitality comes from our connection to others. A person doesn't let go of life because he or she is old; rather, a person is old because he or she lets go of life. Make yourself useful to someone, something, or some cause; be necessary or even indispensable, and you will always have a reason to live and will likely outlive your reclusive neighbors.

A Healthy Life Is One That Is Balanced with Inner Joy, Outer Health, and Social Connectedness

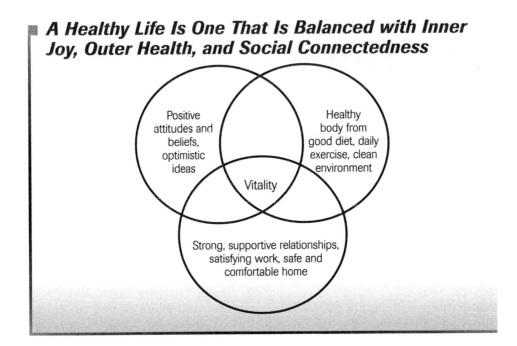

Home Life

Never take anything for granted.

—BENJAMIN DISRAELI

Strong family ties and a satisfying and comforting home life have been consistently linked to living a longer and healthier life. Happily married people live longer than do single people or people in unhappy marriages. Living in a loving home reduces a person's risk for developing heart disease and high blood pressure, aids in recovery and rehabilitation from illness, and speeds adaptation to life's changes, particularly in people after age sixty-five and especially in men.

The secret is to nurture a healthy household, one where open and supportive communication is welcomed. Couples who live with hostility and poor communication also have suppressed immune systems and are more susceptible to colds, infections, and diseases such as cancer. A study from the Karolinska Institute in Sweden also found that unhappily married women were at higher risk for heart disease. They also become more socially isolated. Developing ways to nurture support, love, and encouragement and to resolve disputes is critical not only to the life of the relationship but to the health of the partners.

Developing a loving family life may be more important today than ever before. In past centuries, often several generations lived under one roof. People stayed, grew up, and grew old in the same neighborhoods. These built-in support groups have dwindled as our culture has become more mobile. It may be hard to imagine a need now to actively seek, develop, and nurture friendships for your health in later years, but cultivating those friendships could save your life and help in your quest for vitality.

Our ancestors never expected to live long enough to be grandparents. Today most people should expect to become grandparents and, if they take care of themselves and/or are born with a good set of genes, they can look forward to being great-grandparents—or even great-great-grandparents. Start planning how you want to live those later years as an integrated elder in a growing family.

Friends: How Well Have I Loved?

You are not here to make a living. You are here in order to enable the world to live more amply, with greater vision, with finer spirit of hope, and achievement. You are here to enrich the world, and you impoverish yourself if you forget the errand.

—WOODROW WILSON

More than money, possessions, job, status, or even sex, satisfaction with how well a person has loved and been loved determines the degree of meaning, purpose, and vitality he or she attributes to life.

Friends nourish and soothe the soul, providing a mirror from which to reflect on our path through life and a haven from daily problems. Women's ability to gather good friends might be one of the reasons they live longer than men.

People with strong, supportive relationships with family members and friends have one-quarter to one-half the risk of dying prematurely of lonely people. Women with strong, supportive friendships are less likely to develop fatal cancers; when cancer does strike, they are more likely to survive. They are happier and healthier. In one study from Stanford University, women with breast cancer who joined a support group lived twice as long as patients who received only medical care. Researchers at Rush University Medical Center in Chicago report that stress, poor social support, and negative emotional states (including depression, anger and hostility, and anxiety) increase a person's risk for developing and dying from heart disease.

Maintaining good friends with open and honest communication also appears to shield us from other health problems. Menopausal symptoms are much more prevalent in women lacking strong social networks than in (relatively symptom-free) menopausal women with strong friendships. Even menstrual cramps, PMS symptoms, and complications during pregnancy are more pronounced in women with poor social support. People need friends to stay healthy.

Developing a supportive community of friends helps encourage other healthful behaviors. People with strong social contacts are healthier and more likely to take charge of their health by reducing their dietary fat and increasing fiber intake compared with people who are more isolated. Even sharing life with a pet helps offset the aging process and can bring the humor, joy, meaning, and love necessary to keep us healthy and vital.

People who spend their leisure time in isolating pastimes, such as watching television, are most likely to develop high blood cholesterol levels, which doubles their risk for heart disease. Even moderate amounts of time in these sedentary, solo pursuits increase disease risk and could accelerate isolation and aging in later years, unless these habits are balanced with other, more social, activities.

How Does Your Environment Affect Your Health?

If life is a game, it's the only one I know where the goal is to protect the playing board and preserve the players.

—KURT VONNEGUT

If you're planning to live to be a hundred, you should plan to stay mentally and physically active so you can work at something you enjoy until you're eighty years old or older. People who report contentment and enjoyment in their work are more likely to live longer and healthier than people who are disgruntled with how they spend their time. Up to 190 hours or more each month are devoted to a job. You'd better like it, or the toll that the added stress takes on longevity could undermine the best of dietary and exercise practices.

The extra years you can expect to live when you adopt the healthful habits outlined in this book will mean you have more time to spend in fulfilling pastimes, including work. You'd better have a clear idea of what you want to do with that extra time, since there will be a lot of it. By conservative calculations, anyone planning to live vitally until at least the age of one hundred will have an additional thirty-five years after the current retirement age of sixty-five to fill with meaningful pursuits.

Vital people keep working, change jobs, or attack retirement with the same passion with which they have lived their lives. Here are a few examples:

- Maggie Kuhn was sixty-four when she organized the Gray Panthers in 1970, a group dedicated to fighting age discrimination.
- At age seventy-five, Golda Meir resigned as Israel's prime minister; two years later she accepted a position as head of the Labor Party.
- The French poet, novelist, and playwright Victor Hugo wrote his last great work at age eighty-one.
- Concert pianist Arthur Rubinstein gave one of his finest performances at New York's Carnegie Hall at the age of eighty-nine.

How can your work support your longevity goals? Start today to aim for a type of work that you love. If your work could be anything you wanted, what would you like to do? Would you work outside or inside, with people or alone? Would you be self-employed or work for someone else? Would the job be a volunteer position? What talents and skills would you use? Once you have a clear idea of what you want to do, if it is something other than what you're doing now, start finding ways to bring that job vision into reality. As Kahlil Gibran said, "Work is love made visible."

When All Is Said and Done

Don't lead me; I may not follow. Don't walk behind me; I may not
lead. Walk beside me and be my friend.

—ANONYMOUS

As you venture on your journey toward a long and vital life, accumulate and bring with you the components that will give that life meaning and purpose, including special friends, family, satisfying work, and community involvement. Think of all the facets of a healthy life as threads in a tapestry. How you weave those threads will determine how beautiful and lasting a piece of work is created. For example, sharing meals with loved ones, or even starting a dinner club that meets weekly to share new healthful recipes, is a way to nurture relationships, express connections, and encourage well-being. It also satisfies one of the guidelines of the Antiaging Diet, to enjoy food.

Nurture and build a social team of friends, family members, workmates, neighbors, and other loved ones. Look for healthy relationships everywhere. Embrace those friendships that make you feel good and that encourage you to stretch your wings and support your quest for health and vitality.

A Final Word

*Youth would be an ideal state
if it came a little later in life.*
—HERBERT HENRY ASQUITH

Most people want to hold on to a youthful appearance. How you live can affect how you look. But at a more profound level, how you live, what you think, whom you choose to spend time with, and how you care for your body will be the deciding factors in how you feel, how much you enjoy your time here on earth, and to what extent others and the world are better off because you were here. Choosing healthful habits every day lets growing older become a greater opportunity for self-knowledge, balance, and joy than any other stage in life.

Never allow the tools for longevity to become your primary focus. When fitness and diet become a joyless quest for immortality, the deeper joy of passionate living gets lost in the process. You can never reduce the complexities, the wonder, and the magic of living to simple rules on how to eat or when to exercise. The guidelines in this book are a means to an end, not the end in itself.

Nothing can promise eternal life. Mortality is not an option. Embracing all of the guidelines in this book will push back the inevitable for a few years or even decades but not forever. While we all must face life's exit at some point, by adopting healthful habits, we can live life to its fullest and go out with a blaze of glory, with dignity intact, knowing we did well for ourselves and for others.

Albert Einstein once said, "When the solution is simple, God is answering." That truth applies to living a long and vital life and might be summed up in the following advice: dine well, stay fit, keep laughing, and enjoy life and the people you share it with. Another way of expressing it is to ask yourself, "How do I want to be remembered?" When you answer that question, you'll know how you want to live today.

My wish is that all of your highest dreams come true.

A Week's Worth of Antiaging Meals

These menus supply, on average, 2,000 calories a day. If you are young, active, a man, or taller than the average woman, your caloric needs may be higher. Increase serving sizes, add additional servings of healthy foods, or include a favorite food here and there to make up the difference in calories. Women who require fewer than 2,000 calories a day to maintain a desirable weight should cut back on serving sizes of grains, fruits, and/or meat, not vegetables. Items marked with an asterisk (*) are recipes found in Appendix B.

Day 1

BREAKFAST

1 frozen whole-grain waffle, toasted and topped with:

¼ cup fat-free sour cream

1 cup blueberries

1 cup light fortified soy milk

SNACK

1 apple

A glass of sparkling water with a twist of lemon

LUNCH

1 serving Chilled Cantaloupe Soup with Coconut and Blueberry Puree*

A turkey sandwich made with:

3 ounces turkey breast

3 large lettuce leaves

1 teaspoon Dijon mustard

2 slices whole-wheat bread

15 baby carrots

Iced green tea

SNACK

1 6-ounce container of low-fat strawberry-kiwi yogurt mixed with 1 kiwi, peeled and cubed

Ice water

DINNER AND DESSERT

1 serving Grilled Salmon with Pesto and Lemon Zest*

1 serving Oven-Roasted Brussels Sprouts with Apples and Walnuts*

½ cup cooked instant brown rice

½ cup frozen green peas, steamed

2 cups air-popped popcorn

Nutritional analysis for the day: 2,098 calories; 29 percent fat (67.6 grams); 19 grams saturated fat; 3.3 grams omega-3 fats; 21 percent protein; 50 percent carbohydrate; 46 grams fiber

Day 2

BREAKFAST

1 serving Oven-Roasted Vegetable Frittata*

1 cup calcium- and vitamin D–fortified orange juice

2 slices whole-wheat toast topped with 1 tablespoon jam

Tea or coffee (sweetened with artificial sweetener, if desired)

SNACK

1 ounce nuts

2 tablespoons dried cranberries

Sparkling water

LUNCH

1 chicken-salad sandwich made with:

    2 ounces cubed chicken breast mixed with 2 tablespoons fat-free mayonnaise,

    3 tablespoons diced celery, salt and pepper to taste

    2 lettuce leaves

2 slices whole-wheat bread

1 cup peeled and sliced jicama

1 serving Thai Ginger Cabbage Salad*

SNACK

1 banana

2 tablespoons peanut butter

2 whole-wheat crackers

Green tea

DINNER AND DESSERT

1 serving Fresh Mushroom Soup with Chicken and Thyme*

Spinach salad made with:

    2 cups baby spinach leaves

    ⅓ cup drained canned mandarin oranges

    2 tablespoons diced red onion

    2 tablespoons vinaigrette dressing

Hot cocoa:

    1 cup nonfat milk

    1 packet sugar-free cocoa mix

Nutritional analysis for the day: 2,020 calories; 30 percent fat (67 grams); 12 grams saturated fat; 1.8 grams omega-3 fats; 21 percent protein; 49 percent carbohydrate; 35 grams fiber

Day 3

BREAKFAST

1 cup shredded wheat cereal topped with 1 cup light fortified soy milk

4 apricot halves, canned in light syrup and drained

Tea or coffee (sweetened with artificial sweetener, if desired)

SNACK

1 slice Fruit Pizza*

Sparkling water with a twist of lemon

LUNCH

A pita sandwich—1 whole-wheat pita bread filled with:

   ⅓ cup canned and drained black beans

   4 avocado slices

   2 tablespoons grated cheddar cheese

   ¼ cup chopped cilantro

1 tomato, sliced and topped with fresh basil leaves and 1 tablespoon oil and vinegar dressing

Ice water

SNACK

1 serving Marinated Four-Bean Salad*

½ whole-wheat bagel topped with 1 tablespoon fat-free cream cheese

Ice water

DINNER AND DESSERT

1 serving Roasted Sea Bass with Ginger-Soy Glaze*

1 serving Broiled Asparagus with Sea Salt and Lemon*

1 cup carrot slices, peeled and steamed

Green mashed potatoes made with:

   1 baker potato, peeled, boiled, and mashed with ½ cup steamed chopped chard

   2 teaspoons butter

   Salt and pepper to taste

   Enough nonfat milk to form a creamy consistency (approximately ⅓ cup)

1 serving Fresh Mango Fruit Cups*

1 cup 1 percent low-fat milk, warmed and flavored with almond extract

Nutritional analysis for the day: 1,998 calories; 23 percent fat (51 grams); 15 grams saturated fat; 1.5 grams omega-3 fats; 19 percent protein; 58 percent carbohydrate; 43 grams fiber

Day 4

BREAKFAST

1 serving Creamy Oatmeal with Blueberries* topped with 2 tablespoons chopped pecans

1 cup cubed honeydew melon

Tea or coffee (sweetened with artificial sweetener, if desired)

SNACK

1 cup nonfat cottage cheese

1 cup fresh or canned pineapple

Sparkling water

LUNCH

1 serving Creamy Leek and Squash Soup with Fresh Herbs*

Caesar salad:

    2 cups chopped romaine lettuce

    2 tablespoons low-calorie Caesar dressing

    Fresh-ground pepper

1 piece French bread

Sparkling water

SNACK

6 ounces tomato juice

1 ounce low-fat Swiss cheese

5 whole-grain crackers

Green tea

DINNER AND DESSERT

1 serving Chicken Scallopini with Tarragon-Caper Sauce*

1 serving Baked Circles of Zucchini, Squash, and Fresh Roma Tomatoes*

1 cup cooked rotini pasta mixed with:

 1 tablespoon olive oil

 2 minced garlic cloves

 1 tablespoon grated low-fat Parmesan cheese

1 serving Sunrise Salad*

1 cup 1 percent low-fat milk, warmed and flavored with almond extract

1 cup grapes

Nutritional analysis for the day: 2,022 calories; 27 percent fat (60 grams); 12 grams saturated fat; 1.2 grams omega-3 fats; 20 percent protein; 53 percent carbohydrate; 31 grams fiber

Day 5

BREAKFAST

Breakfast smoothie made with:

 ½ cup nonfat, plain yogurt

 1 banana

 2 tablespoons orange juice concentrate

 2 tablespoons toasted wheat germ

 ¼ cup apricots, canned in juice or light syrup and drained

SNACK

2 fig bars

Sparkling water

LUNCH

Chili chicken sandwich made with (broil if desired):

 2 ounces chicken breast

 2 canned chili peppers

 1 slice low-fat Monterey Jack cheese

 2 slices whole-wheat bread

1 serving Mediterranean Salad*

1 cup lightly steamed broccoli dunked in 1 tablespoon low-calorie ranch dressing

Water

SNACK

1 whole-wheat pita bread dunked in ⅓ cup hummus (made with no oil or fats)

1 cup red bell pepper slices

Water

DINNER AND DESSERT

3 ounces grilled halibut topped with lemon juice and basil leaves

1 serving Sweet Potato Ramekins with Maple Syrup and Chopped Hazelnuts*

1 serving Baked Eggplant with Vegetable Ragu Sauce*

Spinach salad made with:

    2 cups baby spinach leaves

    1 tablespoon Craisins

    1 tablespoon low-calorie Italian dressing

1 serving Chilled Blue Moon Dessert*

Nutritional analysis for the day: 2,070 calories; 25 percent fat (57.5 grams); 12 grams saturated fat; 1.9 grams omega-3 fats; 21 percent protein; 54 percent carbohydrate; 44 grams fiber

Day 6

BREAKFAST

Scrambled eggs made with ⅔ cup liquid egg substitute (spray pan with cooking spray)

1 slice whole-wheat toast topped with 1 tablespoon apple butter

2 medium tomatoes, sliced

1 cup grapefruit juice

SNACK

1 slice Fruit Pizza*

1 cup 1 percent low-fat milk

LUNCH

1 serving Salmon Cakes on a Bed of Salad Greens*

1 piece French bread

1 cup strawberries dunked in 3 tablespoons fat-free dark chocolate syrup

Water

SNACK

1 serving Vietnamese Black Bean Salad*

6 ounces tomato juice

DINNER AND DESSERT

1 serving Santa Fe Sweet Potato Soup*

1 slice whole-wheat bread

Tossed salad made with:

    2 cups chopped romaine lettuce

    2 tablespoons sliced red onion

    2 tablespoons grated carrot

    2 tablespoons salad dressing

Fruit parfait—layer in a parfait glass:

    ½ cup chopped papaya

    ⅓ cup fresh or thawed raspberries

    ½ cup low-fat, plain yogurt

    2 tablespoons light dessert topping

Nutritional analysis for the day: 2,021 calories; 25 percent fat (56 grams); 15 grams saturated fat; 2.7 grams omega-3 fats; 19 percent protein; 56 percent carbohydrate; 37 grams fiber

Day 7

BREAKFAST

1 Flaxseed Blueberry Muffin*

2 tablespoons almond or peanut butter

1 large caffe latte made with nonfat milk

1 orange, peeled and sectioned

SNACK

½ toasted whole-wheat bagel topped with:

  2 ounces smoked salmon/lox

  1 slice red onion

  1 thick slice tomato

  2 tablespoons alfalfa sprouts

10 baby carrots

Sparkling water

LUNCH

Linguini marinara:

  1 cup cooked linguini pasta

  Marinara sauce: Heat 2 teaspoons olive oil in cast-iron skillet. Sauté 2 minced garlic cloves, ½ cup chopped onion, ¼ cup sliced red bell peppers, and ⅓ cup grated carrot until tender, approximately 10 minutes. Add ½ cup bottled pasta sauce and ½ teaspoon Italian seasoning. Simmer until bubbling. Pour over pasta.

1½ cups fresh green beans, steamed and topped with 1 tablespoon slivered almonds

Water

SNACK

1 large apple

2 tablespoons chunky peanut butter

Water

DINNER AND DESSERT

1 serving Moroccan Chicken Stew with Curried Couscous*

1 cup broccoli, steamed and topped with 1 teaspoon sesame seeds

1 serving Fresh Bowls of Berries with Sour Cream and Yogurt*

1 cup nonfat milk, warmed and sweetened with 2 teaspoons sugar and 1 teaspoon almond extract

Nutritional analysis for the day: 2,001 calories; 29 percent fat (64.5 grams); 10 grams saturated fat; 1.1 grams omega-3 fats; 18 percent protein; 53 percent carbohydrate; 47 grams fiber

Antiaging Recipes

Breakfast Ideas

Oven-Roasted Vegetable Frittata

The vegetables in this frittata pack hefty doses of iron, zinc, calcium, and other minerals that aid in wound healing, circulation, and bone health.

2 teaspoons olive oil

½ cup yellow peeled and diced onion

½ cup seeded and diced red or yellow pepper

½ cup diced zucchini

1½ cups liquid egg substitute

½ cup nonfat milk

1 teaspoon each of dried basil and oregano

1 cup diced fresh tomatoes

¼ cup shredded low-fat Parmesan cheese

1. Preheat oven to 400°F.
2. Heat olive oil in a medium-large, ovenproof skillet over medium heat. Add onion and peppers and sauté until soft, about 5 minutes. Add zucchini and cook for 1 minute. Reduce heat to low.
3. Blend egg substitute, milk, and seasonings in a medium bowl, and pour over vegetables in a skillet. Increase heat to medium high. Cook for about 3 minutes, until egg mixture is set. Add diced tomatoes and sprinkle with cheese.

4. Transfer skillet to preheated oven. Bake until top is golden brown, approximately 10 to 15 minutes. Makes 4 servings.

Nutritional analysis per serving: 162 calories; 40 percent fat (7 grams); 1 gram saturated fat; 35 percent protein; 25 percent carbohydrate; 1.3 grams fiber

■ ■ ■

Creamy Oatmeal with Blueberries

Berries are excellent sources of phytochemicals that protect brain tissue from free-radical damage associated with memory loss. The soluble fiber in oats lowers heart disease risk, too!

½ cup water
½ cup fat-free half-and-half
½ cup old-fashioned oats
½ cup fresh or frozen blueberries
Additional fat-free half-and-half to pour over hot oatmeal
Splenda (optional)

1. Combine water and half-and-half in a medium-size saucepan over medium-high heat. Bring to a boil. Add oats and simmer for 4 minutes, stirring frequently. Remove from heat. Let rest for 2 minutes.
2. Placed cooked oats in 2 small bowls, top with blueberries, add additional half-and-half to taste. Sprinkle with Splenda if sweeter taste is desired. Makes 2 servings.

Nutritional analysis per serving: 138 calories; 10 percent fat (1.5 grams); 0 grams saturated fat; 16 percent protein; 74 percent carbohydrate; 3 grams fiber

Flaxseed Blueberry Muffins

These tasty muffins are great for breakfast or as a snack served with soy milk and fruit.

½ cup egg substitute

2 tablespoons sugar-free maple syrup

Juice and zest of 1 medium orange

¼ cup brown sugar

½ cup Splenda

1 teaspoon vanilla extract

2 teaspoons cinnamon

½ teaspoon salt

2 teaspoons baking soda

1 teaspoon baking powder

¾ cup flaxseed meal

1½ cups oat flour

⅔ cup nonfat milk

1 cup fresh or frozen blueberries

1. Preheat oven to 350°F. Spray 12-muffin tin with cooking spray.
2. Combine all ingredients except blueberries in a large mixing bowl. Beat with an electric mixer for 1 minute (or stir by hand for 2 minutes). Don't overbeat. Gently fold in blueberries.
3. Pour mixture into prepared muffin tin, using about ⅓ cup per muffin. Bake for 25 minutes, or until done. Makes 12 muffins.

Nutritional analysis per muffin: 115 calories; 21 percent fat (2.7 grams); 0 grams saturated fat; 18 percent protein; 61 percent carbohydrate; 4.2 grams fiber

Soups

Chilled Cantaloupe Soup with Coconut and Blueberry Puree

*Besides being packed with antioxidants, providing an entire day's require-
ment for vitamin C, and tasting great, this soup is beautiful!*

2 pounds ripe cantaloupe, peeled, seeded, and cut into 1-inch pieces (about 4 cups)

⅔ cup light coconut milk

¼ cup shredded coconut

Juice and zest from 1 lime

½ cup plus 2 tablespoons fresh or frozen blueberries

2 tablespoons water

2 teaspoons Splenda

½ teaspoon vanilla

Fresh mint sprigs for garnish

1. Place diced cantaloupe in a food processor, and process for 1 minute or until pureed. Add coconut milk, coconut, and lime juice and zest, and pulse 10 times. Pour into a medium-size bowl, cover, and chill until ready to serve. (Can chill overnight.)
2. Combine ½ cup blueberries, water, Splenda, and vanilla in a food processor. Process until pureed (add more water if too thick). Pour into a small bowl, and chill until ready to serve.
3. Pour chilled cantaloupe soup into 4 individual small serving bowls, drizzle with blueberry puree, and garnish with remaining blueberries (2 tablespoons) and a sprig of mint. Makes 4 servings.

Nutritional analysis per serving: 114 calories; 28 percent fat (3.5 grams); 3 grams saturated fat; 7 percent protein; 65 percent carbohydrate; 2 grams fiber

Fresh Mushroom Soup with Chicken and Thyme

This filling, tasty soup is excellent served the next day and keeps up to three days in the refrigerator, and it is rich in folic acid, a B vitamin that lowers risk for heart disease, depression, cancer, and memory loss.

2 tablespoons olive oil

1 pound mushrooms, cleaned and sliced thinly

1 large yellow onion, peeled and diced

4 stalks celery, diced

4 cloves garlic, minced

6 cups chicken broth

3 cups diced cooked chicken breasts

1 10-ounce box frozen chopped spinach

1 cup frozen green peas

1 large carrot, peeled and grated

1 teaspoon each of thyme, sage, and curry powder

½ cup fat-free half-and-half

1. Warm olive oil in a large soup pot or Dutch oven over medium heat. Add mushrooms, onions, celery, and garlic. Sauté until soft, about 5 minutes.
2. Pour chicken broth over vegetable mixture, bring to a boil, reduce heat, and simmer for 10 minutes.
3. Add diced cooked chicken, spinach, peas, carrots, and seasonings. Simmer for 10 to 15 minutes.
4. In the last 5 minutes of cooking, add half-and-half. Serve hot. Makes 8 generous servings.

Nutritional analysis per serving: 175 calories; 30 percent fat (5.8 grams); 1 gram saturated fat; 41 percent protein; 29 percent carbohydrate; 3.4 grams fiber

Creamy Leek and Squash Soup with Fresh Herbs

With almost 100 micrograms of folic acid and 3 grams of iron, this soup helps fight fatigue and memory loss. Serve with whole-wheat bread and a tossed salad to round out the meal.

1 tablespoon olive oil

4 leeks, white and light green parts only

5 yellow crookneck squash, washed and finely chopped

2 cloves garlic, minced

4 cups chicken broth (Better Than Bouillon works well—1 teaspoon per cup of hot water)

1 cup fat-free half-and-half

Zest and juice of 1 small lemon

1 tablespoon finely chopped fresh basil

2 tablespoons of any of the following herbs combined, finely chopped: lemon thyme, regular thyme, marjoram, and sage (save ½ teaspoon for garnish)

Salt and pepper to taste

1. Warm olive oil over medium heat in a large soup pot or Dutch oven. Add leeks and sauté until soft, about 5 minutes. Add squash and sauté until lightly browned, about 4 minutes longer. Add garlic and cook for an additional minute.

2. Add chicken broth and simmer, partially covered, until squash is very tender, about 15 minutes. Remove from heat and cool slightly.

3. Using a blender, puree soup in small portions until smooth. Return puree mixture to pot. Stir in remaining ingredients, and season with salt and pepper. Reheat gently over medium-low heat. Ladle into warm bowls, and garnish with remaining herbs. Makes 4 servings.

Nutritional analysis per serving: 190 calories; 25 percent fat (5 grams); 1 gram saturated fat; 20 percent protein; 55 percent carbohydrate; 4 grams fiber

Santa Fe Sweet Potato Soup

This rich, creamy soup is packed with beta-carotene and other antioxidants, as well as fiber and protein. Beta-carotene helps boost immune function, thus protecting against infections and disease. Serve this soup with warm bread and low-fat cheese.

3 tablespoons olive oil

1 cup chopped onion

3 sweet potatoes, peeled and chopped (about 8 cups)

7 cups chicken broth

1 can chilies, chopped, or 1 jalapeño pepper, seeded and thinly sliced

1 10-ounce package frozen corn kernels

½ cup low-fat milk

Salt and pepper to taste

3 tablespoons finely chopped fresh cilantro (optional)

¼ cup fat-free sour cream (optional)

1. Heat olive oil in a large saucepan over medium heat. Add onions and sauté until transparent. Add sweet potatoes and chicken broth. Bring to a boil, lower heat, and simmer until potatoes are tender, about 25 minutes.
2. Place potato mixture in a blender with broth (in small batches), and blend until smooth. Return to saucepan and add chilies and corn. Simmer 10 minutes.
3. Stir in milk, salt, and pepper. Serve immediately. If desired, top with cilantro and sour cream. Makes 8 servings.

Nutritional analysis per serving: 322 calories; 20 percent fat (7.3 grams); <1 gram saturated fat; 15 percent protein; 65 percent carbohydrate; 6.4 grams fiber

Salads

Thai Ginger Cabbage Salad

This crispy salad supplies generous amounts of vitamin C, vitamin E, beta-carotene, and potassium, nutrients essential in protecting the body from age-related damage and in maintaining a normal heartbeat and muscle contraction.

DRESSING:

½ cup fat-free sour cream

¼ cup fat-free mayonnaise

1 tablespoon apple cider vinegar

2 teaspoons Splenda

3 tablespoons peeled and grated fresh ginger

1 large clove of garlic, minced

SALAD:

1 16-ounce bag tricolored slaw mix

1 cup peeled and finely chopped jicama

1 tart apple (such as Granny Smith), unpeeled, cored, and chopped

4 green onions (green tops only), thinly sliced

½ cup finely chopped cilantro

1. To prepare dressing, place all dressing ingredients in a medium bowl and mix well. Cover and chill (up to 24 hours).
2. Place all salad ingredients in a large bowl, and gently mix together. Add chilled dressing and toss well to combine. Serve on chilled salad plates. Makes 6 servings.

Nutritional analysis per serving: 72 calories; 5 percent fat (<1 gram); 0 grams saturated fat; 15 percent protein; 80 percent carbohydrate; 3 grams fiber

Marinated Four-Bean Salad

Beans are the most fiber-packed foods in the diet and also contain iron, zinc, B vitamins, and phytochemicals, such as saponins and phytosterols, that lower cancer and heart disease risk.

1 15-ounce can cut green beans
1 15-ounce can cut yellow wax beans
1 15-ounce can garbanzo beans
1 15-ounce can red kidney beans
1 small red onion, peeled and thinly sliced
1 tablespoon chopped fresh parsley

DRESSING:

¾ cup Splenda
½ cup apple cider vinegar
2 tablespoons olive oil
1 tablespoon balsamic vinegar

1. Drain and rinse beans. Combine all the beans, onion, and parsley in a large bowl. Toss to mix.
2. Combine the dressing ingredients in a small saucepan over medium heat. Simmer and whisk until Splenda dissolves, about 1 minute. Remove from heat and cool.
3. Pour cool dressing mixture over beans, stir to combine, and cover. Refrigerate until ready to eat, from 2 hours to overnight. Makes 8 servings.

Nutritional analysis per serving: 167 calories; 24 percent fat (4.5 grams); <1 gram saturated fat; 18 percent protein; 58 percent carbohydrate; 8 grams fiber

Vietnamese Black Bean Salad

Black beans are cholesterol free, almost fat free, and rich in fiber and nutri-ents, supplying more than half a day's requirement for folic acid and hefty amounts of calcium, magnesium, iron, and zinc in every serving. They also are loaded with phytochemicals, such as saponins and phytosterols, that lower cancer and heart disease risk, and being low in the glycemic index, they help regulate blood sugar as well as appetite.

1 15-ounce can black beans, rinsed and drained

1 cup fresh or frozen corn

½ cup seeded and diced red bell pepper

½ cup diced celery

½ cup diced cucumber

⅓ cup chopped cilantro

6 mint leaves, rolled from stem to tip and thinly sliced (prevents bruising)

DRESSING:

2 tablespoons sesame oil

1½ tablespoons rice vinegar

Zest of 1 small lime

2 teaspoons lime juice

1 teaspoon fish sauce

2 cloves garlic, minced

1½ teaspoons peeled and minced fresh ginger

1. Combine all bean salad ingredients in a medium bowl, toss, and set aside.
2. Whisk together all dressing ingredients in a small bowl.
3. Pour dressing over black bean mixture, toss to coat, cover, and chill at least 2 hours or overnight. Stir before serving. Makes 4 servings.

Nutritional analysis per serving: 190 calories; 27 percent fat (6 grams); <1 gram saturated fat; 17 percent protein; 56 percent carbohydrate; 7 grams fiber

Salmon Cakes on a Bed of Salad Greens

*A diet high in the omega-3 fats found in salmon slows age-related
memory loss and might slow the progression of Alzheimer's disease,
according to numerous studies, including one from the
University of California, Los Angeles.*

1 teaspoon olive oil

½ cup seeded and finely chopped red bell pepper

½ cup finely chopped green onion

½ pound medium-size shrimp, cleaned and deveined

1½ teaspoons minced garlic

2 tablespoons fat-free mayonnaise

2 tablespoons grated Parmesan cheese

1 pound salmon fillet, skin removed, cleaned, patted dry, and chopped

1½ teaspoons chopped fresh dill

Sea salt to taste

2 7-ounce bags prepared baby greens salad mix

LEMON VINAIGRETTE DRESSING:

2 tablespoons fresh lemon juice

1 clove garlic, minced

1. Warm olive oil over medium heat in a large nonstick skillet. Add peppers and onions, and sauté for about 5 minutes or until peppers are soft. Set aside.
2. Place shrimp, garlic, mayonnaise, and Parmesan cheese in a food processor. Pulse several times, until mixture is well combined.
3. Combine the chopped salmon, pepper and onion mixture, and processed shrimp mixture in a large mixing bowl. Blend well, and add chopped dill and sea salt to taste. (May cover and refrigerate up to 24 hours.)
4. Using about ¼ cup salmon-shrimp mixture, make a round, semiflat salmon cake, approximately ½ inch thick. Continue to make salmon cakes until ingredients are used up.
5. Using the same skillet over medium-high heat, cook salmon cakes for about 3 minutes on each side or until salmon is flaky. Remove from skillet, place on a serving platter, cover with foil, and keep warm.
6. To prepare the lemon vinaigrette, whisk together dressing ingredients in the order listed in a small bowl. Set aside.

7. Combine the salad mix and vinaigrette in a large salad bowl. Toss well. Place about 2 cups of the salad mixture on 6 dinner plates, and then top with 2 warm salmon cakes. Enjoy! Makes 6 servings, each including 2 salmon cakes.

Nutritional analysis per serving: 211 calories; 43 percent fat (10 grams); 2 grams saturated fat; 1.3 grams omega-3 fats; 47 percent protein; 10 percent carbohydrate; 1 gram fiber

■ ■ ■

Mediterranean Salad

Cup for cup, red bell peppers are a better source of vitamin C than orange juice and also are rich sources of antioxidant phytochemicals that protect tissues from premature aging and disease.

1 English cucumber, peeled and chopped
1 cup chopped tomatoes
½ cup seeded and chopped red bell pepper
¼ cup peeled and chopped red onion
2 tablespoons chopped olives
2 tablespoons chopped fresh cilantro
1 tablespoon chopped fresh dill
1 teaspoon capers, rinsed and drained (optional)
1 tablespoon fresh lemon juice
1 teaspoon olive oil
1 teaspoon water
2 ounces fat-free feta cheese, crumbled
Sea salt to taste

Combine ingredients in a medium bowl. Stir well to mix. Cover and chill until ready to serve. Makes 4 servings.

Nutritional analysis per serving: 54 calories; 28 percent fat (1.6 grams); 0 grams saturated fat; 27 percent protein; 45 percent carbohydrate; 1.6 grams fiber

Sunrise Salad

This salad is packed with nutrients, including beta-carotene, vitamin C, and folic acid. It's good warm or cold, winter or summer.

1½ cups orange juice (fresh or from concentrate)
8 large carrots, peeled and cut into ½-inch diagonal slices (if in a hurry, use 1 pound of baby carrots, uncut)
2 teaspoons butter
1½ teaspoons grated fresh ginger
¼ teaspoon red pepper flakes (optional)
⅔ cup pea pods, cut in half diagonally
1 11-ounce can of mandarin oranges, drained
½ cup finely chopped fresh parsley
½ teaspoon salt

---

1. Place orange juice, carrots, butter, ginger, and pepper flakes in a deep-dish frying pan. Bring to slow boil and cook for 20 minutes. Add pea pods and cook for another 10 minutes, or until carrots and pea pods are still slightly crisp and juice has evaporated. Remove from heat and cool to room temperature.
2. Add orange slices and parsley, and toss. Salt to taste. Serve at room temperature or chill before serving. Makes 4 servings.

Nutritional analysis per serving: 163 calories; 13 percent fat (2.5 grams); <1 gram saturated fat; 8 percent protein; 79 percent carbohydrate; 6.3 grams fiber

Entrées

Grilled Salmon with Pesto and Lemon Zest

Wild salmon is nature's best source of the omega-3 fats, which lower risk for heart disease and possibly bone loss, memory loss, depression, and arthritis.

1 ½ pounds wild salmon fillet

3 tablespoons commercial basil pesto sauce

Zest of 1 small lemon

Sea salt to taste

Cooking spray

1. Preheat oven to 375°F. Spray a foil-lined cookie sheet with cooking spray.
2. Place salmon on foil-lined cookie sheet. Spread pesto sauce over salmon. Sprinkle with lemon zest. (Can refrigerate up to 1 hour prior to baking.)
3. Bake until fish is flaky but not dry, about 20 minutes (time will vary due to thickness of salmon and is done when fish is barely opaque in center).
4. Remove from oven and sprinkle with sea salt to taste. Serve with lemon wedges. Makes 4 servings.

Nutritional analysis per serving: 368 calories; 58 percent fat (23 grams); 5.6 grams saturated fat; 2.5 grams omega-3 fats; 40 percent protein; 2 percent carbohydrate; 0.5 gram fiber

Chicken Scallopini with Tarragon-Caper Sauce

Served with a tossed salad, steamed vegetables, and brown rice, this
quick-fix meal can be ready in less than 20 minutes.

4 chicken breast cutlets, skinned
1 tablespoon olive oil
½ cup chicken broth
⅓ cup fat-free sour cream
1½ teaspoons Dijon mustard
1 teaspoon dry tarragon
2 tablespoons capers, rinsed and drained

1. Clean and pat dry chicken breast cutlets. If using regular chicken breast, slice in half lengthwise or ask butcher to slice.
2. Warm olive oil over medium-high heat in a large skillet. Add chicken and cook until brown on each side, about 2 minutes per side or until no longer pink. Remove chicken from pan, place on a serving platter, and cover with foil. Keep warm.
3. Add chicken broth in the same skillet over medium-high heat. Using a whisk, stir and scrape bits of chicken left from browning the chicken. Bring mixture to a boil for 1 minute, and then remove from heat. Add sour cream, mustard, tarragon, and capers. Whisk until blended. Pour sauce over warm chicken and serve. Makes 4 servings.

Nutritional analysis per serving: 144 calories; 50 percent fat (8 grams); 1 gram saturated fat; 44 percent protein; 6 percent carbohydrate; 0 grams fiber

Moroccan Chicken Stew with Curried Couscous

*Rich in fiber, B vitamins, and iron, this one-dish meal also is great served
with a spinach salad.*

1 tablespoon olive oil

3 skinless, boneless chicken breasts, cut into 2-inch chunks

2 sweet yellow onions, peeled and chopped

3 cloves garlic, minced

1 tablespoon cinnamon

6 cups low-sodium chicken broth

1 15-ounce can garbanzo beans

3 medium carrots, peeled and cut into ¼-inch slices

1 small green zucchini, cut into ¼-inch slices

2 large tomatoes, chopped

⅓ cup chopped fresh parsley

¼ cup raisins

Juice and zest of 1 small orange

Sea salt and pepper to taste

1 (5.7-ounce) box Near East Couscous mix (Mediterranean Curry Flavor)

---

1. Heat olive oil in a large soup pot or Dutch oven over medium heat. Sear
   chicken for 2 minutes per side, or until no longer pink. Remove from pot
   and set aside.
2. Add onions to same pot and sauté until soft, about 4 minutes. Add all
   remaining ingredients except couscous. Stir, bring to a boil for 5 minutes,
   and reduce heat to medium. Add chicken and simmer for 30 minutes.
3. Cook couscous according to package, except use half the seasoning packet to
   lower sodium content and do not add fat or oil.
4. Ladle stew into individual bowls, place about ⅓ cup prepared couscous in
   center of stew, and serve hot. Makes 8 servings.

Nutritional analysis per serving: 260 calories; 13 percent fat (3.7 grams); 0.7 gram
saturated fat; 32 percent protein; 55 percent carbohydrate; 6.6 grams fiber

Baked Halibut with Tomato Salsa and Shaved Parmesan Cheese

This entrée supplies one-fifth of your total day's need for calcium and generous amounts of B vitamins, iron, zinc, and magnesium.

1 pound fresh halibut fillet, cleaned and patted dry
¾ cup fresh tomato salsa (chunky style), drained
2 ounces fresh Parmesan cheese, shaved
Cooking spray

1. Preheat oven to 375°F. Spray cookie sheet lined with tin foil with cooking spray. Set aside.
2. Place halibut on foil-lined cookie sheet. Pour salsa over top of halibut. Bake in oven for 15 minutes, or until flaky.
3. Remove halibut from oven. Sprinkle Parmesan cheese on top, and return to oven until cheese is melted, about 2 minutes. Serve hot from oven. Makes 4 servings.

Nutritional analysis per serving: 187 calories; 31 percent fat (6.4 grams); 2.7 grams saturated fat; 0.5 gram omega-3 fats; 64 percent protein; 5 percent carbohydrate; 0.5 gram fiber

Roasted Sea Bass with Ginger-Soy Glaze

Ginger helps with nausea and might have anti-inflammatory properties in the treatment of arthritis. Halibut or any firm, white fish will work well for this dish.

4 tablespoons low-sodium soy sauce (citrus soy sauce works well)

¼ cup finely chopped green onion

2 tablespoons honey

1 tablespoon brown sugar

1 teaspoon sesame oil

2 teaspoons peeled and minced fresh ginger

⅛ teaspoon crushed red pepper flakes

Juice and zest of 1 small orange

4 5-ounce sea bass fillets, cleaned and patted dry

Cooking spray

1. Preheat oven to 450°F. Coat a 8 × 8 × 2–inch glass baking dish or foiled cookie sheet with cooking spray.
2. Combine the first 8 ingredients in a small bowl and mix well. Set aside.
3. Arrange fish in a single layer on baking dish or cookie sheet, and drizzle sesame-soy sauce over fish. Roast fish in oven until opaque in center, about 10 minutes. Serve hot. Makes 4 servings.

Nutritional analysis per serving: 218 calories; 14 percent fat (3.3 grams); <0.5 gram saturated fat; 57 percent protein; 29 percent carbohydrate; 0 grams fiber

Vegetables

Sweet Potato Ramekins with Maple Syrup and Chopped Hazelnuts

Sweet potatoes are rich in beta-carotene, an antioxidant that lowers risk for skin cancer and possibly heart disease.

2½ cups sweet potatoes, peeled and cut into 1-inch cubes (about 2 medium sweet
   potatoes)
2 tablespoons fat-free sour cream
2 tablespoons sugar-free maple syrup
½ teaspoon salt
½ teaspoon cinnamon
Pinch of cardamom or nutmeg
Cooking spray

TOPPING:
⅓ cup chopped hazelnuts
⅛ teaspoon cayenne
2 tablespoons sugar-free maple syrup

1. Preheat oven to 350°F. Spray 4 ½-cup ramekins with cooking spray and set aside.
2. Steam potatoes until tender, about 12 minutes.
3. Drain and return potatoes to pan. Add sour cream, maple syrup, salt, cinnamon, and cardamom. Mash to desired consistency. If too thick, add more sour cream or milk.
4. Spoon sweet potato mixture evenly into 4 ramekins.
5. Mix together topping ingredients in a small bowl, and sprinkle over each ramekin filled with sweet potatoes.
6. Place ramekins on cookie sheet and bake until tops are brown, about 15 minutes. Serve hot. Makes 4 servings.

Nutritional analysis per serving: 123 calories; 42 percent fat (5.7 grams); <0.5 gram saturated fat; 8 percent protein; 50 percent carbohydrate; 3 grams fiber

Oven-Roasted Brussels Sprouts with Apples and Walnuts

Brussels sprouts are a member of the cabbage family and are packed with antioxidant phytochemicals called indoles that reduce cancer and heart-disease risk.

1 pound Brussels sprouts, washed and trimmed

2 apples (Golden Delicious), peeled, cored, and thickly sliced

⅓ cup chopped walnuts

1 tablespoon olive oil

2 teaspoons lemon juice

½ teaspoon cinnamon

⅛ teaspoon nutmeg

Sea salt to taste

2 tablespoons sugar-free maple syrup

Cooking spray

1. Preheat oven to 350°F. Spray a large cookie sheet with cooking spray and set aside.
2. Mix together Brussels sprouts, apples, walnuts, olive oil, lemon juice, cinnamon, and nutmeg in a large bowl. Toss well to coat Brussels sprouts.
3. Pour Brussels sprouts onto prepared cookie sheet, sprinkle with sea salt, and bake for about 30 minutes, or until tender-crisp. May need to cover the last 10 minutes to prevent excess browning.
4. Remove from oven. Place mixture on a serving plate or in a medium bowl, and drizzle with maple syrup. Makes 4 servings.

Nutritional analysis per serving: 205 calories; 40 percent fat (9 grams); 1 gram saturated fat; 0.8 gram omega-3 fats; 10 percent protein; 50 percent carbohydrate; 8 grams fiber

Broiled Asparagus with Sea Salt and Lemon

Asparagus is an excellent source of antioxidant phytochemicals and a good source of folic acid, a B vitamin that helps prevent certain cancers, heart disease, and memory loss. Olive oil helps keep blood cholesterol levels low, reducing heart disease risk.

1½ pounds medium-size fresh asparagus, washed and ends snapped off
1 tablespoon olive oil
Sea salt to taste
Zest of 1 small lemon
Cooking spray

1. Turn oven broiler to high. Place oven rack 4 inches from heat source. Spray a large cookie sheet with cooking spray.
2. Place asparagus on cookie sheet in a single layer. Drizzle with olive oil, and shake cookie sheet back and forth until all asparagus are coated. Sprinkle with sea salt.
3. Roast for 4 minutes. Turn asparagus and continue to roast for an additional 3 minutes, or until tender-crisp. Remove from oven, and sprinkle with lemon zest. Serve on a platter or large plate. Makes 4 servings.

Nutritional analysis per serving: 69 calories; 42 percent fat (3.7 grams); <1 gram saturated fat; 19 percent protein; 39 percent carbohydrate; 3 grams fiber

Baked Circles of Zucchini, Squash, and Fresh Roma Tomatoes

The tomatoes in this dish supply lycopene, a carotenoid that lowers heart disease risk in men and women and prostate cancer risk in men.

Cooking spray

1 tablespoon olive oil

1 large sweet yellow onion, peeled and diced

3 cloves garlic, minced

3 medium zucchini, cut into ¼-inch slices

3 medium yellow squash, cut into ¼-inch slices

8 Roma tomatoes, cut into ¼-inch slices

2 teaspoons Italian seasonings

Sea salt to taste

⅓ cup grated Romano cheese

2 tablespoons crumbled fat-free feta cheese

1½ tablespoons chopped parsley

1. Preheat oven to 375°F. Coat a round 10-inch quiche pan with cooking spray, and set aside.
2. Warm olive oil in a large skillet over medium heat. Add onions and sauté for 2 minutes. Add garlic and continue to cook for 1 minute, stirring occasionally. Remove skillet from heat, and set aside.
3. Arrange slices of zucchini, squash, and Roma tomatoes in a circular pattern starting from the outer edges of the quiche pan to the center. (Place vegetables in an upright position, not layering them flat.)
4. Spread onion mixture over the top of zucchini mixture. Sprinkle with Italian seasonings and salt. Cover with foil and bake for 1 hour. When tender-crisp, remove from oven and sprinkle with Romano cheese, feta, and parsley. Return to oven uncovered for 5 minutes, or until top is lightly brown. Serve hot. Makes 8 servings.

Nutritional analysis per serving: 74 calories; 36 percent fat (3 grams); 1 gram saturated fat; 20 percent protein; 44 percent carbohydrate; 2.4 grams fiber

Baked Eggplant with Vegetable Ragu Sauce

Onions, like garlic, help lower heart disease risk, while the lycopene in the pasta sauce lowers heart disease and prostate cancer risk.

SAUCE:

2 tablespoons fat-free chicken broth

1 large yellow onion, peeled and chopped

½ pound mushrooms, cleaned and coarsely chopped

1 medium zucchini, with stem removed and coarsely chopped

1 medium yellow squash, with stem removed and coarsely chopped

1 14-ounce can quartered artichoke hearts in water, drained and chopped

2 25-ounce jars of pasta sauce

1 tablespoon balsamic vinegar

2 teaspoons Italian seasonings

BAKED EGGPLANT:

½ cup liquid egg substitute

½ cup grated low-fat Parmesan cheese

1 large eggplant, sliced into ⅓-inch rounds

1. Preheat oven to 350°F. Spray a large cookie sheet with cooking spray and set aside.
2. Warm chicken broth in a large soup pot or Dutch oven over medium heat. Sauté onions until soft, about 4 minutes. Add mushrooms, zucchini, and squash. Continue to sauté until vegetables are soft, about 2 minutes. Add artichokes, pasta sauce, balsamic vinegar, and seasonings. Stir well, bring to a boil, and reduce heat to medium low. Simmer for 25 minutes.
3. Place egg substitute in a shallow bowl and Parmesan cheese on a large plate.
4. Dip eggplant slices into egg substitute; roll in Parmesan cheese to coat both sides. Place on cookie sheet and bake for 25 minutes, or until crust of eggplant is crispy brown. Remove from oven, cover with foil, and keep warm.
5. Place eggplant slices on plates, and top with about 1 cup of sauce. Sprinkle with extra grated cheese, if desired. Serve hot. Makes 8 servings.

Nutritional analysis per serving: 237 calories; 32 percent fat (8.4 grams); 1 gram saturated fat; 15 percent protein; 53 percent carbohydrate; 9 grams fiber

Desserts

Fresh Bowls of Berries with Sour Cream and Yogurt

This luscious dessert supplies ellagic acid, anthocyanidins, and other phyto-chemicals that protect the body's tissues from age-related damage. You'll also get a full-day's supply of vitamin C and hefty amounts of calcium, vitamin A, fiber, and folic acid.

⅔ cup fat-free sour cream

½ cup fat-free, sugar-free vanilla yogurt

2 tablespoons sugar-free maple syrup

Zest of 1 small orange

4 cups fresh mixed berries (blueberries, strawberries, raspberries, or any other favorites), rinsed and drained (leave berries whole)

Fresh mint for garnish

1. Stir together sour cream, yogurt, syrup, and orange zest in a small bowl. Cover and refrigerate until ready to use.
2. Place berries in a large glass bowl or individual serving dessert cups. Pour sour cream mixture evenly over the top, garnish with a sprig of mint, and serve. Makes 4 servings.

Nutritional analysis per serving: 85 calories; 5 percent fat (<1 gram); 0 grams saturated fat; 21 percent protein; 74 percent carbohydrate; 4 grams fiber

Fruit Pizza

Along with the wealth of antioxidants in this pizza, the bacteria in yogurt crowd out disease-causing bacteria, produce natural antibiotics, and possibly switch off an enzyme that triggers colon cancer.

1 package pizza dough mix for 10-inch to 12-inch pizza, sweetened with 2 teaspoons granulated sugar

2 6-ounce containers lemon-flavored nonfat yogurt

3 cups sliced fresh fruit, including kiwi, strawberries, bananas, halved grapes, mandarin oranges, and cantaloupe balls

3 tablespoons orange juice concentrate

1 tablespoon powdered sugar

1 sprig mint

1. Prepare pizza dough mix according to package directions, with addition of sugar. Shape dough into a large circle on a round pizza pan or stone, forming a ½-inch-high edge. Bake according to package directions. Cool.
2. Spread crust evenly with a layer of yogurt to within ½ inch of raised edge.
3. Beginning with kiwi, arrange each grouping of sliced fruit in concentric circles on top of crust. Mix orange juice concentrate with powdered sugar until smooth. Drizzle over top of fruited torte. Finish with mint sprig in center. Chill. Makes 4 servings of ¼ pizza each.

Nutritional analysis per serving: 309 calories; 9 percent fat (3 grams); <1 gram saturated fat; 14 percent protein; 77 percent carbohydrate; 3 grams fiber

Fresh Mango Fruit Cups

*Mangos are a rich source of beta-carotene and vitamin C, two of the most
powerful antioxidants in the diet. They also taste like heaven!*

2 ripe mangos, peeled and diced
2 cups peeled and diced ripe cantaloupe
Juice and zest of 1 small lime
1 tablespoon fresh mint, leaf rolled from stem to tip, thinly sliced (to prevent bruising)
1 cup fresh or frozen blueberries

1. Combine mango, cantaloupe, juice and zest of lime, and mint in a medium
   bowl. Mix well and set aside.
2. Spoon mango mixture into 4 glass dessert cups, bowls, or parfait dishes.
   Sprinkle with blueberries and serve. Makes 4 servings.

Nutritional analysis per serving: 121 calories; 4 percent fat (<1 gram); 0 grams
saturated fat; 5 percent protein; 91 percent carbohydrate; 4 grams fiber

Chilled Blue Moon Dessert

Along with their brain-protecting antioxidants, blueberries are high in fiber,
potassium, and vitamin C, and like other fruits, they help curb weight gain.
Aim for three or more cups a week.

1 8-ounce container sugar-free, fat-free vanilla yogurt
½ cup fat-free half-and-half
1 cup frozen blueberries

Place ingredients in a blender and blend until pureed. Pour into 2 tall fluted
glasses and serve. Makes 2 servings.

Nutritional analysis per serving: 137 calories; 4 percent fat (0 gram); 0 grams
saturated fat; 22 percent protein; 74 percent carbohydrate; 2.5 grams fiber

Antiaging Superfoods

Tired of only hearing about the foods you can't have, should cut back on, or should avoid like the plague? Well, here's a list of twenty foods that scientists report we should be eating much more of. From chin-dribbling strawberries to sweet, chewy figs, these selections are Mother Nature's superfoods, supplying lots of antiaging nutritional punch for very few calories and little fat.

Bananas. This fruit is one of the few plants that are high in vitamin B_6, a nutrient essential for red blood cell formation, nerve function, energy metabolism, and the regulation of mood and sleep. A banana with a whole-wheat bagel and juice is an excellent after-workout way to restock glycogen stores and fuel your energy level.

Beans, black. Black beans make it to the plate 148 percent more often today than in the early 1990s, yet most people still average only about a cup a year, a pittance compared with the fifty pounds of pork we gobble at the same time. Like most legumes, black beans are cholesterol free, almost fat free, and rich in fiber and nutrients, supplying more than half a day's requirement for folic acid and hefty amounts of calcium, magnesium, iron, and zinc in every serving. They also are loaded with phytochemicals, such as saponins and phytosterols, that lower cancer and heart disease risk, and they are low in the glycemic index, so they help regulate blood sugar as well as appetite. A study from Tulane University School of Public Health in New Orleans found that people who included beans in their diets at least four times a week lowered their risk for heart disease by 22 percent compared with people whose diets included a serving or less each week. "Increasing bean intake as part of a diet rich in fruits and vegetables might help prevent heart disease, lower cholesterol, and may even lower blood pressure, too," says Lydia Bazzano, M.D., Ph.D., Harvard clinical fellow in medicine at Beth Israel

Deaconess Hospital and chief researcher on the study. At least four times a week, use rinsed, canned black beans in salads, burritos, and soups, or sprinkle with cilantro and serve hot on top of rice.

Berries. Berries supply a wealth of phytochemicals, including flavonoids, caffeic acid, ellagic acid, and anthocyanins. "These compounds are potent antioxidants associated with a lower risk for heart disease and cancer, and they protect against highly reactive oxidants that damage the brain," says Gary Stoner, Ph.D., professor in the Department of Internal Medicine at the Ohio State University. Berries also are high in fiber, potassium, and vitamin C, and like other fruits, they help curb weight gain. You have countless options when it comes to using berries: toss them in salads, add them to cereal, layer them with yogurt for a parfait, heat them with Splenda and a bit of cornstarch to make a topping for waffles or desserts, eat them frozen as an alternative to ice cream, dip them in fat-free chocolate syrup, blend them into smoothies, or add them fresh or dried to muffin and pancake batters. You can even mix blueberries into salsas. Dr. Stoner recommends including a cup of fresh or frozen berries in the diet three or four times a week. (See Chilled Cantaloupe Soup with Coconut and Blueberry Puree, Fresh Bowls of Berries with Sour Cream and Yogurt, and Chilled Blue Moon Dessert in Appendix B.)

Brewer's yeast. Though not a typical inclusion in many people's daily fare, a quarter-cup of this nutritional yeast mixed into orange juice contains more zinc than two cups of green peas, five slices of white bread, or twenty-one cups of cabbage. It also contains more vitamin B_6 than twenty-seven pounds of hamburger or forty-five slices of vitamin B_1–enriched white bread. Brewer's yeast is equally high in the other B vitamins, as well as being an excellent source of iron, calcium, and selenium. For that kind of nutritional punch, it might be worth getting used to the taste!

Broccoli. A one-cup serving of steamed broccoli supplies 20 percent of your folic acid needs, 193 percent of vitamin C needs, and 15 percent of the requirements for vitamins B_2 and B_6, all for only 43 calories! Broccoli also contains sulforaphane and indoles, phytochemicals that block the growth of cancerous tumors. Include this powerhouse in your diet at least twice a week.

Chocolate. Maybe it's the phenylethylamine that produces lovelike emotions or the endorphin release that produces feelings of euphoria, or maybe it's just the melt-in-your-mouth taste and aroma. Whatever it is, chocolate is the number-one most craved food, and nothing else satisfies the craving. So work with, rather than against, chocolate cravings. Dip two cups of fresh fruit in a quarter-cup low-fat chocolate syrup, eat chocolate with a meal (you're likely to eat less), or have a cup of low-fat, sugar-free hot chocolate.

Dark orange produce. Even a small serving of deep orange vegetables supplies five times the Daily Value for beta-carotene, which might lower your risk for cancer, boost defenses against colds and infections, and protect the skin from sun damage. "Beta carotene accumulates in the skin providing partial 24-hour protection against sun damage," says Ronald Watson, Ph.D., professor of public health research at Arizona Health Sciences Center in Tucson, who adds that the more carotene-rich produce you eat, the more skin protection you get. Bright orange veggies also supply hefty amounts of vitamin C, potassium, and iron, as well as more fiber than a slice of whole-wheat bread or a bowl of oatmeal. Microwave and top with maple syrup and pecans. Puree and add to soups as a thickener. Use instead of potatoes in salads. Slice sweet potatoes into wedges, salt, and bake at 425°F for fifteen minutes for golden fries. Cook, mash, and use instead of noodles or rice as a base for any dish. Americans average only slightly more than a bite or two of a sweet potato each week. Jeffrey Blumberg, Ph.D., professor in the Friedman School of Nutrition Science and Policy at Tufts University in Boston, says, "Diets containing 10 to 15 milligrams a day of beta-carotene (which also contain lots of other carotenoids and phytochemicals) are associated with a reduced risk of several forms of cancer." That's the daily equivalent of one sweet potato or one cup of butternut squash.

Figs. If you're looking for something sweet and chewy, four dried figs is a healthy choice. For just under 200 calories, this snack provides 7 grams of fiber and more than 10 percent of your daily requirements for vitamin B_6, calcium, iron, magnesium, and potassium.

Greens. It is almost impossible to meet all your nutritional needs without including dark green leafy vegetables. A one-cup serving of cooked Swiss chard supplies 150 milligrams of magnesium, or 47 percent of a woman's and

36 percent of a man's daily recommendation. Dark green leafy vegetables also boost your intake of fiber; vitamin C; folic acid, the B vitamin that lowers risk for heart disease, memory loss, and birth defects; vitamin K, which helps build strong bones; and the minerals calcium, iron, and potassium. But that's just the beginning. A study from Cornell University found that of all the vegetables studied, spinach had the highest score for inhibiting cancer cells. Greens are especially good sources of the phytochemical lutein, which lowers the risk for age-related vision loss. "Generous intakes of spinach, kale, and other lutein-rich foods may reduce the risk of cataract and macular degeneration by up to 40 percent," says Dr. Blumberg. Switch from iceberg lettuce to spinach for salads; layer greens into lasagna; steam, chop, and whip them into mashed potatoes; blend them with tofu for a vegetarian quiche; add them to a stir-fry; add a twelve-ounce box of frozen chopped spinach to scrambled eggs, soups, or stews; use large spinach leaves instead of tortillas as a wrap around leftover meat or beans; or sauté them in a little olive oil and garlic. (Heating greens actually improves their beta-carotene and lutein content, as long as you cook them quickly in a minimal amount of liquid.) "People need 6 to 12 milligrams of lutein every day, but typically consume only a fraction of that," says Dr. Blumberg. That's because we average less than one serving of greens a week. You need at least one serving daily, preferably two (1 serving = 1 cup raw or ½ cup cooked).

Lentils. These legumes are a fat- and cholesterol-free alternative to red meat. One cup of cooked lentils supplies 2.5 milligrams of zinc, as well as ample amounts of calcium, iron, magnesium, folic acid and other B vitamins, fiber, protein, and complex carbohydrates, all for under 225 calories. Besides the proverbial lentil soup, cook a pot of lentils and store in the refrigerator to add to rice dishes, stews, salads, burritos, Indian dals, and chili.

Nuts. An ounce or two of nuts added to the diet several times a week could cut your risk for heart disease by up to 39 percent, as well as lower cancer and diabetes risk. Yet if you're like most Americans, you're averaging less than an ounce of nuts a week, not a day, so are depriving yourself of a rich source of protein, magnesium, vitamin E, and B vitamins. Granted, nuts are high in calories, but the fat in most nuts is heart-healthy monounsaturated fat and appears to help with weight loss. Switch from pretzels to an ounce of nuts or dip baby carrots in peanut butter for a snack. Sprinkle nuts instead of croutons on salad, toss an ounce of nuts on top of cereal instead of sugar, and add them to rice dishes and stir-fries.

Oatmeal. Oatmeal is an excellent source of oat fiber (one cup supplies 24 percent of a person's daily fiber need), which helps lower blood cholesterol and the risk for heart disease. Cooked in low-fat milk and topped with wheat germ, this hot cereal is an excellent way to fuel the morning and help fend off carb cravings later in the day. (See Creamy Oatmeal with Blueberries in Appendix B.)

Orange juice. The classic source of vitamin C has an added nutritional punch. One cup also supplies 109 micrograms of folic acid, a B vitamin that lowers the risk for cancer, heart disease, dementia, and depression yet often is sorely lacking in people's diets. Orange juice also is a source of limonene and bioflavonoids, phytochemicals that activate detoxifying enzymes in the body and possibly lower the risk for cancer.

Quinoa (pronounced "keen-wa"). This birdseed-shaped, mild-flavored grain far surpasses other grains in nutritional content. Ounce for ounce, quinoa contains 700 percent more iron than enriched white rice. It also is an excellent source of protein, calcium, and other minerals. Use as a substitute for rice in all casseroles, stuffed bell peppers, side dishes, or soups and stews, or use as a hot breakfast cereal.

Salmon, wild. In addition to being delicious, a four-ounce salmon steak provides up to 2.2 grams of eicosapentaenoic acid, a type of fish oil known to lower blood cholesterol and triglycerides and possibly raise HDL (good) cholesterol levels. Eaten canned with the bones, salmon is also an excellent source of calcium (three ounces contain more than 200 milligrams). Stick with wild salmon, since it contains lower levels of pesticides compared with farmed salmon. (See Grilled Salmon with Pesto and Lemon Zest in Appendix B.)

Soy milk, fortified. Soy milk has moved from the fringes to mainstream, yet regular consumption only increased 3 percent in 2003, according to the Soyfoods Association of North America, and only one in every six people consumes a glass or more a week. This simple way to add soy to the diet packs a major nutrient punch. Fortified soy milk is a great alternative to cow's milk in supplying calcium and vitamin D, plus it contains phytoestrogens that lower heart disease risk, promises to reduce the risk for memory loss and osteoporosis, and even might help with weight loss. New "light" soy milk in the refrigerator section of most grocery stores has all the benefits of soy with fewer calories than a glass of nonfat milk. Use soy milk instead of milk in recipes or coffee, on cereal, or add to smoothies.

Tomato sauce. People average less than three ounces of canned tomatoes daily, which is nowhere near enough. Tomatoes are an excellent source of lycopene, a potent antioxidant found in the red pigment in plants that might be a heart saver. "Maintaining high blood levels of lycopene could lower heart disease risk in women by up to 50 percent," says Howard D. Sesso, Sc.D., M.P.H., lead researcher on a study from Harvard that identified the heart-saving advantages of lycopene. He adds that the first place to start is to consume more lycopene-rich foods, such as tomatoes and tomato products like tomato sauce or juice. Cooked tomato products have more lycopene than fresh tomatoes, says Dr. Sesso. Another study suggests that lycopene also might reduce the risk for fibroid tumors, which affect up to 45 percent of women. You'll need seven servings or more a week, each containing at least 10 milligrams, or the amount of lycopene in half a cup of tomato sauce or two fresh tomatoes. The redder the fruit, the higher the lycopene, so add vine-ripened tomatoes to salads and sandwiches, since they have more lycopene than tomatoes picked green and allowed to ripen later. Add tomato paste and sauce or canned tomatoes to soups and sauces. For a quick snack, spread tomato-based pizza sauce on a toasted English muffin, top with cheese, and broil until the cheese bubbles. (See Baked Eggplant with Vegetable Ragu Sauce in Appendix B.)

Wheat germ. The older crowd is wheat germ savvy, but anyone under fifty-five still shuns this little nugget, with consumption on the decline since 2002. Yet the heart of the wheat kernel is a gold mine of nutrition. A half-cup serving of toasted wheat germ supplies more than half of your daily magnesium needs, as well as husky amounts of vitamins, including 100 percent of your daily need for folic acid and 50 percent of your vitamin E requirement. Wheat germ also supplies decent amounts of trace minerals, such as iron and zinc. Allergic to wheat? Then switch to flaxseed meal, which is a good source of the cholesterol-lowering omega-3 fats, soluble fiber that lowers diabetes risk, and lignans that cut cancer risk. Sprinkle on oatmeal or yogurt, add to cookie and pancake batters, mix into muffin or meat loaf recipes, or blend with honey and peanut butter for a sandwich spread.

Whole-grain bread (100 percent). While we eat record amounts of refined grains, typical consumption of whole grains is less than one serving a day. Eighty-five percent of our grains are refined, which contributes to a huge fiber shortfall, not to mention the vitamins and minerals that are lost when grains are processed. "Whole grains also supply health-enhancing phytochemicals not found in refined grains," adds Dr. Blumberg. Many refined grains, such as cakes, cookies, doughnuts, and muffins, are so high in fat that they rank number four as a source of saturated fat in our diets. Research repeatedly reports that people who eat the most whole grains have lower risks for stroke, colon cancer, diabetes, high blood pressure, heart disease, and even weight gain. Include two or more servings daily by switching from white bread to 100 percent whole-wheat for sandwiches, French toast, and dinner rolls.

Yogurt, nonfat plain. Low-fat yogurt is one of the best sources of B vitamins, high-quality protein, and calcium. "It's also a useful alternative to milk for people who are lactose intolerant, and if it contains the probiotic bacteria that flourish in the intestinal tract, then yogurt helps prevent constipation and diarrhea, as well as helping to treat food allergies," says Barry Goldin, Ph.D., in the Department of Public Health and Family Medicine and Community Health at Tufts. These bacteria crowd out disease-causing bacteria, produce natural antibiotics, and possibly switch off an enzyme that triggers colon cancer. To cut back on sugar, choose plain, nonfat yogurt and sweeten it with an all-fruit jam. Look for yogurt that lists *acidophilus* and *bifido* as ingredients. Layer yogurt with fruit for a quick snack; use it instead of sour cream for dips, salad dressings, and toppings; top hot soup with low-fat yogurt instead of sour cream; mix equal parts low-fat mayonnaise and yogurt for coleslaw or potato salad; substitute yogurt for buttermilk in muffin or pancake batters; or serve low-fat yogurt over cereal and fruit for breakfast. There are no hard-and-fast rules for yogurt intake. Dr. Goldin recommends regular servings throughout the week to maintain a strong population of healthy bacteria in the gut.

Organizations, Books, and Related Materials

Aging

AARP, 601 E Street NW, Washington, DC 20049. (888) 687-2277. www.aarp.org.

Administration on Aging, Washington, DC 20201. (202) 619-0724. www.aoa.gov.

Aging Network Services, 4400 East-West Highway, Suite 907, Bethesda, MD 20814. (301) 657-4329. www.agingnets.com.

National Alliance of Senior Citizens, 1744 Riggs Place NW, 3rd Floor, Washington, DC 20009. (202) 986-0117.

National Association of Area Agencies on Aging, 1730 Rhode Island Avenue NW, Suite 1200, Washington, DC 20036. (202) 872-0888. www.n4a.org.

National Council of Senior Citizens, 8430 Colesville Road, Suite 1200, Silver Spring, MD 20910. (310) 578-8800. www.network-democracy.org/social-security/bb/whc/ncsc.

National Council on the Aging, P.O. Box 411, Annapolis Junction, MD 20701-0411. (800) 373-4906. www.ncoa.org.

National Institutes of Health, National Institute on Aging, Information Center, Building 31, Room 5C27, 31 Center Drive, MSC 2292, Bethesda, MD 20892. (800) 222-4225 (for information on publications) or (301) 496-1752 (for the Center). www.nia.nih.gov.

Older Women's League, 1750 New York Avenue NW, Suite 350, Washington, DC 20006. (202) 783-6686 or (800) 825-3695. www.owl-national.org.

Arthritis

Arthritis Foundation, P.O. Box 7669, Atlanta, GA 30357-0667. (404) 872-7100. www.arthritis.org.

Arthritis Society, National Office, 393 University Avenue, Suite 1700, Toronto, ON M5G 1E6. (416) 979-7228. www.arthritis.ca.

Cancer

American Cancer Society, Inc., National Headquarters, 1599 Clifton Road NE, Atlanta, GA 30329-4251. (404) 320-3333 or (800) 227-2345 (to locate a local Cancer Society office). www.cancer.org.

American Institute for Cancer Research, 1759 R Street NW, Washington, DC 20009. (800) 843-8114. www.aicr.org.

National Cancer Institute, Cancer Information Service, Building 31, Room 1OA24, 9000 Rockville Pike, Bethesda, MD 20892. (800) 422-6237. www.nci.nih.gov.

Wellness Community, 919 18th Street NW, Suite 54, Washington, DC 20006. (202) 659-9709. www.thewellnesscommunity.org.

Diabetes

American Diabetes Association, 1701 North Beauregard Street, Alexandria, VA 22311. (800) DIABETES. www.diabetes.org.

Exercise

American College of Sports Medicine, 401 West Michigan Street (or P.O. Box 1440), Indianapolis, IN 46206. (317) 637-9200. www.acsm.org.

Evans W, Rosenberg I: *Biomarkers: The 40 Keys to Prolonging Vitality*. New York: Fireside Books, 1991.

National Institute on Aging: *Fitness over Fifty*. New York: W. W. Norton & Co., 2003.

President's Council on Physical Fitness and Sports, 200 Independence Avenue SW, Washington, DC 20201-0004. (202) 690-9000. www.fitness.gov.

Rippe J: *Fit over Forty*. New York: William Morrow, 1996.

Health and Medicine

American Holistic Medical Association, 12101 Menaul Boulevard NE, Suite C, Albuquerque, NM 87112. (505) 292-7788. www.holisticmedicine.org.

Center for Mind-Body Medicine, 5225 Connecticut Avenue NW, Suite 414, Washington, DC 20015. (202) 966-7338. www.cmbm.org.

National Institutes of Health, Office of Alternative Medicine (OAM) Clearinghouse, P.O. Box 7923, Gaithersburg, MD 20898. (888) 644-6226. www.ods.od.nih.gov.

National Women's Health Network, 514 10th Street NW, Suite 400, Washington, DC 20004. (202) 347-1140. www.womenshealthnetwork.org.

National Women's Health Resource Center, 157 Broad Street, Suite 315, Red Bank, NJ 07701. (877) 986-9472. www.healthywomen.org.

Hearing

Better Hearing Institute, 515 King Street, Suite 420, Alexandria, VA 22314. (703) 684-3391. www.betterhearing.org.

International Hearing Aid Society, 20361 Middlebelt Road, Livonia, MI 48152. (810) 478-2610. www.ihsinfo.org.

Heart Disease and Hypertension

American Association of Cardiovascular and Pulmonary Rehabilitation, 401 North Michigan Avenue, Suite 2200, Chicago, IL 60611. (312) 321-5146. www.aacvpr.org.

American Heart Association, 7272 Greenville Avenue, Dallas, TX 75231-4596. (800) AHA-USA1 (to locate a local Heart Association office). Also provides the free booklet *How to Choose a Nutrition Counselor.* www.americanheart.org.

National Heart, Lung, and Blood Institute Information Center, P.O. Box 30105, Bethesda, MD 20824-0105. (301) 592-8573. www.nhlbi.nih.gov.

National Hypertension Association, 324 East 30th Street, New York, NY 10016. (212) 889-3557. www.nathypertension.org.

WomenHeart: The National Coalition for Women with Heart Disease, 818 18th Street NW, Suite 230, Washington, DC 20006. (202) 728-7199. www.womenheart.org.

Menopause

North American Menopause Society, 5900 Landerbrook Drive, Suite 195, Mayfield Heights, OH 44124, or P.O. Box 94527, Cleveland, OH 44101-4527. (440) 442-7550. www.menopause.org.

Mental Health

Alzheimer's Association, 225 North Michigan Avenue, Chicago, IL 60601. (800)
    272-3900 or (312) 335-8700. www.alz.org.

American Psychological Association, 750 First Street NE, Washington, DC 20002-4242.
    (202) 336-5500. www.apa.org.

Depression and Bipolar Support Alliance, 730 North Franklin Street, Suite 501,
    Chicago, IL 60610-7224. (800) 826-3632. www.dbsalliance.org.

National Foundation for Depressive Illness, Inc., P.O. Box 2257, New York, NY 10116.
    (800) 248-4344. www.depression.org.

National Institute of Neurological Disorders and Stroke, P.O. Box 5801, Bethesda, MD
    20824. (800) 352-9424. www.ninds.nih.gov.

National Institute on Aging Alzheimer's Disease Education and Referral Center, P.O.
    Box 8250, Silver Spring, MD 20907-8250. (800) 438-4380. www.alzheimers.org.

Nutrition and Diet

American Dietetic Association, 120 South Riverside Plaza, Suite 2000, Chicago, IL
    60606. (800) 877-1600 (nutrition hotline, 10 A.M. to 5 P.M. EST, Monday through
    Friday). www.eatright.org.

Dietary Guidelines for Americans, Consumer Information Center, Pueblo, CO 81009.
    (Guidelines free with SASE.) www.health.gov/dietaryguidelines.

USDA Dietary Guidelines and MyPyramid. www.mypyramid.gov.

Osteoporosis

National Osteoporosis Foundation, 1232 22nd Street NW, Washington, DC 20037-
    1292. (202) 223-2226 or (800) 464-6700 (for listings of the nearest bone density
    testing site). www.nof.org.

Osteoporosis and Related Bone Diseases National Resource Center, 1150 17th Street
    NW, Suite 500, Washington, DC 20036-4603. (800) 624-BONE or (202) 223-9994.
    www.osteo.org.

Other Disorders and Problems

National Kidney and Urologic Diseases Information Clearinghouse, 3 Information Way, Bethesda, MD 20892-3560. (800) 891-5390. www.kidney.niddk.nih.gov.

National Organization for Rare Disorders, 55 Kenosia Avenue, P.O. Box 1968, Danbury, CT 06813-1968. (203) 744-0100. www.rarediseases.org.

Skin

American Academy of Dermatology, 930 North Meacham Road, P.O. Box 4014, Schaumburg, IL 60168-4014. (847) 330-0230. www.aad.org.

Skin Cancer Foundation, 245 Fifth Avenue, Suite 1403, New York, NY 10016. (800) SKIN-490 or (212) 725-5176. www.skincancer.org.

Sleep Disorders

American Sleep Association, 614 South 8th Street, Suite 282, Philadelphia, PA 19147. (443) 593-2285. www.americansleepassociation.org.

Stress

American Institute of Stress, 124 Park Avenue, Yonkers, NY 10703. (914) 963-1200. www.stress.org.

Anxiety Disorders Association of America, Department B, 8730 Georgia Avenue, Suite 600, Silver Spring, MD 20910. (240) 485-1001. www.adaa.org.

Vision

American Academy of Ophthalmology, P.O. Box 7424, San Francisco, CA 94120-7424. (415) 561-8500. www.aao.org.

National Eye Institute, Information Office, 31 Center Drive, MSC 2510, Bethesda, MD 20892-2510. (301) 496-5248. www.nei.nih.gov.

Vitality

Benson H: *Timeless Healing: The Power and Biology of Belief*. New York: Scribner, 1996.

Burns D: *Feeling Good: The New Mood Therapy*. New York: William Morrow, 1990.

Jeffers S: *Feel the Fear and Do It Anyway*. New York: Fawcett Columbine, 1987.

Maslow A: *Toward a Psychology of Being*, 2nd ed. New York: D. Van Nostrand, 1962.

Moore T: *The Re-Enchantment of Everyday Life*. New York: HarperCollins, 1996.

Omega Institute, 150 Lake Drive, Rhinebeck, NY 12572. (845) 266-4444. eomega.org.

Seligman M: *Learned Optimism*. New York: Pocket Books, 1992.

Spiritual Eldering Institute, 970 Aurora Avenue, Boulder, CO 80302. (303) 449-7243. spiritualeldering.org.

Selected References

Chapter 1

Anderson N, Blennow K: CSF biomarkers for mild cognitive impairment and early Alzheimer's disease. *Clin Neurol* 2005;107:165–173.

Blennow K: Cerebrospinal fluid protein biomarkers for Alzheimer's disease. *Neurorx* 2004;1:213–225.

Gundgaard J, Nielsen J, Olsen J, et al: Increased intake of fruit and vegetables: Estimation of impact in terms of life expectancy and healthcare costs. *Publ Heal N* 2003;6:25–30.

Liang J, Bennett J, Krause N, et al: Old age mortality in Japan: Does the socioeconomic gradient interact with gender and age? *J Geront B* 2002;57:S294–S307.

Macintyre S, McKay L, Ellaway A: Who is more likely to experience common disorders: Men, women, or both equally? Lay perceptions in the West of Scotland. *Int J Epid* 2005;34:461–466.

Minino A, Arias E, Kochanck K, et al: Death: Final data for 2000. *Natl Vital Stat Rep* 2002;50:1–119.

Nieschlag E, Kramer U, Nieschlag S: Androgens shorten the longevity of women: Sopranos last longer. *Exp Clin Endo D* 2003;111:230–231.

Vaupel J, Carey J, Christensen K: Aging: It's never too late. *Science* 2003;301:1679–1681.

Winklhofer-Roob B, Meinitzer A, Maritschnegg M, et al: Effects of vitamin E depletion/repletion on biomarkers of oxidative stress in healthy aging. *Ann NY Acad* 2004;1030:361–364.

Chapter 2

Aigner T, Rose J, Martin J, et al: Aging theories of primary osteoarthritis: From epidemiology to molecular biology. *Rejuv Res* 2004;7:134–145.

Balaban R, Nemoto S, Finkel T: Mitochondria, oxidants, and aging. *Cell* 2005;120:483–495.

Bokov A, Chaudhuri A, Richardson A: The role of oxidative damage and stress in aging. *Mech Age D* 2004;125:811–826.

De la Fuente M: Effects of antioxidants on immune system ageing. *Eur J Clin N* 2002;5:S5–S8.

Effros R: From Hayflick to Walford: The role of T cell replicative senescence in human aging. *Exp Geront* 2004;39:885–890.

Goldstein S, Gallo J, Reichel W: Biologic theories of aging. *Am Fam Phys* 1989;40:195–200.

Hadley E, Lakatta E, Morrison-Bogorad M, et al: The future of aging therapies. *Cell* 2005;120:557–567.

Harman D: The free radical theory of ageing. *Antiox Redox Sig* 2003;5:557–561.

Hasnis E, Reznick A: Antioxidants and healthy aging. *Isr Med Ass* 2003;5:368–370.

Hayflick L: DNA replication and traintracks. *Science* 2002;296:1611–1612.

Hayflick L: The future of ageing. *Nature* 2000;408:267–269.

Hayflick L: The illusion of cell immortality. *Br J Canc* 2000;83:841–846.

Hayflick L: The not-so-close relationship between biological aging and age-associated pathologies in humans. *J Geront A* 2004;59:B547–B550.

Inoue M, Sato E, Nishikawa M, et al: Free radical theory of apoptosis and metamorphosis. *Redox Rep* 2004;9:237–247.

Joseph J, Shukitt-Hale B, Casadesus G: Reversing the deleterious effects of aging on neuronal communication and behavior: Beneficial properties of fruit polyphenolic compounds. *Am J Clin N* 2005;81:313S–316S.

Manczak M, Jung Y, Park B, et al: Time-course of mitochondrial gene expression in mice brains: Implications for mitochondrial dysfunction, oxidative damage, and cytochrome c in aging. *J Neurochem* 2005;92:499–504.

Mattson M: Emerging neuroprotective strategies for Alzheimer's disease: Dietary restriction, telomerase activation, and stem cell therapy. *Exp Geront* 2000;35:489–502.

McGahon B, Murray C, Horrobin, et al: Age-related changes in oxidative mechanisms and LTP are reversed by dietary manipulation. *Neurob Ag* 1999;20:643–653.

Montgomery R, Borgatta E: Plausible theories and the development of scientific theory. The case of aging research. *Res Aging* 1986;8:586–608.

Noonberg A, Goldstein G, Page H: Premature aging in male alcoholics: "Accelerated again" or "increased vulnerability"? *Alc Clin Exp Res* 1985;9:334–338.

Ohyashiki J, Hayashi S, Yahata N, et al: Impaired telomere regulation mechanism by TRFI (telomere-binding protein), but not TRF2 expression, in acute leukemia cells. *Int J Oncol* 2001;18:593–598.

Olshansky S, Hayflick L, Carnes B: Position statement on human aging. *J Geront A* 2002;57:B292–B297.

Schipper H: Brain iron deposition and the free radical-mitochondrial theory of ageing. *Age Res Rev* 2004;3:265–301.

Wickens A: Ageing and the free radical theory. *Respir Physiol* 2001;128:379–391.

Wilson D, Hall M, Stone G: Test of some aging hypothesis using two-dimensional protein mapping. *Gerontology* 1978;24:426–433.

Chapter 3

Adams P: Humour and love: The origination of clown therapy. *Postgr Med J* 2002;78:447–448.

Bartlett S, Piedmont R, Bilderback A, et al: Spirituality, well-being, and quality of life in people with rheumatoid arthritis. *Arth Rheum* 2003;49:778–783.

Bennett H: Humor in medicine. *South Med J* 2003;96:1257–1261.

Consedine N, Magai C, King A: Deconstructing positive affect in later life: A differential functionalist analysis of joy and interest. *Int J Aging* 2004;58:49–68.

Davidhizer R: "On the scale of 1 to 10 I'm a 13: The benefits of being happy." *J Pract Nurs* 2003;53:18–21.

Gee L, Abbott J, Conway S, et al: Quality of life in cystic fibrosis: The impact of gender, general health perceptions and disease severity. *J Cyst Fibros* 2003;2:206–213.

Giangrego E: Laughing fits: Laugh your way to good health. *CDS Rev* 2004;97:22–24.

Goodman J, Fry W: Toward optimal health: The experts discuss therapeutic humor. *J Womens H* 2004;13:474–479.

Hamilton D, Haennel R: The relationship of self-efficacy to selected outcomes. *Can J Car Nurs* 2004;14:23–32.

Helliwell J, Putnam R: The social context of well-being. *Phi T Roy Soc Bi* 2004;359:1435–1446.

Hoffmann H, Kupper Z, Kunz B: Hopelessness and its impact on rehabilitation outcome in schizophrenia: An exploratory study. *Schizophr R* 2000;43:147–158.

Jones T, Rapport L, Hanks R, et al: Cognitive and psychosocial predictors of subjective well-being in urban older adults. *Clin Neurps* 2003;17:3–18.

Leust A: What makes bodies beautiful. *J Med Philos* 2003;28:187–219.

Lewandowski W: Patterning of pain and power with guided imagery. *Nurs Sci Q* 2004;17:233–241.

Lilja A, Smith G, Malmstrom P, et al: Psychological profile in patients with stages I and II breast cancer: Associations of psychological profile with tumor biological prognosticators. *Psychol Rep* 2003;92:1187–1198.

MacDonald C: A chuckle a day keeps the doctor away: Therapeutic humor and laughter. *J Psych Nurs Ment H* 2004;42:18–25.

Mahon N, Yarcheski A, Yarcheski T: Happiness as related to gender and health in early adolescents. *Clin Nurs Res* 2005;14:174–190.

Mahony D, Burroughs W, Lippman L: Perceived attributes of health-promoting laughter: A cross-generational comparison. *J Psychol* 2002;136:171–181.

Menee V: The relation between everyday activities and successful aging: A 6-year longitudinal study. *J Geront B* 2003;58:S74–S82.

Morris E: The relationship of spirituality to coronary heart disease. *Altern Th H* 2001;7:96–98.

Perneger T, Hudelson P, Bovier P: Health and happiness in young Swiss adults. *Qual Life R* 2004;13:171–178.

Roysamb E, Tambs K, Reichborn-Kjennerud T, et al: Happiness and health: Environmental and genetic contributions to the relationship between subjective well-being, perceived health, and somatic illness. *J Pers Soc* 2003;85:1136–1146.

Ryff C, Singer B, Dienberg Love G: Positive health: Connecting well-being with biology. *Phi T Roy Soc Bi* 2004;359:1383–1394.

Scharloo M, Kaptein A, Weinman J, et al: Patients' illness perceptions and copying as predictors of functional status in psoriasis: A 1-year follow-up. *Br J Derm* 2000;142:899–907.

Schattner A: The emotional dimension and the biological paradigm of illness: Time for a change. *Q J Med* 2003;96:617–621.

Skinner T: Psychological barriers. *Eur J Endoc* 2004;151:T13–T17.

Steele A, Wade T: The contribution of optimism and quality of life to depression in an acute coronary syndrome population. *Eur J Card N* 2004;3:231–237.

Steptoe A, Wardle J, Marmot M: Positive affect and health-related neuroendocrine, cardiovascular, and inflammatory processes. *P Natl Acad S* 2005.

Chapter 4

Alper C, Mattes R: Effects of chronic peanut consumption on energy balance and hedonics. *Int J Obes* 2002;26:1129–1137.

Anson R: Absolute versus relative caloric intake: Clues to the mechanism of calorie/ aging-rate interactions. *Ann NY Acad* 2004;1019:427–429.

Bhattacharyya T, Merz M, Thomas J: Modulation of cutaneous aging with calorie restriction in Fisher:344 Rats: A histological study. *Arch Facial Plast Surg* 2005;7:12–16.

Dillon S, Burmi R, Lowe G, et al: Antioxidant properties of aged garlic extract: An in vitro study incorporating human low density lipoprotein. *Life Sci* 2003;72:1583–1594.

Etminan M, Takkouche B, Caamano-Isorna F: The role of tomato products and lycopene in the prevention of prostate cancer. *Canc Epid B* 2004;13:340–345.

Hak A, Ma J, Powell C, et al: Prospective study of plasma carotenoids and tocopherols in relation to risk of ischemic stroke. *Stroke* 2004;35:1584–1588.

Heber D: Vegetables, fruits and phytoestrogens in the prevention of diseases. *J Postgrad Med* 2004;50:145–149.

Jiang R, Manson J, Stampfer M, et al: Nut and peanut butter consumption and risk of type 2 diabetes in women. *J Am Med A* 2002;288:2554–2560.

Liu R: Potential synergy of phytochemicals in cancer prevention: Mechanism of action. *J Nutr* 2004;134:3479S–3485S.

Low Y, Taylor J, Grace P, et al: Phytoestrogen exposure correlation with plasma estradiol in postmenopausal women in European prospective investigation of cancer and nutrition may involve diet-gene interactions. *Canc Epi Bio* 2005;14:213–220.

McCaffree J: What you should know about calorie restriction. *J Am Diet A* 2004;104:1524, 1526.

McCann S, Freudenheim J, Marshall J, et al: Risk of human ovarian cancer is related to dietary intake of selected nutrients, phytochemicals and food groups. *J Nutr* 2003;133:1937–1942.

Mennen L, Sapinho D, de Bree A, et al: Consumption of foods rich in flavonoids is related to a decreased cardiovascular risk in apparently healthy French women. *J Nutr* 2004;923–926.

Montonen J, Knekt P, Jarvinen R, et al: Dietary antioxidant intake and risk of type 2 diabetes. *Diabet Care* 2004;27:362–366.

Murtaugh M, Ma K, Benson J, et al: Antioxidants, carotenoids, and risk of rectal cancer. *Am J Epid* 2004;159:32–41.

Nelson S, Bose S, Grunwald G, et al: The induction of human superoxide dismutase and catalase in vivo: A fundamentally new approach to antioxidant therapy. *Free Rad Biol* 2006;40:341–347.

Rae M: It's never too late: Calorie restriction is effective in older mammals. *Rejuv Res* 2004;7:3–8.

Rattan S: Aging intervention, prevention, and therapy through hormesis. *J Geront* A 2004;59:705–709.

Ros E, Nunez I, Perez-Heras A, et al: A walnut diet improves endothelial function in hypercholesterolemic subjects: A randomized crossover trial. *Circulation* 2004;109:1609–1614.

Saravanan G, Prakash J: Effect of garlic (allium sativum) on lipid peroxidation in experimental myocardial infarction in rats. *J Ethnophar* 2004;94:155–158.

Sesso H, Buring J, Norkus E, et al: Plasma lycopene, other carotenoids, and retinol and the risk of cardiovascular disease in women. *Am J Clin* N 2004;79:47–53.

Smith J, Heilbronn L, Ravussin E: Energy restriction and aging. *Curr Opin Clin* N 2004;7:615–622.

Tamimi R, Hankinson S, Campos H, et al: Plasma carotenoids, retinol, and tocopherols and risk of breast cancer. *Am J Epid* 2005;161:153–160.

Tapiero H, Townsend D, Tew K: The role of carotenoids in the prevention of human pathologies. *Biomed Phar* 2004;58:100–110.

Chapter 5

Bondy S, Lahiri D, Perreau V, et al: Retardation of brain aging by chronic treatment with melatonin. *Ann NY Acad* 2004;1035:197–215.

Copeland J, Chu S, Tremblay M: Aging, physical activity, and hormones in women: A review. *J Aging Phys Act* 2004;12:101–116.

Dharia S, Parker C: Adrenal androgens and aging. *Semin Rep* M 2004;22:361–368.

Gaytan R, Prisant L: Oral nutritional supplements and heart disease: A review. *Am J Ther* 2001;8:255–274.

Genazzani A, Stomati M, Bernardi F, et al: Long-term low-dose dehydroepiandrosterone oral supplementation in early and late postmenopausal women modulates endocrine parameters and synthesis of neuroactive steroids. *Fert Steril* 2003;80:1495–1502.

Harman S, Blackman M: The effects of growth hormone and sex steroid on lean body mass, fat mass, muscle strength, cardiovascular endurance and adverse events in healthy elderly women and men. *Hormone Res* 2003;60:121–124.

Harman S, Blackman M: Use of growth hormone for prevention or treatment of effects of aging. *J Geront* A 2004;59:652–658.

Ishii N, Senoo-Matsuda N, Miyake K, et al: Coenzyme Q10 can prolong C. elegans lifespan by lowering oxidative stress. *Mech Age D* 2004;125:41–46.

Johnson M, Bebb R, Sirrs S: Uses of DHEA in aging and other disease states. *Age Res Rev* 2002;1:29–41.

Kohut M, Thompson J, Campbell J, et al: Ingestion of a dietary supplement containing dehydroepiandrosterone (DHEA) and androstenedione has minimal effect on immune function in middle-aged men. *J Am Col N* 2003;22:363–371.

Linnane A, Zhang C, Yarovaya N, et al: Human aging and global function of coenzyme Q10. *Ann NY Acad* 2002;959:396–411.

Nippoldt T: Dehydroepiandrosterone supplements: Bringing sense to sensational claims. *Endocr Pract* 1998;4:106–111.

Perls T: Antiaging quackery: Human growth hormone and tricks of the trade: More dangerous than ever. *J Geront A* 2004;59:682–691.

Reisman N: Legal issues associated with the current and future practice of antiaging medicine. *J Geront A* 2004;59:674–681.

Reiter R, Tan D, Pappolla M: Melatonin relieves the Neutral Oxidative Burden that contributes to dementias. *Ann NY Acad* 2004;1035:179–196.

Rosenfeldt F, Pepe S, Linnane A, et al: Coenzyme Q10 protects the aging heart against stress: Studies in rats, human tissues, and patients. *Ann NY Acad* 2002;959:355–359.

Savine R, Sonksen P: Growth hormone: Hormone replacement for the somatopause? *Hormone Res* 2000;53:37–41.

Yamada Y, Nakajima A, Sekihara H: Anti-apoptotic effect of dehydroepiandrosterone and its role in an aging society. *Intern Med* 2004;43:158–160.

Youl Kang H, Hwan Kim S, Jun Lee W, et al: Effects of ginseng on growth hormone, testosterone, cortisol, and insulin-like growth factor 1 responses to acute resistance exercise. *J Strength C* 2002;16:179–183.

Zita C, Overvad K, Mortensen S, et al: Serum coenzyme Q10 concentrations in healthy men supplemented with 30 mg or 100 mg coenzyme Q10 for two months in a randomized controlled study. *Biofactors* 2003;18:185–193.

Chapter 6

Albandar J, Steckfus C, Adesanya M, et al: Cigar, pipe, and cigarette smoking as risk factors for periodontal disease and tooth loss. *J Periodont* 2000;71:1874–1881.

Appleby P, Davey G, Key T: Hypertension and blood pressure among meat eaters, fish eaters, vegetarians and vegans in EPIC-Oxford. *Publ Heal N* 2002;5:645–654.

Ashton E, Dalais F, Ball M: Effect of meat replacement by tofu on CHD risk factors including copper induced LDL oxidation. *J Am Col N* 2000;19:761–767.

Cade J, Burley V, Greenwood D, et al: The UK Women's Cohort Study: Comparison of vegetarians, fish-eaters, and meat-eaters. *Publ Heal N* 2004;7:871–878.

Chang-Claude J, Hermann S, Eilber U, et al: Lifestyle determinants and mortality in German vegetarians and health-conscious persons: Results of a 21-year follow-up. *Canc Epid B* 2005;14:963–968.

Chao A, Thun M, Connell C, et al: Meat consumption and risk of colorectal cancer. *J Am Med A* 2005;293:172–182.

Clifton P, Keogh J, Noakes M: Trans fatty acids in adipose tissue and the food supply are associated with myocardial infarction. *J Nutr* 2004;134:874–879.

Dos Santos Silva I, Mangtani P, McCormack V: Lifelong vegetarianism and risk of breast cancer: A population based case-control study among South Asian migrant women living in England. *Int J Canc* 2002;99:238–244.

Dyerberg J, Eskesen D, Andersen P, et al: Effects of trans and n-3 unsaturated fatty acids on cardiovascular risk markers in healthy males. An 8-week dietary intervention study. *Eur J Cl N* 2004;58:1062–1070.

Elias S, Innis S: Bakery foods are the major dietary source of trans-fatty acids among pregnant women with diets providing 30 percent energy from fat. *J Am Diet A* 2002;102:46–51.

Giacomoni P, Rein G: Factors of skin aging share common mechanisms. *Biogerontol* 2001;2:219–229.

Gillen L, Tapsell L: Advice that includes food sources of unsaturated fat supports future risk management of gestational diabetes mellitus. *J Am Diet A* 2004;104:1863–1867.

Hu F, Rimm E, Stampfer M, et al: Prospective study of major dietary patterns and risk of coronary heart disease in men. *Am J Clin N* 2000;72:912–921.

Hu F, Stampfer M, Manson J, et al: Dietary saturated fats and their food sources in relation to the risk of coronary heart disease in women. *Am J Clin N* 1999;70:1001–1008.

Hu F, Willett W: Optimal diets for prevention of coronary heart disease. *J Am Med A* 2002;288:2569–2578.

Ibrahim A, Natrajan S, Ghafoorunissa R: Dietary trans-fatty acids alter adipocyte plasma membrane fatty acid composition and insulin sensitivity in rats. *Metabolism* 2005;54:240–246.

Kabagambe E, Baylin A, Siles X, et al: Individual saturated fatty acids and nonfatal acute myocardial infarction in Costa Rica. *Eur J Cl N* 2003;57:1447–1457.

King I, Kristal A, Schaffer S, et al: Serum trans-fatty acids are associated with risk of prostate cancer in Beta-Carotene and Retinol Efficacy Trial. *Canc Epid B* 2005;14:988–992.

Ledda A: Cigarette smoking, hypertension and erectile dysfunction. *Curr Med Res Opin* 2000;16:13–16.

Lopez-Garcia E, Schilze M, Meigs J, et al: Consumption of trans fatty acids is related to plasma biomarkers of inflammation and endothelial dysfunction. *J Nutr* 2005;135:562–566.

Mancini M, Stamler J: Diet for preventing cardiovascular diseases. *Nutr Met Ca* 2004;14:52–57.

Mozaffarian D, Pischon T, Hankinson S, et al: Dietary intake of trans fatty acids and systemic inflammation in women. *Am J Clin N* 2004;79:606–612.

Placzek M, Kerkmann U, Bell S, et al: Tobacco smoke is phototoxic. *Br J Derm* 2004;150:991–993.

Sabate J: The contribution of vegetarian diets to human health. *Forum Nutr* 2003;56:218–220.

Stender S, Dyerberg J: Influence of trans fatty acids on health. *Ann Nutr M* 2004;48:61–66.

Tanasescu M, Cho E, Manson J, et al: Dietary fat and cholesterol and the risk of cardiovascular disease among women with type 2 diabetes. *Am J Clin N* 2004;79:999–1005.

Tucker K, Hallfrish J, Qiao N, et al: The combination of high fruit and vegetable and low saturated fat intakes is more protective against mortality in aging men than is either alone: The Baltimore Longitudinal Study of Aging. *J Nutr* 2005;135:556–561.

Vegetarianism: Addition by subtraction: An increasing number of studies are finding health benefits from a low or no-meat dict. *Harv Health Lett* 2004;29:6.

Chapter 7

Barkeling B, Linne Y, Lindross A, et al: Intake of sweet foods and counts of cariogenic microorganisms in relation to body mass index and psychometric variables in women. *Int J Obes* 2002;26:1239–1244.

Coppen A, Bolander-Gouaille C: Treatment of depression: Time to consider folic acid and vitamin B_{12}. *J Psychopharm* 2005;19:59–65.

Drewnowski A, Specter S: Poverty and obesity: The role of energy density and energy costs. *Am J Clin N* 2004;79:6–16.

Elliott S, Keim N, Stern J, et al: Fructose, weight gain, and the insulin resistance syndrome. *Am J Clin N* 2002;76:911–922.

Knekt P, Ritz J, Pereira M, et al: Antioxidant vitamins and coronary heart disease risk. *Am J Clin N* 2004;80:1508–1520.

Knoops K, de Groot L, Kromhout D, et al: Mediterranean diet, lifestyle factors, and 10-year mortality in elderly European men and women. *J Am Med A* 2004;292:1433–1439.

Ludwig D, Peterson K, Gortmaker S: Relation between consumption of sugar-sweetened drinks and childhood obesity. *Lancet* 2001;357:505–508.

Meier C, Woitge H, Witte K, et al: Supplementation with oral vitamin D_3 and calcium during winter prevents seasonal bone loss. *J Bone Min* 2004;19:1221–1230.

Meydani S, Leka L, Fine B, et al: Vitamin E and respiratory tract infections in elderly nursing home residents. *J Am Med A* 2004;292:828–836.

Michaud D, Liu S, Giovannucci E, et al: Dietary sugar, glycemic load, and pancreatic cancer risk in a prospective study. *J Natl Canc* 2002;94:1293–1300.

Millen A, Kodd K, Subar A, et al: Use of vitamin, mineral, nonvitamin, and nonmineral supplements in the United States: The 1987, 1992, and 2000 National Health Interview Survey results. *J Am Diet A* 2004;104:942–950.

Ninfali P, Mea G, Giorgini S, et al: Antioxidant capacity of vegetables, spices, and dressings relevant to nutrition. *Br J Nutr* 2005;93:257–266.

Peeters A, van der Molen E, Blom H, et al: The effect of homocysteine reduction in B-vitamin supplementation on markers of endothelial dysfunction. *Thromb Haem* 2004;92:1086–1091.

Raben A, Vasilaras T, Moller A, et al: Sucrose compared with artificial sweeteners: Different effects on ad libitum food intake and body weight after 10 weeks of supplementation in overweight subjects. *Am J Clin N* 2002;76:721–729.

Schulze M, Manson J, Ludwig D, et al: Sugar-sweetened beverages, weight gain, and incidence of type 2 diabetes in young and middle-aged women. *J Am Med A* 2004;292:927–934.

St-Onge M, Rubiano F, DeNino W, et al: Added thermogenic and satiety effects of a mixed nutrient vs a sugar-only beverage. *Int J Obes* 2004;28:248–253.

Winklhofer-Roob B, Meinitzer A, Maritschnegg M, et al: Effects of vitamin E depletion/repletion on biomarkers of oxidative stress in healthy aging. *Vitam E He* 2004;1031:361–364.

Zandi P, Anthony J, Khachaturian A, et al: Reduced risk of Alzheimer disease in users of antioxidant vitamin supplements: The Cache County Study. *Arch Neurol* 2004;61:82–88.

Chapter 8

Atlantis E, Chow C, Kirby A, et al: An effective exercise-based intervention for improving mental health and quality of life: A randomized controlled trial. *Prev Med* 2004;39:424–434.

Blair S, LaMonte M, Nichaman M: The evolution of physical activity recommendations: How much is enough? *Am J Clin N* 2004;79:913S–920S.

Blumenthal J, Sherwood A, Babyak M: Effects of exercise and stress management training on markers of cardiovascular risk in patients with ischemic heart disease: A randomized controlled trial. *J Am Med A* 2005;293:1626–1634.

Carnethon M, Jacobs D, Sidney S, et al: A longitudinal study of physical activity and heart rate recovery: CARDIA, 1987–1993. *Med Sci Spts* 2005;37:606–612.

Clarke M: The effects of exercise on skeletal muscle in the aged. *J Musc Neur Int* 2004;4:175–178.

Courneya K, Karvinen K, Campbell K, et al: Associations among exercise, body weight, and quality of life in a population-based sample of endometrial cancer survivors. *Gynecol Onc* 2005;97:422–430.

Dziura J, de Leon C, Kasi S, et al: Can physical activity attenuate aging-related weight loss in older people? *Am J Epidem* 2004;159:759–767.

Hogan M: Physical and cognitive activity and exercise for older adults: A review. *Int J Aging* 2005;60:95–126.

Holcomb C, Heim D, Loughin T: Physical activity minimizes the association of body fatness with abdominal obesity in white, premenopausal women. *J Am Diet A* 2004;104:1859–1862.

Kirby S: The positive effect of exercise as a therapy for clinical depression. *Nurs Times* 2004;101:28–29.

Kohut M, Senchina D: Reversing age-associated immunosenescence via exercise. *Ex Immunol Rev* 2004;10:6–41.

Landi F, Russo A, Bernabei R: Physical activity and behavior in the elderly: A pilot study. *Arch Ger G* 2004;9:235–241.

Lindholm E, Brevinge H, Bergh C, et al: Relationships between self-reported health related quality of life and measures of standardized exercise capacity and metabolic efficiency in a middle-aged and aged healthy population. *Qual Life R* 2003;12:575–582.

Livingstone M, Robson P, Wallace J, et al: How active are we? Levels of routine physical activity in children and adults. *P Nutr Soc* 2003;62:681–701.

Lucas J, Schiller J, Benson V: Summary health statistics for U.S. adults: National Health Interview Survey, 2001. *Vital Health Stat* 2004;218:1–134.

Manger T, Motta R: The impact of an exercise program on posttraumatic stress disorder, anxiety, and depression. *Int J Em Ment H* 2005;7:49–57.

Melzer K, Kayser B, Pichard C: Physical activity: The health benefits outweigh the risks. *Curr Opin Clin Nutr* 2004;7:641–647.

Messier S, Loeser R, Miller G, et al: Exercise and dietary weight loss in overweight and obese older adults with knee osteoarthritis: The Arthritis, Diet, and Activity Promotion Trial. *Arth Rheum* 2004;50:1501–1510.

Nicklas B, Ambrsius W, Messier S, et al: Diet-induced weight loss, exercise, and chronic inflammation in older, obese adults: A randomized controlled clinical trial. *Am J Clin N* 2004;79:544–551.

Parise G, Brose A, Tarnopolsky M: Resistance exercise training decreases oxidative damage to DNA and increases cytochrome oxidase activity in older adults. *Exp Geront* 2005;40:173–180.

Quartetti H: Live fit. Moving into midlife: Short on time and long on stress, 40- and 50-somethings need exercise more than ever. *Diabet Forecast* 2005;58:60–62.

Radak Z, Chung H, Goto S: Exercise and hormesis: Oxidative stress-related adaptation for successful aging. *Biogerontol* 2005;6:71–75.

Renehan A, Howell A: Preventing cancer, cardiovascular disease, and diabetes. *Lancet* 2005;365:1449–1451.

Riebe D, Garber C, Rossi J, et al: Physical activity, physical function, and stages of change in older adults. *Am J Heal B* 2005;29:70–80.

Samad A, Taylor R, Marshall T, et al: A meta-analysis of the association of physical activity with reduced risk of colorectal cancer. *Colorect Dis* 2005;7:204–213.

Seguin R, Nelson M: The benefits of strength training for older adults. *Am J Prev M* 2003;25:141–149.

Sigh M: Exercise and aging. *Clin Geriat* 2004;20:201–221.

Stewart K, Turner K, Bacher A, et al: Are fitness, activity, and fatness associated with health-related quality of life and mood in older persons? *J Cardiop Reh* 2003;23:115–121.

van Baak M, van Mil E, Astrup A, et al: Leisure-time activity is an important determinant of long-term weight maintenance after weight loss in the Sibutramine Trial on Obesity Reduction and Maintenance (STORM Trial). *Am J Clin N* 2003;78:209–214.

Wendel-Vos G, Schuit A, Tijhuis M, et al: Leisure time physical activity and health-related quality of life: Cross-sectional and longitudinal associations. *Qual Life R* 2004;13:667–677.

Whitaker E: The bicycle makes the eyes smile: Exercise, aging, and psychophysical well-being in older Italian cyclists. *Med Anthr Q* 2005;24:1–43.

Williams P: Vigorous exercise and the population distribution of body weight. *Int J Obes* 2004;28:120–128.

Chapter 9

Albers R, Bol M, Bleumink R, et al: Effects on supplementation with vitamins A, C, and E, selenium, and zinc on immune function in a murine sensitization model. *Nutrition* 2003;19:940–946.

Anderson K, Greenblatt D: Assessing and managing drug-nutrient interactions. *J Am Pharm A* 2002;42:S28–S29.

Birt D, Hendrich S, Wang W: Dietary agents in cancer prevention: Flavonoids and isoflavonoids. *Pharmacol & Therap* 2001;90:157–177.

Chan L: Drug-nutrient interaction in clinical nutrition. *Curr Opin Clin N* 2002;5:327–332.

Chandra R: Impact of nutritional status and nutrient supplements on immune responses and incidence of infection in older individuals. *Age Res Rev* 2004;3:91–104.

Ekiz C, Agaoglu L, Karakas Z, et al: The effect of iron deficiency anemia on the function of the immune system. *Hemat J* 2005;5:579–583.

High K: Micronutrient supplementation and immune function in the elderly. *Clin Inf D* 1999;28:717–722.

Jenkins D, Kendall C, Connelly P, et al: Effects of high-isoflavone (phytoestrogen) soy foods on inflammatory biomarkers and proinflammatory cytokines in middle-aged men and women. *Metabolism* 2002;51:919–924.

Kew S, Mesa M, Tricon S, et al: Effects of oils rich in eicosapentaenoic and docosahexaenoic acids on immune cell composition and function in healthy humans. *Am J Clin N* 2004;79:674–681.

Kwak H, Hansen C, Leklem J, et al: Improved vitamin B_6 status is positively related to lymphocytes proliferation in young women consuming a controlled diet. *J Nutr* 2002;132:3308–3313.

Maka D, Murphy L: Drug-nutrient interactions: A review. *AACN Clin Issues* 2000;11:580–589.

McCabe B: Prevention of food-drug interactions with special emphasis on older adults. *Curr Opin Clin N* 2004;7:21–26.

Meydani M: Dietary antioxidants modulation of aging and immune-endothelial cell interaction. *Mech Age D* 1999;111:123–132.

Miles E, Banerjee T, Dooper M, et al: The influence of different combinations of gamma-linolenic acid, stearidonic acid and EPA on immune function in healthy young male subjects. *Br J Nutr* 2004;91:893–903.

Mirtallo J: Complications associated with drug and nutrient interactions. *J Infus Nurs* 2004;27:19–24.

Rostan E, DeBuys H, Madey D, et al: Evidence supporting zinc as an important antioxidant for skin. *Int J Dermat* 2002;41:606–611.

Sacheck J, Blumberg J, Milbury P, et al: Vitamin E reduces muscle damage and biomarkers of oxidative stress after exercise. *FASEB J* 2002;16:1137 (meeting abstract).

Safir N, Wendel A, Saile R, et al: The effect of selenium on immune functions of J774.1 cells. *Clin Ch L M* 2003;41:1005–1011.

Simopoulos A: Omega-3 fatty acids in inflammation and autoimmune diseases. *J Am Col N* 2002;21:495–505.

Sorensen J: Herb-drug, food-drug, nutrient-drug, and drug-drug interactions: Mechanisms involved and their medical implications. *J Altern C* 2002;8:293–308.

Tauler P, Aguilo A, Fuentespina E, et al: Diet supplementation with vitamin E, vitamin C and beta carotene cocktail enhances basal neutrophil antioxidant enzymes in athletes. *Eur J Physiol* 2002;443:791–797.

Thomsen D, Mechlsen M, Hokland M, et al: Negative thoughts and health: Associations among rumination, immunity, and health care utilization in a young and elderly sample. *Psychos Med* 2004;66:363–371.

Venkatraman J, Pendergast D: Effect of dietary intake on immune function in athletes. *Sports Med* 2002;32:323–337.

Wu D: Modulation of immune and inflammatory responses by dietary lipids. *Curr Op Lip* 2004;15:43–47.

Yaqoob P: Fatty acids and the immune system: From basic science to clinical applications. *P Nutr Soc* 2004;63:89–104.

Chapter 10

Adlercreutz H: Phytoestrogens and breast cancer. *J Steroid B* 2003;83:113–118.

Aggarwal S, Takada Y, Singh S, et al: Inhibition of growth and survival of human head and neck squamous cell carcinoma cells by curcumin via modulation of nuclear factor-kappaB signaling. *Int J Canc* 2004;111:679–692.

Berendschot T, Broekmans W, Klopping-Ketelaars I, et al: Lens aging in relation to nutritional determinants and possible risk factors for age-related cataract. *Arch Ophth* 2002;120:1732–1737.

Bischoff H, Roos E: Effectiveness and safety of strengthening, aerobic, and coordination exercises for patients with osteoarthritis. *Curr Op Rh* 2003;15:141–144.

Boon H, Wong J: Botanical medicine and cancer: A review of the safety and efficacy. *Expert Op Pharmacothe* 2004;5:2485–2501.

Burke K, Clive J, Combs G, et al: Effects of topical L-selenomethionine with topical and oral vitamin E on pigmentation and skin cancer induced by ultraviolet irradiation in Skh:2 hairless mice. *J Am Acad D* 2003;49:458–472.

Campbell J, Canene-Adams K, Lindshield B, et al: Tomato phytochemicals and prostate cancer risk. *J Nutr* 2004;134:3486S–3492S.

Cevette M, Vormanan J, Franz K: Magnesium and hearing. *J Am Acad Audiol* 2003;14:202–212.

Cho E, Seddon J, Rosner B, et al: Prospective study of intake of fruits, vegetables, vitamins, and carotenoids and risk of age-related maculopathy. *Arch Ophth* 2004;122:883–892.

Christensen R, Astrup A, Bliddal H: Weight loss: The treatment of choice for knee osteoarthritis? A randomized trial. *Osteo Cart* 2005;13:20–27.

Chrysohooou C, Panagiotakos D, Pitsavos C, et al: Adherence to the Mediterranean diet attenuates inflammation and coagulation process in healthy adults. *J Am Col C* 2004;22:152–158.

Chung K, Lee C: Over-the-counter sleeping pills: A survey of use in Hong Kong and a review of their constituents. *Gen Hosp* 2002;24:430–435.

Cleland L, James M, Proudman S: Omega-6/omega-3 fatty acids and arthritis. *World Rev N Diet* 2003;92:152–168.

Clifton P, Keogh J, Noakes M: Trans fatty acids in adipose tissue and the food supply are associated with myocardial infarction. *J Nutr* 2004;134:874–879.

Clifton P, Noakes M, Sullivan D, et al: Cholesterol-lowering effects of plant sterol esters differ in milk, yoghurt, bread and cereal. *Eur J Clin N* 2004;58:503–509.

Curhan G, Willett W, Knight E, et al: Dietary factors and the risk of incident kidney stones in younger women. Nurses' Health Study II. *Arch Intern Med* 2004;164:885–891.

Curhan G, Willett W, Speizer F, et al: Intake of vitamins B_6 and C and the risk of kidney stones in women. *J Am Soc Nephrol* 1999;10:840–845.

Dai Q, Franke A, Jin F, et al: Urinary excretion of phytoestrogens and risk of breast cancer among Chinese women in Shanghai. *Canc Epid B* 2002;11:815–821.

Darlington L, Stone T: Antioxidants and fatty acids in the amelioration of rheumatoid arthritis and related disorders. *Br J Nutr* 2001;85:251–269.

Dauchet L, Ferrieres J, Arveiler D, et al: Frequency of fruit and vegetable consumption and coronary heart disease in France and Northern Ireland: The PRIME study. *Br J Nutr* 2004;92:963–972.

Davey M, Teubner D: A randomized controlled trial of magnesium sulfate, in addition to usual care, for rate control in atrial fibrillation. *Ann Emerg M* 2005;45:347–353.

Delmas P: Treatment of postmenopausal osteoporosis. *Lancet* 2002;359:2018–2026.

Donaldson M: Nutrition and cancer: A review of the evidence for an anti-cancer diet. *Nutr J* 2004;3:19.

Eilat-Adar S, Goldbourt U, Resnick H, et al: Intentional weight loss, blood lipids and coronary morbidity and mortality. *Cur Op Lip* 2005;16:5–9.

Engler M, Engler M, Malloy M, et al: Antioxidant vitamins C and E improve endothelial function in children with hyperlipidemia. *Circulation* 2003;108:1059–1063.

Farrenrons J, Barnadas M, Lopex-Navidad A, et al: Sunscreen and risk of osteoporosis. *Dermatology* 2001;202(1):27–30.

Fitzpatrick R, Rostan E: Double-blind, half-face study comparing topical vitamin C and vehicle for rejuvenation of photodamage. *Derm Surg* 2002;28:231–236.

Fleischauer A, Simonsen N, Arab L: Antioxidant supplements and risk of breast cancer recurrence and breast cancer–related mortality among postmenopausal women. *Nutr Cancer* 2003;46:15–22.

Flood A, Peters U, Chatterjee N, et al: Calcium from diet and supplements is associated with reduced risk of colorectal cancer in a prospective cohort of women. *Canc Epid B* 2005;14:126–132.

Ganji V, Kafai M: Frequent consumption of milk, yogurt, cold breakfast cereals, peppers, and cruciferous vegetables and intakes of dietary folate and riboflavin but not vitamins B-12 and B-6 are inversely associated with serum total homocysteine concentrations in the US population. *Am J Clin N* 2004;80:1500–1507.

Giuliano A, Siegel E, Roe DJ, et al: Dietary intake and risk of persistent human papillomavirus (HPV) infection: The Ludwig-McGill HPV Natural History Study. *J Infec Dis* 2003;188:1508–1516.

Gowda R, Khan I: Magnesium in treatment of acute myocardial infarction. *Int J Card* 2004;96:467–469.

Hall N, Gale C: Prevention of age related macular degeneration. *Br Med J* 2002;325:1–2.

Hegde K, Varma S: Protective effect of ascorbate against oxidative stress in the mouse lens. *Bioc Biop A* 2004;1670:12–18.

Heinrich U, Gartner C, Wiebusch M, et al: Supplementation with beta carotene or similar amount of mixed carotenoids protects humans from UV-induced erythema. *J Nutr* 2003;133:98–101.

Hiraoka-Yamamoto J, Ikeda K, Negishi H, et al: Serum lipid effects of a monounsaturated (palmitoleic) fatty acid-rich diet based on macadamia nuts in healthy, young Japanese women. *Clin Exp Ph* 2004;31:S37–S38.

Hites R, Foran J, Carpenter D, et al: Global assessment of organic contaminants in farmed salmon. *Science* 2004;303:154–155.

Itoh Y, Yasul T, Okada A, et al: Preventive effects of green tea on renal stone formation and the role of oxidative stress in nephrolithiasis. *J Urol* 2005;173:271–275.

Jacques P, Taylor A, Moeller S, et al: Long-term nutrient intake and 5-year change in nuclear lens opacities. *Arch Ophth* 2005;123:517–526.

Jampol L: Antioxidants and zinc to prevent progression of age-related macular degeneration. *J Am Med A* 2001;286:2466–2468.

Jensen M, Koh-Banerjee P, Hu F, et al: Intakes of whole grains, bran, and germ and the risk of coronary heart disease in men. *Am J Clin N* 2004;80:1492–1499.

Jiang R, Manson J, Stampfer M, et al: Nut and peanut butter consumption and risk of type 2 diabetes in women. *J Am Med A* 2002;288:2554–2560.

Jurz B, Jost B, Schunke M: Dietary vitamins and selenium diminish the development of mechanically induced osteoarthritis and increase the expression of antioxidative enzymes in the knee joint of STR/1N mice. *Osteo Cart* 2002;10:119–126.

Karanja N, Erlinger T, Pao-Hwa L, et al: The DASH diet for high blood pressure: From clinical trial to dinner table. *Clevel Clin J* 2004;71:745–753.

Kessler T, Jansen B, Hesse A: Effect of blackcurrant-, cranberry-, and plum-juice consumption on risk factors associated with kidney stone formation. *Eur J Clin N* 2002;56:1020–1023.

King D, Egan B, Geesey M: Relation of dietary fat and fiber to elevation of C-reactive protein. *Am J Cardio* 2003;92:1335–1339.

Klein S, Sheard N, Pi-Sunyer X, et al: Weight management through lifestyle modification for the prevention and management of type 2 diabetes: Rationale and strategies. *Am J Clin N* 2004;80:257–263.

Knoops K, de Groot L, Kromhout D, et al: Mediterranean diet, lifestyle factors, and 10-year mortality in elderly European men and women. *J Am Med A* 2004;292:1433–1439.

Kreuzer M, Heinrich J, Kreienbrock L, et al: Risk factors for lung cancer among nonsmoking women. *Int J Canc* 2002;100:706–713.

Laaksonen D, Niskanen L, Nyyssonen K, et al: C-reactive protein in the prediction of cardiovascular and overall mortality in middle-aged men. *Eur Heart J* 2005;26:1783–1789.

Linde K, Berner M, Egger M, et al: St John's wort for depression: Meta-analysis of randomised controlled trials. *Br J Psychi* 2005;186:99–107.

Linseisen J, Piller R, Hermann S, et al: Dietary phytoestrogen intake and premenopausal breast cancer risk in a German case-control study. *Int J Canc* 2004;110:284–290.

Liu R: Health benefits of fruit and vegetables are from additive and synergistic combinations of phytochemicals. *Am J Clin N* 2003;78:517S–520S.

Lu M, Taylor A, Chylack L, et al: Dietary fat intake and early age-related lens opacities. *Am J Clin N* 2005;81:773–779.

McCann S, Freudenheim J, Marshall J, et al: Risk of human ovarian cancer is related to dietary intake of selected nutrients, phytochemicals and food groups. *J Nutr* 2003;133:1937–1942.

McFadden S, Woo J, Michalak N, et al: Dietary vitamin C supplementation reduces noise-induced hearing loss in guinea pigs. *Hear Res* 2005;202:200–208.

Mennen L, Sapinho D, de Bree A, et al: Consumption of foods rich in flavonoids is related to a decreased cardiovascular risk in apparently healthy French women. *J Nutr* 2004;923–926.

Messier S, Loeser R, Miller G, et al: Exercise and dietary weight loss in overweight and obese older adults with knee osteoarthritis: The Arthritis, Diet, and Activity Promotion Trial. *Arth Rheum* 2004;50:1501–1510.

Messina M, Ho S, Alekel D: Skeletal benefits of soy isoflavones. *Curr Opin Clin N* 2004;7:649–658.

Millen B, Quatromoni P, Nam B, et al: Dietary patterns, smoking, and subclinical heart disease in women: Opportunities for primary prevention from the Framingham Nutrition Studies. *J Am Diet A* 2004;104:208–214.

Mireles-Rocha H, Galino I, Huerta M, et al: UVB photoprotection with antioxidants: Effects of oral therapy with d-alpha-tocopherol and ascorbic acid on the minimal erythema dose. *Act Der-Ven* 2002;82:21–24.

Mitchell P, Smith W, Cumming R, et al: Nutritional factors in the development of age-related eye disease. *Asia P J Cl* 2003;12:S5.

Miyata S, Noda A, Ito N, et al: REM sleep is impaired by a small amount of alcohol in young women sensitive to alcohol. *Intern Med* 2004;43:679–684.

Moeller S, Taylor A, Tucker K, et al: Overall adherence to the dietary guidelines for Americans is associated with reduced prevalence of early age-related nuclear lens opacities in women. *J Nutr* 2004;134:1812–1819.

Mokdad A, Ford E, Bowman B, et al: Prevalence of obesity, diabetes, and obesity-related health risk factors, 2001. *J Am Med A* 2003;289:76–79.

Montonen J, Knekt P, Jarvinen R, et al: Dietary antioxidant intake and risk of type 2 diabetes. *Diabet Care* 2004;27:362–366.

Mori M, Aizawa T, Tokoro M, et al: Soy isoflavone tablets reduce osteoporosis risk factors and obesity in middle-aged Japanese women. *Clin Exp Ph* 2004;31:S39–S41.

Moskowitz R: Role of collagen hydrolysate in bone and joint disease. *Sem Arth Rh* 2000;30:87–99.

Murtaugh M, Ma K, Benson J, et al: Antioxidants, carotenoids, and risk of rectal cancer. *Am J Epidem* 2004;159:32–41.

Oh K, Hu F, Cho E, et al: Carbohydrate intake, glycemic index, glycemic load, and dietary fiber in relation to risk of stroke in women. *Am J Epid* 2005;161:161–169.

Olsen A, Tonneland A, Thomsen B, et al: Fruits and vegetables intake differentially affects estrogen receptor negative and positive breast cancer incidence rates. *J Nutr* 2003;133:2342–2347.

Parker E, Folsom A: Intentional weight loss and incidence of obesity-related cancers. *Int J Obes* 2003;27:1447–1452.

Peeters A, van der Molen E, Blom H, et al: The effect of homocysteine reduction in B-vitamin supplementation on markers of endothelial dysfunction. *Thromb Haem* 2004;92:1086–1091.

Pereira M, Kartashov A, Ebbeling C, et al: Fast-food habits, weight gain, and insulin resistance (the CARDIA Study): 15-year prospective analysis. *Lancet* 2005;365:36–42.

Piotrowski A, Kalus J: Magnesium for the treatment and prevention of a trial tachyarrhythmias. *Pharmacothe* 2004;24:879–895.

Ramos E, Middleton F, Laviano A, et al: Effects of omega-3 fatty acid supplementation on tumor-bearing rats. *J Am Coll S* 2004;199:716–723.

Resatoglu A, Demirturk O, Yener N, et al: Magnesium decreases cardiac injury in patients undergoing coronary artery bypass surgery. *Ann Saudi M* 2004;24:259–261.

Ressel G: American Cancer Society releases guidelines on nutrition and physical activity for cancer prevention. *Am Fam Phys* 2002;66:1555–1562.

Sadat M, Jalali M, Siassi F, et al: The impact of vitamins and/or mineral supplementation on blood pressure in type 2 diabetics. *J Am Col N* 2004;23:272–279.

Sagara M, Kanda T, Njelekera M, et al: Effects of dietary intake of soy protein and isoflavones on cardiovascular disease risk factors in high risk, middle-aged men in Scotland. *J Am Col N* 2004;23:85–91.

Schulze M, Manson J, Ludwig D, et al: Sugar-sweetened beverages, weight gain, and incidence of type 2 diabetes in young and middle-aged women. *J Am Med A* 2004;292:927–934.

Seddon J, Cote J, Rosner B: Progression of age-related macular degeneration: Association with dietary fat, transunsaturated fats, nuts, and fish intake. *Arch Ophthal* 2003;121:1728–1737.

Seeram N, Adams L, Hardy M, et al: Total cranberry extract versus its phytochemical constituents: Antiproliferative and synergistic effects against human tumor cell lines. *J Agr Food* 2004;52:2512–2517.

Sesso H, Buring J, Norkus E, et al: Plasma lycopene, other carotenoids, and retinol and the risk of cardiovascular disease in women. *Am J Clin N* 2004;79:47–53.

Sharabi Y, Grotto I, Huerta M, et al: Susceptibility of the influence of weight on blood pressure in men versus women: Lessons from a large-scale study of young adults. *Am J Hyper* 2004;17:404–408.

Sheard N, Clark N, Brand-Miller J, et al: Dietary carbohydrate (amount and type) in the prevention and management of diabetes. *Diabet Care* 2004;27:2266–2271.

Shiga T, Wajima Z, Inoue T, et al: Magnesium prophylaxis for arrhythmias after cardiac surgery: A meta-analysis of randomized controlled trials. *Am J Med* 2004;117:325–333.

Stein C, Colditz G: Modifiable risk factors for cancer. *Br J Canc* 2004;90:299–303.

Strassburg A, Krems C, Luhrmann P, et al: Effect of age on plasma homocysteine concentrations in young and elderly subjects considering serum vitamin concentrations and different lifestyle factors. *Int J Vit N* 2004;74:129–136.

Streppel M, Arends L, van 't Veer P, et al: Dietary fiber and blood pressure. *Arch Int Med* 2005;165:150–156.

Tamimi R, Hankinson S, Campos H, et al: Plasma carotenoids, retinol, and tocopherols and risk of breast cancer. *Am J Epidem* 2005;161:153–160.

Taylor E, Stampfer M, Curhan G: Dietary factors and the risk of incident kidney stones in men. *J Am Soc Nephrol* 2004;15:3225–3232.

Taylor E, Stampfer M, Curhan G: Obesity, weight gain, and the risk of kidney stones. *J Am Med A* 2005;293:455–462.

Theile J, Dreher F, Packer L: Antioxidant defense systems in skin. *J Toxicol* 2002;21:119–160.

Tucker K, Chen H, Hannan M, et al: Bone mineral density and dietary patterns in older adults: The Framingham Osteoporosis Study. *Am J Clin N* 2002;76:245–252.

Turk J: Melatonin supplementation for severe and intractable sleep disturbance in young people with genetically determined developmental disabilities. *J Med Genet* 2003;40:793–796.

Uusi-Rasi K, Sievanen H, Pasanen M, et al: Association of physical activity and calcium intake with the maintenance of bone mass in premenopausal women. *Osteo Intern* 2002;13:211–217.

Valero M, Fletcher A, De Stavola B, et al: Vitamin C is associated with reduced risk of cataract in a Mediterranean population. *J Nutr* 2002;132:1299–1306.

Vrentzos G, Papadakis J, Malliaraki N, et al: Diet, serum homocystcine levels, and ischaemic heart disease in a Mediterranean population. *Br J Nutr* 2004;91:1013–1019.

Wallace L, Ballard J: Lifetime physical activity and calcium intake related to bone density in young women. *J Womens H* 2002;11:389–398.

Wu A, Wan P, Hankin J, et al: Adolescent and adult soy intake and risk of breast cancer in Asian-Americans. *Carcinogen* 2002;23:1491–1496.

Yamori Y, Moriguchi E, Teramoto T, et al: Soybean isoflavones reduce postmenopausal bone resorption in female Japanese immigrants in Brazil: A ten-week study. *J Am Col N* 2002;21:560–563.

Zegedi A, Kohnen R, Dienel A: Acute treatment of moderate to severe depression with hypericum extract WS 5570 (St John's wort): Randomised controlled double blind non-inferiority trial versus paroxetine. *Br Med J* 2005;330:503.

Zhang M, Yang Z, Binns C, et al: Diet and ovarian cancer risk: A case-control study in China. *Br J Canc* 2002;86:712–717.

Chapter 11

Ahluwalia N, Vellas B: Immunologic and inflammatory mediators and cognitive decline in Alzheimer's disease. *Immunol All* 2003;23:103–115.

Alves C, Andreatini R, da Cunha C, et al: Phosphatidylserine reverses reserpine-induced amnesia. *Eur J Pharmacol* 2000;404:161–167.

Benloucif S, Orbeta L, Ortiz R, et al: Morning or evening activity improves neuropsychological performance and subjective sleep quality in older adults. *Sleep* 2004;27:1542–1551.

Englehart M, Geerlings M, Ruitenberg A, et al: Dietary intake of antioxidants and risk of Alzheimer disease. *J Am Med A* 2002;287:3223–3229.

Fukui K, Omoi N, Hayasaka T, et al: Cognitive impairment of rats caused by oxidative stress and aging, and its prevention by vitamin E. *Ann NY Acad* 2002;959:275–284.

Grundman M, Delaney P: Antioxidant strategies for Alzheimer's disease. *P Nutr Soc* 2002;61:191–202.

Heude B, Ducimetiere P, Berr C: Cognitive decline and fatty acid composition of erythrocyte membranes: The EVA Study. *Am J Clin N* 2003;77:803–808.

Hillman C, Belopolsky A, Snook E, et al: Physical activity and executive control: Implications for increased cognitive health during older adulthood. *Res Q Exerc Sp* 2004;75:176–185.

Jorissen B, Brouns F, van Boxtel M, et al: Safety of soy-derived phosphatidylserine in elderly people. *Nutr Neuros* 2002;5:337–343.

Kennedy D, Scholey A, Wesnes K: Modulation of cognition and mood following administration of single doses of ginkgo biloba, ginseng, and a ginkgo/ginseng combination to healthy young adults. *Physl Behav* 2002;75:739–751.

Kritz-Silverstein D, Von Muhlen D, Barrett-Connor E, et al: Isoflavones and cognitive function in older women: The Soy and Postmenopausal Health in Aging (SOPHIA) Study. *Menopause* 2003;10:189–190.

Liu R: Health benefits of fruit and vegetables are from additive and synergistic combinations of phytochemicals. *Am J Clin N* 2003;78:517S–520S.

Maskarinec G, Robbins C, Riola B, et al: Three measures show high compliance in a soy intervention among premenopausal women. *J Am Diet A* 2003;103:861–866.

McCaddon A, Regland B, Hudson P, et al: Functional vitamin B_{12} deficiency and Alzheimer disease. *Neurology* 2002;58:1395–1399.

McDaniel M, Maier S, Einstein G: "Brain-specific" nutrients: A memory cure? *Nutrition* 2003;19:957–975.

Mecocci P: Oxidative stress in mild cognitive impairment and Alzheimer disease: A continuum. *J Alz Dis* 2004;6:159–163.

Morris M, Evans D, Bienias J: Vitamin E and cognitive decline in older persons. *Arch Neurol* 2002;59:1125–1132.

Morris M, Evans D, Bienias J, et al: Consumption of fish and n-3 fatty acids and risk of incident Alzheimer disease. *Arch Neurol* 2003;60:940–946.

Morris M, Evans D, Bienias J, et al: Dietary intake of antioxidant nutrients and the risk of incident Alzheimer disease in a biracial community study. *J Am Med A* 2002;287:3230–3237.

Morris M, Evans D, Tangney C, et al: Relation of the tocopherol forms to incident Alzheimer disease and to cognitive change. *Am J Clin N* 2005;81:508–514.

Morris M, Jacques P, Rosenberg I, et al: Hyperhomocysteinemia associated with poor recall in the third National Health and Nutrition Examination Survey. *Am J Clin N* 2001;73:927–933.

Munoz F, Sole M, Coma M: The protective role of vitamin E in vascular amyloid beta-mediated damage. *Subcell Bioch* 2005;38:147–165.

Polidori M: Antioxidant micronutrients in the prevention of age-related diseases. *J Postgr M* 2003;49:229–235.

Rinaldi P, Polidori M, Metastasio A, et al: Plasma antioxidants are similarly depleted in mild cognitive impairment and in Alzheimer's disease. *Neurobiol Aging* 2003;24:915–919.

Seshadri S, Beiser A, Selhub J, et al: Plasma homocysteine as a risk factor for dementia and Alzheimer's disease. *N Eng J Med* 2002;346:476–483.

Solfrizzi V, Panza F, Capurso A: The role of diet in cognitive decline. *J Neural Tr* 2003;110:95–110.

Strassburg A, Krems C, Luhrmann P, et al: Effect of age on plasma homocysteine concentrations in young and elderly subjects considering serum vitamin concentrations and different lifestyle factors. *Int J Vit N* 2004;74:129–136.

Vreugdenburg L, Bryan J, Kemps E: The effect of self-initiated weight-loss dieting on working memory: The role of preoccupying cognitions. *Appetite* 2003;41:291–300.

Weuve J, Kang J, Manson J, et al: Physical activity, including walking, and cognitive function in older women. *J Am Med A* 2004;292:1454–1461.

Zandi P, Anthony J, Khachaturian A, et al: Reduced risk of Alzheimer disease in users of antioxidant vitamin supplements: The Cache County Study. *Arch Neurol* 2004;61:82–88.

Chapter 12

Barkeling B, Linne Y, Lindross A, et al: Intake of sweet foods and counts of cariogenic microorganisms in relation to body mass index and psychometric variables in women. *Int J Obes* 2002;26:1239–1244.

Dohm F, Beattie J, Aibel C, et al: Factors differentiating women and men who successfully maintain weight loss from women and men who do not. *J Clin Psychol* 2001;57:105–117.

Elliott S, Keim N, Stern J, et al: Fructose, weight gain, and the insulin resistance syndrome. *Am J Clin N* 2002;76:911–922.

Field A, Manson J, Taylor C, et al: Association of weight change, weight control practices, and weight cycling among women in the Nurses' Health Study II. *Int J Obes* 2004;28:1134–1142.

Gluck M, Geliebter A, Lorence M: Cortisol stress response is positively correlated with central obesity in obese women with binge eating disorder (BED) before and after cognitive-behavioral treatment. *Ann NY Acad* 2004;1032:202–207.

Gorin A, Phelan S, Wing R, et al: Promoting long-term weight loss control: Does dieting consistency matter? *Int J Obes* 2004;28:278–282.

Guo S, Chumlea W, Roche A, et al: Age- and maturity-related changes in body composition during adolescence into adulthood. *Int J Obes* 1997;21:1167–1175.

McGuire M, Wing R, Klem M, et al: Behavioral strategies of individuals who have maintained long-term weight losses. *Obes Res* 1999;7:334–341.

McGuire M, Wing R, Klem M, et al: What predicts weight regain in a group of successful weight losers? *J Cons Clin* 1999;67:177–185.

Raben A, Vasilaras T, Moller A, et al: Sucrose compared with artificial sweeteners: Different effects on ad libitum food intake and body weight after 10 weeks of supplementation in overweight subjects. *Am J Clin N* 2002;76:721–729.

Shick S, Wing R, Klem M, et al: Persons successful at long-term weight loss and maintenance continue to consume a low-energy, low-fat diet. *J Am Diet A* 1998;98:408–413.

Simkin-Silverman L, Wing R: Weight gain during menopause: Is it inevitable or can it be prevented? *Postgr M* 2000;108:47–50, 53–56.

Wadden T, Vogt R, Foster G, et al.: Exercise and the maintenance of weight loss: 1-year follow-up of a controlled clinical trial. *J Cons Clin* 1998;66:429–433.

Wallner S, Luschnigg N, Schnedl W, et al: Body fat distribution of overweight females with a history of weight cycling. *Int J Obes* 2004;28:1143–1148.

Zandi P, Anthony J, Khachaturian A, et al: Reduced risk of Alzheimer disease in users of antioxidant vitamin supplements: The Cache County Study. *Arch Neurol* 2004;61:82–88.

Chapter 13

Barton D, Loprinzi C, Quella S, et al: Prospective evaluation of vitamin E for hot flashes in breast cancer survivors. *J Clin Oncol* 1998;16:495–500.

Birkhauser M: Depression, menopause and estrogens: Is there a correlation? *Maturitas* 2002;41:S3–S8.

Davis J, Alderson N, Welsh R: Serotonin and central nervous system fatigue: Nutritional considerations. *Am J Clin N* 2000;72:573S–578S.

Delilbasi C, Cehiz T, Akal U, et al: Evaluation of gustatory function in postmenopausal women. *Br Dent J* 2003;194:447–449.

Huntley A, Ernst E: Soy for the treatment of perimenopausal symptoms. *Maturitas* 2004;47:1–9.

Ivarsson T, Spetz A, Hammar M: Physical exercise and vasomotor symptoms in postmenopausal women. *Maturitas* 1998;29:139–146.

Jenkins D, Kendall C, Marchie A, et al: Effects of a dietary portfolio of cholesterol-lowering foods vs lovastatin on serum lipids and C-reactive protein. *J Am Med A* 2003;290:502–510.

Krebs E, Enesrud K, MacDonald R, et al: Phytoestrogens for treatment of menopausal symptoms. *Obstet Gynecol* 2004;104:824–836.

Littman A, Kristal A, White E: Effects of physical activity intensity, frequency, and activity type on 10-year weight change in middle-age men and women. *Int J Obes* 2005;29:524–533.

MacGregor C, Canney P, Patterson G, et al: A randomized double-blind controlled trial of oral soy supplements versus placebo for treatment of menopausal symptoms in patients with early breast cancer. *Eur J Canc* 2005;41:708–714.

Markus C, Panhuysen G, Tuiten A, et al: Does carbohydrate-rich, protein-poor food prevent a deterioration of mood and cognitive performance of stress-prone subjects when subjected to a stressful task? *Appetite* 1998;31:49–65.

Nikander E, Rutanen E, Nieminen P, et al: Lack of effect of isoflavonoids on the vagina and endometrium in postmenopausal women. *Fertil Steril* 2005;83:137–142.

Petri Nahas E, Nahas Neto J, DeLuca L, et al: Benefits of soy germ isoflavones in postmenopausal women with contraindication for conventional hormone replacement therapy. *Maturitas* 2004;48:372–380.

Phipps W, Duncan A, Kurzer M: Isoflavones and postmenopausal women. *Treat Endocr* 2002;1:293–311.

Sternfeld B, Wang H, Quesenberry J, et al: Physical activity and changes in weight and waist circumference in midlife women. *Am J Epidem* 2004;160:912–922.

Ueda M: A 12-week structured education and exercise program improved climacteric symptoms in middle-aged women. *J Physl Anthr Appl Hu* 2004;23:143–148.

Verma P, Mahajan K, Mittal S, et al: Salt preference across different phases of menstrual cycle. *In J Physl P* 2005;49:99–102.

Chapter 14

Bacon C, Mittleman M, Kawachi I, et al: Sexual function in men older than 50 years of age: Results from the health professionals follow-up study. *Ann Intern Med* 2003;139:161–168.

Derby C, Mohr B, Goldstein I, et al: Modifiable risk factors and erectile dysfunction: Can lifestyle changes modify risk? *Urology* 2000;56:302–306.

Esposito K, Ciotola M, Marfella R, et al: The metabolic syndrome: A cause of sexual dysfunction in women. *Int J Impot* 2005;17:224–226.

Esposito K, Ciotola M, Marfella R, et al: Sexual dysfunction in women with the metabolic syndrome. *Diabet Care* 2005;28:756.

Esposito K, Giugliano D: Obesity, the metabolic syndrome, and sexual dysfunction. *Int J Impot* Res 2005;May 19.

Esposito K, Giugliano F, Di Palo C, et al: Effect of lifestyle changes on erectile dysfunction in obese men: A randomized controlled trial. *J Am Med A* 2004;291:2978–2984.

Evans M: Lose weight to lose erectile dysfunction. *Can Fam Phy* 2005;January:47–49.

McKay D: Nutrients and botanicals for erectile dysfunction: Examining the evidence. *Altern Med Rev* 2004;9:4–16.

Murphy L, Lee T: Ginseng, sex behavior, and nitric oxide. *Ann NY Acad* 2002;962:372–377.

Chapter 15

Bennett H: Humor in medicine. *South Med J* 2003:96:1257–1261.

Bennett M, Zeller J, Rosenberg L, et al: The effect of mirthful laughter on stress and natural killer cell activity. *Altern Th H* 2003;9:38–45.

Blumenthal J, Sherwood A, Babyak M, et al: Effects of exercise and stress management training on markers of cardiovascular risk in patients with ischemic heart disease: A randomized controlled trial. *J Am Med A* 2005;293:1626–1634.

Bonadonna R: Meditation's impact on chronic illness. *Holist Nurs Prac* 2003;17:309–319.

Boudreaux E, O'Hea E, Chasuk R: Spiritual role in healing: An alternative way of thinking. *Prim Care* 2002;29:439–454.

Christie W, Moore C: The impact of humor on patients with cancer. *Clin J Oncol N* 2005:9:211–218.

Dallman M, Pecoraro N, Akana S, et al: Chronic stress and obesity: A new view of "comfort food." *P Natl Acad S* 2003;100:11696–11701.

Drapeau V, Therrien F, Richard D, et al: Is visceral obesity a physiological adaptation to stress? *Panmin Med* 2003;45:189–195.

Emmons R, McCullough M: Counting blessings versus burdens: An experimental investigation of gratitude and subjective well-being in daily life. *J Pers Soc* 2003;84:377–389.

Gluck M, Geliebter A, Lorence M: Cortisol stress response is positively correlated with central obesity in obese women with binge eating disorder (BED) before and after cognitive-behavioral treatment. *Ann NY Acad* 2004;1032:202–207.

Grossman P, Niemann L, Schmidt S, et al: Mindfulness-based stress reduction and health benefits: A meta-analysis. *J Psychosom Res* 2004;57:35–43.

Ironson G, Balbin E, Stuetzle R, et al: Dispositional optimism and the mechanisms by which it predicts slower disease progression in HIV. *Int J Behav Med* 2005;12:86–97.

Lane R, Laukes C, Marcus F, et al: Psychological stress preceding idiopathic ventricular fibrillation. *Psychos Med* 2005;67:359–365.

MacDonald C: A chuckle a day keeps the doctor away: Therapeutic humor and laughter. *J Psychos Nurs Ment H* 2004;42:18–25.

Mahony D, Burroughs W, Lippman L: Perceived attributes of health-promoting laughter: A cross-generational comparison. *J Psychol* 2002;136:171–181.

Mamtani R, Mamtani R: Ayurveda and yoga in cardiovascular diseases. *Cardiol Rev* 2005;13:155–162.

Matthews KA, Raikkonen K, Sutton-Tyrrell K, et al: Optimistic attitudes protect against progression of carotid atherosclerosis in healthy middle-aged women. *Psychos Med* 2004;66:640–644.

Olsson H, Backe H, Sorensen S, et al: The essence of humour and its effects and functions: A qualitative study. *J Nurs Manag* 2002;10:21–26.

Peeke P, Chrousos G: Hypercortisolism and obesity. *Ann NY Acad* 1995;771:665–676.

Rafanelli C, Roncuzzi R, Milaneschi Y, et al: Stressful life events, depression and demoralization as risk factors for acute coronary heart disease. *Psychoth Ps* 2005;74:179–184.

Robinson-Smith G: Prayer after stroke: Its relationship to quality of life. *J Holist Nurs* 2002;20:352–366.

Schou I, Ekeberg O, Ruland C, et al: Pessimism as a predictor of emotional morbidity one year following breast cancer surgery. *Psychoncol* 2004;13:309–320.

Smith B, Zautra A: The role of purpose in life in recovery from knee surgery. *Int J Behav Med* 2004;11:197–202.

Smith N, Young A, Lee C: Optimism, health-related hardiness and well-being among older Australian women. *J Health Psychol* 2004;9:741–752.

Walton K, Fields J, Levitsky D, et al: Lowering cortisol and CVD risk in postmenopausal women: A pilot study using the Transcendental Meditation program. *Ann NY Acad* 2004;1032:211–215.

Chapter 16

Blom M, Janszky I, Balog P, et al: Social relations in women with coronary heart disease: The effects of work and marital stress. *J Card Risk* 2003;10:201–206.

Centers for Disease Control and Prevention (CDC): Social support and health-related quality of life among older adults: Missouri, 2000. *MMWR Morb Mortal Wkly Rep* 2005;54:433–437.

Choi H, Lee D, Lee K, et al: A structural model of menopausal depression in Korean women. *Arch Psy N* 2004;18:235–242.

Deeks A: Is this menopause? Women in midlife: Psychosocial issues. *Aust Fam Phys* 2004;33:889–893.

Everson-Rose S, Lewis T: Psychosocial factors and cardiovascular diseases. *Annu R Pub H* 2005;26:469–500.

Murphy P, Prewitt T, Bote E, et al: Internal locus of control and social support associated with some dietary changes by elderly participants in a diet intervention trial. *J Am Diet A* 2001;101:203–208.

Orth-Gomer K, Wamala S, Horsten M, et al: Marital stress worsens prognosis in women with coronary heart disease: The Stockholm Female Coronary Risk Study. *J Am Med A* 2000;284:3008–3014.

Polakoff P: Satisfaction with work is strongest factor in predicting longevity. *Occ He Saf* 1989;58:37–38.

Steptoe A, Doherty S, Kerry S, et al: Sociodemographic and psychological predictors of changes in dietary fat consumption in adults with high blood cholesterol following counseling in primary care. *Health Psychol* 2000;19:411–419.

Appendix C

Anderson J, Hanna T, Peng X, et al: Whole grain foods and heart disease risk. *J Am Col N* 2000;19:S291–S299.

Arjmandi B, Khalil D, Smith B, et al: Soy protein has a greater effect on bone in postmenopausal women not on hormone replacement therapy, as evidenced by reducing bone resorption and urinary calcium excretion. *J Clin End* 2003;88:1048–1054.

Bazzano L, He J, Ogden L, et al: Legume consumption and risk of coronary heart disease in US men and women. *Arch In Med* 2001;161:2573–2578.

Bloedon L, Szapary P: Flaxseed and cardiovascular risk. *Nutr Rev* 2004;62:18–27.

Clarkson T: Soy, soy phytoestrogens and cardiovascular disease. *J Nutr* 2002;132:S566–S569.

Demark-Wahnefried W, Robertson C, et al: Pilot study to explore effects of low-fat, flaxseed-supplemented diet on proliferation of benign prostatic epithelium and prostate specific antigen. *Urology* 2004;63:900–904.

DeMoreno A, Perdigon G: Yogurt feeding inhibits promotion and progression of experimental colorectal cancer. *Med Sci Monit* 2004;10:BR96–BR104.

Frankenfeld C, Patterson R, Kalhorn T, et al: Validation of a soy food frequency questionnaire with plasma concentrations of isoflavones in US adults. *J Am Diet A* 2002;102:1407–1413.

Hou D: Potential mechanisms of cancer chemoprevention by anthocyanins. *Curr Mol Med* 2003;3:149–159.

Jacobs D, Pereira M, Meyer K, et al: Fiber from whole grains, but not refined grains, is inversely associated with all-cause mortality in older women. *J Am Col N* 2000;19:S326–S330.

Joseph J, Denisova N, Arendash G, et al: Blueberry supplementation enhances signaling and prevents behavioral deficits in an Alzheimer disease model. *Nutr Neuros* 2003;6:153–162.

Kasum C, Nicodemus K, Harnack L, et al: Whole grain intake and incident endometrial cancer: The Iowa Women's Health Study. *Nutr Cancer* 2001;39:180–186.

Kris-Etherton P, Zhao G, Binkoski A, et al: The effects of nuts on coronary heart disease risk. *Nutr Rev* 2001;59:103–111.

Kritz-Silverstein D, Von Muhlen D, Barrett-Connor E, et al: Isoflavones and cognitive function in older women: The Soy and Postmenopausal Health in Aging (SOPHIA) Study. *Menopause* 2003;10:189–190.

Liu S: Intake of refined carbohydrates and whole grain foods in relation to risk of type 2 diabetes mellitus and coronary heart disease. *J Am Col N* 2002;21:298–306.

Liu S, Manson J, Stampfer M, et al: Whole grain consumption and risk of ischemic stroke in women. *J Am Med A* 2000;284:1534–1540.

Lucas E, Lightfoot S, Hammond L, et al: Flaxseed reduces plasma cholesterol and atherosclerotic lesion formation in ovarectomized Golden Syrian hamsters. *Atheroscler* 2004;173:223–229.

Lyons M, Yu C, Toma R, et al: Resveratrol in raw and baked blueberries and bilberries. *J Agric Fd Chem* 2003;51:5867–5870.

Perdigon G, de Moreno A, Valdex J, et al: Role of yoghurt in the prevention of colon cancer. *Eur J Clin N* 2002;56(suppl):S65–S68.

Pins J, Geleva D, Keenan J, et al: Do whole-grain oat cereals reduce the need for antihypertensive medications and improve blood pressure control? *J Fam Pract* 2002;51:353–359.

Putnam J, Allshouse J, Kantor L: U.S. per capita food supply trends: More calories, refined carbohydrates, and fats. *FoodReview* 2002;Winter:2–11.

Rachid M, Gobbato N, Valdex J, et al: Effect of yogurt on the inhibition of an intestinal carcinoma by increasing cellular apoptosis. *Int J Imm Pharma* 2002;15:209–216.

Roberts S: High glycemic index foods, hunger, and obesity: Is there a connection? *Nutr Rev* 2000;58:163–169.

Rock C, Lovalvo J, Emenhiser C, et al: Bioavailability of beta carotene is lower in raw than in processed carrots and spinach in women. *J Nutr* 1998;128:913–916.

Sesso H, Buring J, Norkus E, et al: Plasma lycopene, other carotenoids, and retinol and the risk of cardiovascular disease in women. *Am J Clin N* 2004;79:47–53.

Slavin J: Mechanisms for the impact of whole grain foods on cancer risk. *J Am Col N* 2000;19:S300–S307.

Stone K, Duong T, Sellmeyer D, et al: Broccoli may be good for bones. *J Bone Min* 1999;14:F272.

Wien M, Sabate J, Ikle D, et al: Almonds vs complex carbohydrates in a weight reduction program. *Int J Obes* 2003;27:1365–1372.

Zheng W, Wang S: Oxygen radical absorbing capacity of phenolics in blueberries, cranberries, chokeberries, and lingonberries. *J Agric Fd Chem* 2003;51:502–509.

Index